GIVE
YOUR CHILD
MUSIC

Pop song

GIVE YOUR CHILD MUSIC

JILL PHILLIPS

PAUL ELEK
LONDON

First published in Great Britain 1979 by
Paul Elek Limited
54–58 Caledonian Road, London N1 9RN

© 1979 Jill Phillips

Frontispiece photograph reproduced by permission of Mayotte Magnus;
other photographs reproduced by permission as follows:
Lance Browne (pages 26 and 86);
Tony Stokes (pages 27, 28 and 76);
Steinway & Sons (pages 91 and 92);
Margaret Williams (page 105);
Jorge Lewinski (page 127).
All other photographs, and music notation, by the author.
Drawings by pupils of Bessemer Grange Junior School, Dulwich.

ISBN 0 236 40145 9

Text set in 11/12 pt VIP Plantin, printed by photolithography,
and bound in Great Britain at The Pitman Press, Bath

for
TOM
and for
Ruth and Leo

'. . . somehow children
         children opened the imagination . . .'

A Humument TP

CONTENTS

Acknowledgements   9

INTRODUCTION   11
Development of sensory perception in babies—shared activities—the elements of sound—Common Sense takes over—are you musical?

Chapter 1 LEARNING TO CONTROL SOUND   17
The sounds around—collecting sounds—games to play—musical patterns—composing—full use of the piano—the 'prepared' piano—your own instruments

Chapter 2 TEACHING YOUR CHILD TO READ MUSIC   29
Formal notation—time-names—games to play—pitch—your own music book—some easy first pieces—silence in music—using 'real' music

Chapter 3 HOW TO CHOOSE AN INSTRUMENT: OR, FIRST FIND YOUR TEACHER   66
*The right order—when should formal lessons begin?—which instrument?—facts you should know—advantages and disadvantages—*CHOOSING A TEACHER*—locating the best teacher—the local music festival—making contact with the teacher of your choice*

Chapter 4 HOW NOT TO BUY AN INSTRUMENT   85
Discussion with the teacher—pitfalls—'suitable for beginner'—the piano—central heating—humidity—removals—stringed instruments—woodwind—brass—percussion—other instruments

Chapter 5 THE FIRST LESSON: SOME NECESSARY QUESTIONS   104
Discussion—preparing a list of questions—your role—how long will the lesson be?—a week's work—performance—care of instruments—classes—examinations—sight reading—playing for pleasure

Chapter 6 SANE AND SYMPATHETIC ARRANGEMENTS FOR PRACTICE   113
Why do people 'give up'?—examining your own experiences—the author's experience—what to avoid—what to provide—practice—sharing difficulties and triumphs—a positive practice session—tuning—loving the sound—interpretation

Chapter 7 MAKING AND LISTENING TO MUSIC
TOGETHER   126
*Using music publishers' catalogues—simple adaptation—how to rehearse
a small ensemble—becoming a great audience—understanding a
performance—development of active interest in all fields—attending a
concert—new music—allowing a laugh or two*

Chapter 8 MUSIC IN SCHOOLS: WHERE CAN IT BE FOUND?   138
*Music within a general education—research throughout the world—the
position in Britain—choosing a school—grants, awards and
scholarships—Choir schools—the Yehudi Menuhin School—St Mary's
School—the Purcell School—Chetham's Hospital School—Wells
Cathedral School—summary—financial support*

CONCLUSION   157
*Reasons for writing this book—self-help—exchange of information
amongst parents, teachers, students and play-group leaders—retention of
curiosity and desire to learn—prodigious talent—Music . . . a gift from
God or from Granny?*

Glossary   163
Booklist   165
List of Useful Addresses   167

ACKNOWLEDGEMENTS

Whilst writing this book I have had the pleasure of speaking at length to and checking facts with students, music teachers, headmasters, instrument makers and repairers, mathematicians, medics and a host of others. Instrumental specialists have been consulted throughout. Friends have passed on problems, experiences and tips—they have found me isolated quarters where I could escape from the telephone and the insurance man, fed me and bolstered up my confidence. For this my heartfelt thanks. I hope they will forgive me if I have space only to mention by name Shirley and David Cargill, Kato Havas, Sheila Thompson, John Tilbury and Kipper and David Walker; I should also like to record my gratitude to Antony Wood of Elek, for his sympathetic handling of the manuscript.

My most grateful thanks however must be reserved for Margaret Napier and Leonard Worsley, who for long years exercised all those qualities one could hope to find in the perfect teacher, and who allowed my children and myself the privilege of learning with them.

Without my husband's persistence and support this book would never have been written.

Author's Note

For the sake of clarity, I have referred to the imaginary child throughout as 'he' and 'him', and to the imaginary teacher as 'she' and 'her'. This is merely a distinction of convenience and nothing else is meant by it. A flurry of 'he/she' and 'him/her' would have been within the letter of the Sex Discrimination Act, but would finally have irritated the reader.

Publisher's Note

Words referenced thus ^G are explained in the Glossary (pages 163–64). Names of publishers of books mentioned in the text will be found in the chapter-by-chapter Booklist (pages 165–66), which also lists further books.

INTRODUCTION

'Take that out of your mouth' screamed the mother to her small child as she loaded her purchases tantalisingly on to his pram. It was too much for him to bear. The colours, the rustly papers, the smells which suddenly surrounded him, were all forbidden. He went stiff, then red, before opening his mouth in a bawling expression of protest. His mother was prepared for that; deftly she whipped out of her pocket a much used dummy and rammed it into the great cavern of her baby's mouth. A look of surprise flitted into his eyes before they went dead; he began to suck hard with disappointment. The tears and the interest dried up and the little scene was over.

The parent of the newly born child is content that his senses are merely present; the developing baby is not—his need is to employ them to the utmost. He tastes, touches, smells, hears and sees everything within his expanding fields of perception. He examines with care, and gives his attention to each tiny detail. Lying warm and comfortable in his pram, with the scent of autumn and the songs of birds all around, he will watch a leaf swinging—just about to fall—until he goes to sleep, perhaps an hour or so later. His mother will observe his contentment—may even look to see what he sees—but to consider giving her attention to the leaf for more than a second or two would seem to her to be an absurd waste of time. Yet the child 'understands' that leaf completely.

The child's pleasure grows with his developing sensual awareness and his unconscious achievements in those fields. It is not long before he becomes aware that a large proportion of his experiments are considered 'naughty', even downright 'bad'. Unless this realisation is sympathetically handled, his original delight in all things new turns sour; either he is inhibited by fear from further experiment, or he begins to use his guile merely to attract attention. Either way, sensual pleasure, so often a cause for adult concern, will already arouse in him feelings of guilt from which he will not easily recover.

This may seem a far cry from a child's musical development; but I must stress that his earliest experiences are of paramount importance since they lay the foundations of an active and uninhibited involvement with sound which can seldom be replaced by the later imposition of formal music-making upon his small person.

'Primitive' tribes have no problem. Their way of life demands the constant use of all their separate senses, enabling them to embrace their various art-forms as the natural expression of their own identity, and their yearning towards the mystical.

Since our 'civilised' way of life has placed a premium on 'common' sense, it may be difficult to disentangle the five components without loss of security. Not impossible, however. The newly blind person amongst us finds compensatory powers in his growing acuteness of hearing, smelling, touching and tasting. The earlier the necessity for this development arises, the more successful will be his response: without sight, a critical ability develops, enabling him to re-experience with his remaining senses many of the delights of his early childhood. As compensation for his disability it has little to offer, but as a lesson to us, it is valuable.

In helping our children to acquire 'common' sense, we must be careful to avoid impairment of their separate sensual abilities. Their education could become the means of our re-education; the benefit can be just as much ours as it will be theirs.

The development of critical powers demands a measure of self-discipline. In acquiring them, the child finds himself worthy of respect. No better security exists.

Music has a unique advantage over the other arts in that it can become the means of demonstrating these powers very early in life, thereby allowing a child to participate at a real level of adult communication, very often before he reaches secondary school age.

The following chapters are designed to provide parents with ideas with which they may assist the musical development of their children. They do not purport to provide a 'method' of working, since parents should find that their own and their children's ideas prove to be of greater value.

Before I embark on suggestions for a positive approach to music-making, let us pause for a moment to examine the nature of the fear experienced by so many when musical education is discussed. As soon as their opinion is invited, with no examination of the phrase, most parents will pronounce themselves 'unmusical'. Even if they themselves enjoy *listening* to music, they feel that there is no way of sharing this enjoyment with their child without the intervention of an expert, or other than by simply waiting for him to grow up.

What then of the fields of enjoyment in which apparently fewer problems are encountered?

Words, forming the basis of our communication with each other, can be used to tell stories, poems, jokes or riddles. They can be used seriously or in fun. The measure of a child's achievement in learning a language is immense. The success is due to a maximum degree of sharing.

Painting initially presents few problems. A child is given lovely large dollops of brightly coloured paints, and he produces big bright pictures. It is obvious to the parent that he is playing with colours, and ordering them as he sees fit. Whatever the result, a normal parent will remark on his achievement, probably trying to find out what it is the child has depicted. Even if the parent is way off the mark, and the picture is merely an

expression of his sheer delight in the colours, a child will joyfully join in the guessing game and the discussion of all aspects of the picture. Probably mum will show the picture to dad when he comes home from work, and the process of sharing will begin all over again. (As he gets bigger, however, the child will notice that his parents themselves do not 'waste time' painting pictures, and gradually his pleasure diminishes, until it is shared only at school. In order to share to the maximum degree, he paints pictures that become indistinguishable from those of his classmates. After that, only a few children take real pleasure in the world of vision.)

Music, in these basic terms, is a non-starter. The child's preoccupation with the raw materials of sound often goes completely unnoticed. His pleasure in rattles for instance, is not shared aurally with his parents—they watch, but do not listen to the source of his delight. Sounds of his environment, exciting to him, do not reach his parents' ears unless they have a message to convey. Gradually the child realises that his parents do not hear anything which is not either meaningful, or loud, or unexpected.

Seeing her baby's attention caught, a mother will *look* to find the source of his interest. It does not occur to her to *listen*—in any case, the moment may have passed when she could share the experience.

So whilst the smallest painted ant beside his big painted house is praised for its attention to detail, the child realises that his musical 'ants' have to be pretty enormous before they're noticed at all. As a result, the noise level shoots up, and he gets told to 'shut up', or to 'go into the garden with all that noise'. His fascination is gradually dulled, and by the time he's 'old enough to have piano lessons now', music has vanished from his soul.

The key to enjoyment is obviously to do with sharing and communication. A small child allowed to help mum or dad cook or mend the car is going to grow up with an interest in and respect for these activities. That is perfectly obvious. Sharing these things comes naturally to most parents.

But how, if you can't 'do' it, do you share music?

The answer is so simple.

First by learning to hear, then by learning to control sound. For music is just controlled sound.

Given the run of the kitchen and pantry, a young child is unlikely to come up with 'haute cuisine' cooking. Given a box of paints, a young child is unlikely to produce a Velasquez. Nor will his first words add up to a sonnet.

Listen to your child: he can speak English before he goes to school. You did not have to be a poet or a professor of languages in order to enable him to do so. Although you are not Escoffier or even Fanny Cradock, you can share, without any feeling of inadequacy, your child's delighted sense of achievement in making a simple rock cake.

Similarly, you do not have to be a wonderful musician, or even a practising musician of any kind, to share with your child his early experiments with, and pleasure in, sound.

Let us now consider those aspects of sound which are open to control. It should be then quite an easy matter to invent some games to play with them.

To begin with, here is a short, somewhat long-faced definition of sound—which you can forget as soon as you understand and can use it.

Sound has three elements: *pitch*, *timbre* and *dynamic*. The space it occupies is *time*.

Pitch is the highness or lowness of a sound. It is caused by regular vibrations through the air; these cause a sympathetic reaction upon the ear-drum, which transmits the information received to the brain.

Two or more pitches can react simultaneously upon different areas of the ear-drum, enabling the brain to recognise a multitude of sounds. If the vibrations received are irregular or infrequent, there is no recognisable pitch, and the resultant sound is termed 'noise'.

There is no reason to exclude noise from your music-making.

Timbre is the word used to denote the 'colour' of a sound. It varies according to the nature of the materials used and the method employed to produce the sound. It is the result of the natural harmonics or overtones and their varying strengths which are produced by the instrument and its activator.

Dynamic is the loudness or softness of a sound, and is controlled by the initial speed of attack—followed in the case of a sustained, non-percussiveG sound by firm application of pressure or speed to preserve the impetus.

A young child is fully aware of all these qualities. He is naturally interested in any sound that catches his attention. He will experiment with pitches, noises, timbres and dynamics. He is a great imitator, as is evident from his capacity to learn to speak. He plays with vocal sounds that please him; gradually he eliminates those which do not play a part in his native language.

Whilst paying particular attention to the formation of his first 'real' words, he is also able to imitate the 'tunes' of the complete sentences he hears around him.

The musician in him is fully occupied.

Once the child can speak, his parents commonly ignore all those other sounds which still excite and interest him; unencouraged and unshared, this larger vocabulary of sound dwindles away. (Some children store these unused sounds and their secret enjoyment of them until later—witness the vocal games played by some comedians.)

Except where this awareness of sound lies fallow, no number of formal 'music' lessons can compensate a child for the very personal involvement which he risks losing during his earliest years.

There are yet those adults who will complain that they have never 'understood' music.

Do they 'understand' colour? They have probably never felt the need to do so. And yet they enjoy it.

I recently met a man who could not see green. Driving through the countryside, I felt an immense sadness that he could not experience the abundance of beauty which I took for granted. Following my sadness through, I realised that he could not see either all the green particles which occur in quite different colours. How very vividly since then I have seen what he could never see.

What is it then, that those who 'don't understand' music are lacking? It is merely the experience of music.

The reason for this is not hard to find; they have stopped allowing their world of sound to develop. Unlike my friend, they *have* the equipment, but have allowed it, in the acquisition of their 'common' sense, to go rusty: it has long stopped accepting information that is not *useful*.

And the Arts are not useful: their purpose is a spiritual one. (It may be of use to have a few enlightened spirits around, but that is something else.)

The equipment can be revived. Your child will have aural experiences he would like you to share. To describe them is beyond him—beyond everybody. They exist only in terms of sound. Since you do not seem to hear them, he has no means of sharing. He notices, imitates, plays with sound. You don't. You keep your sound locked up in a little black box. Sometimes you open it and make it produce nice tunes for him; that's good. But he has good sounds too. You never know they exist; so you must learn once more to listen.

Allow yourself the luxury of total relaxation for two or three minutes. Close your eyes and let the sounds you have chosen to ignore for years flood your consciousness. Don't consider the source or reason for the sounds—just examine them. Examine their pitch, dynamic and timbre. Listen hard to discover the tiniest variation. A running tap, a fridge that cuts in and out again, a bicycle bell, the factory hooter can all be as enthralling as the birdsong you sometimes allow to cross the threshold of your consciousness because it is a 'beautiful' sound of nature.

Because you have exercised control over your hearing, you have created a piece of music.

All these sounds are a real part of your child's world: a part you have chosen to prune away as being excessive to your needs.

It may be that time and place have conspired against you, and that the only sounds you hear are (as yet) ugly. Try somewhere else, or at a different time.

Eventually you should begin to 'understand'.

Chapter 1

LEARNING TO CONTROL SOUND

Once you have begun to be aware of the music for free, you will more easily notice the times when your child is listening. When this happens, stop what you're doing for a moment to show him that you hear as well. If you can imitate the sound with your voice, do so. If he's interested, he will probably try too. Very often the more grotesque the imitation the greater will be his enjoyment of it.

As you take your child shopping in the pram, join in with the sounds around you. (You'll probably cause a few raised eyebrows, but there's no harm in seeming a little eccentric.)

A generator in our road hums two notes to itself day and night. As we used to pass it, my two children and I joined in. At first we copied the notes it sang, then added two others to make a chord. Eventually one of us would make up a tune, one a rhythm, the other complete a chord. Finally we became aware of all the other sounds which lent their presence to make each performance a unique affair.

When you pass an identifiable site, or visit a new place, listen critically to the sounds it makes. Without the deafening roar of unmuted drills, a building site is usually a fascinating place to stop and listen, since it is often busy with all sorts of unexpected sounds, as well as things to see.

Once attuned to the possibilities, make a collection of sounds for your child to play with. Put the objects on a tray or into a box, to be brought out as an exciting alternative to his painting materials or bricks. You will find plenty of things to use, but here are a few examples:

1 A balloon.
2 A small battery, or clockwork motor.
3 A bamboo flute.
4 An elastic band.
5 Things to bang and things to stroke.
6 Bottles of various shapes and sizes. (Filled with varying amounts of water, they produce different pitches when struck, or blown across the open neck.)
7 As many types of striker as you can find or make. (Try to provide some with hard heads and some with soft.)
8 Any old musical instrument, regardless of condition. Especially valuable are those with a sounding board and strings, such as a skiffle box, a mandolin, auto harp, or the inside of a piano. (See section on the piano later in this chapter.)
9 Musical toys of a sturdy nature. (There is nothing worse than a favourite sound whose source breaks and cannot be replaced.)

10   Paper, foil and other rustly items.

It is a good idea to provide these items very gradually, so that the child learns to hear that each source of sound can provide him with a variety of possibilities.

Do not confine your enjoyment to the *sound* qualities of the things you use, but let the child absorb *all* their pleasurable aspects, so that his understanding includes every type of experience they have to offer him.

When he is ready, you can help him to begin his first attempts at physical control of sound.

You could, for instance, prepare a selection of things to tear. Paper, a worn sheet, corrugated cardboard soaked in water, etc, etc. Show the child how to tear a piece of paper very slowly—then how to rip it up very fast. Try with the sheet and the cardboard. See how slowly he can tear the item without stopping his action. Have a competition to see who can tear a page of newspaper the slowest—then the quickest. Amongst the sensations he can enjoy will be the change in timbre and dynamic. Indicate the difference to him, and get him to listen to you. Tell him to shut his eyes and think of one of his stories—perhaps the sounds you make can illustrate one of the things that happens. If not, don't force the issue—carry on with the tearing game.

Make some rules for him to follow—as soon as he breaks a rule he is 'out'. If you tear item Number 1 slowly, he must tear item Number 2 slowly. If you tear item Number 2 quickly, he should tear item Number 3 slowly.

Get somebody to join in with a tin plate and a spoon—perhaps to put a stop to any sound when a particular rhythm appears. If the tearing stops with the wrong rhythm, the player is 'out'. (This develops an ability to listen over a period of time—let it be short at first.)

If you have a tape recorder, you should try to make a 'piece' which lasts about two to three minutes. (For having ordered sound, you have created a piece of music.) Playing back such a piece to the child will enable him to examine the sound alone. Ask him to tell you about what happens—try to encourage him to tell you about the sound rather than the actions that caused it.

Perhaps you could use something else in the kitchen—the tap, for instance. Some taps are better than others—yours might be very boring! We had a wonderful tap once; it could sound like Maria Callas or a choking buffalo, and would, if desired, shake the house. It was capable of anything. I think it was the finest instrument we ever had. I have a recording of its beautiful singing somewhere. Sadly the plumber found it in our absence, and put it right.

Don't always use sound in isolation. Help the child to select from his box some sound 'effects' which he can use to illustrate a well-known story as you read it to him. Help him to sort out the appropriate sounds before you

begin—and make a 'performance'. If some sounds seem to be missing from
his collection, try to think of a way in which they may be made. If the child
can himself think of a way of producing the missing sound, so much the
better. If you can record your performance, do so. Get him to listen
carefully to see if the sounds are just right, or whether he can make them
better in any way. Once he has decided upon a performance, rehearse it
carefully, so that he can share it with a parent returning from work, or with
a friend who comes to visit.

If you can store up his performances on tape, he will be thrilled to have
them played back to him as a bedtime treat—or if he is not well and must
stay in bed. The added pleasure of his own participation will lend to these
stories a particular magic which is missing from the commercial cassettes
which are becoming so popular. He will pay very careful and critical
attention to his part in the story, and will very often want to improve his
next attempts.

It may be a good idea too, to illustrate a favourite picture with sound. In
this way, the result will be purely abstract, and you could perhaps play a
guessing game with visitors, who must listen hard to tell which picture is
being played.

Over a long period of time, you could begin to add the presence of a 'real'
musical instrument to your games. It doesn't have to be played 'properly',
but it must always be controlled—just as all the other sounds have been.

It is said that some children can never achieve the control necessary to

play an instrument—but it doesn't seem to me that there is much difference between controlling one simple action and controlling any other. The recent Gulbenkian Report on Training Musicians (1978) would seem to suggest that in order to be considered as a future 'gifted' musician, amongst other qualities (some of an equally dubious nature) a child should be possessed of a naturally occurring kinetic skill and manipulative ability of a high order. When my children were very young I didn't know that; if I had, my daughter would never have been given a cello. I confess that I am somewhat surprised that her cello is still with us, since she falls over everything else, and always has done. As for kinetic skill—it took me a year to teach her how to catch a ball (the year after all her friends could do it, that is) and she has yet, at the age of fourteen, to succeed in transferring any given item from the frying pan to a plate without having to scrape it off the floor.

Since this knowledge has come my way, I have many times observed that some of the world's greatest musicians seem to find it rather difficult to coordinate their limbs when not actually playing their instruments. Perhaps one should not take the experts all that seriously. If the child enjoys his 'sound games', he will enjoy their extension into the field of instrumental sound—whether or not he has the 'approved' qualifications.

There is a very nice cheerful book which you might enjoy when your child has become quite proficient in his games and wants to play something a little more adventurous. It is written for older children, so that they can play music with their friends, but I suspect that it would be much better used by children with some adult direction. The book is called *Fun To Make Music* by Anthony Kemp. It includes many simple ideas for excellent instruments—and a handy man or woman would be able to make the more complicated suggestions quite easily. There are lots of ideas for pieces of music, using 'graphic' or 'prose' notations.[G] This means that you don't have to be able to 'read music', in the conventional sense, to be able to perform the scores. Nowadays these types of score are quite usual—even in the most 'serious' sorts of music.

However you arrange your musical activities together, it is very important not to try and do too much too quickly. The best help a child can have is to be allowed lots of time to take in all the aspects of each new addition to his games before moving on. You should help him to make as many interactions between the sounds he knows as he is able. Otherwise the 'games' will get out of hand, and he will lose his critical powers. There is lots of time—don't use up your ideas all at once. Go at the pace the child dictates; this will give you, also, the time to learn to listen acutely.

One way of doing this is to encourage the child to describe the sounds in his box. You should disappear with the box behind a screen, or a big armchair, and make a sound. First of all, he might say that the sound is 'long', 'short', 'very long' or 'very short'. Then you could ask him if the

sound is 'high' or 'low'. Later on he can tell you if it is loud or soft, sad or happy, strong or weak, serious or funny, smooth or lumpy, red, yellow, blue, green, mauve, square, round, straight, etc, etc.

It is important that the source of the sound is out of sight, so that the child does not associate his description with the look of the object responsible. (Making sounds behind a screen is better than asking him to close his eyes, because not only does it avoid 'peeping', but it also lends an air of mystery to the game.)

Once the child begins to recognise sounds as having different characteristics, you could make drawings of the sounds as he describes them.

Try making a pattern with the sounds he describes—very simple indeed to begin with. Then play the piece you have written. Help him to do the same. He has written a piece of music. He is a composer! Perhaps he could try and play some of his other drawings? Decide first of all which way they should be read—from top to bottom, right to left, or inside out. Ask him if he wants you to join in with any of the parts.

I include on the next page an example of a piece of music based on a drawing by a seven-year-old boy: 'Totemtanz'. It has been performed with enjoyment by children as young as three and as old as sixteen years. An

accompanying rhythm invented by the older children was very sophisticated, but the younger ones invented their own, which of course changed
with each practice!

Don't give up playing games with sound when your child begins to study
'real' music. There is really no difference in essence, and they are an
invaluable training for a young musician—so many children do not have the
advantage of hearing what they play. A young pianist, for example, has
very remote control over the sound he may make—he has only to depress a
key, and the sound is made. There is nothing that he can do to alter it.
Since piano teachers generally teach on their own instruments, they have
little idea what sound the child's own instrument makes; they can only
issue him with instructions as to how to control actions to produce the right
notes, according to the composer's directions. They very seldom stop to ask
a child to listen critically to the sound he is producing. It is possible the
child does not even notice after a while that his own piano sounds
completely different from his teacher's—he is more concerned with
practising the physical actions of getting the 'notes' in the right order and
time. No longer are notes *sounds* to him. They have turned into little black
dots. When that happens, there is little chance of enjoying 'real' music any
more.

TOTEMTANZ

The drawing opposite has been done by a seven-year-old child. It can be
used to make a piece of music in any way you choose. First decide upon the
kind of impression the image conveys (as you will see the main features are
numbered). You might decide that the eyes look rather melancholic, the
nose rather squirmy or energetic and the mouth somewhat fierce. The other
features make the face seem busy and some of the lines suggest animals.

Find sounds to convey the feelings you have chosen about the piece, and
write them down against each number so that you can remember them—or
change your mind if you decide one of the sounds is inappropriate.

The next thing to think about is whether you will provide a background
to your series of aural events; there is a rhythm which those who can read
music may choose to use—or of course you could make up your own, which
need not be in only one part. And there is a striped awning which suggests
perhaps a kind of tribal association which you could consider.

All you have to do now is to decide whether you are going to read the
'music' from top to bottom, right to left or from the outside in or inside out.
Perhaps you could try any or all of these possibilities.

A tape recording could be made so that you can exercise some criticism
over the results in order to raise your sights and standards.

The next thing to do is to perform your child's own pieces.

TOTEMTANZ

repeat ad lib.   (notes marked thus: — should be heavily stressed)

THE PIANO

In many households the piano exists as part of a heritage, or as a homely addition to the furnishings, long before children or music lessons are ever dreamt of. If it is there it should be used—for it is a veritable box of delights. People get hung up about their pianos. They think of them in sentimental terms, and stop their children from enjoying them until they can 'play properly'.

The fact is, pianos are hardy creatures. Obviously, as an amateur, you will not be persuaded to take outrageous risks with your instrument, and neither should you be; if this were to be the case you would not enjoy the sounds you can make. But you could consider your attitude more closely, to see that it is not responsible for inhibiting your own or your child's enjoyment for no reason other than tradition or taboo.

A piano is full of magic. You must have noticed a young child selecting the 'funny' notes for special attention. These are the sounds which may be caused by a broken string setting up sympathetic vibrations within the other strings, and clanging against them—or perhaps a broken hammer which clicks as it reaches the key-bed. If you play the piano in the conventional manner, these sounds will jar upon your nerves, for they may prevent you from playing for your own pleasure. They could also serve to remind you that you have not yet asked the tuner to call—which may in itself cause you irritation.

But to a child, these sounds have no such meaning. They are different, and fascinating. To him, the sound he has caused is as enchanting as the discovery of a brand new timbre to a great composer.

Listen with him, and enjoy it.

A piano does not have to be damaged to produce wonderful new sounds. Many times I have attended school functions where a harpsichord effect has been faked simply by laying tissue paper over the strings of the piano when it seemed more appropriate to the situation. You would certainly not balk at the idea of experimenting with different weights of paper placed in such a way. Why not other objects?

In Chapter 4 you will find instructions for opening up both an upright and a grand piano to expose the strings and the sounding board. Once this is done, wedge the sustaining pedal (the one on the right) well down into position. (This must be done very carefully indeed with an upright, for the strings which you will play are situated just behind the pedals, and tiny fingers and unprotected toes may get pinched if the action is stiff.)

Now take a piece of stiff cardboard, and slowly stroke the lowest strings. Because the other strings are free to vibrate, this sound is very mysterious. It does not stop straight away as the percussive sound of a hammer striking the string does, and your child will be able to examine it as it proceeds—for as long as he wants.

Next gently pluck one of the low strings—watch it vibrate—this may be the first time your child has been able to 'see' sound in the making.

Wait until the sound has died away completely, and then pluck the string again. This time have ready a small piece of plastic—perhaps a picnic knife. Gently place the plastic against the vibrating string. Try with other objects, and examine the different timbres. Try with the higher strings; the sound won't last so long. If you are lucky enough to have a grand piano, there are lots of things you can do using the horizontal position of the strings. For instance, one of the loveliest sounds in the world can be made by gently setting in rocking motion a fairly light bottle on the higher middle strings, and differently weighted and proportioned bottles in other areas. With the right bottle in the right place, it will continue rocking in 'perpetual' motion, so long as the sustaining pedal is held down or wedged in place.

Move the bottles around on the strings. Dark and mysterious at the bottom—screechy and terrifying at the top.

Roll a bottle or a round paper weight across the strings, from one end to the other. (All such items should of course be clean and dry.)

Tap the sounding board very gently with a finger (avoiding the nail which will scratch the thin varnish), or a soft-headed striker. (Do be careful not to be rough with the sounding board, for it is usually very thin to allow for maximum vibration—and cannot be easily or cheaply replaced—but do not ignore its possibilities.)

With a variety of strikers, gently tap in different places. All the strings will respond if the pedal is down.

Take your time, and listen to every aspect of the sounds you make. When your child has had enough, you will know. Do not use up all the possibilities at once, but examine the implications and variations of all that you do.

Make your own experiments. If you are careful and sensitive, absolutely no harm will come to the instrument, for your instinct will inform you when there is danger of going too far.

Perhaps you could help your child to illustrate some of his stories with sounds made entirely inside the piano. With a tape-recorder you could do a number of animated readings which will give him great pleasure.

There is no reason why you should not use 'preparations' to produce exciting variations of timbre. Such 'preparations' are merely an extension of the mute which can be used on all kinds of other instruments to soften or to change the sound normally produced.

Mutes can be made of any suitable materials—as is required. Here is a quotation from an old classic book about the violin. 'As effective a mute as any may be extemporised by placing a penny or half-crown behind and against the bridge, setting it under the A string with its edges resting on the E and D.' (*Violin Making: As It Was And Is*, edited by Heron Allen, 1885.)

John Tilbury, a leading exponent of new music, watched by his daughter as he 'prepares' a piano for performance. (It is not advisable for amateurs to undertake such radical treatment unless they know exactly what they are doing.)

String players usually carry a selection of mutes so that they may choose the most appropriate to their task. Brass players may use commercial mutes, or may operate one hand inside the bell of the instrument to change the tone. You can do the same with the piano; for instance, a thin piece of metal carefully threaded under and over the three strings of a high register

An instrument made by Hugh Davies, using domestic oddments over a crude sounding board. Amplification is by means of a small contact microphone which can be seen at the junction formed by the comb and the coiled spring.

note can produce a stunning sound. Find the best place for it—it will sound different with even the slightest change of position. If the key is depressed normally, the well-positioned 'preparation' will produce a magical sound. A three-year-old would appreciate its fantastic qualities, and may like to use it for instance as the sound of a fairy's wand. An older child should enjoy it for its own sake.

Nuts and bolts, or any other found object of an appropriate size and shape, may be inserted between the lower single strings to enable the keyboard player to produce a whole orchestra of new sounds. (The preparations should always be inserted by a capable adult, who will not risk 'losing' them inside the instrument. It is as well to check the number of insertions against the number of extractions at the end of the day.)

I suppose that sooner or later 'Piano Preparations' will become commercially available, just like violin mutes, and then eyebrows will no longer be raised at their appearance in the concert hall, for they will have passed into the acceptable realm of established usage. Until this happens, surprise yourself with the successful marriage of the piano with a specially devised collection of junk.

If you are electrically minded, or can fit the simplest plug, try fitting a contact microphone to various parts of the piano, and to other sources of tiny sounds. This acts as a kind of sound-microscope, and just as most people are thrilled by seeing the perfect and beautiful blown-up images of quite ordinary matter, so may they be equally thrilled by hearing the surprising beauty of tiny sounds magnified into life.

(Of course, if you are using a grand piano, you should make arrangements for the small child to stand where he can see and take part in the wealth of music you have found for him. Perhaps he could be given a whole

Hugh Davies helping a child to make an electronic harp.

area of his own to operate, once he has been helped to consider its possibilities.)

It is quite possible that parents and children could become so interested in the new kinds of music they find presented to them by these means that they could begin to make their own instruments based on strings, sounding boards and contact microphones, such as those made by the composer and inventor of amazing instruments, Hugh Davies, which always attract a great deal of enthusiasm from the children who have been lucky enough to encounter them.

I would suggest though, that each new sound source is fully explored and made use of in a piece of music as you go along. One of the saddest tales I have to tell is of a museum with a famous and beautiful collection of instruments which are barely, if ever, heard by the large number of children who see them. If they are inspired by their school's visit to make their own instruments, the curator has never heard of any which were ever played. They hang—like those in the museum—on the wall or in cases, silent for ever.

Chapter 2

TEACHING YOUR CHILD TO READ MUSIC

Before I have time to lose any readers, let me assure you that reading 'conventional' music notation is very, very easy.

Seeing in this chapter the appearance of the dreaded black dot, some of you may feel inclined to skip it and abandon all hope. Before you do so however, read on a little. If you really can't take it, or if you are psychologically unprepared, you can always choose to leave it to a teacher later on. It would be a pity if this were to happen, for reading music can be great fun. It is also a great achievement for a child to make, and is much simpler than reading words.

If you want to read a word, you must be able to combine all the separate sounds of the letters in the right order before you can make sense. A complete musical sound however, is portrayed by just one symbol.

Publishers of children's books realise that a child needs to see big letters, with lots of space around them. Unfortunately, publishers of children's music don't seem to have caught on. You will have to write the notes yourself so that your child can take them in; make the note-heads really big. Buy a big scrap book, and a black felt marker.

N.B. Before you read any further, please realise that every single stage that you reach with your child will be as a result of many many sessions. Of course you will not, if you are unused to reading notation, be able to understand the whole of this chapter in the time you will take to read the words. You may have two or three years in which to develop an ability to read music with your child. In which case, you should imagine the material given in this chapter spread over that sort of period.

Here is a note. It is complete. You can play it on a drum.

Does it frighten you? You can draw a face on it if you want to.

And here are two notes joined together.

I shall give the Hungarian time-names, since I shall be recommending that you make use of Kodaly's[G] material later on.

The first note I introduced shall be named 'taa', and the pair which followed shall be called 'ti-ti'.

Your first 'note games' will consist of writing 'taa' and 'ti-ti' on two big cards, and asking your child to call them by these names.

The cards will look like this (sizes are only rough guides):

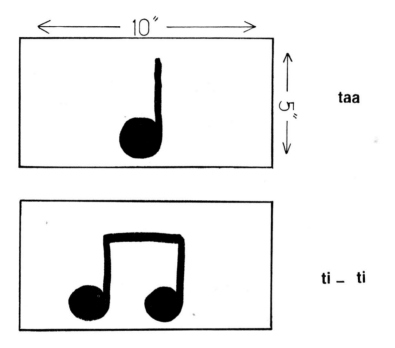

Once he is absolutely sure of what they are called, you can introduce the first rhythm games. For unlike words, you can take one aspect of musical notation at a time, and it will make complete sense.

Taa and ti-ti have the same value in time.

Pretend you are soldiers. March around the room saying:

ONE two *three* four ONE two *three* four ONE two *three* four

Perhaps you can find some music to march to?

Next try:

TAA taa *taa* taa TAA taa *taa* taa TAA taa *taa* taa

And then:

TI-ti ti-ti *ti*-ti ti-ti TI-ti ti-ti *ti*-ti ti-ti TI-ti ti-ti *ti*-ti ti-ti

In this way the child will become familiar with the names of the notes he is about to read. Don't introduce them too soon.

When he is ready, write on the first page of his scrap book a group of four big taa notes. You will find that he has no difficulty in reading it. This group of four beats, you should call a 'bar'. (See Example 1.) The bar[G] is traditionally the basic measure of time in western music.

Next write out and show the child a group of four pairs of ti-ti notes (Example 2). He will know just how to say them. Don't forget to give the eight notes lots of space.

Make a big 'flash card' on which is written a bar of taa notes, and another on which is written a bar of ti-ti notes. (Keep the number of beats in each to four at the moment.)

Find a 'banging' instrument and striker, and give them to your child.

Produce one of the flash cards from behind your back, and ask him to bang out the notes as he says their names. Produce the other card and let him do the same—as he improves he could use a different instrument for each group.

Try to keep a steady rhythm going.

Make up lots of different rhythms, using both taas and ti-tis. See Example 3. (The names and numbers are for your benefit—the child should just see the notes.)

Work with flash cards may become quite advanced. This picture shows a class of children at Chetham's Hospital School; the children are singing a song, at the same time clapping an independent rhythm from the shuffled flash cards held in front of them.

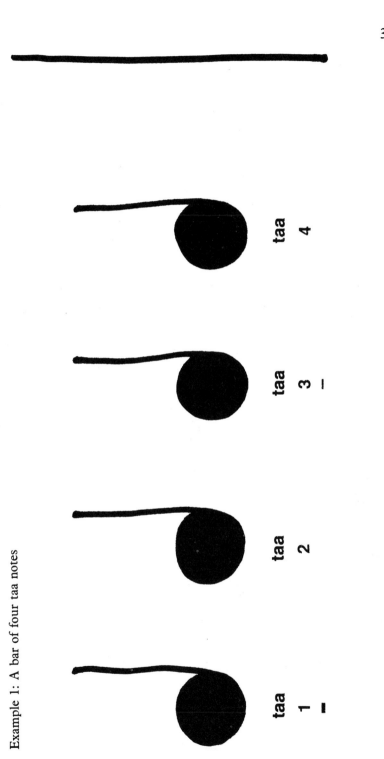

Example 1: A bar of four taa notes

Example 2: A bar of four pairs of ti – ti notes. You should make
them as big as the taa notes

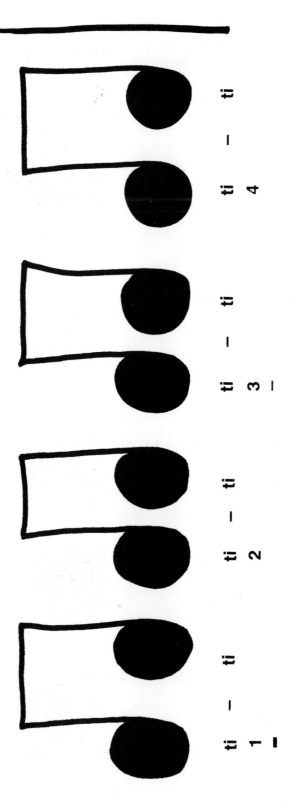

ti – ti   ti – ti   ti – ti   ti – ti
1   2   3   4
–   –   –

Example 3: Some rhythms using both taa and ti – ti notes

a)

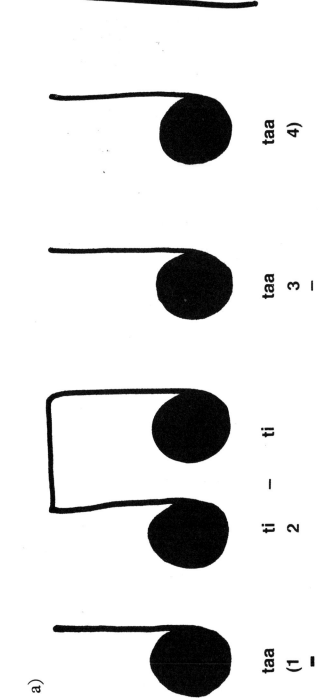

taa	ti	–	ti	taa	taa
(1	2			3	4)
–				–	

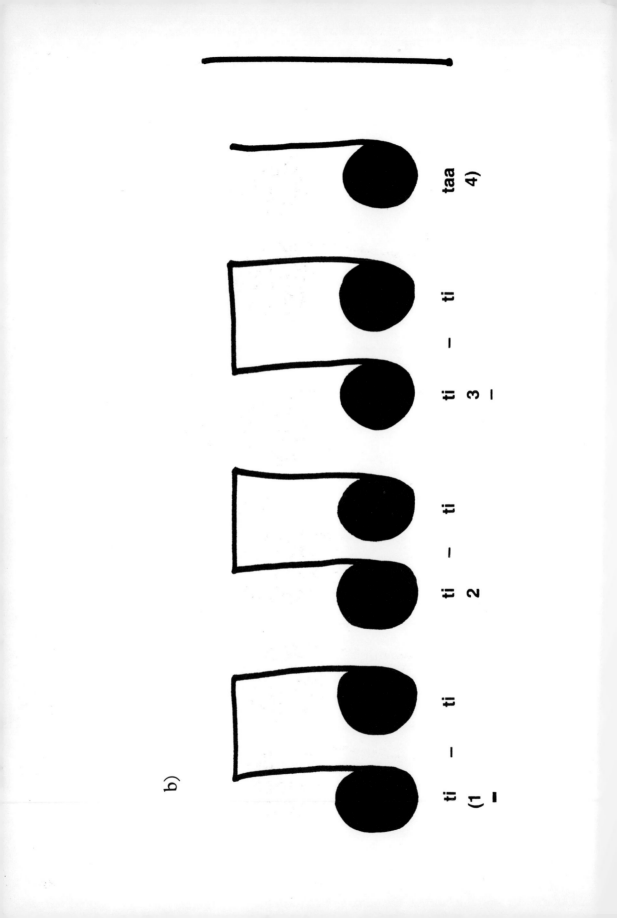

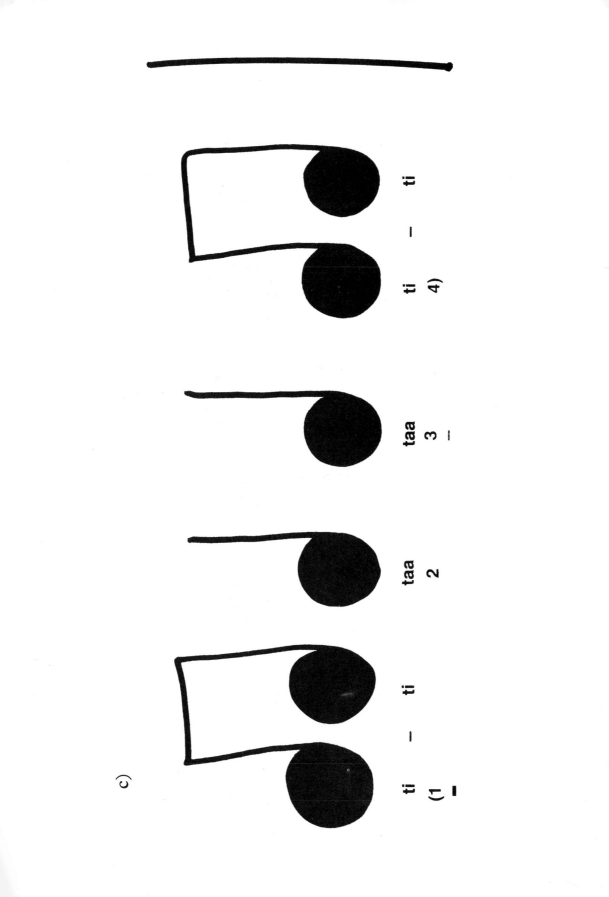

These games can go on for months, or years—depending on the age and aptitude of your child.

There are hundreds of different combinations of taas and ti-tis. As your child becomes familiar with notation, you could make the notes smaller and the pieces longer.

Gradually he will not need to say the time-names at all. But if you experience any difficulty in playing the sounds, you should return to saying the names first of all. Also, with any new material that is tried, the time-names should first be spoken in the 'speaking' game.

On the next two pages are some very simple march rhythms. Each bar[G] has a line after it, to enable you to get the accents in the right place. There is a double bar line at the end of each piece. It could be a good idea to draw these in with a different coloured felt pen, so that they don't get muddled up with the notes.

You will also notice that the figure 4 appears at the beginning of each little piece. This is to tell you that there are four beats in each bar, so that you can prepare it in your head by saying 'ONE two three four' before you begin.

I have made each piece four bars long. This will give them a nice feeling of balance. When you make up your own pieces, you should model them on the same shape to begin with.

Although more than one piece appears on one page of this book, you should write out each one on a page of its own in your child's book of pieces. Make the book as cheerful as possible, but keep the notes clear.

Do not try to do too much in one session. Perhaps you could use one rhythm at a time in a more colourful setting—as part of a story, or together with a composition your child has already played.

Even if you don't do any more than play with the rhythms I have suggested, you will have conquered your own fear of notation. It is likely that your child had no such fear to begin with.

Five Little March Rhythms

(3)

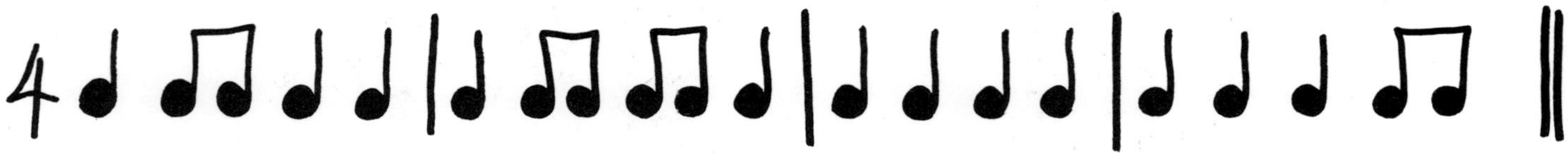

(4)

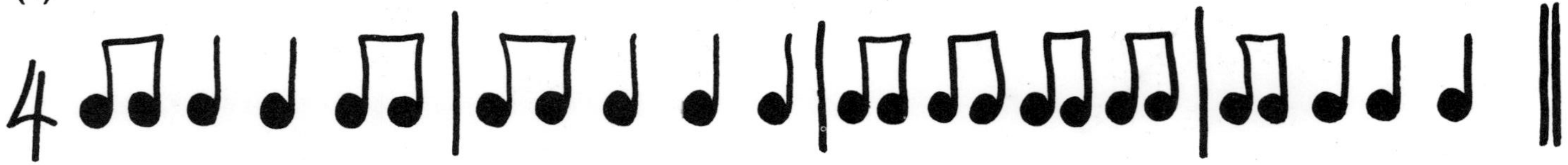

(5)

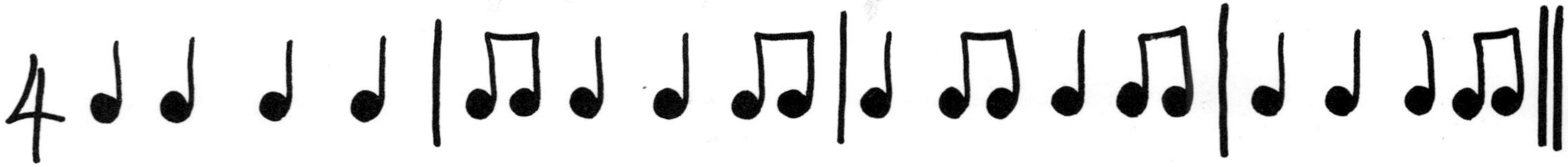

Do you feel like going on?

If so, perhaps you could use a waltz instead of a march. This is in 3 time, that is, it has *three* beats in a bar. You should prepare yourself by saying, '*one* two three *one* two three *one* two three *one* two three' before you begin to say the notes. This will help you to get the rhythm right. You will notice that there is only one beat with an accent this time—making this rhythm even simpler than the march.

On the next two pages are some waltz rhythms. This time the number 3 appears at the beginning, to say that there are three beats in each bar. There are still four bars in each piece for the sake of a good balance.

Make the notes nice and big, one piece at a time in your child's music book. When you have played these pieces, help the child to compose some of his own.

Try to get some recorded marches and waltzes, and see if your child can 'accompany' them with one or another of his rhythmic pieces.

Six Little Waltzes

(1)

(2)

(3)

43

When you have had lots of time to practise these, and your own pieces, you are ready to include two more rhythms in your music making:

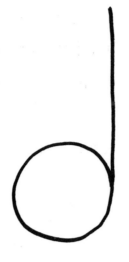

taa-aa

This 'taa-aa' is, as you will guess, worth two beats.
   And:

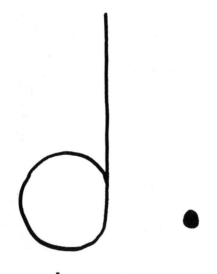

taa-aa-aa

'Taa-aa-aa' is worth three beats. (A dot after any note represents half the time value of that note.)

Here is an example of a piece which uses the new two-beat note 'taa-aa'. You will find others in the next group of examples.

taa-aa taa-aa taa taa taa taa ti – ti ti – ti taa taa taa ti – ti taa-aa
(1 2 3 4 1 2 3 4 1 2 3 4 1 2 3 4)

And here is a piece which uses 'taa-aa-aa'. There are more examples in the next group.

taa-aa-aa   taa-aa-aa   taa ti – ti   ti – ti   taa-aa-aa
(1 2 3 1 2 3 1 2 3 1 2 3)

Don't muddle your child by letting him see the names of the notes—he will be happier simply to be told what they are.

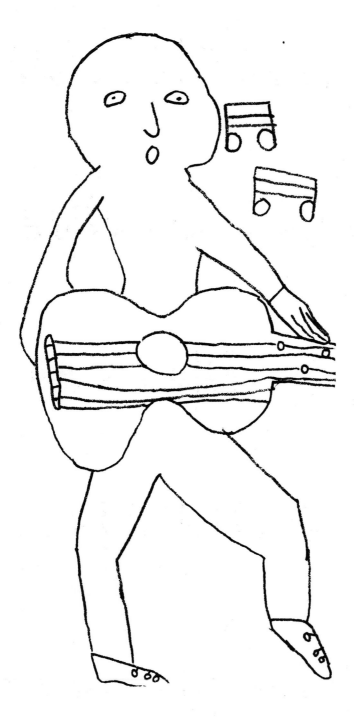

Five New Rhythm Pieces

(1)

(2)

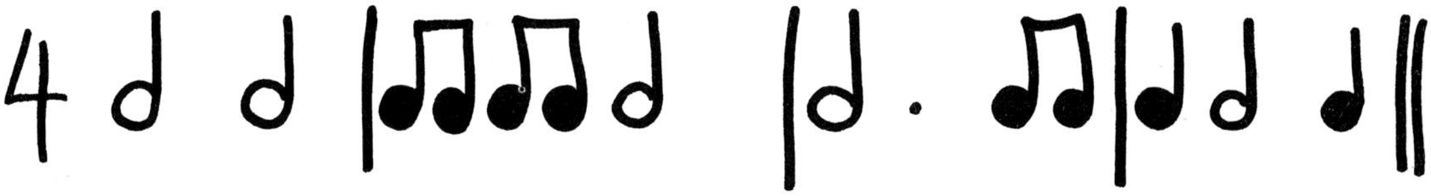

(3)

(4)

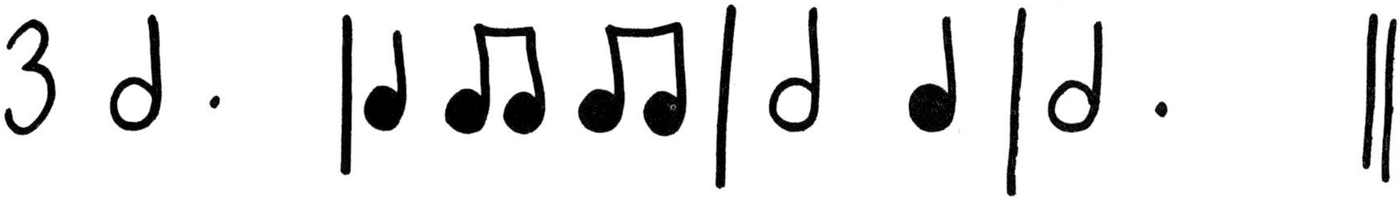

(5)

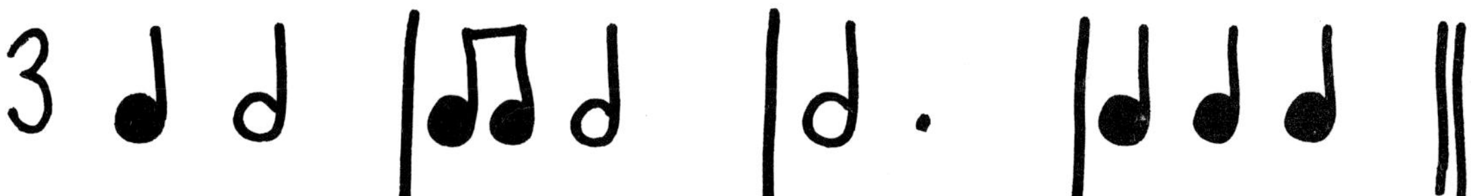

It is now time to introduce the longest note you will need. It is called 'taa-aa-aa-aa', and is worth four beats. It cannot therefore be included in your waltz rhythms, which have only room for three beats in each bar. When it appears, it takes up the whole of a four-beat bar. It usually occurs at the end of a piece—in the middle it would sound too much like a long rest. So when you use it, unless you have another part going at the same time, keep it until the end of your march rhythms.

Here it is:

taa-aa-aa-aa

It looks a bit like an egg lying on its side—don't make it round like the notes which have stems.

Here are some examples which use the four-beat note alongside all the others you have learnt:

(1)

(2)

(3)

And here are some rhythms in 2 time, which sound like little soldiers with short legs marching briskly along. Before you begin, say 'one two one two one two one two' to put you in the right mood. (There is no room for either 'taa-aa-aa' or 'taa-aa-aa-aa' to appear in any of these bars.)

Before you proceed to anything more complicated, you should try fitting together two pieces which have the same number of beats in a bar. If they go at the same pace, they *should* reach home together.

When you have become experts at this game, you could try fitting together three or more parts.

Here is an example. You should compose lots more of your own (use the pieces you have already written—don't bother writing them out again).

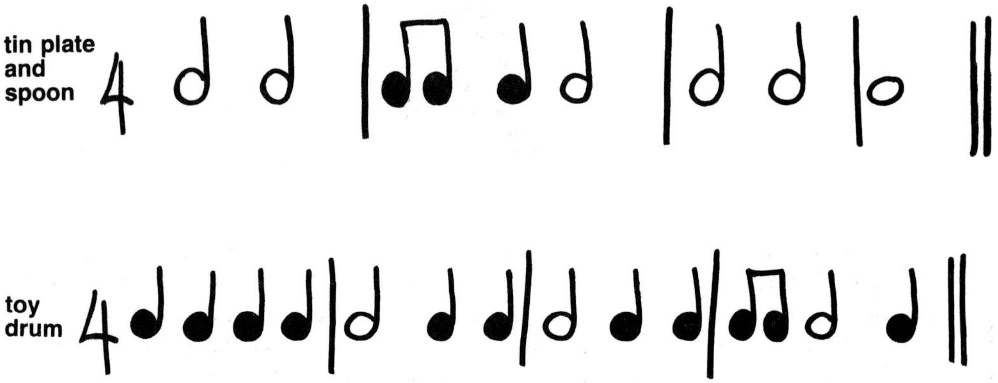

tin plate
and
spoon

toy
drum

Make sure that you both count yourselves in, very firmly, with 'ONE two *three* four' before you begin.

You can make quite complex pieces of music in this way. Repeat each piece four times. Introduce some louds and softs into the playing. It should be a lot of fun.

If however, you find this muddling, leave it for a few months, and carry on with the simpler exercises and games. Don't ever go on for longer than your child wants to—and as soon as he seems muddled, stop. When you have a few moments to yourself, check that all your instructions have been correctly given and that you are sure of yourself. There is no reason to tell your child that you find music 'difficult'—it could make him see problems where he saw none before.

If you can encourage another parent or two to join in (or even better, if you can persuade a play-group leader to participate) do so, for music is a sociable activity, and the sooner it may be enjoyed in such a way, the better the progress will be.

If you find that music is easier than you thought, you should introduce pitch into your sessions.

This necessitates drawing a set of lines; the notes are written under, on or

over the lines. For the moment, we shall only use the notes under and on *one* line. If you know the music notation system called 'tonic sol-fa', you should call them 'doh' and 'ray'. (I shall use phonetic spelling.)

If you don't know the notes 'doh ray', they occur as 'save our' in the British National Anthem ('God *save our* gracious . . .'). They are the first two notes of any normal scale.

When you are dealing with pitch, you should use big notes again—even though they have probably got a good deal smaller through practice. In this way, the child will easily see that a note that *looks* higher also *sounds* higher.

Because we are dealing with only two pitches for the moment, we only really need one line. But I am going to ask you to draw a group of five, because that is what is used in notation. Five lines make up what is termed a 'stave'.G Since doh and ray occur at the low end of the musical scale, this will give you a chance to become familiar with a rational base for action.

In your child's music book, draw a group of five lines, about eight inches long, and one inch apart.

Because the space between the lines is one inch, this is also to be the diameter of the note-heads.

Draw doh, just touching the bottom line, and ray, which has the bottom line running right through the middle.

Now put the stems to the note-heads. Make sure that they reflect the different heights of the note-heads. The top of ray's stem should be about half an inch higher than that of doh. (If this all sounds terribly fussy and difficult, just look at the illustration. You will soon get the hang of making the notes correctly, quite automatically, and freehand.)

There should be no difficulty in telling which note is higher, either from looking at the note-head, or from looking at the top of the stem.

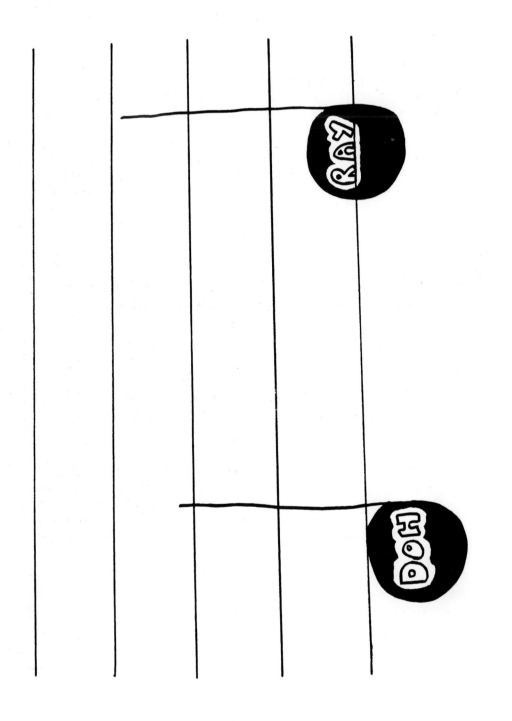

(The reader who already reads music will notice that there is no sign of a clef.^G This is because a clef 'fixes' a note at a certain pitch. This is not a good idea. Doh should be sung at your child's natural pitch. Do not give the notes 'letter-names'.)

When you have a nice big picture of doh and ray side by side, get a long thin stick, and put the 'music' firmly up at your child's eye level, at a comfortable reading distance away.

Point to one note, then the other—singing the names as you point. Ask the child to join in as soon as he can. (Pitch according to the child's singing voice.)

Get a good steady rhythm going, and play around with the notes—sometimes pointing to the same note two or three times in a row.

You could begin with a march rhythm. It could go something like this. (Don't muddle the child by showing him any writing except the notes in his book—just the two of them.)

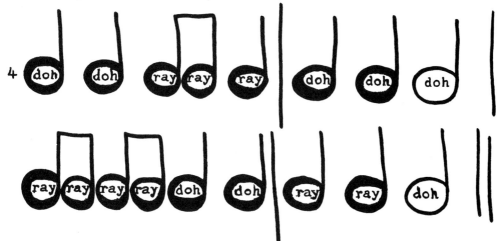

You should make up the tunes as you go along. Ask the child to choose a march or a waltz. 'Play' the notes with the stick very slowly but steadily.

When he is ready, give him two milk bottles, tuned to a doh and a ray (by using differing amounts of water), and let him play the tune as well as singing it. (This could be some weeks after you first start playing pitch games.)

Eventually you will be ready to sing and play some real pieces.

Here is how you might tackle them.

First write out the music in the music book – nice and big.

Next, help the child to do all the following exercises:

1 *Say* the time-names.
2 *Clap* the time whilst saying the time-names.
3 *Clap* the time.

4   *Sing* the pitch names.
    (You can help him to keep the proper rhythm by pointing to the notes
    in the right time. You should also help him pitch the notes by making
    your pointer go up or down with the notes.)
5   *Sing* the pitch names with no help from the pointer.
6   *Sing* the time-names in the right pitch.
7   *Play* the piece on two milk bottles.

This may need a bit of practice at first. You should make sure you know
the drill before you play with your child. Perhaps you could try it out with a
friend first.

Here are some other examples of doh and ray you might use later
on—they merely represent two pitches at a certain distance from each
other; relationships with other pitches are logical, and you should not
worry about them yet.

Obviously once you have chosen a doh and a ray, they must remain at the
same pitch for the duration of each piece of music.

I suggest that you keep the note-heads on or below the middle line, since
the stems must be reversed above this point. (Of course, if you know the
rules, go ahead.)

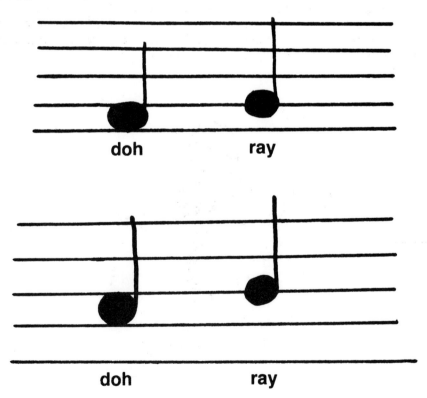

doh   ray

doh   ray

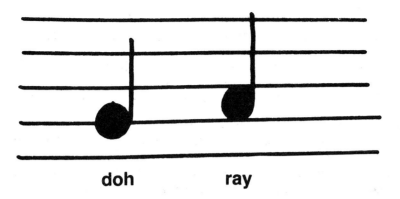

doh   **ray**

There follow some examples of pieces to play. You should make up lots of your own. Give them titles, and make them as expressive as you can when performing them. Show the child how to use different 'instruments', and how to make them play louder or softer.

Perhaps you could begin to decorate the music book with the child's pictures, drawn to illustrate the titles. Stick the drawings opposite the pieces; this will make the book of music begin to be very special.

Because doh and ray are movable, it could be a good idea, when your child feels secure, to place them on a higher line and adjacent space, so that when he later encounters other dohs he doesn't get muddled.

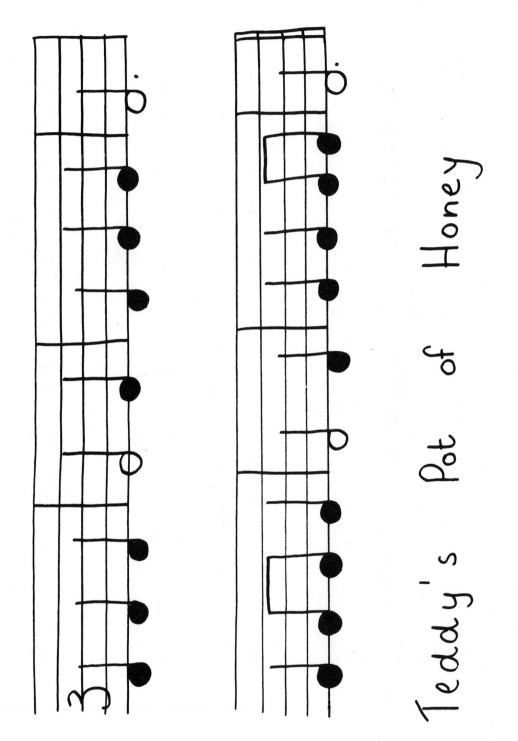

Teddy's Pot of Honey

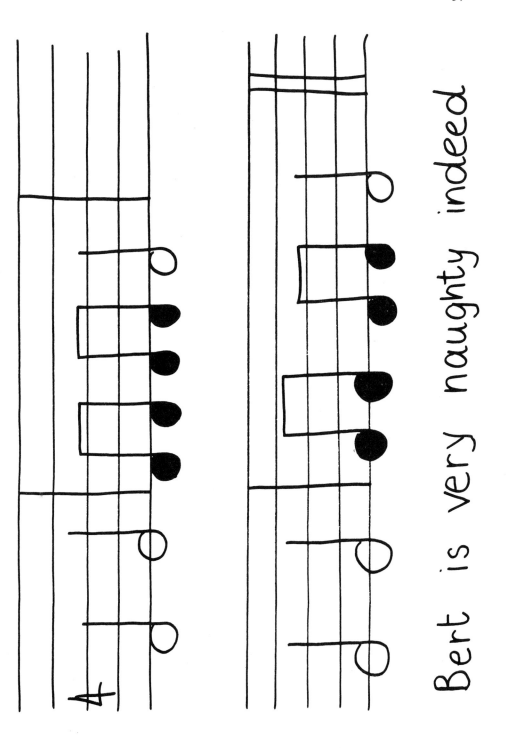

57

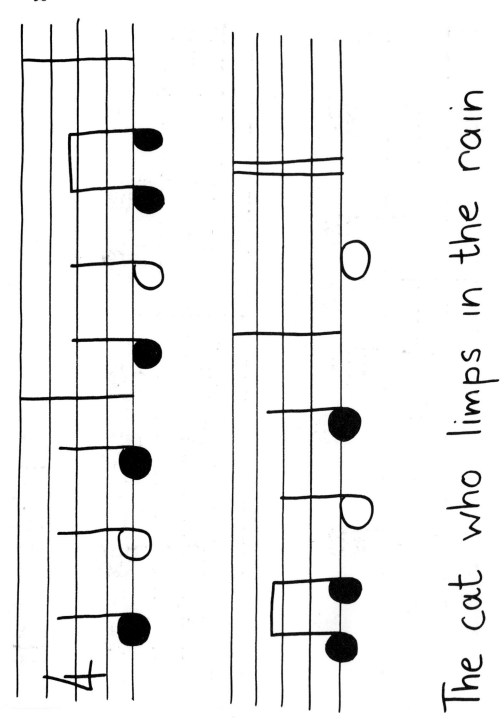

The cat who limps in the rain

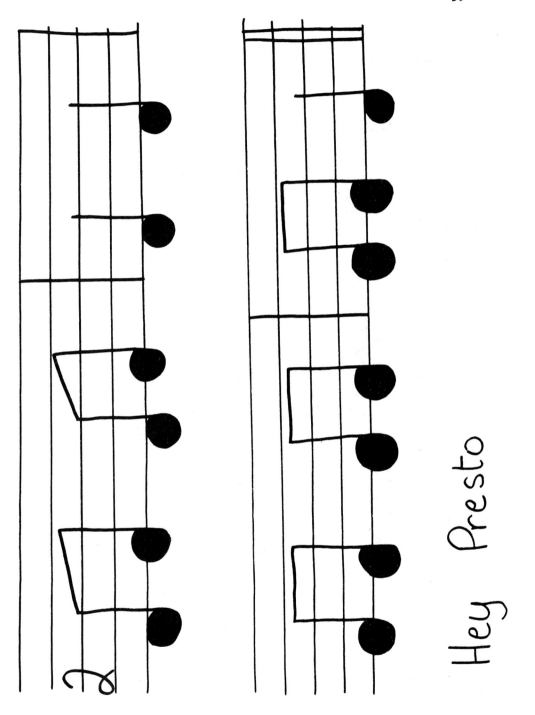

Hey Presto

(Notice how in the last example, when doh and ray are joined as a ti-ti, the joining line slants from one stem to the other.)

Before going on to introduce any more notes, you should know how silence is written. Silence in music is very important indeed. It gives the sound time to breathe, and it can sometimes be very surprising.

We must measure silence in exactly the same way as we measure sound. Each measure of sound has a representative time-name. Likewise, each measure of silence—known as a 'rest'. The names are very similar. Instead of 'taa', we can say 'saa'. It is better if the sound 'aa' is whispered. You should not lose any of the rhythmic impulse though—it is not a sloppy sound at all.

Obviously we shall not need a 'si-si', because that adds up to a 'saa'. Ti-si and si-ti are common however, and look like this:

$$\text{♪} \text{⅂} = \text{ti-si};\qquad \text{⅂} \text{♪} = \text{si-ti}.$$

This is not difficult to understand when you come to use it.

Here are the silences, and their names. I have put them beside the matching notes, so that you can tell easily which is which.

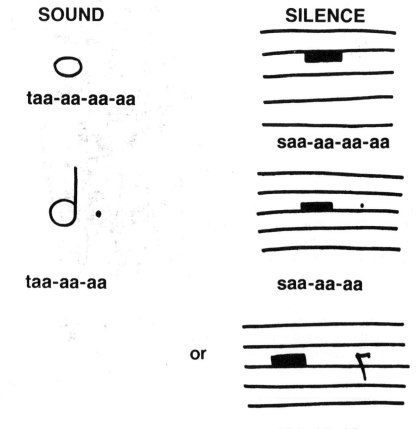

SOUND	SILENCE
taa-aa-aa-aa	saa-aa-aa-aa
taa-aa-aa	saa-aa-aa
or	saa-aa-aa

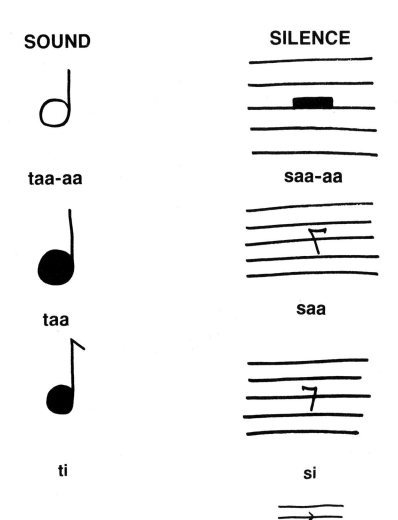

SOUND	**SILENCE**
taa-aa	saa-aa
taa	saa
ti	si

(The printed version of saa looks like this:

You should know, in order to read it, but it is better to stick to the 'backwards number 7' when you are writing.)

I have written the rests on the stave in their right places. (If saa-aa-aa-aa or saa-aa were not stuck to the proper lines, they could easily be muddled up. You can remember that saa-aa-aa-aa has had to stay there so *long* that he has fallen off his line!)

Here are some examples of rests in music.

The alternation of vocal sound, as you say the time-names, with the whispered rest-names can be very exciting. Give the 's' sound a good push to begin the silence, and don't let your voice be heard at all.

I will begin with some rhythms to say, and then go on to use the rests in pitched music. You should practise the rhythms of the tunes before you try to sing them.

Rhythms with rests

(1)

(taa taa   saa-aa   ti – ti   ti – ti   taa   saa)

(2)

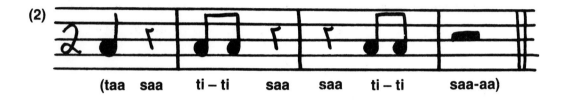

(taa   saa   ti – ti   saa   saa   ti – ti   saa-aa)

(3)

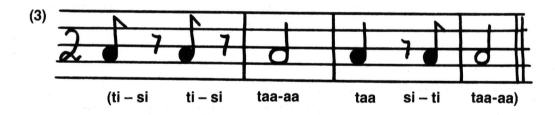

(ti – si   ti – si   taa-aa   taa   si – ti   taa-aa)

(4)

(taa-aa   ti – si   saa   taa   ti – ti   saa   taa)

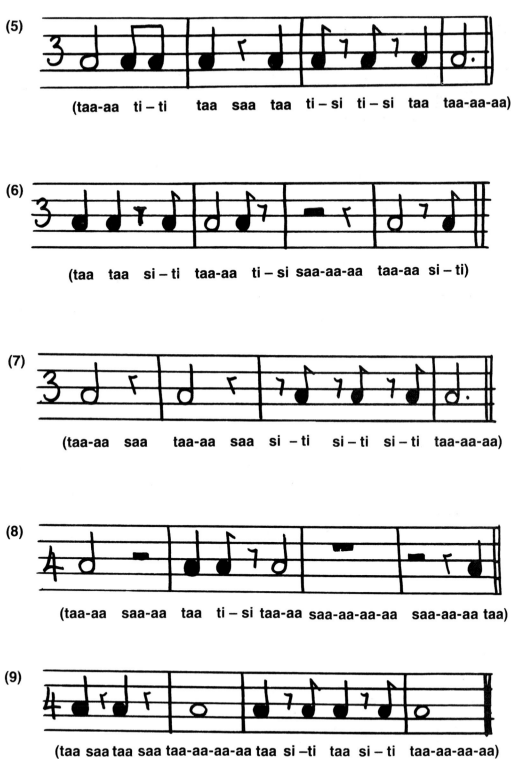

(5) (taa-aa ti – ti   taa   saa   taa   ti – si   ti – si   taa   taa-aa-aa)

(6) (taa   taa   si – ti   taa-aa   ti – si saa-aa-aa   taa-aa   si – ti)

(7) (taa-aa   saa   taa-aa   saa   si – ti   si – ti   si – ti   taa-aa-aa)

(8) (taa-aa   saa-aa   taa   ti – si taa-aa   saa-aa-aa-aa   saa-aa-aa taa)

(9) (taa saa taa saa taa-aa-aa-aa taa si –ti   taa si – ti   taa-aa-aa-aa)

Tunes with silences

I have covered a great deal of ground with the last few examples. You should approach each new rest with as much preparation as you gave to the new notes. It is not within the scope of this book to give as many examples as you will need. Should you reach this stage you have achieved a very great deal. It may have taken you well over a year, and you can now buy printed music which you will be able to sing together.

I suggest you purchase the *Nursery Rhymes* of Kodaly, and *The Kodaly Way to Music*, adapted for English schools by Cecilia Vajda. The nursery rhymes are quite lovely. They begin by using only the two notes we have practised. The only drawback is that the notes are very small. You should copy them out very big into your child's music book before you begin to learn them.

The best manner of approach is to read the words through with your child, so that he can tell what kind of music it will be, and then carry out the following steps. (Don't use a piano to help—it does all the work for him, and takes away his chance to achieve such a lot.) Take only half the song to begin with, then go on in the same way.

1. *Say* the time-names.
2. *Clap and say* time-names.
3. *Clap* time.
4. *Clap* from memory.
5. *Sing* to pitch-names.
6. *Say* the words in the time, as written.
7. *Sing* the words as written.

Repeat with the second half.

You should take as much time as your child needs over each of these steps, and don't go on for longer than he wants to.

The nursery rhymes soon introduce the note 'me'. If you know how it sounds, you can blaze your way ahead. If not, you should work with a friend, or perhaps it is time to start looking for a teacher.

Meantime, you have come a very long way indeed. If you yourself suffered under the 'Crotchet, quaver, minim, semi-breve, treble clef, bass clef, ABCDEFG . . .' syndrome from your own very first lesson, you may be a little surprised at how easy it has all been.

If you have decided that reading music together is not for you—do not worry. Your child still enjoys sound, and has not lost anything. In any case, please read on . . .

Chapter 3

HOW TO CHOOSE AN INSTRUMENT: OR, FIRST FIND YOUR TEACHER

Your child, you have decided—or he has—is now ready for formal instruction upon an instrument. The problem is, which?

On the face of it, this may seem simple. Don't you just choose the one you like best?

Well—no.

A great deal depends upon the age and physical development of the child, and the availability of a first-class teacher. This is of prime importance. A good teacher will elicit the best your child can give, whereas a poor teacher can do irreparable harm.

Let me explain.

As you will gather from Chapter 6, practice sessions are geared mainly towards two things: the development of an ability to hear and control sound and (since playing an instrument is not a *natural* skill) the acquisition of a technique which will be able to cope *automatically* with all the problems of performance.

It is to this end that one forms habits.

Habits are consciously acquired, learned, or just slipped into; they make possible the efficient performance of everyday tasks. Inefficient habits are corrected as soon as their inefficiency is recognised. A conscious but generally not taxing effort is required to change them.

In the case of learning to play an instrument however, years could elapse before one realises that one's technique will never be capable of sustaining the performance inside one's head. To *un*learn habits developed (sometimes with difficulty) over a period of years, to begin anew, leaving aside the sound—the *music*—so nearly within one's grasp, would break one: it could break your child.

A GOOD TEACHER IS ESSENTIAL.

But the first thing to do, if your child is old enough to have some say in the matter, is to engage his interest in a selection of available and appropriate instruments. Help him to sort out, from the list below, a number of instruments that he would be the right sort of age, size and disposition to start learning.

(The fact that, for example, a quarter-size violin is available, does not mean that he *must* start learning at the age of three, although it may suggest a historical association with youthful prowess, and the probable advantage of a fairly early start. Bear in mind also that neither children nor instruments come in uniform sizes, and large and small versions of each are available at every stage. In some cases a car is necessary for frequent transportation of otherwise unmanageable equipment. The following list is therefore intended only as a very rough guide.)

I shall deal first with those instruments usually to be found in a 'symphony orchestra' since the large and ever-growing number of amateur orchestras makes available to so many the opportunity of sharing some of the world's very greatest masterpieces with others who play for the sheer joy and love of music.

ORCHESTRAL INSTRUMENTS

Strings	*Quarter size*	*Half size*	*Three-quarter size*	*Full size*
Violin	3–5 yrs	6–8 yrs	9–12 yrs	13+ yrs
Viola	Advised to begin with violin and transfer to viola at about 13+ years. (Tone quality is lost by stringing a violin as a viola, although a place may perhaps be gained in an orchestra by so doing.)			
Cello	4–6 yrs	7–9 yrs	9–12 yrs	13+ yrs
Double Bass	—	13–15 yrs	16–17 yrs	17+ yrs
	(An excellent instrument for a late starter with a fair-sized physique.)			

Woodwind

No small woodwinds are available on which to learn. Young children are advised to learn to read music by those means which are easily available to them, perhaps in school. Many schools run recorder classes, and supposing the teacher to be sensitive, these may enable the students to reach a high degree of musical attainment, whilst reserving until later the choice of whether to proceed with an orchestral woodwind instrument.

Another, easier alternative is to learn to play the tin whistle, which does not have the tuning requirements of the recorder, and for which there is a repertoire of folk material which may prove most successful with a young player. Perhaps teachers have not given to this instrument the attention which it deserves; in particular it offers the player an immediately accessible method of sound production, whereas with other woodwinds each note must be 'formed' correctly by the shape of the mouth before it can successfully be sounded.

The flute does not require a strong physique, but all other wind instruments demand a certain amount of back pressure, and some teachers do not care to take asthmatic students. If this is a problem, you should seek medical advice before you decide on a wind instrument.

The oboe, the clarinet and (particularly) the bassoon require a fairly large finger span; 'cushioned' finger-pads are an added advantage. For intending players of these instruments, a firmly set pair of front teeth is also necessary. (Make sure your child's dentist knows if he plays a wind instrument before embarking on major treatment in this area.)

The age of transfer to a woodwind instrument could be at about 11 years. (Although one virtuoso flautist was said to have played the piccolo at the age of four!)

Brass

As is the case with woodwinds, no small-size instruments are available for learning purposes, although the higher-pitched brass instruments are themselves quite small; in fact an intending player may begin to learn just as soon as he can boast a good strong pair of firmly set front teeth. (Your dentist should be able to tell you when they are ready.)

The cornet, trumpet, and tenor and baritone French horns can therefore normally be started from about 9+ years.

In addition to an appropriate dental condition, the euphonium, trombone and tuba require a long right arm and/or a large hand. (I think it depends on the instrument in question which hand this should be!)

Players of higher brass very often transfer to these instruments as they themselves get bigger, although it is of course not necessary to change, and they can be learnt from scratch.

All these instruments require back strength.

Percussion

This is a delightful subject for a child to study, since it allows him scope for indulging in both 'pop' and 'serious' music. It is not often considered as a possibility for serious study. Indeed, percussionists complain that they are often lumbered with children who merely have no other instrumental skill, and wish to play in the orchestra. Very often though, their enthusiasm grows with their new interest, and they can turn out to be quite good.

No special physical attributes are called for, and a player may begin at any age.

It is desirable that a serious student should at some time become familiar with a keyboard instrument, since xylophones and other percussion instruments are built to the same pattern. It is also an asset to be able to read notation, for many percussionists are not trained teachers, and would find a pupil who could already read music much easier to teach than one who could not.

Each percussion teacher would have his own way of approaching the subject. Often he may begin the tuition with a snare drum, adding a bass, and then a 'high-hat' pedal with which to operate the cymbals. If he is interested in symphonic music, he will eventually, like the boy in the picture, graduate to the kettle drums, or timpani.

If this sounds terribly noisy, don't despair, for a practice-pad is easily made, or can be purchased very cheaply; your teacher will explain how—or where. Percussion is an excellent field for building up your equipment as it suits your purse.

Finding a teacher may present a problem, since many percussionists do not emerge through the channels I will suggest. If your local education authority inspector can't help, it is a good idea to ask for advice at the local music shop, or to put an advert in their window.

The *Music Education Handbook* gives the names of journals which would contain pertinent advertisements.

Harp

Although the amount of traditional material available for this instrument is enough to satisfy most needs of a private nature, many orchestral concerts are arranged in which the services of a harpist are not called for. If the player wishes to extend his repertoire to cover the classical field, he must realise that the scope is not great; there are only usually one or two harpists involved in a normal-sized orchestra and although there is some new music being written, there is not much of a 'classical' nature in the chamber music sphere.

However, national festivals in Wales and Ireland, in particular, give harpists the opportunity of playing to an enthusiastic audience. A keen player may find himself involved in recitals with perhaps poets and singers.

Since the methods of approach are so different, prospective harpists should write for advice to the United Kingdom Harpists Association, stating the kind of music in which their interest mainly lies, and asking for advice on instruments and teachers most suitable to their needs. The Association (see List of Useful Addresses) runs a lively little magazine, which you may care to read for a time before making a final decision.

NON-ORCHESTRAL INSTRUMENTS

Piano

No small piano *keyboards* are commercially available. (A 'baby' grand has short, thick strings, resulting in a smaller appearance, but the keyboard is the same as in all other pianos.)

Begin early if possible. (5–10 years is usual, but you can begin with advantage at 3 years, or as late as you still want to.)

Organ

Learn to play the piano first. Although the technique is different, it will be subsequently easier to acquire.

The notation is a further extension of keyboard notation. The pedals will be out of reach until about the age of 13 years.

For teaching, apply to a good church organist.

Harpsichord, Clavichord, etc.

Specialist instruments do not really come within the scope of this book, but these instruments could possibly provide a solution to learning a keyboard instrument where there is little space, or difficult neighbours.

Lessons will however probably have to be taken with a piano teacher, since the number of specialist teachers of these instruments is small; the manner of performance and the music written for them is quite different, and you must make sure that the teacher feels confident to tackle the problems. Tuning can now be facilitated by means of a recently introduced tuning device, which a specialist shop would stock.

Guitar

'Student' size, 6–10 years. Full size, 10+ years.

This can be a really sociable and enjoyable instrument to play. It is useful for simple accompaniment to solo or group singing, and can be invaluable to an intending teacher; she will find its informality more popular amongst her pupils than say, the piano. For students of promise the guitar can be

This child is playing an old American organ; she has chosen the timbres she wishes to use and has pulled out the appropriate 'stops'. She experiences no difficulty in reading the large notes in her scrapbook.

capable of great expression, and a large repertoire of classics is available.

On the other hand, for somebody with relatively little time to spare, the instrument gives a quick and rewarding return. 'Pop' music would of course be lost without its electric version.

I would recommend to anybody who has to study the theory of music for examination purposes, to spend some time working out the sounds of chords with the guitar—for in that way all those mathematical formulae begin to make sense.

Recorder: descant, treble, tenor, bass

This is a really lovely instrument at its best. Serious composers have quite recently begun to write once more for it, although there is of course a wealth of early music available.

Children with a fair hand-span can begin playing the descant recorder at about 6 years. Once established, the manner of playing can be transferred to the larger-sized (and consequently lower-pitched) instruments, from about the age of 11 years.

Should you become a serious player of the recorder, you will have to do a fair amount of work, since some of the more advanced pieces demand very intricate fingering. But the scope is large, and an enthusiastic family can start its own consort at any time. There is much more easy music which can be enjoyed at a high musical level for recorders than for any other instrument.

Bagpipes

Although there is no strong tradition of bagpipe playing in southern England, there certainly is in other parts of Britain. The pipes are generally learned as a matter of family tradition, and few aspiring pipers will need advice as to whether or not they are piping material. At its best, piping can sound as lovely as anything on this earth—at its worst it can be awful. You will have to be prepared to put in a great deal of work before you make a piper. The sound of the learner seems to carry a long way, although you may obtain a practice chanter for quieter fingering practice (this is a pipe without a bag).

You will need a great deal of back strength, and firmly set teeth to begin.

Teachers may be located by means of Scottish and Irish National clubs, or others where there is a strong local tradition.

Voice

This is a tricky subject, since the voice is the only instrument which cannot itself be replaced if bad tuition has caused its misuse and consequent ruination.

I would personally never recommend an immature voice to be 'trained'. By trained, I mean learning to 'project' the voice. This has always seemed to me to produce 'hot-house' voices, unable through early forcing to sustain the rigours of normal vocal behaviour—and singers who are inclined to wobble uncontrollably. Of course, the professional wobbler has her supporters, and is often at the end of a short career all too eager to pass on her awful secrets.

It must be said that there are excellent and responsible teachers to be found. But few of them will take responsibility for a female voice under the age of 18—and male voices do not mature sometimes until the age of about 25, especially if they have been strained in any way during the breaking period.

Early singing lessons, if they are taken, should concentrate on the correct manner of breathing, diction, and development of interpretative skills. All

these are beneficial both to the instrument and to the musician. Adult operatic fields should be avoided at all costs.

Children can sing many types of music beautifully, and adults with no more training than that which I have mentioned, can often find great pleasure in belonging to a choral group.

(For somebody who wishes to experience working with a great conductor, and has not had the opportunity to play in an orchestra, singing can be a wonderful way to do so. There are many large and famous choral societies throughout Britain, to which you may apply for audition. It is often necessary to be able to sight-read. Failing this, there are many smaller choirs who will be pleased for anybody to join them, and quite often the weekly rehearsal turns out to be a most enjoyable social occasion.

There are small madrigal^G groups too, if this is a field which you enjoy. The 'trained' singer is usually unwelcome in these groups, since such a voice will stick out —a kind of vocal BO, hard to bear, and impossible to mention.)

Electronics

Here is a whole new field, where those hitherto frustrated musicians with technical, mathematical or electronic knowledge have an initial advantage over the musically literate. It is a field of experiment, but which may yet prove to be as attractive to the true music-lover as the traditionally scored works of previous centuries.

Dexterous fingers are necessary, but beginners of any age with an ability and desire to invent and experiment are capable of producing pieces with a freshness of appeal that makes their developing skill immediately rewarding.

Classes for beginners, and more advanced courses for the technically

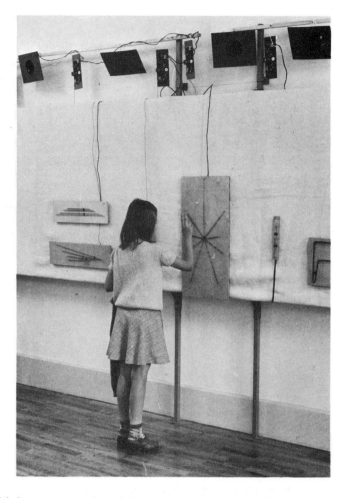

competent, are held in many universities, adult education centres and technical colleges, where absolute beginners can sometimes find themselves working alongside professional composers.

If your family travels a great deal, it is necessary to take into consideration the transport of instruments which cannot pass as 'hand-luggage'. Porters cannot always be trusted to treat any large item with care, and passenger space must be paid for. For instance, a bass player or a cellist must expect to pay full fare for his instrument to travel inside trains or planes, or else suffer the consequences. (My daughter's cello, en route from one part of Africa to another, was found to be dripping—after freezing in the hold of the plane and rapidly thawing on arrival.)

Orchestras indeed often charter planes, so that their instruments may occupy space inside the cabin alongside the players.

*   *

Having thought which of the many possibilities seem to be the most appropriate, available and desirable, you must take into account the uses to which the selected instruments may eventually be put.

Ever since the Beatles (so long ago!) incorporated a top class string quartet into their Sergeant Pepper record, the use of orchestral instruments in popular music has made a long-awaited come-back. In jazz, almost the complete range of such instruments is now in use. But the availability of 'traditional' music will probably always draw you towards one type of instrument or another. The nature and length of the history of your choice of instrument will be reflected in its available repertoire. A flute or violin for instance, will have a large classical repertoire which can almost be guaranteed to last a lifetime. The clarinet on the other hand, is an eighteenth-century invention, whose proper repertoire only begins at that point in history. The tuba does not have a large solo repertoire, and since the harp has been used for centuries to accompany the player in song or to improvise freely, its notated repertoire is rather small. The *Emerson Catalogue of Music for Woodwind and Brass* can be studied with pleasure and profit. (This should be sent for—see List of Useful Addresses.) Another catalogue of more general application is that produced by J. B. Cramer & Co. Ltd (see List of Useful Addresses) called *Ideas in Music*; most parents and teachers would find things to enjoy with their children included here. Separate catalogues must be consulted for other categories of instrumental music—most should be available from a good music shop.

It is somewhat surprising if you are a buyer of books, to find that if your musical requirements are not immediately available in the locality, you should approach the publisher direct. He will post a copy of whatever it is you need once arrangements for payment have been made. Should you not know the publisher of the music in question, you can always find out by asking at your local music library—or by contacting the Westminster Central Music Library (see List of Useful Addresses) whose staff are always extremely helpful, and who will be pleased to advise you. If the publisher is foreign and has no premises of his own in Britain, another publishing house will act as his agent; most libraries or big music shops should be able to help you track down what you need—but failing local services, you could always ask at the Westminster Central Music Library.

Of course, *great* players of all instruments are always needed; especially if the player is prepared to play new music of eventual historical significance—breaking new ground and extending the traditional limits of his instrument. But in this field, a comfortable living is not to be made, so it helps if you're rich—or a saint.

The probability of greatness is, however, remote. So it would be wise to consider mainly the areas where a *good* standard of playing is always to be welcomed—and further, those which are less likely to be over-subscribed.

For instance, the clarinet has attracted many players in the recent past because of its cheapness. But there are only four clarinets in any normal-sized orchestra, and the range of solo and ensemble music is limited. This leaves many players with little to do but teach—which could make it a dead end for someone who reaches the level of mere competence. On the other hand, the large number of string players can be accounted for in many ways—an orchestra swallows good players wholesale, chamber groups abound, and the amount of music available to play at home with or without friends is enough to satisfy the most ardent player.

The viola player is always in great demand. It is difficult to find a violist whose time is not fully accounted for.

(I am, in the main, referring to amateur music-making. Unfortunately, the situation of players who wish to play music as a profession is very different. The number of first-class orchestras seems always to be diminishing. Colleges of music turn out hundreds of hopeful players each year, who have little chance of playing for their living. It is not uncommon for forty applicants or more to apply for a back-desk position with one of the big orchestras when vacancies are advertised. There are of course other ways of employing instrumental skills, but often skilled players do not wish to consider them.)

Fashion sometimes plays a part too in the choice of an instrument—today, for example, there seems to be a glut of young flautists. Or a school may suggest your child learns to play a particular instrument to which he seems positively attracted—perhaps a bassoon. Even if a loan is arranged, access to the instrument must eventually be withdrawn (perhaps after only a year or two), in which case parents should be forewarned that a new bassoon can be expected to cost currently in the region of £800–£900. It is worthwhile making enquiries before a child becomes really involved. Music schools and colleges would be happy to give such information. (A rough guide to proportional differences in cost may be made by sending for a current price-list from a firm such as Boosey & Hawkes (see list of Useful Addresses), which stocks a comprehensive range of instruments. Wider comparisons of price and quality of particular instruments should of course still be made by prospective buyers.)

The amateur pianist has a wealth of solo music from which to choose. The demand for accompanists or sonata partners is high and a competent player, particularly if he can sight-read well, is not often lost for an evening's entertainment.

Certainly the piano is the most self-sufficient of all the instruments. There are many good teachers to choose from—and many more bad ones, so be careful. It is not an easy instrument to learn; there is a history of dropping out unrivalled by any other instrument.

The present revival of traditional folk music makes it possible for players of tin whistles, accordions, concertinas, mandolins, banjos, harmonicas and

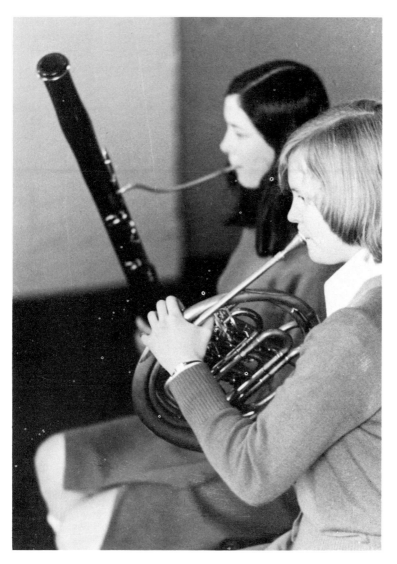

the like to find both music to play and players to make music with much more easily than has been the case for decades.

The current growth of interest in Indian and African music has produced players and teachers where there were none before.

The aspiring lutenist no longer has to work out his own system of playing, and there are yet discoveries to be made and remade in all kinds of musical fields, where the player has a bent for research.

Jazz will, in addition, begin to attract many young players as they make its acquaintance.

Problems and preferences are, however, personal. In the end you must make your choice. But before you do so, you must yet make the most important decision of all—who will teach your child?

*   *

There are many ways of finding a teacher. Indeed, there is quite likely to be a nameplate dripping with 'qualifications'* in your road. To this address, you will notice a succession of small people trooping dutifully to their lessons each Saturday morning. Of course, it could be somebody wonderful to whom they troop. Personal recommendations may have been forthcoming from all your neighbours. But how can you judge? Do the children who attend the teacher's lessons take graded examinations regularly? That can often be a *bad* sign. Strict adherence to an examination system can be the most soul-destroying way of approach. Do they all enjoy their lessons? This is a better sign. But how are you to know that *your* child will get on with the teacher so well?

Once in the door, many parents have already committed themselves. They feel it is rude to enquire, or to ask for a 'test' period. And yet this choice of teacher is the most important step to a successful association with music you will ever take. It is absolutely *essential* that your choice of teacher is right.

Professional bodies of musicians and teachers will willingly supply you with names and addresses of teachers in your area. The addresses of some leading bodies in the UK, such as the Incorporated Society of Musicians and the Music Teachers' Association, will be found in the List of Useful Addresses at the end of this book. The addresses of all member societies of the Rural Music Schools Association are to be found in the *Music Education Handbook*. As well as these, or if your area is unrepresented by such a society, the Local Education Authority Music Inspector should be able to help. (County Hall would put you in touch with him/her.) Music magazines (listed in the *Music Education Handbook*) can be found to represent most musical interests: their editorial staff can often prove very helpful.

(If you find your teacher through one of these channels, you should remember that not all teachers are known, and the societies do *not* in general make recommendations. If a teacher pays a subscription, or is on the 'approved list', you will merely be informed of her whereabouts. The

---

* 'Qualifications' may be more or less obscure. Those most commonly associated with instrumental teaching include Fellows (F), Graduates (G), Associates (A) and Licentiates (L) of the colleges and academies of music which issue them. Thus an ARCM is an Associate of the Royal College of Music, an LRAM is a Licentiate of the Royal Academy of Music, and an ABCA is an Associate of the British College of Accordionists. These qualifications may or may not qualify the holder to teach, or be held in conjunction with a teaching diploma. (A comprehensive list is to be found in the *Music Yearbook* and in the *Music Education Handbook*.)

list of seven names I received when looking for a violin teacher contained two deceased, one gas-meter robber and absconder, three 'no forwarding address', and finally one who was too busy but whom I eventually persuaded wasn't! The whole exercise is like pinning a tail on a donkey—it could fit.)

By far the most satisfactory method I have come across of finding the right teacher is to attend local music festivals.

Although you may think that the only festivals of music and arts are to be found in Wales—at the big eisteddfods—or in Edinburgh, this is certainly not the case. Local festivals are held all over the British Isles. In Scotland, they are generally held at the time of the village and district Highland Games. In the rest of the British Isles they are usually held as part of a larger Festival of Music, Speech, Drama and Dancing. Your local library should be able to provide you with details; in tourist areas, the Tourist Board should have them.

If you live in a big city, it is possible that details are not available in this way. You should contact the British Federation of Music Festivals (see List of Useful Addresses), which publishes an inexpensive yearbook giving details of all the known festivals in Britain. Such a list is also to be found in the *Music Year Book*, which you should certainly be able to consult in your local library.

The festivals often take place in the spring, and you should make your initial enquiries well in advance. Having located your nearest festivals, obtain a syllabus for each, and sort out the items of most interest to you.

Very often some of the winning performances are repeated at a grand concert, at which cups and medals are presented. But although these affairs are enjoyable, you will be most interested in the heats. These may be held in local primary or secondary schools, or village halls—after school hours or on Saturdays. Usually the only audience consists of parents, teachers or friends of the competitors. Whatever your interest in the field, it is likely to be represented in some way.

Large choirs of mature Gilbert & Sullivanites, small madrigal groups, mixed chamber ensembles,G colliery bands, college or school music societies, pensioners' music-hall clubs—all rehearse enthusiastically throughout the year to attain their best standards for the Festival.

But best of all, for your purposes—innumerable children's solo classes: tiny children, going through their earliest paces; virtuosi sparkling their way through cascades of impossible arpeggio passages—and every one of the stages in between. Classes are titled according to age, or according to the number of years' tuition. Some of the classes are 'open', and children compete with adults to achieve their highest standards. Sometimes there are classes for families to compete against each other.

After each heat has been held, an adjudicator—usually a very well-known musician and teacher—is called upon to give his comments. These

can be very helpful to the casual observer. The criticism is most often, of course, directed at the teacher. Points of excellence are discussed, and areas where more attention should be given are revealed.

Very often the children cluster in little groups around their teachers. It is possible to observe the relationships which each teacher has with her pupils.

All this, without having to reveal your personal interest. Complete anonymity is maintained until the time you choose to make your own enquiries.

Of course, some teachers do not enter children for such festivals; and some, having done so, do not attend the heats. (I have a great deal of sympathy for those teachers who maintain that music is not about competitions—indeed I hold this opinion very strongly myself. But many such teachers have been encouraged by the fact that the adjudicator is usually extremely responsible and helpful, to make the best use of the opportunity for their pupils to play before such an eminent musician, and a ready-made audience of strangers.) Some children enter themselves, and you may be able to enquire from a parent if not from the teacher, about the teaching which has most impressed you during your observations.

(It must be said at this point that competitions of all kinds—from the local village affair to the national 'Young Musician of the Year' contest recently introduced by the BBC and watched by millions of people—very often tend to create animosity, and are often considered by many to be unfairly judged. Youngsters who enter any musical competition must be well advised of this beforehand, so that they do not suffer intense disappointment or embarrassment as the result of an apparently inappropriate placing.)

If one teacher is particularly successful, it is possible that she will have a waiting list. It may be wise, therefore, to make enquiries in other fields, so that you are not left high and dry when the festival finishes.

Certainly your attendance will provide you with a great deal to think about, and probably a great deal of enjoyment too.

Any enquiries you may wish to make should be made at once, for the teachers are not named, or even necessarily known to the administrators.

It sometimes makes a great deal of difference to a teacher's willingness to take on another pupil, if the parents show an intelligent interest in the ways they can support the lessons at home. Although you have been privileged to observe many aspects of the teacher's work, she has not been able to gauge your attitude in the same way.

During a festival, the teacher's attention will be fully engaged. It is better, therefore, to confine your initial enquiries to her name and address. You should make your own notes during the festival to remind you of her particular qualities.

Afterwards, you should write to those teachers whose achievements both in personal relationships with their pupils and in their pupils' playing ability have impressed you most, setting out your own position, and letting it be known that you are willing to give as much support to your own child as the teacher thinks he will need. Be careful not to overestimate your child's ability, or to swamp him with your own aspirations. Perhaps you could suggest the teacher may like to have your child for a trial period to begin with, being very careful of course, not to allow your child to think that he is *himself* on trial.

Having thus made sure that your child will have the best possible chance, you will be in a position to tackle ensuing hurdles with very much more confidence.

Chapter 4

HOW NOT TO BUY AN
INSTRUMENT

This chapter has a negative title in order to stop prospective purchasers rushing headlong into trouble.

Having issued a preliminary warning, I can say that the sane thing to do is to locate your teacher first of all, and then to make an appointment to discuss the possible purchase of a suitable instrument. It may be that the teacher will advise you not to make a purchase at all until she knows more about the aptitude of her prospective new pupil.

DO NOT BUY WITHOUT HER ADVICE.

Obviously if the instrument in question is an heirloom, or has otherwise 'come into your possession', you have little choice. If you feel like taking a chance in exceptional circumstances, by buying blind you could strike lucky with your purchase. (I am relieved to say that we have ourselves done so once or twice.)

The most usual situation is quite simple. With lessons about to commence, an urgent shopping expedition is arranged. This often results in a hasty, and commonly quite unsuitable acquisition of an instrument, so that the child is 'ready' for his first lesson. It is a natural mistake to make, but it can prove expensive—and not only in terms of cash.

I wish that teachers, when accepting a pupil for lessons, would say to a parent 'If you haven't bought an instrument yet, I would like to talk to you about it before I begin to teach your child'. Unfortunately it seldom occurs to them to do so; you must take the initiative and ask for their advice.

In the same way as *you* have learnt from experience where to buy spanners or eggs cheaply, whom to trust and where to find the best quality goods, so has the professional musician, regarding the tools of his or her trade.

It would seem obvious that you should make careful enquiries about the purchase of a musical instrument—but people don't.

Just to give you an idea of what you may be up against, here are a few of the most commonly encountered pitfalls, and some facts to help you avoid them.

'Suitable for Beginner'. Everybody has come across this phrase. Advertisements, junk shops, music shops and you yourself are likely to use it freely.

What does it mean?

You mean 'cheap'. You mean cheap because the child has not yet

Do not buy without advice.

'proved' himself to be an expert player. Neither do you know whether his interest will continue to grow with his independence. You don't want to spend a lot of money on an instrument whose destiny may prove to be no more or less than that of a delightful toy—as likely to lose favour as any other.

Or, seeing the phrase by chance, you will buy on impulse—recognising a basic description of your child's condition. You would prefer a bargain, but you will settle for not spending a lot of money.

The vendor also means 'cheap'. He could mean cheap for any number of reasons. Let us consider a few of them.

The most common meaning outside of music shops proper is that the instrument looks scruffy, but makes a noise. This is your best bet. But with thousands of experts combing the field, you would be exceptionally lucky to find something good, unless the shop is in the middle of nowhere, or the instrument has just arrived. If the shop is, indeed, in the middle of nowhere, the vendor will know where the instrument came from. If you make further enquiries, you could find out whether such a home was likely to yield a good instrument. There could be other signs around the shop which would give you a clue as to whether this was so. If the shop is not in the middle of nowhere, the instrument is likely to disappear well within a week if it is any good. Of course, it may have been hidden under a pile of old rubbish—but the dealers know that too.

Is the instrument unsaleable? Just such a ticket as caught your eye is likely to get rid of it more quickly.

If the vendor is an 'Antique Dealer', he will have made the instrument look its enticing best. It need not necessarily be any better than a scruffy model in the junkshop next door. But he could have had repairs undertaken. If so, you will pay. He may specialise in instruments. In this case, he has an obligation to issue accurate descriptions of his goods. If you get an instrument from such a dealer, ask him to receipt you with a full description.

Only recently we had a simple trick played on us by a 'specialist' dealer in the south of England. After looking everywhere for a suitable bow, we chose one my daughter liked very much. It was £160 . . . by no means cheap, but she had won the money for the purpose. We were told it was 'by' a very famous French maker. I asked for a descriptive receipt so that I could hand it to the trust which had given my daughter the money. It was handed to me sealed. When I opened the envelope, the receipt stated that the bow was 'said to be' by the maker concerned. You may say that if she liked the bow, there was little difference. But she is very young, and may well want to change to a heavier bow in the future. In this case, the bow would not be worth the money we paid. Luckily I had only paid a deposit, which was returned when the dealer refused to back up his word with his description.

Does the dealer really *know* that the instrument he offers for sale is 'suitable for a beginner'—of whatever age, size or aptitude?

Perhaps the instrument in question is a 'kit'. In this case, you will expect it to be in good condition, for it will not be old. It will be factory-made, and you can easily compare the price with that of a comparable instrument sold new in the music-shops. Of these, more later . . . do not buy without advice.

You may see the words 'Playing condition: suitable beginner'. This is no more informative. Examine the phrase and you will see the gaping loophole.

If you find such an instrument really interesting, ask the dealer to put it aside *until you have had a chance to take advice* on the matter. Unless there is a queue at his door, no reasonable dealer would refuse. Leave a returnable deposit, if you like—so that he knows you will come back. But do not, on your return, feel obliged to him for the extent of his patience. It is his job to sell—and if the instrument is any good he will not lose.

PIANOS

In this field, you must be particularly careful not to buy without advice if possible, since pianos, because of their size, feature not only as instruments, but also as prominent pieces of furniture in their surroundings. Many manufacturers of recent date have played a successful commercial game with this fact, sacrificing sound quality to a 'fashionable' appearance. The dead sound, not immediately apparent to the untrained ear, eventually proves the function of the instrument to be merely decorative, and the glamour soon wanes.

The lucky few who have no problems of money, space or neighbours may go straight to the showrooms of Steinway, Bechstein or Blüthner to find the perfect instrument (see List of Useful Addresses). Here they will get what they pay for—a superb instrument in perfect condition, whether it be new or reconditioned. In addition, they will receive an assurance of an on-going concern for its welfare. From such places a new 'boudoir' grand could cost upwards of £6000; a reconditioned 'boudoir' grand may be in the region of £3000. The latter are in great demand.

Another venue for splendid makes of piano is the Morley Galleries in Lewisham (see List of Useful Addresses). Here may be found the most comprehensive range of keyboard instruments in Britain. New and reconditioned instruments of all kinds and prices are always available, and a serious buyer would do well to send for their informative prospectus (which carries a small charge) before embarking on a purchase, wherever he eventually chooses to make it. In addition, the Piano Advisory Service exists to offer expert advice on all aspects of the instrument (see List of Useful Addresses).

An excellent idea has been passed on to me by a friend. I quote her letter: 'Friends who recently had to buy a piano, decided to find a tuner first, then enlisted his help (and paid him for his time) before committing themselves to an instrument—this seems a very good idea, as he can't then say there's a lot wrong with it when he comes to tune it; and anyway he has a practised eye and ear when inspecting for faults . . .'

Many of us however, must do our shopping in the local second-hand furniture store. Pianos of distinction have become more expensive even here, in recent times, since for a period of fifteen years during and immediately following the war, manufacture of instruments was at a standstill.

I shall devote a fair amount of space to helping you see what, in the piano, you are looking at. This is for three main reasons.

First, the piano is not cheap; it is the instrument most often bought on impulse (usually because it has an attractive appearance) and it can so easily become a white elephant.

90

Second, of the more usual instruments it is mechanically the most complex.

Third, it is the nice-looking piano at a seemingly reasonable price which is the most likely instrument to attract a large number of prospective customers. It may not therefore be possible to reserve it until you have taken professional advice.

Before you go piano-hunting, it would be an excellent idea to take stock of all your friends' pianos first. Take a large duster, and don't wear your best clothes. (Particularly when visiting an upright.)

An upright piano is one which has the strings strung vertically. A grand piano has horizontally strung strings.

Grand pianos are divided by size into three categories. These are termed 'concert grands', 'boudoir grands' and 'baby grands'. The names mean no more than 'enormous', 'pretty big' and 'middling big to small' grands. If you wish to know the exact size, you must ask, or measure it yourself.

(Whilst you have measurements in mind, you should take stock of the route into your house which a piano will have to take. If the instrument is to be moved by yourselves rather than by the vendor, it is worthwhile engaging a firm which specialises in piano removals. Make sure that you measure all the awkward corners at their narrowest point, and consider the space you will have for manoeuvre. It is sometimes possible to haul a piano up to a high window by means of ropes—but not, for instance, if there is a porch sticking out underneath the window. Removal by crane is possible if such obstacles present a problem. A specialist firm will advise. (Indeed, sightings of the hitherto extremely rare piano-bearing helicopter are becoming almost commonplace in some parts of the world.) A grand piano is sometimes easier to manoeuvre because the legs come off.

Before you can see the inside, you will have to know how to expose it. (In a reputable piano shop all parts may be shown on request; or you could of course choose to be advised by a local piano-tuner.)

Here is how to open a grand piano.

1. Open the lid over the keyboard.

2. Turn back the front part of the main lid. This should reveal the music stand, lying flat.

3. From a position central to the keyboard, slide the music stand (still lying flat) towards you. It will come right out.

4. Standing at the curve of the piano, lift the doubled up lid at its heaviest point. There will be a prop lying just inside the case.

5. Prop the lid up at the highest position.

This is what you will see:

Steinway grand: 1—strings. 2—bridge. 3—hitch-pins. 4—wrest-pins. 5—frame (iron). 6—sounding board (wood; below strings). 7—hammer-heads (below strings). 8—dampers (above strings).

Here is how to open an upright piano. Make sure you know how to put each part back in reverse order.

1. If the lid of the keyboard is open, close it.

2. Open the top of the case by folding the front part back on its hinges.

3. Locate the fittings (usually swivel pegs) which hold the upper front panel in place. Unlock them. Allow the panel to lean slightly forward. Lift the panel up and out.

4. Open the lid over the keyboard. From the top and back grasp the double layer, and slide the keyboard lid up and out of its grooves, making sure to keep it level.

5. Locate the locks on either side of the lower front panel and free them. Lift the panel up and out.

This is what you will see:

Steinway upright: 1—strings. 2—bridge. 3—hitch-pins (left: behind bass strings; right: exposed). 4—wrest-pins. 5—frame (iron). 6—sounding board (wood). 7—hammer-heads. 8—dampers (between hammer-heads and strings). 9—pedals: sustaining, soft.

i. The strings

The strings in the 'bass area' are copper-covered; at the very bottom they are long, thick, and one to each pitch. As the pitch rises the length and thickness of the strings decrease, but the available volume is maintained by increasing the number of strings to each pitch from one to two, and finally to three. In the 'middle' and 'top' areas the (uncovered) steel strings, three to each pitch, continue to become progressively shorter and thinner. They are stretched over a bridge, from the hitch-pins at one end to the wrest-pins at the other.

If all the strings are broken, or if they or the pins are all rusty, this will be a major repair. If one or two strings are in bad condition—or broken—although this may play havoc with the sound, they can easily be mended.

Some old pianos are 'straight' strung. Most are 'overstrung'. It is better to have an overstrung piano (where the covered strings cross over the steel strings) because this gives a better length of string, more responsive to fine tuning; it also means that sympathetic vibrations are better, which makes for a richer sound altogether.

ii. The frame

The frame is the roughly harp-shaped form over which the strings are stretched. It is the item to which you should give your closest attention.

Before about 1900, it was not unusual for instruments to be built with a wooden, or half-wooden frame. At that time, there was no fierce central-heating, and concert-pitch was a fraction lower than today.

If the instrument has such a frame, and has not received constant attention, it may not be possible to tune it up to pitch without danger of the wood splitting. In this case, it cannot be played together with other instruments without sounding flat.

Check also for signs of warping. If the frame is warped, the strings cannot be tuned properly.

You would be wise to look for an instrument with an iron frame. An iron frame, with inexpert handling (and this means also from the shop to your house), can easily crack. If it does, the instrument is more or less finished.

Unscrupulous dealers have been known to give a cracked frame a new coat of the traditional gold paint to hide the damage. Therefore, if the overall condition of the piano suggests that the frame should still appear to be in its original condition, you should look very carefully to see whether a hair-line crack has appeared in the paint. If it has, it may be that worse damage has been disguised.

iii. The sounding board

This is another item to which you should pay closest attention. If it is cracked, the sound may be affected. A (fairly expensive) repair can sometimes be made however, if the quality of the instrument warrants it.

iv. The hammers

If only one or two hammer-shanks are broken the repair could be quite simple. They can be removed and replaced for the cost of the new mechanism and the labour entailed.

Each hammer-head, you will notice, is covered with felt; the impact of the felt on the string is partly responsible for the tone of the instrument. If the felts are badly indented by constant contact with the individual strings, the sound will be hard, and the felts may need replacing. If the felts themselves are hard, although not badly indented, this will also cause the tone to be unattractive. This condition however can be very simply remedied by an expert; he can 'tone' the felts by pricking them into a softer condition. (They must be done absolutely evenly, and it is not a job for an amateur.) Such treatment can change a hard, unattractive tone into a most beautiful sound.

Look out for damage caused by moth, rats or mice—this could be expensive. Individual moth-eaten felts can be replaced. (All felt parts are vulnerable in this way, and should be checked—including the strips around the pedals.)

v. The dampers

These are felt-covered. Although they may seem inaccessible to you, they may be removed for repair.

vi. The pedals

I shall treat the grand and upright models separately with regard to this subject, since the actions are quite different, and the presence of a third pedal may complicate the issue.

The grand

Most pianos have only two pedals. The pedal on the right is called the 'sustaining' pedal. (*Please* don't call it the 'loud' pedal—its action causes a sound to last longer, whether it be a soft sound or a loud sound. It makes *no* difference to the dynamic (or loudness) of the initial attack at all, except that it allows sympathetic vibrations from other strings to enrich the sound produced). The pedal on the left is the 'soft' pedal.

The action of the sustaining pedal is to remove all the dampers from their resting place against the strings when depressed, and to replace them when brought up. If any sounds continue to be heard when the pedal is brought back, it may be that one or two dampers are sticking, or that the whole mechanism needs an overhaul. You must make your own judgement.

The soft pedal, when depressed, should shift the complete action—including the keyboard—to one side. This causes the hammers, when activated, to strike only a part of each string or set of strings, thus causing a softer sound.

If the instrument has a third, middle, pedal, this will be for either sustaining selected sounds (Steinway), or for practice purposes.

If the piano is a Steinway, you can check the action of the middle pedal by selecting and playing a group of notes, and depressing the pedal in order to sustain them. The sound, when you remove your hands, will continue—just as it would if you played the sustaining pedal on the right. But if you look at the action, you will see that only those dampers belonging to the selected notes will be held off the string. Such a middle pedal enables a chord to be held throughout a series of changing harmonies. (As in Debussy's 'La Cathédrale Engloutie'.)

If the middle pedal is a practice pedal, there will be a lever to fix the action, thus freeing both feet. The purpose of this pedal is to impose a strip of felt—a mute—between the hammers and the strings. Although the tone is changed, the whole range of the instrument is still available at a much lower level of dynamic.

This can be a very desirable feature if you have difficult neighbours. It is usually to be found in older instruments, but manufacturers are once more beginning to incorporate it into their designs.

The upright

The sustaining pedal of an upright has basically the same action as that of a grand.

The soft pedal has a completely different action. In this case the whole action, excluding the keyboard (which is fixed) moves nearer to the strings. Thus acceleration is decreased, and the dynamic reduced.

In some old uprights, the action of the soft pedal is similar to that of the practice pedal described above. With the introduction of a felt mute, the timbre is completely changed. The soft pedal can never therefore be used in a performance which requires mere dynamic change. This action should be avoided.

A third pedal on an upright is generally a practice pedal.

vii. All wooden parts—including the case

Look out for worm.

*   *

Should you become really interested in pianos, you could visit showrooms and factories of the best-known makers. Another good venue can be the big sale rooms on 'viewing' days. You can always send for catalogues of forthcoming sales.

When you do finally make your purchase, it should be the very best you can afford. (From the reputable firms, it is often possible to make hire-purchase arrangements, and from a few it is possible to arrange sale or return.)

Keep the piano (and of course any other instrument) in a reasonable place with regard to temperature, humidity and comfortable access for your child. Bear in mind that whereas excessive heat or a badly placed heater can cause wood to warp, excessive humidity or a badly placed humidifier can just as easily cause metal to rust. It is no good thinking that a humidifier cancels out all the bad effects of a heater, or merely replaces lost moisture. If all appliances are on at full blast you create equatorial jungle conditions where, if it seems to take ten minutes to grow a lettuce, it takes only half as many seconds to abandon all hope of tuning an instrument. I know; I tried in Gabon. You should ask for advice from an expert attached to the firm supplying your humidifier, and expect to use it in conjunction with a hygrometer for best results. The wooden parts of pianos made since the late fifties have included kiln-drying as part of the normal manufacturing process; this reduces moisture content and makes new instruments better able to withstand a centrally heated environment. Proper precautions must however still be taken.

Arrange for a properly qualified piano tuner to call on a regular basis. (He should belong to the Piano Tuners' Association, which will advise on request; otherwise ask the very best local dealer to help. Tuners will often operate from his premises.) The tuner will be able to assess how often (according to use and personal housing conditions) tuning should be carried out. On average it is about every six months. On no account employ casual labour, or allow your piano to be tuned by a stranger without a reliable recommendation. My own tuner has just terrified me on your behalf with the story of a self-proclaimed piano tuner who goes around the locality thoroughly banging in the wrest-pins (which should be so gently turned) with a hammer; unsuspecting piano owners are said to pay him for having the privilege of having their instruments ruined. And I have myself seen a piano which had been completely dismantled by an unknown gentleman who had disappeared with some of the bits, never to be heard of again.

Don't take the risk.

STRINGED INSTRUMENTS

Here we encounter the opposite problem to that of the highly complex piano. These are instruments of such striking simplicity that good or bad, old or new, can all look exactly alike to the unpractised eye.

This statement should be enough to warn you off.

I will go further.

Inside a stringed instrument, if you look through the curly holes in the top (known as F-holes), you are quite likely to see the maker's label. You might think you could believe what it says—especially if the label is printed in wobbly 18th-century letters, and signed in ink. It probably says:

'Antonius Stradiuarius Cremonensis
Faciebat Anno . . .
(and the date)'

W. H. Hill & Son, the famous violin dealers, receive an average of six letters a day asking them to verify such a pedigree. (I haven't written, and we have two.) In fact these labels still appear inside factory-made instruments—although they are now typewritten!

A smart dealer could let you 'discover' such an instrument for yourself. And pay for the privilege.

Don't be misled by the gleaming varnish and the red plush either—that can all be laid on.

Then there are the factory-made 'kits', which consist of violin, bow and case. Suitable for a beginner again. Well, some of them are not bad—the Chinese seem less inclined to want to sabotage the music-making of the West than most. But before these instruments can be properly tested, they

have to be put right. Some shops provide this service. Do not buy without
at least asking whether this has been done, and obviously, on the specific
advice of your teacher. Even when the necessary adaptations have been
made, identical-seeming instruments can sound quite different. A really
top-class set of strings makes no end of difference to such an instrument. It
is always, whatever instrument you may eventually purchase, worthwhile
buying the best strings. The 'Student' variety can be abominable. The
teacher will advise you which strings to buy for the best results. If this
means cutting them down to fit a small instrument, this is what you must
be prepared to do. They are not cheap, and manufacturers should make

them in all sizes—but they don't. When you must replace a string, make sure that it 'matches' the set on the instrument. It is a good idea to keep a note of the strings in use.

Beware of 'school' instruments. Few such objects are worth any value in terms of sound. Since nobody has a special interest in them, they are likely to reflect the lowest standards, and they are often responsible for putting a child off for life.

The viola comes in two sizes. Each model is called 'full-size', but some players prefer the smaller model to that designed by Lionel Tertis in comparatively recent times. Tertis designed a large-sized 'standard' model, which is capable of producing a big tone. Some people think that this model sacrifices tone-quality—others like it for the balance it gives to the viola section of an ensemble.

Before you buy, know what you are buying.

The teacher will be familiar with trade magazines, local dealers, other teachers and even instrument-makers. She will have a better chance of finding the instrument you require.

Accessories must also be considered.

A good bow, in good condition, is a top priority. If you suspect that you will not have the patience to visit the local instrument repairer when your child's bow needs rehairing, you should consider the fibre-glass model from Boosey & Hawkes. This comes complete with a hank of new hair which can be fitted in a matter of minutes. In addition to this advantage, the bow cannot warp. (A child's bow often warps as a result of not loosening the hair when his practice is at an end.) This bow (the Golden Strad) is now available for all sizes of stringed instruments, from quarter-sized violin to full-sized bass. It is also very cheap to buy.

Mutes, shoulder pads, rosin—there is a large variety of each to choose from. Until your child can express a personal preference, rely on the teacher for advice.

(Anybody who needs to transport stringed instruments into hot or cold parts of the world should seek advice on maintenance beforehand.)

WOODWIND

In this department too, the pitfalls are numerous.

Cheap new instruments are commonly made of unseasoned wood. The market in seasoned wood has not been able to keep in pace with demand. The price of a new instrument generally reflects the amount of seasoning the appropriate wood has received, and the amount of care taken in the fitting of the action.

An instrument which has had little seasoning is liable to crack, and/or warp with use. (There is no guarantee that an expensive one would not do so either, but one would hope that the manufacturer would be prepared to replace without question in this case.)

Manufacturers are increasingly drawn towards the production of instruments in synthetic materials. (Boosey & Hawkes seem to have made the most progress in this field, and now have a clarinet available.)

A really good buy can be a pre-war instrument which has been well maintained. This will have been made of properly seasoned wood.

But some instruments have become obsolete. The so-called 'Simple System' clarinet, for instance, is generally no longer in use. It is not simple at all to play, and only a very few players of the old school still use it. The model you will need is a 'Boehm system'. Most beginners use a 'B♭' instrument to begin with, and purchase the others as they become necessary.

The oboe is still made in different versions. The teacher will tell you which one to get, for he may not be able to play the one you turn up with!

The bassoon also exists in two main versions. In Britain the German 'Heckel' model is preferred, but there are some who play the French model.

The flute, currently most often made in metal, presents a whole new set of problems. Once again, you must avoid the obsolete. Very old flutes are not commonly encountered, but there are flutes still to be easily found which, although identical in appearance to the current concert model, are pitched high, rendering them useless for ensemble work. Also, beware of the 'military' models, which abound. You will need a Boehm system pitched correctly.

Often a 'beginner' is advised to purchase a 'Student' model by Yamaha; new, at current prices, this will cost about £100. As he progresses, he may be told to purchase a better quality Yamaha, at about £500. This will contain more silver, and more careful workmanship. But if he is vigilant, he could come across a pre-war, seasoned wooden instrument at the correct pitch, for as little as £120. With this he has the same quality of sound as a metal instrument, but a different tone (which he may prefer). These prices will not, of course, remain stable for long, but may prove useful as a proportionate guide to different kinds of purchase. Advice on treatment in extreme climatic conditions should be sought if necessary.

There are on the market some *very* cheap metal flutes, whose action twists out of shape at the first or second blow. They cannot be put right. Don't buy one.

BRASS

Before you buy a brass instrument, you should be sure that your child is going to be able to play it. Many teachers require a number of sessions with a new pupil before they can tell what his aptitude will be.

Metal instruments are subjected to a good deal of moisture, and with a great deal of playing they eventually suffer from metal-fatigue. Players must replace their instruments during the course of a playing career—sometimes quite often. It is common therefore to come across old instruments in a worn condition. It is not common to find a brass instrument in a second-hand shop which is going to prove to be just what you've been looking for.

Of course you *may* come across a good instrument, but it is unlikely. Brass instruments are easily dented. Having dents removed is not a cheap business.

Cheap instruments may come apart at the seams.

The teacher will know exactly what to get, and from where. Don't buy without his advice.

PERCUSSION INSTRUMENTS

Here is a market in which you would be well advised to buy second-hand equipment. Although equipment may have been badly treated during the course of a short and unsuccessful career, it is usually easy to tell if it is in good condition.

What you must do first however, is to make sure you know what you need. A whole lot of expensive-looking equipment could put a child off. If he begins with a snare drum, then he will only need a snare drum. If he gets all the rest too, he may be bewildered, and his practice will become dissipated.

Replacing a broken drumskin can be quite expensive—especially if the drum is large. If you buy a broken drum, have a good look at the hoop, to make sure it isn't warped, before you buy it. If the hoop itself is broken, don't buy the drum. You will easily find a better one.

As far as the purchase of other percussion instruments goes, buy what you like, at the child's and the teacher's discretion. It is largely a matter of personal taste.

Don't rush into a mammoth purchase of large numbers of expensive new items. Buy one thing at a time, and only augment the collection as progress is achieved. An excellent and informative book on the subject has been written by the well-known percussionist and teacher James Blades (see Booklist for details).

OTHER INSTRUMENTS

From what I have said in the preceding paragraphs, you will see that buying an instrument is something you must do with your eyes open.

If you decide to buy, for instance, a sitar, or a banjo, or an accordion, it is, I hope, likely that you have made contact with an excellent teacher first. In any case, you should not purchase a specialised instrument without making sure you will be able to arrange lessons. If you have arranged lessons, you should be in fairly safe hands regarding the purchase of a suitable instrument.

*   *

The purpose of this chapter has not been to tell you what to look for—it has been to tell you to take expert advice. If it has resulted in the avoidance of a disastrous purchase, then it has succeeded.

One most valuable service offered by some serious music-shops is the hiring of musical instruments with the eventual possibility of purchase at a reduced rate. This is an excellent service, but once again the teacher should be asked to advise, in order that any adjustments which must be made can be fully discussed with the hirer before final arrangements are settled.

Once you have made your purchase (the best you can afford—most instruments keep their price if they are good ones), ask the dealer and the teacher for advice on insurance. A portable instrument in particular, in the hands of a young child, is at risk. You should take care to obtain immediate insurance cover.

Chapter 5

THE FIRST LESSON: SOME NECESSARY QUESTIONS

Whatever arrangements have been made for the purchase of an instrument, the first 'lesson' should be reserved for discussion. If you have helped your child to enjoy music since he was tiny, do not consider that your job is now done. Although it will not be your policy to 'interfere', you have, nevertheless, an obligation to continue your support. The relationship the child is about to form is the most important of his musical career. It is not, as so many parents are inclined to think, a good idea to abandon him on the doorstep.

You should prepare yourself and your child for this first encounter as you would for any important interview. You may in so doing, take the teacher by surprise—but it should be for her too a pleasant and welcome experience.

Arm yourself with a list of what you have done together. (If for instance, you have learnt rhythmic patterns by means of time-names, say so. Not all teachers use them, but would be willing to employ them at least during a transitionary period.) As well as this summary, prepare a list of questions. This will demonstrate to the teacher a positive interest in her own approach, and give her a good chance to explain how she works.

(So very many teachers complain that a pupil's lack of progress is due to indifference in the home, and yet so few teachers go out of their way to encourage a two-way relationship in support of the child. In this respect, a termly report is just not good enough.)

Here are some questions I have found it useful to ask during the course of my children's lessons. You may have different questions; whatever they are, do ask them. This will make the relationship positive from the start.

1. *Should I attend the lessons to take notes, or to take notice?*

To some teachers, the idea of a parent attending lessons is just not on. Since you have taken such care in choosing a teacher, you should trust her to make the right decision. For many children, a parent's presence may be inhibiting—for others it may lend the support he needs. (Cheerful notes and little cartoon reminders can be valuable ways of jogging small memories during a long week.)

Perhaps it may be a good idea to attend the first few lessons and see how it goes. Should the teacher eventually opt for lessons alone with the child, do not consider this to be a negative move; my son has chosen to learn alone for as many years as my daughter has found my presence helpful. In fact I had to remove myself from my daughter's lessons in the end, to enable her to stand on her own feet.

A cello lesson. The child's father takes notes as her teacher makes detailed observations on her progress.

2. *If I don't attend lessons, is there any way in which I should help?*

I think most teachers would welcome some degree of assistance with a young pupil. If the lessons are weekly, a child's interest is almost bound to flag over such a long period.

Perhaps the teacher may suggest making a tape-recording of the lesson. If she does, you should ask exactly how it should be used. It may be possible for a teacher to programme the whole week's work in a most interesting way with such an aid.

Or perhaps the teacher may have very definite views on arrangements for practice. If so, you should support her. Unfortunately few teachers have been trained to consider a child's work in the home, and leave all arrangements to be made without her assistance. You should consider each aspect of your child's work and prepare any questions you think relevant.

If, for instance, your child is to learn an instrument in a sitting position, you must know the exact height of the chair or stool from the floor. If little feet swing off the floor, you should ask what support they should be given. You should expect to be notified of any change.

Or, if the child is to model his stance on that of his teacher, you should ask whether a large mirror would help him to check his position.

In the next chapter you will find some suggestions of general interest.

Since all teachers have their own ways of approach, you must continue to make enquiries of a more specific nature should any doubt arise.

3. *How long will a lesson normally last? Should I arrange a 'staggered' lesson?*

Obviously the child's age and ability to concentrate must be taken into account. Half an hour at a time is the most a very young child can take; this may not, however, contain sufficient material for him to tackle during a whole week. It is probably a case for trial and error. At some time, a young child may be able to concentrate so well that his lesson may be extended to cover all the material. This must depend on the availability of the teacher who must make such a decision. You should ask her at intervals whether she wishes to review the arrangements.

4. *What should we do if the work set has not been covered during the week?*

This will depend on the relationship that develops between the child and the teacher. If the child is in the habit of working well, and needs more time, the teacher may suggest giving a lesson a miss. If, however, he is going through a sticky patch the teacher may well prefer to repeat a lesson and assure the child of her continuing support. In such a case, you should rely completely on the teacher, who is an individual, and who will have her own ideas on the subject. (Do however assure the teacher that she will not suffer financial loss if a lesson is not taken.)

Do not threaten to stop lessons unless progress is maintained. This is a

major decision, and should not be taken lightly. Such threats will undermine your child's trust in you.

If a teacher finds herself constantly having to undo the results of a week's 'practice', she will make her own decision as to whether it is a good idea to continue. She should also be trusted to inform you if she thinks your child would do better with another teacher.

But by the time this sort of drastic decision must be taken, you should have a very fair idea of your child's enthusiasm and commitment to his music, so that any such decision will be responsibly considered.

5. *Do you provide opportunities for the performance of pieces your pupils are learning?*

Whilst still in the very early stages, this question is relatively unimportant. Later on, it becomes all-important.

Once all the little black dots have been accurately accounted for, and an interpretation of the composer's intentions has been thought out and worked over, the music is ready; it awaits the life-giving adrenalin which inspires a performer at the supreme moment of *sharing* with an audience.

The audience may be one or two people, or it may be a thousand or more. But upon that audience rests a great responsibility: from it, the performer draws the sympathy for the inspiration of the moment. A coughing, sweetpaper-rattling, programme-rustling audience can ruin months of patient and loving preparation. A sympathetic audience can however lift a performance to heights it perhaps never could otherwise have reached.

There are various ways in which a teacher can provide performing experience for her pupils—even those who are just embarking on their music-making career. One, already discussed, is the annual music festival; another is a concert the teacher may herself organise for parents and friends. Yet another, the examination syllabuses provided by various examination boards. (Of these, more later.)

At first, a pupil will have very little to play to an audience; it is amazing how very fast the music one has taken such pains to learn goes by. It is better therefore to incorporate early performances within a larger programme—thus preserving for each pupil the sense of occasion. Almost as important as the audience itself is the date set for the event. Work must be geared to that date very carefully, so that it coincides with the moment of ultimate achievement; the programme must be completely prepared—and yet not stale; a delicate task indeed.

6. *How should we take care of the instrument?*

Although a few instruments do not need constant attention, most do. The teacher should suggest a routine by which the player learns to care quite

Every player should know how to care for his instrument, and be prepared to undertake responsibility for it.

consciously for his instrument. If this is left to the parent, the child may well suspect that an unnecessary fuss is being made. The teacher could also point out that care for the instrument not only results in a good sound, but very often in a beautiful appearance too.

Assembling and taking apart woodwind instruments needs special care, and instruments should never be left carelessly 'lying around'. Appropriate humidifiers designed for particular instruments may be necessary; ask the teacher's advice. Certainly a secure and well-fitting case is needed for all portable instruments.

7. *Do you teach in classes?*

You will surely know by this time if this is so. If it is, the teacher should be prepared to explain her way of teaching very fully.

There are advantages and disadvantages of learning in a class. The nicest aspect is the enjoyment a child will have from working at a discipline with other children. But you should ascertain that the class will be small enough for individual faults to be corrected and individual triumphs to be noticed. You should also know what happens if one child is outstandingly quick—or slow.

Although you will be sharing the fee with other parents, it is more important to know that the teacher is *good*, rather than that she is merely *cheaper* than others.

Because it is becoming so widespread, the 'Suzuki Method' of violin teaching springs to mind. Properly carried out, it has many advantages. The children learn to enjoy sound, each other's company and their parents' support. Daily (individual) and weekly (group) lessons are backed up by a series of records, to which the child must regularly listen and to whose sound he must aspire.

Parents are given precise instructions as to how to direct their child's practice.

The language of notation is *used* before it is read, since Suzuki maintains that children develop their powers of hearing and physical coordination very quickly if they do not have to divide their attention in order to read the notes.

(Personally, I see no difficulty in learning to read notation as a separate activity—preferably vocal—but Suzuki prefers to leave it until later.)

One aspect of this system which I have observed on many occasions, and which I deplore, is the chopping and changing of parts, according to a given signal. Perhaps the children are tiny, and do look very sweet marching spritely round the room swapping the parts of a Bach two-part invention. But it is not *music* that they thus perform—it is something much more akin to a circus trick.

I have also come across examples of the Suzuki music books in the hands of children whose parents have never attended a single lesson. This is gross misuse of the material.

If your child does learn in a class, do make sure that his *musical* aptitude is being developed, and that his personality is not being swamped.

8. *Do you enter pupils for instrumental examinations?*

Of the few remaining British activities upon which the sun yet does not set, are those of the music examining boards. Regularly at home and abroad, in centres as diverse as Swansea and Swaziland, Torquay and Tokyo or Slough and the Seychelles, throughout the Americas, or in any unexpected corner of the world, you may find teams of examiners representing the Associated Board of the Royal Schools of Music, Guildhall School of Music, Trinity College of Music or the London College of Music; between them they will hear annually many thousands of students, mostly young, but frequently not so young.

Your child is quite likely to encounter this network, possibly many times

during his period of instrumental study. In order to make best use of the system, a wise teacher will have studied the standards and requirements of each syllabus available to her before deciding which, if any, examination to use for any given pupil.

For example, a teacher may have brought a young pupil to a very advanced level of performance. The child will be learning naturally how to interpret all kinds of notation with regard to the period of music he is playing. If such a promising pupil is taking occasional Associated Board examinations he will at a certain level (Grade V) be required to sit a comparable examination in theory before being allowed to proceed to the higher instrumental grades.

Or, as is often the case, this particular level of playing coincides with external school examinations, and a child who loves playing will have an unwanted academic obstacle thrust in his way at the very time he could do without it.

A teacher who is aware of all available systems will be able to enter him for Guildhall or Trinity College examinations, whose requirements for practical subjects up to the final grade are directly related and confined to the pieces being played. This system is, in my opinion, far more satisfactory, since it provides the less academically inclined, the very young and the hard-pressed, with proof of advanced playing skill which would otherwise be denied them. By the time an advanced player reaches the final grade, he has usually absorbed enough theoretical information through his instrumental studies for the necessary theory examination (still Grade V) to be merely a formality.

(I hope that one day this block may be removed. The silliest aspect of it all is that a candidate may be permitted to sit all the theory examinations, up to and including Grade VIII, without being able to *hear*, let alone *produce* a note of music!)

Each examining body grades its syllabus from low to high, Grade VIII being the final in most subjects. The first available examination is not always Grade I, and not all grades are necessarily represented.

Here are some examples:

Guildhall: Piano

Introductory.
Preliminary.
Junior.
Grades I, II, III, IV, V, VI, VII.
Grade VIII (A), designed as preparation for the Teacher's Diploma.
Grade VIII (B), designed as preparation for the Performer's Diploma.

Associated Board: Guitar

Grades III, IV, V, VI and VIII.

Trinity College: Wind

Grades III, IV, V, VI and VIII.

London College: Recorder (Treble and Descant)

Preliminary.
Grades I, II, III, IV, V, VI, VII, VIII.

Candidates may enter for any subject at an appropriate level, unless restricted by theoretical requirements already explained. (It is possible for a candidate to enter himself, but his teacher's signature adds authority to the entry form.) The examining bodies will send a current syllabus for the nominated subject, free on request.

The usual solo instrumental examination has four sections, designed to encourage candidates towards the development of an all-round musicianship. They are:

The performance of (usually three) set pieces, of contrasting character.
Scales, arpeggios (broken chords), technical exercises.
Playing at sight.
Ear tests.

You should ask the teacher what store she sets by each of these aspects of her work, for they are all essential, and too often some are overlooked.

How common it is, for instance, to come across a person who learnt to play the piano for many years. She no longer plays, for the original performance of her schoolgirl repertoire has broken down, and she has little technique to apply to the learning of new pieces, and no ability to read even the simplest notes without hours of preparation. And yet she may have gained a distinction in Grade VIII! It is as if the end has been reached at this point.

You should ensure that all your child's energies will *not* be directed towards the merely temporary performance of the most complicated pieces he can take on, in order to reach a meaningless paper level of performance.

(Once an orchestral instrumentalist reaches an adequate level, many of these worries automatically disappear, for he will sight-read and listen hard at orchestra rehearsals. This fact goes a long way towards explaining why so very many pianists 'drop out' whilst their 'orchestral' friends carry on.)

You can help, or can perhaps enlist the aid of an older child, in giving your child aural tests under the precise instructions of the teacher. (All examining boards publish examples.)

If you can play ever such simple duets with the child—not those that must be learned, but those that can be almost read at sight—this provides the best playing motive of all; not only is the child sight-reading (a wonderful feeling of attainment), but he is *sharing* directly with you.

It can be of great benefit to a more advanced pupil to be given this task if you are unable to do it—but try to take an active interest anyway, and don't wait until your child is sufficiently 'advanced' before you offer support, for it is certain to be later than necessary!

The teacher should certainly be able to suggest ways of helping if you ask.

Many teachers do not like to teach theory at all, and some cannot. You may have to ask for outside help (and pay for it) if the teacher wishes to stick to a particular examining board.

I am also told, on excellent authority, that many parents (who cannot be expected to appreciate the marked difference in the various editions of music available) are sent to obtain music for examination purposes with no specific instructions and with no idea of the prices involved. The teacher should always give precise instructions and advice if she is unable to make the purchase herself.

9. *Do you encourage your pupils to indulge in corporate music-making?*

Obviously this question is related to a later date, by which time you will know the answer! But it may be permitted for your child to attend an ensemble rehearsal if he will not interrupt or become bored. There is nothing better than to see real music being enjoyed by his own teacher's pupils. For those whose teacher is not able to provide such an opportunity, Chapter 7 suggests ways in which you might like to try to set up your own little group.

Chapter 6

SANE AND SYMPATHETIC ARRANGEMENTS FOR PRACTICE

Millions of people in recent times have been given the chance of learning to play an instrument. Most of them 'gave up'.

If you ask a child why he is 'giving up', he will probably say 'It's not very interesting'. If you ask an adult, he may say 'I couldn't be bothered to practise'.

These two answers are very interesting.

Quite recently the child had found the prospect of learning his instrument so exciting that he was able to override his parents' protests, and convince them that he really would work, and he would not give up. When he does, he is embarrassed, and searches for a way to allow him reasonably to break his promise. Hence 'It's not very interesting'. Very often 'it' is extended to mean 'all music', and the subject is completely written off—it becomes 'sissy', and parents are told that 'none of my friends does *that* sort of thing any more'.

The adult, on the other hand, rues his decision. He looks back and 'wishes he had carried on'. He blames himself for 'not being bothered'. He does himself an injustice.

Both answers have much truth in them—although it is quite hard to see.

'It's not very interesting' and 'I couldn't be bothered to practise' add up to the fact that the whole thing was *as boring as hell*. This is the real truth that nobody will face. In the beginning is the magic—at the end is the magic. But in the middle is a lot of hard work which *a child cannot be expected to sustain by himself.*

I am not saying that *music* is boring. I am saying that the way in which a child is expected to live through hours and hours and hours of tedious, undirected so-called 'practice' while his friends play outside or watch the telly is nonsense—and shouldn't be allowed.

I am saying that neither Music nor You were at fault. To a certain extent, it may have been the teacher. But in the vast majority of cases it was Practice which was boring.

Now, consider the implications of this fact, when you hear the child say 'It's boring', and the adult say 'I couldn't be bothered to practise'. The child does not really mean 'Music is boring', and the adult does not mean 'I was feckless'. They both mean 'practising is boring'.

Now you are in a position to ask yourself *'Why?'*.

You should try to examine your own experience to discover what went wrong. If you have no experience, you should talk to others who have. If you are amongst the lucky few who survived, look for the reasons. Find out the good and the bad, and use your findings to support your child.

In order to help you, I will tell you of my own experience. It has made me a rotten pianist, but it has enabled me to give my children a better deal.

At the end of this chapter, I shall describe a positive approach to practice. This will not be intended as 'instructions'—rather as suggestions as to how *you* and *your child* can work out a good system.

During the war, as a small child, I lived with an aunt. She screwed my hair up in rags every night so that I should have pretty ringlets. If I didn't scream too much, I was permitted to listen to her daughter play 'Sheep may safely graze' on the piano. Even with a raging headache, this was a wonderful experience. I wasn't allowed to touch the piano.

After the war, I remember longing for Sunday afternoons to finish so that my father would play his records of Gigli, Jussi Björling, Paul Robeson and other great singers. I loved to sing too. Sometimes we would listen to 'Palm Court', a programme of light classical music on the wireless. When I was ten, 'Ballet Shoes' was serialised by the BBC's late lamented programme 'Children's Hour'. I used to run home from school as fast as I could to hear the marvellous magic music which preceded the story. I wrote to ask what it was. It was from Wolf-Ferrari's *Jewels of the Madonna*. I cried when the serial ended and I would hear this music no more. I love it still. (There must be few who have not experienced such simple and uncomplicated pleasure in music. The 'gift' is not reserved for a tiny minority.)

When I was eleven, a piano arrived. I had no warning of this amazing event. I was surprised not to be reprimanded for dawdling, but sent to 'see

what's in the sitting room'. I was very thrilled.

During the next few days I ran home to poke around with the notes, finding little bits of tune here and there. I looked for some big fat bass notes to accompany my 'tunes', but at this the saucepan on the adjoining scullery wall would wallop out its disapproval.

A teacher was found. She was very well-qualified, very old, and very cheap.

A dull-looking 'Tutor' was purchased, and the lessons commenced. The teacher slept through an increasing measure of the allotted half-hour. I did mention the fact, but no action was taken. Each lesson I was given a 'piece' to struggle with, and told to 'go up to there for next week'. With the aid of a confusing text, I managed to work out what the notes were, but the fingering remained a mystery. Each week I 'played my piece', and was straightaway given another one. I was not told how to correct mistakes, and I was not given any technical work. The pupil who followed me into the parlour was the handsome young cub-master, who could play quite well. Sometimes he came early. When this happened, the teacher would rummage around for an old song, and hand him the music. Then she would say to me 'Sing dear'. I sang, he played, she slept. One day she died.

This tale, so short in the telling, took years to live through.*

Each day after school I was expected to 'do my practice'. This became hateful to me. I never wondered why. It was not then given to children to question arrangements made on their behalf.

There is no doubt that I had an awful teacher. But that was only part of the story. In order to encourage me, my parents bought a record called 'Sparky's Magic Piano'. I listened enthralled. I was already convinced that I would become a great pianist. The record confirmed my belief. I had only to practise. It might take a few years, but it *would* happen. And now here was this little boy, just about my age—it even said so—'Sparrky was ay liddel boye, jerst abowt yooer age . . . he hed been taking peeairno lessons for arlmowst ay yeer now, and waas already on his therrd peece . . .' I remember it to this day. *I* had been taking piano lessons for almost a year, and I must have been on my thirtieth piece! I was obviously much more advanced than he was. He made an awful racket. He became a wonderful pianist in a dream, and when he woke up, he was told that his dream would come true, if he only kept up his practice. And so we hear him

* A parallel experience was related to me in a letter I recently received from a friend, which I quote:

'I had piano lessons for three years and hated it—I was worse at the end than when I started. The only thing I can remember about my music teacher is that he always had a cup of tea and a digestive biscuit. So what? Well, he put the digestive biscuit *in* the cup of tea, stirred it up, let it settle in a sediment, drank the tea—and scooped out the sediment with his teaspoon. He spat the tealeaves back into the cup. He sounded like a duck with consumption. I was so fascinated by his performance that I watched out of the corner of my eye and I never noticed *my* performance. This is *absolutely* true!'

again—breaking down in the same old place, not correcting, but just stumbling along. At no time was he ever told *how* to practise. He and I doggedly continued to march on the spot. I believe he is still there. He is now about your child's age, bewitching him as well, quite likely.

I would like to hear a sequel to this story. Unfortunately like Peter Pan, he will never grow up. If he had grown up, I should take delight in the fact that he never even became as good as me! This story is a killer. If you do have it, you must help your child to laugh at Sparky—for his promise will never be fulfilled. But I believed. I got all the music that he had played in his dream, and 'learnt' it. I attacked the notes with great passion—convinced that they would come right in the end. They never did. As the years passed I began to suspect that something had gone wrong. It is only in the last few years, with my own children's music at stake, that I have been able to come to terms with what it was.

The piano was in the sitting room. This was located at the end of a long dark passageway. It shared a common wall with the scullery. The sitting room was kept clean and polished to sit in on Sundays, when a fire was lit, and my parents dozed in the armchairs. Apart from Sundays, this room was never used. It was absolutely freezing—even in mid-summer. It backed onto the garden, but there was no way out. It was brown and unfriendly. Even the cows on the wall looked sad. The piano faced a wall. On it stood my music. Any other music, like that in my head, or that which occasionally dared to stray to my fingertips, was forbidden. Unauthorised excursions outside the realm of the printed black dots merely irritated the saucepan. This was the only thing that took any notice of me.

For the allotted time, I froze, and was bored.

After the death of my first teacher, I transferred to the teacher at school. She had some pupils who played beautifully; I did not become one of them. This teacher however impressed me, for not only did she tell me WHAT to do, but she also told me WHY.

What she said made sense, but my habits stuck, and I was not able to conceive that if I was to learn to play her way, I might succeed.

She told me WHY I should learn scales, and so for a bit I tried them, willing them to come right. She told me WHY I shouldn't use the sustaining pedal, and so I tried that too—but though the sound was no longer confused, it was not romantic either, and no longer disguised so many wrong notes. I could not break my habits, for I had nothing but long-term promises to put in their place.

With this amazing 'technique', A level music, and a passionate love of it, I eventually came, incredibly, to attend the Royal College of Music.

Here I encountered the late Cyril Smith.

This great musician was consulted by the most able players on the development of their already advanced powers of interpretation. He was seldom called upon to correct actual errors in the notes they had learnt; he was renowned for his insight into the real stuff of music. He must have been appalled at the task which faced him on my arrival. But the most amazing thing happened. Observing the multitude of faults, he made a start—beginning with the use of the sustaining pedal. It was the most valuable lesson of any sort that I had ever had; it was the first time that I had ever been expected to respond to the process of learning. Because it was so important to me, I shall quote a part of that lesson, as I recall it.

C.S. 'Put the music away for the moment—have you heard of direct pedalling?'

J.P. 'No.'

C.S. 'Then do as I say. Hold the pedal ready and play any note with your middle finger, right hand. Before you take it up, depress the pedal. Leave the pedal, take the finger up. Place your finger above the next note—slowly now, no hurry. Listen—as your finger goes down, lift your pedal. Ready? Keep the finger—depress the pedal. Do it again. Up with the finger; Down, Updown up, Down Updown up . . . Go up to C and then come down again.'

I played the scale of C very slowly, using one finger and direct pedalling. At last I had been given a single, uncomplicated task, and had been told HOW to do it. Later on I was to be told HOW to break a piece into sections, HOW to locate trouble spots, HOW to analyse problems and HOW to tackle them. I was told HOW to memorise and HOW to prepare a piece for performance. It had set me free—I began to look for ways of doing things myself. I had learnt how to think! It was too late for me to accept the discipline of learning how to play the piano myself—I was as a beginner amongst near-professionals. I scrambled through an ARCM teaching diploma ('Because she was cheerful', reported Antony Hopkins to an amazed Cyril Smith) and went on to teach, whilst only just beginning to learn how to learn.

To reiterate the lesson it took me so long to learn:

It is not only necessary to be told WHAT to do. A child should be told WHY, and shown HOW. In that way he can eventually learn to teach himself, and there is no better lesson to be had. Although he must work hard, he will never be bored. Some children will find other interests which mean more to them than music. Some children will have little interest in *playing* music, but might still enjoy listening. Some will need a great deal of help, a very few will need none. Whichever way your child develops, if he does want to study music at all, you must keep yourself tuned in to his needs. And you must be prepared to put in a great deal of your own time—certainly whilst he is young. It will be worth it however, since by the time he reaches an age where he may decide to 'give up', he could have reached such a high standard that the idea would never occur to him.

I suspect that my son might have 'given up', had he not tasted the fruits of his ability so young. He is very quick, and forms quite independent interests of his own, which follow one after the other in rapid succession. It is good to see how much of the world he enjoys. But he would have realised that there wasn't time for everything, and might have taken a very long time to form his own conclusions as to where his main interests lay. Meantime music, which has already given him so much, could have become a casualty of his wider independence. My daughter, on the other hand, takes one thing at a time. I think she probably would have persevered even if she had made a late start.

Some families have only one child to whom music is *really* important. This can be difficult to deal with, because not only does music involve a parent's time—it can also cost a lot of money. If you have always been at pains to provide your children with what they *need*, they may understand the principle. (Perhaps one child grows faster than another—in which case he will need clothes and shoes to be replaced more often than his brothers or sisters.) If on the other hand, you go in for a 'fair shares for all' policy, it may prove difficult to avoid jealousy. Perhaps only one child seems to cause you more effort and money, in which case it may be worthwhile switching to a policy of 'To each according to his needs' . . . so long as you know what they are. The difficulty which music can present lies in the fact that it might have to be treated seriously whilst a child is very young. If he misses out at the crucial point, his chance could disappear for ever. This is easy to see, but can be quite difficult for brothers and sisters to come to terms with.

*   *

Presuming you have no particular difficulties, how can you make it possible for your child to enjoy his practice?

If you have shared music with your child up to the time when he began lessons, you should not stop now. He may have a more formal set of tasks to perform, but in essence, he is still 'controlling sound'.

The work should be carried out in a warm, well-aired and familiar place. The child should be completely comfortable. He should be helped towards forming a habit of his practice time. He does not usually get out of bed wondering if he will be bothered to go to school today, or if his mum will be bothered to give him any food. Although he may not feel like going to school, or mum may not feel like feeding him, nonetheless these things happen. They are habits, and, as I have mentioned, they make life easier by removing the necessity to *decide* on every tiny action as it occurs each day.

I have found it an excellent idea to situate this work period in the early morning, before school. This needed from me a great effort of will, as I am not at my best at this time. However, the effort proved to be worth the trouble. Not only were the children fresh, but at this time their friends were not playing, watching the telly, or doing anything else of interest. There was no sacrifice called for. If the work covered during this time was

good, it was almost always followed by a really splendid day at school. On
the days which were not so successful—and there were many—I had to try
to get the children to readjust themselves on the way to school. Although
the journey was short, it was very valuable. If you choose to adopt this
method, you should keep an eye on that journey to school—it could be
important. If the work in the morning was really bad, we tried to do some
in the evening. This was rarely successful. (Although a child may be
willing, it is a time when a parent's attention is usually fragmented.)

Because practising became a Habit, my children found it easy to observe
their own progress. They could see that they were steadily achieving
something really good. There were landmarks, like the one when two very
much older children joined in to do some early chamber music. One of
them even made a record with the tiny players. And then there was the
realisation that some of *our* friends were coming to play with *them*! Music
that is! (A music student I recently asked about landmarks told me that a

great day for her was when her teacher gave her 6d for practising her piece very slowly for the first time.) I worked with the children directly—alternating my attention—for about five years, by which time they were eight and nine years old, and could more or less direct their own practice. (Then I reverted to my former state of early morning stupor, shouting occasional instructions from the bedroom!)

Obviously older children would not need such a long period of supervised practice. Perhaps a nice new alarm clock would do the trick.

So what form might your assistance take?

If the teacher has planned the week's work for you, you are really in luck. If not, she has probably made some notes in the Notebook you will almost certainly be asked to provide—or if you have attended the lesson, then you have your own notes and your own memory to aid you. If there is no record of the lesson at all, you will have to ask your child for details. Do this directly after the lesson, but make it a pleasant task. Perhaps, if it is to become regular, you should arrange to have a nice tea whilst you discuss the work in hand. You could tell your child it is a 'business tea'; that will make him feel grown up. He should take this task very seriously, for you will need to know the teacher's exact instructions. 'I've got to go up to there' is, as I hope I have helped you to understand, useless. If the child doesn't know the reason for his work, it may be because to tell him WHY may have muddled him—his teacher can tell him when he is ready. But he *must* know HOW to perform each given task.

Once you fully understand the week's work, you should enlist your child's aid in making a plan. Gauge how long his concentration will last, and don't make heavy demands upon it. Decide which practice is to be done daily and write out, in an attractive way, the order in which he says it should be done. If he has a longish piece, or study, divide it into sections according to the difficulty of each part. You may (with his assistance, perhaps) divide such a piece into four sections. If most of the difficulty lies in two bars, make them the object of a whole day's study. In this way, he could learn parts 1 and 2 on days 1 and 2; day 3 could be set aside for revision. Parts 3 and 4 on days 4 and 5; day 6 for revision. By day 7, he should be able to play the whole piece through. (Another advantage of early morning work is that the day of the lesson is not lost to practice.)

You will notice that, knowing HOW and applying the knowledge to a different section each day, your child will avoid the trap of playing a piece from beginning to end every time, without regard to accuracy. You should try to dovetail the sections in a sensible manner, so that the child doesn't stumble at the joins. You could assist him to work over these points from different starting points, until they are fluent. It is a good idea too, to cover most of the work from memory. If the child is helped to see how this may be done, he will eventually develop an ability to play without thinking of his actions. In this way his mind is left free to direct the performance. Such an ability is not accidental—it comes with the habitual exercise of the memory.

All that is required of you is interest in and real involvement with the child himself—you need *know* nothing at all about the instrument in order to give valuable help. Indeed, the most useful aspect of this exercise is the child's own conscious and fresh consideration in detail of each task he has been asked to perform.

Let us take as an example of an early practice, a day following a young child's violin lesson (you may arrange to break the practice up with breakfast in the middle; if so, this should be prepared whilst the child washes and dresses). When he is ready, the room should be already comfortable, the music ready and in order, and the notes to hand. Possibly the child has been asked to practise holding his instrument correctly. In this case a mirror will help. It should be at just the right height for him to see his position without changing it. This will not be the normal position for a mirror in the room, unless it is full-length.

First of all, ask the child exactly what he must do. He should try to tell you in words—perhaps using his violin to demonstrate each aspect. Question him on details, and make sure he knows what he is going to try and do. (We will presume the child is playing his first notes—he may have had a dozen or so lessons.) Get him to pick up the violin as he has been instructed. Ask him to close his eyes, and then say 'Does it *feel* right?'. He should not answer immediately, for he will have to think quite hard about that. When he says 'Yes', show him how he looks in the mirror. (Avoid moving him!) Ask him 'Does it look right—like your teacher?'. If he says 'No', get him to say what looks wrong. He should then correct his position, and close his eyes again. If he has made an alteration, you should tell him to pay particular attention to the 'feel' of the correction. When he is satisfied that he has got the right 'feel', he should put the instrument down and walk around the room at a normal, relaxed pace. Then, returning to his position in front of the mirror, he should pick up his instrument again, close his eyes, and get the right 'feel'. Allow him time to think about it. When he is ready, he should look and check. This time, *you* may have noticed a difference. If he doesn't mention it, point it out and ask him which is the right way. (Perhaps his legs have stiffened for instance—and he hasn't noticed.) When you have done this, direct his attention to the next requirement. He should now give all his attention to that.

He may or may not be using the bow—he may or may not be using a finger to pluck the strings. Let us presume that he has a little piece to play by plucking the open strings. First he should tell you which finger is going to pluck, and where on the string it must act. Because the violin is played so near to the eyes, the child will receive a foreshortened view of the instrument. He may indicate one place, and, with violin under his chin, pluck in quite a different place. You should ask him to show you where his teacher said he should play—holding the violin out in front of him. Then, with violin in position, you should help him find the right place. Explain that his eyes may deceive him, and show him in the mirror where he is to play. He should not look at his instrument while he plays, because the information he receives will be false. (In any case, players do not play in this way—if they are not playing from memory, they are reading music. They do not *look* for the notes—they learn where they are by *feel*.)

Now you can ask the child to close his eyes, hold his instrument so that it feels right, and bring his right hand up to pluck the string in the right place. Each of the four strings has a different playing position. He may need only one of them. If he needs two or more, he should be helped to learn where they are by feel.

When the child is satisfied with this, he has perhaps had enough. A whole practice, and only one or two plucked notes to show for it? Not at all. If you had not been there to help him, he might have raced away to all kinds of faulty positions. He would have certainly covered the week's work on the first day, even if it was to prove to you that he could make sounds with his instrument. Bad habits would have begun, which would have to be dealt with in the next lesson. As it is, he will have achieved a very real success.

Every aspect of every tiny action must be considered independently. If the child is naturally able to do the right thing in certain areas, let him. Praise him for it, and explain that you needn't spend time examining what's wrong—because it seems to be right. This will speed things up and delight him. Always praise his progress.

This example has only been given as a guide for *you and your child* to think positively about each practice. It is by no means 'The way in which the week's practice should proceed after the twelfth lesson in the violin'. Of course it isn't. But I cannot hope to provide you with detailed instructions for *your child*, *his teacher* and *you* to follow. Every child, every teacher, every instrument is unique. You must work out your way, according to your own child's needs.

Young players may, according to their instrument, need to tune it before they begin to play; they will need help. Some instruments need tuning by an adult because a child just hasn't got the necessary strength. You should ask your child to criticise the tuning. I promise that you will both get better at it. (The bonus, in the shape of increased appreciation of the tiniest subtleties of the greatest playing, is worth the trouble.)

When your child is finally able to produce a beautiful sound from his instrument, allow him to direct his complete attention to the sound he has learned to make. Get him to 'love' the sound from the moment of its birth. Eventually he will be able to play a piece through. If you can play the piano (and of course, if you have one), even just a little, you will find lots of very easy things to play together. When the child's attention can be directed fully at the sound he is making, you should help him to work out an 'interpretation' of his piece. Use the title, if it is imaginative, to work out a story. If the title doesn't grip you, make up your own. Pay attention to the dynamics marked, and perhaps exaggerate them so that they don't get lost. (I have found it a good idea always to go *beyond* the sound we sought, so that we can take a step backwards to it if necessary.) I illustrate this exercise with my daughter's story and drawing for 'Two Minuets', by an obscure German composer called Hesse. It is much better called by her title 'The Two Fat Ladies Piece'. She was seven, and had been learning for nearly three years. (See next two pages.)

This aspect of your help may go on for a very long time—or may not. My son has had his own entirely abstract view of sound for years, whereas my daughter is just beginning to develop it, and still enjoys working with me on the pieces she plays. (It is interesting to note that 'supervised practice' is a most important aspect of the timetables of all schools providing special music courses for their pupils—from the very youngest, to those about to embark on advanced studies of the highest order.) All children have different needs. The task is a delicate one—but taken seriously, it offers great rewards. I hope your child won't 'give up'.

THE TWO FAT LADIES PIECE

by Ruth Phillips

<u>Story</u>   J.A. Hasse
                    Zwei Tänze
        1.st half
One day six fat lady's, were dancing at the ege
of a wood when a wolf came out of it, at
first he was a bit scared becouse the lady's
mint heard him. but then he got more surer
then he was very serten, so he marched in
but in a flash he was gone

                    2nd half

a mother wolf was looking - after her cubs
she was looking allaround her but saw
yellow eys allaround so snarled but this
went on soon father wolf came along (he
was very proud of his cubs)(and he
thought mother wolf was very silly. the
eys came back he had to growl too.
mother wolf took over again

big flash 3rd part and back come fat
lady's

Chapter 7

MAKING AND LISTENING TO MUSIC TOGETHER

This chapter is concerned with the greatest pleasure that music has to offer—that of sharing with others. Although corporate music-making may be in the nature of a bonus for children whose parents or friends also play an instrument, certainly all parents can enjoy the experience of listening to music with their children, whether it be at home or in the concert hall. It may be the case that a parent who does not play, may even so be willing to form and direct a small ensemble—perhaps with occasional help from her child's teacher. If not (or until this is possible), you may prefer to confine your corporate activities to hearing others play—which is discussed later.

MAKING MUSIC TOGETHER

As your child progresses, he will be able to give more and more attention to the sound he is making. By this time his teacher will probably be giving him little pieces to read at sight. If you are able to play an instrument, it is a good idea to play some really simple pieces through with him for sheer enjoyment—with no thought for 'improvement'. Easy duets are widely available; very often one part is extremely simple, whilst the other may be of moderate difficulty. There are however many pieces written for two or more complete beginners. If your family and its friends boasts more than two players (and participants may be of any age or ability), you should try to obtain some simple trios or quartets. There is no doubt that a child's pleasure increases as he is able to take part in more complex ensembles. (You must realise of course that a piano has to be properly tuned in order to be played with other instruments—nothing is more depressing than the sight of a small wind-player trying to match his tuning to that of a piano at half-mast.)

Publishers are now expanding their lists of 'educational' and ensemble music, and you should write to as many as possible to alert them to your requirements. Only in this way do they become aware of prospective markets for their commissioned works. Most publishers will advertise in music magazines. You should be able to trace the kind of music you will need by finding a magazine that suits your joint interests. Once again the *Music Education Handbook* must be recommended—this time for its comprehensive list of such publications, which range from *Accordion Times* through *Drums and Percussion* to *Early Music* and *Guitar*. One very fruitful field to explore is that of recorder music. It can be found in two, three, four or more parts, and if the keys are suitable for all instruments, it can be played by most mixed ensembles. (When all players are beginners, and learning instruments from different 'families'—e.g. some strings, some brass—it may be more difficult to find music that can be played together. Or if one of your players uses a bass, tenor or transposing^G clef, somebody may have the task of shifting it into the right place for him to read. Perhaps

Ensemble—the author with her family.

one or two notes may then be found to be out of the compass of the instrument. A helpful teacher should be able to substitute acceptable alternatives. Should all this seem beyond you, ask your child's teacher if she knows a student or somebody else who would help. It is worth it.) Schott's catalogue (see List of Useful Addresses) is very useful. The pieces are helpfully graded for most purposes. Pieces in educational catalogues as well are graded from 'very easy' through all stages to 'difficult'.

A most delightful new publication designed for use by mixed ensembles of the most basic kind is *Class in Concert*; although the title suggests school, there is no doubt that this enterprising and beautifully illustrated set of three graded kits could be used by parents and children at home with the greatest enjoyment.

One of the very best ventures in the field of catalogues is that compiled by the Emersons, which deals exclusively and in helpful detail with all standards of woodwind and brass music. It is to be hoped that experts in other fields will be encouraged to follow their example.

If you are willing to try, here are a few hints which may help you to get a small ensemble started. (You will certainly get better at the job, and begin to find your own ways of helping the particular players you are working with.) Find a really simple piece—one with lots of repeats if possible. Try to avoid music in which one player (especially if he is the least able) has a lot of rests; this can be both boring and muddling for a youngster, who will have to spend a great deal of time merely counting away other peoples' music. A good choice would be an easy Minuet or Trio. This can be divided into four short sections, so that a convenient stopping place is always near. When the whole piece is finished, it turns out to be $2\frac{1}{2}$ times as long as the notes the players have learnt. This is always a popular move! (Minuet I consists of parts A and B; Minuet II (or Trio) consists of parts C and D; the complete performance takes the form AABBCCDDAB.) When you have found what appears to be an appropriate piece, consult each player in turn, to see whether he can play all the notes in his part.

Take the parts one at a time in order of difficulty. (Meaning of course that the *player* who will find his part the most difficult should be taken first.) If the child enjoys singing, get him first to sing the tune he will play, together with you, being very careful to make the notes absolutely the right length. Find out about louds and softs. When he is ready, get him to try and play the tune. Don't make the session too long—enjoy it.

When this has been done, repeat the process with any other part which may prove difficult. If one player finds his part *very* difficult, give him lots of help in between sessions with other players. Be sure that each part is rhythmically secure—don't worry too much about everything else being spot on—there is plenty of time to deal with other aspects.

Try taking two parts together—perhaps the most secure together with the least secure. This will give a great deal of confidence to a shaky player. Play around with other combinations of parts until everybody knows roughly how the piece fits together. If you can help the players 'colour' their parts with louds and softs, so much the better. If not, don't worry—that will come with confidence. When everybody has had a chance of putting his part with another, try putting the whole piece together. If it goes wrong, it doesn't matter at all—in fact it could quite possibly be the ablest musician in the group who gets so excited listening to all that is happening, that he slips up. Try again until the parts fit. Then you can begin to talk about an interpretation—perhaps when the laughter subsides?

At this stage it is well to consider just whom you have playing in the ensemble. It could be that you have very young children, one or more teenagers and an adult. When dealing merely with the notes, each player is on a fairly equal basis—experience does not intervene when the subject material is abstract. As soon as you reach the interpretative stage however, you must be very careful not to alienate older children, perhaps by referring to 'fairy-tale' effects or the like. It is far better to approach the older children beforehand, and ask them if they could find a way of making the piece make sense to younger players. This is particularly necessary if you have been dealing with young children all day—it is very easy to damage a teenager's pride. If *they* come up with the solution, then they have scored a double triumph, and you have not lost them for ever. Taking your cue from them, you could easily ask their opinion as to any sections which may have been left out of the discussion.

Eventually the players will begin to direct themselves. Once the notes have been learnt, and stray rhythms put right, such a group is well on the way to becoming a proper chamber ensemble.

It can help to have a 'conductor' who has become familiar with the score at the beginning; this gives confidence, but as soon as you are able, designate a 'leader', and let him see if he can hold the players together from 'inside' the music. Eventually the players will develop an aural response to each other's playing, and need only refer to you when they really can't work out a problem by themselves. Let the length of each session depend on the concentration of the youngest player—as soon as it begins to stray, finish playing, for nobody will want to go on too long with anybody who doesn't want to continue.

A good time to begin such a group would be in the weeks preceding Christmas. Get the music in good time, for the shops run out of the most popular material just after the beginning of the Christmas term, as schools stock up with everything in sight. There are more lovely arrangements of carols than of any other simple music—and it helps that young children know and love the tunes they will play. It may be a good idea to rehearse lots of carols with different combinations of instruments, and to invite more children to share by singing some of them with the players.

If your child really does enjoy playing with others (and there are very few that don't), it may be a good idea to choose a week-long or weekend course that he can attend. Here again, the *Music Education Handbook* will come in handy, for it lists very many of the courses that young children can attend—even if they are absolute beginners, and just like playing with sound. There are Music Workshops for children from nine years of age, music camps (held under canvas), and courses for orchestras and chamber groups for children of eleven years and upwards whose standard of playing is good enough. For more advanced players, suitable courses are found also abroad. Then there are the Music Schools and Centres themselves, which are affiliated to the Rural Music Schools Association. The *Music Education Handbook* lists them as well.

LISTENING TO MUSIC

However advanced your own music-making may become, or even if it never gets off the ground, you will no doubt take pleasure in listening to music.

Your child is unlikely to become a great player or composer. But whatever his practical attainments turn out to be, he need not lose the experience of greatness. For he may become a great listener. This is not a passive role. More than anything else, musicians need to be heard by sensitive and sympathetic audiences. Without them, their central role as performers or their original role as composers is as nothing. A good audience will give. They will follow every line of thought as it develops.

Music at its greatest gives us huge abstract concepts to grapple with —argument at its peak. The greatest performances throw new light on the arguments, pushing hidden facets to the surface, moulding massive volumes of sound into new meaning. Music exposes all human passions to the public ear. It can be violent, tender, angry, cold, beautiful—all that life can be.

The composer and the interpreter both expose their whole being to their audience. They do it on trust. Having made an appointment with fate, the performer must be ready to give himself completely. An audience should be prepared to receive him at the same level of commitment. As the musicians use their life-experiences to provide the music, so should an audience use theirs to understand.

Music speaks directly to the soul; it communes with the *capacity* for human experience we all share. It is not necessary for audiences to live lives of extreme passion in order to recognise that such extremes are present in themselves. It is the purpose of Art to help our spiritual growth; to help us to see, hear, touch, taste and smell, and to help us to love.

How common it is to find an audience prepared only to give themselves intellectually. Witness the crowds of people who 'look' at pictures, catalogue in hand. They look at the number beside the picture, read the title in the book, may even stop to read when it was painted, check the name of the painter, and move on to the next. They learn nothing, they feel nothing. They may emerge with a smattering of general *facts*, but no more knowledge of themselves—and they are swindled.

Witness the audiences who take their seats at the last moment, pro- grammes in hand. As the conductor takes his place, they open their programmes to read what is to be played. Sometimes they read the programme notes right through whilst the exposition flows over the tops of their heads. Very often they listen to the first few bars to see if they know the tune; when it becomes fragmented, they turn to their programme notes to *read* what is happening! 'The development section is preceded by a bridge passage using the second half of the first subject. This moves through various keys before arriving at the key of F sharp minor. Muted strings now play the oboe motif; it is a very moving moment . . . ', they might read.

What do they think music is about?

They seem quite oblivious of the fact that there is an attempt at private communion going on all around them.

Some concerts seem to attract a larger or smaller army of spectacle-wearers. Inevitably and almost in unison a battalion or two will accompany the first few bars of each piece by opening handbags, extracting spectacle-cases, putting spectacles on, rattling programmes, taking spectacles off, snapping them shut, putting them back in cases and bags, and springing clasps to close.

Concert promoters should insist on the insertion in their programmes of a note to the effect that music is for listening to, and not for reading about. I should like to see on the cover the sentence 'Please do not disturb others by reading your programme during the performance.'

I do not wish to say that you shouldn't read about music. What I *am* saying is that you should not replace the experience of sound with a description of it. If you do this, music has no reason for being.

You will have no trouble persuading your child of this fact. He wouldn't dream of restricting his response to his intellect. You should follow his example, and allow yourself to listen.

How then can you provide listening experience for your child?

There are excellent children's sections in most record libraries, but you need not confine your listening to what they provide. Here you might find music which composers have written especially for children, pieces which tell stories (with or without words), and pieces that 'paint pictures in sound'. Usually there is an explanation of what the composer had in mind—elephants, the sea, or the way in which Peter and his friends caught the wolf. These pieces make direct application to the child's world of fantasy, and can be very enjoyable. Because commercial enterprises are

rapidly becoming aware of the profit to be made in such a children's
market, lots of new pieces are becoming available; not many of them are
very good. Your child will sort them out with little difficulty.

Much enjoyment is to be had from music in the adult section of a library.
Consider your child's requirements. A piece should be fairly short, so that
if he chooses to listen all through, his concentration is not strained. He
must be given the opportunity to hear it many times if he wishes. It should
not contradict his present mood if he is content. You should share his
experience with him if that is what he wants. You should allow him to
choose whether he wants to do something else whilst the music is played.

If you are obviously enjoying the music, your enjoyment will rub off on
the child. Nothing need be said; he will be content.

A child's earliest experiences of listening may well be to his mother, as
she sings him to sleep. Both feel warm and content. Later on she may play
'singing games' with him. She does not say 'Now we are going to play a
music game. You must try to feel what the little piggy feels as he is on his
way to market.' That would be preposterous. No, the game is played
spontaneously. If mother and child are feeling good, a game might be
played. So should it be later. 'Do you want some music on while you're
painting?', or 'I feel like some music—don't you? What sort would you
like?' should be enough to transmit your pleasure to the child. He might
not care one way or the other. In this case 'Do you mind if I listen to some
music while you're doing that?' would indicate your pleasure, and a respect
for what he is doing. Very often children appear not to be listening the first
two or three times they hear a piece, but stop what they're doing to pay
attention the next time round. If the music is good, and if you are enjoying
it, the child will eventually share your interest. He may want to dance a
wild dance to the music. If so, he is giving his whole body and mind to it.
Join in. Don't be inhibited—nobody else will see you! Try to abandon
yourself like him. Then you will know what the music says to him.

Perhaps he will become interested in the different timbres of the
instruments he hears. Try and follow up his interest by obtaining pictures
of the instruments for him. A good bookshop will be able to tell you what
books are best. You could order them from the library. Once the child
knows what the instruments look like, you could play the music *A Young
Person's Guide to the Orchestra* by Benjamin Britten, allowing him to
indicate the instruments he knows, and showing him the others. This is a
really delightful piece. The first part makes use of the 'Variation' form, so
there is only one main tune to take in, whilst the music is concerned with
the characters and colours of all the orchestral instruments. The last section
is a 'fugue', which allows each section of the orchestra to enter in its own
fashion, one after the other, building up to a huge climax in which
everybody plays. Although it is 'educational', it is also real music, and you
can listen to it in many ways—as a guessing game, as answer to your child's

enquiries as to what instrument makes which sound, for joining in with, or for just enjoying.

Some pieces that you might consider listening to with your child are the 'Minuet and Trio' movements of the larger-scale works of the great composers. Haydn, Mozart and Schubert would be good composers to begin with. Symphonies, string quartets, and instrumental solo music can all be used. Very often the last movements of such works are popular with children, for they are often light-hearted and cheerful.

Besides the Minuet and Trio, you could look for 'Rondo' (a sophisticated kind of 'round'), or 'Variation' (one theme, treated in many ways—some happy, some sad, some serious, etc.) forms. These are all easily digested by young listeners. Try to avoid really large-scale works to begin with, for the movements may be too long. (Shorter movements from the earlier Beethoven symphonies—up to No. 6—will be appropriate, but the later string quartets, for example, will not usually be right for a young child.) Short instrumental solos, well chosen, can be enjoyed, as may music for brass bands.

Negro spirituals, blues, traditional jazz and the best pop songs all have treasures to yield. The field is enormous. Don't take on too much at a time. Your child needs the security of coming to terms with each new delight. Very often adults know a piece very well, and assume that their child learns to love it after one or two hearings. This is not generally the case. Give a child lots of time; he will need it.

Eventually, your child will want to attend a concert. This calls for very particular preparation. I cannot say at what age this should best be arranged, for all children are different. You should know when he is ready. Parents can get it wrong. The promise of an 'outing' which adults attend seems a rare treat. Parents may select a concert that contains a piece the child knows and likes, and certainly one that they will themselves enjoy. The day of the concert arrives. At bed-time, instead of retiring as usual, the child puts on his best clothes and is ready for a treat. At first, it is all very exciting. The big hall, lots of grown-ups, the appearance of the musicians, tuning up, seeing players with their instruments in the flesh, trying to locate the instrumental sounds he can now recognise; the conductor arrives on the rostrum, the lights dim. Marvellous.

They play an overture—nice and short. Loud applause, and the child joins in, ecstatic, shifting his body round in the seat, wriggling with excitement. The conductor turns back to the orchestra and raises his baton for the second time. This time the child is in for a shock. Long after he thinks it should have ended, the music goes on. When it finally stops, there is no applause. He looks at a parent who puts finger to lips. The music begins again—very slowly. He begins to fidget. When this movement ends—another—and another. By this time the child is desperately casting around for a means of escape. He thinks of the lavatory, and mimes his needs to his parents. He receives a definitive shake of the head, and an awful frowning glare. His parents by this time sit rigid in their seats—willing the child to keep still. They might give him some sweets, and whisper that it's nearly over. He looks hopeful, longing for the conductor to go away. He doesn't. Now the child yawns, and his eyes begin to close. He finds the seat uncomfortable, and fidgets around.

Eventually the music finishes; gratefully the child stretches his legs, and joins in the applause; at least he is allowed to move—even to speak. The interval arrives. He remembers his promise to sit still and be quiet, like a grown-up. Eager to please, and desperate to prove himself, he contradicts his parents when they suggest that they should go home because he has had enough. No, this was never mentioned; he has failed if they go now. After the interval, they come back for more. If that isn't the way to kill off for good a child's enjoyment of music, I don't know what is. I have seen it happen more than once.

You can avoid such a situation so easily. If the child is young, or very active, it is a good idea to arrange to take him to an outdoor concert, where small sounds do not disturb. If there are none available in your district, you might consider taking him to an afternoon children's concert. I'm not too keen on these myself, because there are so many unaccompanied children that the distractions may prove too great—especially if the conductor hasn't gauged his audience correctly. But they can be fun. If your child has been brought up to honour the occasion as an exchange of trust, as I have described, he might well be so shocked at the behaviour of other children that he will hate the whole episode. If however, you do decide that he is ready to experience a 'real' concert, you should prepare him properly. Tell him of the occasion well in advance, and let him know what you have decided to do. Then he will be able to cope without disappointment; he will not let you down.

First, he should know what pieces he will hear. You may decide to take him to the first half of a concert only. Explain that you have every intention of leaving at the interval—and that the decision was not made because you don't think he would be 'good'—rather because you want him to *enjoy* the music. It doesn't matter if he still wants more—he will want to go again, and that's good. Then, obtain the music he will hear from a record library—he may know some of it already. Allow him to become familiar with it. Tell him that a real concert is quite different from hearing recorded sound—for different conductors and performers have different ideas on different days. If you can only obtain one piece, try to make it the longest work on the programme. A child has very little idea of time, and even if you tell him that the piece lasts from supper-time to bed-time, he will not expect that to be as long as it turns out. When he is thoroughly familiar with a piece, pretend to be at a concert performance of it. That will mean sitting very still and calm, and listening to everything that is going on. He should try to keep his questions back until the end. (You could try this exercise with a very short piece first, gradually lengthening the time he must sit until he has managed to succeed for the duration of the piece you will hear.) Never allow a child to think that he has failed. Find what you can to praise, and don't try again until he is ready. To give him heart, you can explain that it is far easier to sit still in a concert hall, because he will *see* what is going on too. (I'm afraid you should get good seats for the occasion, otherwise he may become totally disenchanted.)

You must also prepare for the fact that the concert will probably take place when the child is normally asleep. You can arrange practice-runs for this situation. Perhaps you could issue an 'Invitation to Dine' at 8 p.m. one evening. For this, the child must make sure that he will be good company for you. When he returns from school, you should have a light tea prepared for him. He must pretend it is his supper. You could turn the clocks on to his normal bed-time to help him make believe. Let him have a bath, and put on his pyjamas. Tuck him up in bed, and read a bed-time story. Get him to close his eyes and tell him to feel every part of him is very very heavy. Perhaps you could sing him a lullaby. He may join in this game so successfully that he will actually go to sleep. (One April Fool's day, we managed to convince our children it was bed-time at 3.30 in the afternoon.) I'm not suggesting that you 'con' your child—but that you help him to con himself into believing it is bed-time. Assure him that you will let him know well in time for him to dress for Dinner. He can then wash, and put on his best clothes to join you. You could make it a little special for the occasion. If he really can't sleep, there is little you can do about it. He ought to relax as much as he is able, and you will be able to see if he lasts long enough at dinner to make the concert possible. Try a few dummy-runs, and see if you can find the best formula for rest.

I started taking my children to hear live music by keeping a look-out for less formal occasions—rehearsals at music colleges, and short lunch-hour recitals, etc. They were very young—less than four years old. But by then, they had a practical interest in music which made it much more interesting for them. I also made sure that they never looked as though they would create a disturbance. If you do take small children to a concert, you should ask them to behave in an appropriate manner as soon as they enter the hall. It is important to allay the fears of your neighbours *before* they begin to worry—then they can enjoy the music too.*

If you make great use of records or cassettes, you could unwittingly convey the impression that all good composers are dead; this is not so. I have been delighted to find real beauty creeping back into much new music. It is the thing I seek above all else. There are some composers living

* For older children and young adults, mention should be made of the Youth Concession Schemes, such as Youth and Music, which will be found listed in both the *Music Yearbook* and the *Music Education Handbook*.

today whose music I love. They are not the 'easy' ones—those who live off the back of the composers of the last generation. Rather are they those who are inclined to take risks—advancing the art and often leaving me behind; and yet I have learned to trust them.

Unfortunately, music companies do not turn over a large stock of new music, for they make little profit from it. It is the same old story. (Your child will be moved by the story of Mozart's last years, during which he produced some of the loveliest music the world has been privileged to hear. He died in poverty—contemporary audiences could have saved him. Or the story of how reputable and established composers of Beethoven's day considered his last quartets to be the work of a madman. Or even, this century, how Stravinsky's music for *The Rite of Spring* caused a riot.)

The fact is that with regard to new music, history has not yet sorted out the good from the bad, and you must do it for yourself. Usually the new music which is accepted is the easy kind. All the old conventions, but new tunes. Audiences know where they are. But the composers of lasting value are those who take the risks. They may make mistakes frequently, but sometimes they make marvellous discoveries. You may not be present at the birth of a masterpiece, but you should try to make the effort to learn the vocabulary. If composers do not live, then music becomes an antiquarian activity. Even if you don't want just yet to introduce your child to music of unknown quality, try to let him know that music is still alive, and still being written.

One last word about concert-going. Do not expect to like all 'famous' music; some of it is not very good; some of it takes time to know. Don't allow yourself or your child to be bullied into obligatory appreciation of all 'great' composers. I recently attended a Promenade Concert at which the first half of the programme was devoted to little-known music by one of my very favourite composers; there were quite a number of children present. The music turned out to be really boring, the performance pedantic—and a wobbly singer was included for good measure. I felt sorry that the children had been so let down. I did not stay for the second half—but I expect they did.

Remember also that music is not always deadly serious. It can be quite preposterous—like the virtuoso pieces of the nineteenth century; it can be gay or happy. If it is funny, laugh—at least inside your head. Allow yourself to enjoy it. Then your child will learn to know what music is about.

As a member of a 'great' audience, he will be fulfilled without playing a note.

Chapter 8

MUSIC IN SCHOOLS: WHERE CAN IT BE FOUND?

It would seem to be an indisputable fact that music offers a firm basis for a general education unequalled by any other subject.

Some of the more obvious benefits a child will positively enjoy, are the developments of his self- and corporate-discipline, quick and sensitive reaction, reasoning power, abstract and spatial thought, imagination and memory. And yet if your child receives an excellent musical education in his school, he is very, very lucky.

Throughout the world huge efforts are being made to improve music in schools. A great deal of research has been carried out since the 1940s, some of which has had spectacular long-term effects. With the emergence of 'new' music for instance, the traditional limitations which prevented all but the more advanced players from enjoying music at a high level of performance seem to be lifting.

When an area of such immense potential is tapped, the true researcher will open up huge new areas for action. In order to test the results of his work, he must obtain the cooperation of large numbers of field-workers. The danger of such a project lies not in itself, but in its imitators; those who are unable to offer a creative whole, but are willing to scrap the possiblity of fairly solid achievement in favour of a mere flirtation with fashion. And yet a feeling for any true method of instruction, be it old or new, so long as it does not produce failures, is good.

The most startling general improvement has been made in Hungary, as a result of Kodaly's inspiration in setting up a network of Music Primary Schools where the general education is based on singing, and where children have the opportunity to learn to play an instrument from a very early age. From small beginnings, the results so impressed the authorities that the system now includes upwards of 120 such schools, music nursery schools, music secondary schools or conservatoires, music training colleges and the Academy at Budapest. The network still expands, countrywide, and the importance of music in the conventional school has increased.

As well as this, Carl Orff's Schulwerk[G] is at last being fully implemented in some primary schools in Munich.

Experiments in America have confirmed (if confirmation is needed) the benefits of a music-biased education, to the extent that the IQ scores of its privileged recipients are seen to show a marked improvement. For sheer musical achievement, we have seen the results of the Russian policy of intensive training of musicians from an early age. Certainly an impressive number of the world's greatest musicians are from the Soviet Union (although the tragedy of a state which can give so much yet is afraid to inherit the mature fruits of its bounty, is past understanding).

France has announced her intention of embarking upon an intensive course of action based upon the work of both Kodaly and Orff, and dramatically hopes for the establishment of five thousand choirs and a thousand orchestras and chamber groups in French schools within the next three years. We can only wish her luck!

Here in Britain we are renowned for our Choral Tradition. Maybe not for long though, for the removal of direct grant status from the many excellent Choir Schools threatens to mark their gradual disappearance, although a determined effort is being made by most to carry on.

Public Schools retain their own highly respected traditions both of singing and orchestral work, whilst the new crop of fee-paying schools weighs in with a determined bid to found and foster their own honourable customs.

In addition to all this, we have the exciting establishment and growth of five schools of major significance in the field of music-biased education. Of these, more later.

With so much solid attainment to our credit, why the despondency? Merely that the above-mentioned schools, so vitally important to the state of music in our land, are now all in the private sector. By a special Act of Parliament, two schools alone retain direct grant status—the smallest music school (Yehudi Menuhin School), and the Royal Ballet School.

There are music scholarships, some quite well-endowed, at most of the old and some of the new independent schools. In addition, most (although unfortunately not all) of the Local Education Authorities will support a place at a Choir- or music-biased school which has been won on merit.

Of the rest, there are some schools whose music equals and even surpasses that in many of the independent schools.

Dartington College of Arts has implemented much valuable research into the field of music with the handicapped and ESN child. Some schools have built up their own unique field—perhaps in African music, West Indian Steel Band music, or music workshop situations, where pupils are encouraged to make and play their own instruments, and to compose their own music . . . In all these places, music lives—a relevant, passionate and fulfilling life of immense vigour. But they are the exception. It is possible for whole counties to be thus exceptional, and to have worked out the value of music for their schools and future citizens. But the fact remains that most of the children in our state schools get, musically, a very raw deal indeed.

Music plays very little part in our normal school life. It is an extra—a leisure activity—to be indulged in out of school hours. The situation is exacerbated by the cuts recently imposed upon school finances from on high. Here once more is a story from my own experience, which, I am told, is typical of recent events.

From the large number of primary schools in our part of London, we chose the only one which had music for all children as part of its curriculum. (When I say music, I don't mean learning the hymns for the week, or playing around with an instrument trolley.) Each class had a lesson with the excellent specialist teacher, and a part-time teacher came to help with the choir and the recorder group. Since my children could play violin and cello, the recorder group became an orchestra, and a splendid little drummer emerged, together with other enthusiastic percussionists. Instruments were privately financed or donated—and music flourished. Other children, their enthusiasm fired by watching the small instrumentalists, requested tuition. They were told that instruments were not available, and teachers unobtainable. When my children left, the orchestra once more became the recorder group, even though their places could have been easily filled by others wanting to learn. The school's music nevertheless thrived. All children received class tuition, and those who wanted could also sing in the choir or play in the recorder group.

In 1976 the staff quota was cut. The specialist teacher now has a full-time class of her own, and can only give class music to one other class. The choir survives, rehearsed in the teacher's free time, and most children have no music at all.

I have heard of schools whose head teachers seem to work magic. They employ a staff whose ability and enthusiasm for music matches their own. When a member of staff leaves, she will be replaced by an equally capable teacher. Somehow or other, these schools manage to employ, besides a musical staff, a full complement of visiting instrumental teachers. And yet a neighbouring school will state categorically that since it has a full quota of staff, it is not allowed to employ one visiting instrumental teacher!

I cannot understand a system which, whilst decrying privilege, nonetheless manages merely to deprive some children of what would seem to be available to others. There is a shortage of instrumental teachers, we are told. And yet players even with teaching diplomas, willing to give regular lessons to individuals or small groups of children at school, are not allowed to do so for more than ten hours per week unless they are qualified *school*-teachers!

The sad fact is that there is some music in some schools. You must make your own enquiries as to whether there is some music in your child's school. Here are some of the points you can look out for.

It is a good sign if large, or even small-scale concerts or musical productions are put on with enthusiasm for parents and friends. But do not let this mislead you into thinking that all the children have class music. This kind of performance is very often mounted by staff in their free time simply to make up for the fact that there is no other music for the children.

Are music classes given by a specialist teacher, or are class teachers responsible? In the latter case, you should find out whether there is a curriculum for music throughout the school, allowing for development, or whether each teacher acts independently—if at all. It is this last situation which is possibly the least satisfactory. Children may be subject to the same extremes as can be seen in the larger sphere of general education—'Traditional' methods (often sound, but living in the past) versus 'Experimental' methods (whose success depends on whether the experiments work, and whether the experimenters notice).

I would suggest that if music is important to your child, you should not worry too much which method is used, so long as you can be assured that there *is* a solid plan of some sort which you believe capable of extending his appreciation of music without severing his belief in either the old, or the new. If the school has an orchestra, you may find your child is 'selected' to learn to play a given instrument. If this is the case, do make sure that the instrument is suitable and that your child wants to play *it* rather than any other. It can happen that a vacancy will eventually occur in the school orchestra and the teacher picks a 'musical' child to follow up. If the instrument in question turns out to be the wrong one for the child, he will not only lose his chance of playing that instrument—he may also lose the one chance of playing *any*.

If your child's school says it 'does Orff Schulwerk', ask how much of it is done, for it is a method for daily instruction, and although schools may 'use' the material (and some of the instruments), very few schools indeed use it as intended—although most teachers would like the opportunity to do so. It is as well to know too, where a secondary education may be had which carries on where the primary school left off—but that can be said of any subject.

There is some good news! Most LEAs provide grants for children who have reached a certain standard of instrumental playing and seem likely to continue. Teachers must be 'approved' by the authority. If your child's teacher is not, and doesn't want to be approved for any reason (she might, for example, already have a full complement of pupils), and if your child is doing very well, you would be advised to carry on paying. You may find out about this from your local LEA music inspector. Your child's head teacher can obtain details. Sometimes an authority will approve a grant for your child to attend at one of the main Music Conservatories' Junior Departments, usually held on Saturdays. The Royal College of Music in London for instance, has children from 28 different boroughs and county authorities, even from as far away as Portsmouth! Most are paid for by their LEA.

The ILEA runs a music-biased course of studies within the comprehensive school at Pimlico. Children from any London borough who wish to be considered for a place should ask their primary school head to apply for necessary forms early in the spring term of their final year. (Playing

standard should be about Grade III on an orchestral instrument, and applicants should have had some piano tuition.)

If you suspect that your child has a passionate interest in music, you will need to make very early enquiries as to how he may best be helped. It is no good coming across vital information only to realise that it should have been sought years before. In order to put such knowledge at your disposal, I have gathered as many facts about schools and people who can advise as possible.

DO NOT HESITATE TO ASK FOR ADVICE AND INFORMATION. Not only does this cost you nothing, but it may be the means of finding the most appropriate education for your child, whilst drawing attention to the need that exists for better all-round provision.

You may of course find that your ideal solution is going to cost a fortune which you haven't got. I am truly sorry if this turns out to be the case—but at least you *know* that, and are not left wondering what you could or should have done. Some of you will find that your LEA will pay, some will find that it won't. Others will find a scholarship takes care of all financial worries—and some just half of them. In rare cases, you may find yourself in receipt of a direct governmental grant.

Here then, for parents, and for teachers who have a professional need for such information—also for those who are merely interested—are the first clues as to where music is certain to be found.

Local information may be obtained from the LEA music inspector. Otherwise, the first necessity is to obtain the *Music Education Handbook*. It contains indispensable lists. Look at them *all*. See whether you need anything you didn't know you could find. The specific lists I have in mind at the moment are the list of fee-paying schools offering music scholarships, the list of Choir Schools and the list of general schools with special music curricula.

With regard to the fee-paying schools offering music scholarships, you should enquire as you feel inclined or attracted. The schools are as you will find them—not biased towards music, but often making excellent provision for it. Competition for places is often very high, and not all schools suit all children. For instance a school with an intake of academically precocious children could find the 'music scholar' funny—especially if he has not been taught in the same way as they have. This could result in the child becoming an outsider. Questions of suitability cannot be answered by anybody but yourselves. Unless your child obtains a scholarship from the school, you should expect no financial aid.

The Choir Schools do have a common purpose, basing their timetables upon the musical requirements of the Church; what you may find surprising is that they do not confine admissions necessarily to vocally gifted boy boarders. (Your husky-voiced daughter, although perhaps eligible for a place, will not, however, be eligible for a choral scholarship; and the supplementary awards paid by some LEAs to the scholars—who must usually board, and be available at Easter and Christmas—will not be paid in her case.)

I think it is interesting, even for those who have no intention of applying for entry, to know what a Choir School is. Commonly held suppositions can be, as mine were, way off the mark. On the other hand, a particular Choir School might be just the thing for your child, and you may never have found out. Here then is the general information available from the Choir Schools Association. You should ask the schools for dates of voice trials if relevant to your needs. Details of scholarships can be found in the current *Music Education Handbook*, and each school prospectus will inform you of conditions for the entry of non-choristers. Some Choir Schools offer unspecified 'music' or leaving scholarships. The ages of entry differ with each school and should be checked well beforehand. I quote from the Choir Schools Association's official leaflet:

'The common interest of Choir Schools, whether they are attached to Cathedrals, Collegiate Churches or Chapels, or parish Churches, is that they educate boys who sing daily services in choirs. This tradition of choral singing in Britain is without parallel in the world. But in spite of this interest, great care is taken that other activities have their full and proper place in school life . . .

'One group of Choir Schools consists of independent preparatory schools which accept pupils at about the age of seven or eight and keep them until they are thirteen. In these schools they have the advantage of being educated in small classes. A few of these schools are for choristers only, but most take in other pupils, the majority of whom will go on to the independent public schools by means of the common entrance examination or a scholarship; others may enter a school in the maintained system.

'The other group of Choir Schools provides education as far as A level and university entrance. These are larger secondary schools with junior departments, where a chorister may in many cases continue his singing for longer, until his voice breaks.

'Most Choir Schools accept both boarders and day pupils but many insist upon choristers being full boarders. It should be noted that a few are for day pupils only. Some also take girls who, although not eligible for entry to a choir, may otherwise participate fully in the general and musical life of the schools.

'Musical opportunities in Choir Schools are outstanding, as they are well placed to attract good teachers. Most choristers learn one or two instruments from the start, and thus stand a good chance of winning valuable music scholarships to public schools or to the senior department of the school they already attend, at about the age of twelve or thirteen.

'The academic results of choristers are good. Although they spend many hours a week singing, time-tables are arranged so that their normal work and games do not suffer. The intellectual discipline and training of a choir sharpens the wits and is a firm foundation for academic success. No other activity in which a boy regularly takes part requires such concentration, attention to detail and, above all, sense of awareness, as the daily performance of complex music which must be judged entirely by adult standards.

'The fees in Choir Schools are similar to those charged in other independent schools, but scholarships are provided for choristers which reduce the total cost considerably. Some local education authorities contribute towards the fees of boys who have been awarded choral scholarships.

'Choral scholarships are awarded after voice trials, which are held once or twice a year, on dates which are indicated in this leaflet and also advertised in the national, church and music press, and also occasionally at other times, by arrangement. Choirmasters and organists are looking for boys who will be about eight or nine, sometimes a little older, on entry to a choir. A clear and tuneful voice and a well-defined sense of rhythm are essential. A good standard of reading and general intelligence is expected. Every effort is made to gauge a boy's potential.

'For complete details and a prospectus, application should be made to the headmasters of the individual schools, which should preferably be visited by parents and candidates before a voice trial.'

There are in Britain, but open to children of any nationality, five schools offering to highly selected children an education with a pronounced bias towards music. This is a comparatively recent development and is wholly to be welcomed. It is hoped that with proven success, such schools will beget others, and that the process of selection will widen to include large numbers of children who would wish to benefit from such an opportunity as they can offer. Between them, these schools encourage all kinds of musical activities and modes of learning—supplementing their expertise in traditional methods with a real involvement in new music (to the extent of employing responsible but risk-taking young composers), and in one case, furthering a deep and informed commitment to the work of Kodaly, newly structured to support and strengthen an already impressive curriculum. It is important that both professionals and public are aware of the work of these schools, and it is to this end that the following discussion is mainly directed—even though there are only at present about 1275 children in attendance at them.

Each of the five schools operates with regard to the recognition that musical aptitude should if possible be encouraged early in a child's life. In each case, therefore, entry is available to children from the age of seven or eight years. As a child grows older, his attainment in practical music-making is expected to have advanced correspondingly before acceptance can be considered. Each school has its own, very different expectations as to the standard of playing required; these are discussed in the sections on individual schools which follow.

If you suspect that your child has a pronounced musical aptitude, you should seek a second opinion from your LEA music inspector or other professional musician. If they support your opinion, you may apply to the Yehudi Menuhin School or to Chetham's Hospital School for advice as to how it may best be nurtured. (The earlier this is done the better—even though your child may not have commenced the formal study of an instrument. Local music inspectors should be expected to advise, and are generally happy to do so.)

Obviously the schools are primarily interested in children who may eventually attend their schools, but they are also interested in the welfare of any child who seems to have an outstanding potential, and are keen to see that it is developed wherever possible.

It is commonly assumed that before admission to any of these schools can be considered, a child should become a most advanced instrumentalist. This is not necessarily the case, as I will explain. Very often a child will lose his interest, and with it his chance of becoming a fine player as a result of poor teaching; it is far better to make early enquiries than to hang around waiting for the child to attain a hypothetical standard of performance which will 'prove' his ability.

The schools are discussed in order of size; the number of 'music-biased' places does not necessarily coincide with the number of pupils in attendance.

The Yehudi Menuhin School

This school was begun in 1963 by Yehudi Menuhin with the help of his friend and colleague Marcel Gazelle. At the time of its foundation there was barely any provision outside Russia for musically 'gifted' children. As a result it attracted world-wide competition for the few and highly-prized

places it offered to young string players and pianists.

A super-competent staff is backed up by regular visits from the eminent teachers of cello and piano, William Pleeth and Louis Kentner, whilst Yehudi Menuhin himself occasionally visits the school or plays in concerts with the students.

The age-range of the girls and boys is from eight to seventeen years. Places are available for boarders only, since the timetable demands an early start to the day, and a fully integrated community life. For this reason also, numbers are strictly limited. Presently there are forty-two children in attendance.

The rules are fairly loosely constructed to allow for maximum development and freedom; there is no uniform.

The school is situated in its own grounds in Surrey.

All pupils are selected on musical potential alone—no academic tests are given. It has been found that children who have developed those qualities which indicate a deep understanding or appreciation of music, are mostly able to apply them throughout their schoolwork. Indeed, although children are at diverse ages and stages of their education when they enter the school, the classes are so tiny that with naturally high motivation and interest, most academic requirements are fairly easily met—even though time available for study is necessarily severely restricted.

The timetable is divided into two. From Monday to Friday, $3\frac{1}{2}$ hours each are daily devoted to music and to academic work. The orchestra rehearses on Saturday mornings, and the children may go home or visit friends during the rest of the weekend. They have their own telephone. Amongst favourite leisure pursuits are swimming in the school's own pool, and amateur dramatics. There is not a great deal of opportunity for other physical exercise.

The school exists to enable its pupils to become first-class practising musicians. Some proceed to music colleges throughout the world—already they have a high record of scholarship places; others may go direct to study with a particular teacher. University entrance is also possible for those who wish to pursue their education in a wider sphere. (Recently a former student won one of the first scholarships available to women at King's College, Cambridge.) The school offers at its highest level an education comparable to the most advanced tuition available in colleges of music.

There are two auditions. A preliminary audition is held in November, and the final selection is made in February or March for entry the following September. (Applications should be submitted by October preceding entry.) In exceptional circumstances a certified tape recording may be sent.

Competition is very high. There are generally from two to five places available each year, as they are vacated. It is the school's policy to try to replace vacancies by the same instrument, so that a balanced intake is retained. Obviously if two outstanding candidates apply for one place, this policy is reconsidered.

At present roughly one hundred applications are received each year, of which about fifty may be heard. The Music Director is most anxious that those children who apply should not be made to feel that they have 'failed' if they are not offered a place. In every case, he will offer advice if the parents wish it. Sometimes parents are unaware of other possibilities, and he is able to suggest a more appropriate course of studies. He would also wish to point out that the younger a child applies, the better his chance of entry, and the more the school can offer.

It has been known for a child to be admitted to the school on the strength of his recorder playing and his musical responses at the audition.

Fees are high, but British tax-payers have the benefit of a governmental direct grant, relating fees to tax paid, and non-British children can sometimes find sponsors in their own country. Second and subsequent children at the school pay half-fees. The school has never turned away a child for lack of money.

Children perform regularly at home and abroad, and the Friends of the Menuhin School enjoy observing the steady development of its pupils through attending concerts held especially for them. Membership is open to all, and any funds raised are put to good use, providing essential equipment for the school. A prospectus and staff list are available on request from the school secretary.

St Mary's School, Edinburgh

This school made a recent transition from being a conventional Choir School to being a specialist music school with places (some boarding) for about forty children in addition to the original twenty or so choral places. Its status within the Scottish educational system and details of its future are still to be determined. Enquiries should be addressed to the school secretary.

The Purcell School (formerly the Central Tutorial School for Young Musicians)

From very small beginnings (four children at Conway Hall) the Central Tutorial School for Young Musicians was founded in 1962 by the late Irene Forster and by Rosemary Rapaport, who directed the first classes. It rapidly expanded, and was housed at Morley College until lack of space made it necessary to move to Hampstead. Here by 1973 the number of pupils had increased to fifty.

Now the school has moved once again in order to accommodate yet more pupils, and to expand the range of its interests. At its new address it can offer over one hundred children the chance of a music-biased education in splendid surroundings near London.

The Purcell School is a day school, and children of all nationalities are welcomed. The headmaster points out that although exceptional provision is made for the musical child, the school will now admit children with other major interests. In this way he hopes to provide a school which reflects more nearly the situation in the 'outside world'. The school offers 'a good general education to university standard'. Instrumental lessons are taken privately with teachers outside the school. The Director of Music will advise on appropriate teaching if it is not already being obtained. In this way a small school is able to provide chances for a large selection of instrumentalists to benefit from the various musical activities which the school can provide, without having to employ teachers on a permanent basis. Being near London, it does not usually prove difficult for such instruction to be obtained.

The age range of the girls and boys is from eight to eighteen years. There is no school uniform, and discipline is stated to be firm but sensible. Petty regulations are avoided. Pupils are selected by interview, and attention is paid to reports from previous schools. All children are expected to learn a musical instrument.

Where children wish to specialise early in music, practice time can be accommodated within the school timetable. Although a norm cannot be stated, music can account for about a third of the timetable. The school boasts two orchestras; children who reach 'a certain standard' have the opportunity to play in chamber groups, and the whole school rehearses together as a choir. School parties attend concerts, and on occasion lectures

and concerts are given by visiting players. Academic work is done in small classes, and coaching in subjects outside the normal curriculum can sometimes be arranged at an extra fee.

The school encourages the study of music within a balanced framework of academic and artistic subjects. On leaving students may expect to consider entry to university, music colleges and other institutions of further education. Application for entry should generally be made by February, but entry lists are left open to allow for cases of special need. Sixth form entry is available.

A prospectus, staff list and information relating to fees can be obtained from the school secretary. Students who enter on serious musical grounds may apply for a bursary, which is available to them at all stages of their school careers, should they not initially prove successful. Some LEAs provide assistance with fees for children of musical promise.

Children whose parents wish to consider their entry to the Purcell School are advised to consult the headmaster, who will advise whether application should be made. The school has a mailing list, to which anybody may subscribe. Details of informal concerts are mailed, and these concerts are open to the public.

Chetham's Hospital School of Music, Manchester

Chetham's role as a national school for young musicians gradually evolved from a growing interest in music as a leisure activity. A long history (the school was founded in 1656) of boys' general education experienced a sudden twist of fate just after the last war; Manchester Cathedral requested the neighbouring school to provide choristers for its services.

This association was successful, and the music thus introduced rapidly expanded to cover a wide range of other musical subjects. Soon the school could boast three orchestras. The obvious seriousness with which the school had begun to take music attracted to it boys whose own musical inclination was equally committed.

In the mid-sixties a historic decision was taken to provide a school which could offer a sympathetic course of studies to any child who wished, and was able to pursue music seriously—regardless of nationality, sex or creed. The age range would be from seven to nineteen years. In 1975 Chetham's completed its seventh fully musical intake; thus all present pupils have been selected on a basis of musical aptitude alone. There are now 275 children attending the school, of whom one hundred are boarders. There are five orchestras, four choirs and numerous ensembles. Each child normally studies an orchestral instrument and the piano.

An excellent music staff includes many who are associated with the Royal Northern College of Music, the Hallé Orchestra and the BBC Northern Orchestra. Outside London, nowhere else in Britain could such a rich variety of opportunity be made available.

School uniform is worn, and children are expected to conform to sensible standards of behaviour.

Parents who wish to apply for places should write to the Bursar, who will forward application forms. Applications are studied by the Director of Music, who decides whether an audition may suitably be given. (A child who may perhaps play only the recorder, and whose performance in the musical challenges issued at the audition is positive, will be offered a place, and the opportunity to study another instrument; a child who has been pushed and hustled through an advanced instrumental exam, but whose feeling for sound has been stifled, will not.) Once more, the younger a child applies, the better can the school help him to fulfil his potential. Parents should *not* be encouraged to place theoretical 'achievement' above real interest and involvement.

The Music Director points out that this natural feeling for sound can occur against all odds. It has been known to survive in utterly deprived conditions—as has been proved by some of the more vigilant local authority inspectors who have recognised potential and notified the school. Unfortunately not all inspectors are inclined to seek out such children as could benefit, and it is mainly left to parents to apply for places. This has been known to result in parents seeking an alternative to the state system—pushing their children into situations with which they can't cope—thus killing any hope of real attainment.

Primary school teachers should be aware of the opportunities for young children of musical promise at Chetham's, for very often it does not occur to parents to notice their child's preoccupation with sound until it is too late.

Applications may be submitted at any age. A substantial number of sixth-formers arrive each year for specialised study.

Roughly one third of the timetable is given to musical subjects. The general education is of a standard suitable to each pupil's requirements, and special courses are devised to suit any child whose needs depart from the norm. A full range of subjects is taught to advanced level, and other courses including CSE are available. Children are taught in classes of up to 25 pupils.

A great variety of physical exercise and education is available, and there is an enviable selection of activities, including squash, fell-walking, rock-climbing, canoeing, fencing, badminton, trampoline, gym, judo and orienteering.

This school provides the richest variety of opportunity for all its many pupils. Not all children expect or desire to become executants—some will become teachers, inspectors, administrators, concert managers, music therapists, or experts in the field of music for the handicapped.

The possibility of greatness is not overlooked.

Any child who wishes to compose, or who seeks advice in instrument-making, would be encouraged to do so. (It is to be hoped that such an environment may eventually produce one or two great critics—which music desperately needs. This however depends on further education and experience, and cannot be definitely considered at such an early stage.) An example of the positive attitude taken by Chetham's towards music-orientated careers is the appointment of a young teacher who studied the Kodaly approach to music in Hungary for a year, and who has returned with some very particular ideas as to its application in schools in this country. Not only does his work advantage all potential players, but it also serves to a great extent to illustrate the advantages of excellent class teaching.

This is one of the most valuable aspects of the work done at Chetham's, for it enables the privileged minority of children able to attend the school to share their advantages over a much wider field. When the time comes for these young people to attend teacher-training colleges they will demand a very high standard of teaching indeed.

A few children, after leaving, elect to follow careers other than those associated with music, and it is to the school's credit that it is so.

Information regarding fees, together with prospectus and staff lists, may be had from the school secretary. Most LEAs provide assistance with fees. Some, disgracefully, do not.

The school involves itself in many public concerts, and intends to expand its contacts with junior schools and other interested bodies in the area.

Wells Cathedral School

Wells Cathedral School is an Independent School. It contains a Choir School, and provides music-biased courses for a selected number of pupils, according to their needs. There are no religious restrictions on entry. The academic requirements for entry to the school are high. Although it is stated that academic tests are not taken into consideration when selecting children for specialist music places, no child will be admitted who is likely to be unable to keep up with his class in academic work.

The age range of the girls and boys is from eight to eighteen years. There are 600 children in the school, of whom 200 are girls. Of the children in attendance, 275 are boarders accommodated in eight separate boarding houses. Just under half the pupils have music tuition of one sort or another.

School uniform is worn, and rules are of the type which one expects to find in a school of this size and nature.

There are twelve places for 'specialist' violinists, and some for 'specialist' cellists. Choristers are also considered as 'specialist' musicians, and have a music-biased course of studies.

Apart from these children, there are two other categories of musician in the school. 'Serious' musicians are able to study a variety of orchestral instruments, and their studies are biased towards music according to their needs. They are not required to practise quite so much as 'specialists'. 'General' musicians are those who take music as a part of their general studies, and learn an instrument in addition to their normal school work. With so much diversity of approach towards the place of music in each child's school timetable, it is impossible to state just how much, even on average, is devoted to music. In general, the Director of Music says that each musician within the school has the opportunity of taking as much music as he wishes, after serious consultation with the staff involved. A fairly strict level of attainment in GCE is however maintained, and students are not encouraged to over-specialise in the early years. The school is well-endowed, and almost any subject may be studied in depth.

The school's policy is to allow each of its pupils to mature in an environment which reflects all areas of serious study. The standard of a child's playing is taken into account when he enters the school. The staff will not admit children who have had years of poor teaching, since they are not willing to spend a great deal of time undoing the damage—even though the child may appear to be 'gifted'.

'Specialist' musicians are therefore expected to be able to play their instrument well on entry; the school suggests a rough yardstick of about Grade V by the age of ten. They must also be able to keep their end up when it comes to academic prowess. Application for these places is advised early—normally between the ages of eight and twelve years.

Entry to the school is possible in all categories between the ages of seven and sixteen years. There is a fairly complex system of payment. If the child's LEA does not support his 'specialist' place, the school is willing to consider sponsorship according to parental income. One further scholarship of £100+ is available to a non-specialist player. Only a small number of specialist places are annually available, but there is no limit to the number of 'serious' or 'general' musicians, who enter the school on the basis of academic ability. Scholarships are available to these students too, should their academic work be outstanding. Some LEAs will support a 'serious' musician.

Such a system, complex though it undoubtedly is, does allow a large number of children to enjoy music-making at a high level within the school.

There are currently three orchestras, six chamber groups, and a number of wind and brass groups. A full choir practises daily, and there is a choral society. Concerts are given at home and abroad. Many well-known players and orchestras visit the cathedral, and the children attend concerts regularly. Consultant music staff are well-known players and teachers.

Details of fees and information are available from the school secretary. Parents interested in the music courses must make sure that the 'Music Prospectus' is sent, together with all the separate sheets of information dealing with the other music courses available.

Briefly then, to summarise the facts with regard to music in schools.

If music has become important to your child, you will want him to attend a school which is at least sympathetic to his needs, and at best provides him with an excellent musical education as a part of his general curriculum. In addition, he may require instrumental tuition, which must also be of the highest standard.

Should your LEA provide musically to each according to his needs, you are extremely fortunate, and not quite typical. It is to be hoped that with a growing awareness of what music has to offer, this state of affairs will quickly become the norm. However, should your child require special attention in musical subjects which is not otherwise available to him, you must be prepared to pay for it. Scholarships and bursaries are available, but competition is high. Do not introduce talk of success or failure, since this can only be damaging. If you wish to enter your child for a competitive situation, make sure he is properly prepared to do his best, and is not upset by the results.

Here are the basic facts about the alternatives:

Independent Schools

The fee-paying schools have their own individual merits. Scholarships may be available, including music scholarships. School music may not, even so, be of major significance. Day places and boarding places according to the school. LEAs most unlikely to help.

Choir Schools

Boy choristers may pay anything or nothing for the privilege of an education which can be of the highest standard. They will be required to board, from about the age of seven years. An LEA may well supplement a choral scholarship. Other choristers (not scholars), non-choristers and girls may be permitted to take advantage of a Choir School education, with varying degrees of bias towards music, but they should not expect financial aid. Day places and boarding places according to the school.

Of the five schools discussed above in detail, the Menuhin School has no day places, the Purcell School has no boarding places.

The Menuhin School and the Wells 'Specialist' scheme exist to encourage the development of young string *players* and pianists. Each has a very restricted entry indeed. Of all who apply, the joint admission to these places is generally less than ten children per year.

Wells has however an almost unlimited number of places for children of high academic ability who play music well and wish to study it seriously.

Undoubtedly the largest number of places for the greatest variety of careers in music exists at Chetham's. The standard of teaching is in most cases outstanding. Manchester is not beautiful, but it can be intellectually stimulating, and at least a part of the school is very beautiful indeed! Both day and boarding places are available.

If you happen to live near Harrow, the Purcell School can offer proper support to a child who wishes to pursue a serious course in music, or who may eventually decide to do so.

In each case, you may receive financial support. The Menuhin School is direct grant (payment according to means).

In all other cases, a scholarship, bursary or your LEA could foot all or some of the bill. Or they may not.

It seems quite apparent to me that the direct grant status should be extended to cover all specialist music schemes of such seriousness: why one receives such support whilst the others do not is a mystery. The Gulbenkian Report on Training Musicians (1978) states unequivocally that each student who gains a place at one of these last-named schools should receive financial support. Since nobody seems to disagree it would seem to be time that something was done about it.

CONCLUSION

It has been difficult to imagine, whilst writing this book, who my eventual readers might be.

My reason for writing it was quite simple—it didn't exist.

During the last few years, when my need was greatest, I should have been delighted to find whole books or series of books on some of the subjects I have raised. I should certainly have bought large quantities of 'Picture Scores' had they existed; my children would have loved to help me choose their first vocal and instrumental pieces from stacks of attractive scores, specially edited in large cheerful notes, for tiny players. But now, several years later, there is still barely any material to consider, and parents are still having to make it for themselves.

As far as choosing teachers was concerned, we stumbled along—making several mistakes, but being dogged enough to persevere until we struck gold.

Specialist education for children who were considered to be sufficiently 'musical' was a revelation accidentally heard about one afternoon whilst listening to 'Woman's Hour'.

And so it went on. It seemed that absolutely vital decisions had to be made almost daily, without recourse to anybody else's experience or help.

The professional Educators acknowledge the amazingly rapid rate of learning which takes place in the pre-school years. They have done little however, to enable parents to encourage and share their young children's progress.

On the contrary, we are still commonly given to understand that only when a child can leave his parents to attend school, is he old enough to receive Education! Sometimes this is too late.

Recently a great deal of interest has been aroused by the fact that a child who has suffered from catarrh or sinus trouble in his earliest years is quite likely to encounter difficulty with reading and writing. Research by Dr Audrey Wisbey has shown us that a child in whom such trouble goes unchecked is liable to lose his ability to hear the higher frequencies in the sounds we encounter all the time. (If you turn the Bass control on your radio right up, and the Treble control right down, and then imagine the effect exaggerated until the words become unintelligible, you can quite easily see what she means.) If this condition is recognised early enough, a parent can help a child to overcome literacy difficulties before they develop into a fully-fledged problem. (Since the affected child cannot hear accurately, he cannot imitate. Thus his speech becomes slurred, and reading cannot be attempted.) Dr Wisbey suggests that children 'Learn to sing, to learn to read'. By learning to copy sounds accurately, they are able to isolate the source of possible future trouble, and (with great pleasure) arrest its development.

I hope very much that the information and ideas which I have set out will be useful to all those who have to do with children. For from the warding-off of illiteracy to the development of a self-discipline capable of sustaining the very highest levels of thought and action, music has everything to offer.

Much of what I have written has been as a result of my personal experience; you may not like—or may disagree with—some of my ideas and suggestions. I hope and expect that you will be confident enough to adapt, if not completely change whatever you think should be adapted or changed, to suit temperaments and needs. I have tried merely to set readers upon a path of self-help—showing them where, when and how they should begin to look for what they themselves require.

I hope that teachers, students and play-group leaders will be encouraged to exchange opinions with each other and with parents, thus spreading local information, ideas and interest, and removing the feeling of isolation so often experienced by children who 'do music'.

It has been suggested that parts of this book may be found a little difficult to follow by parents who have not themselves received some instruction in music. I do hope that this is not the case. If it turns out to be so, perhaps such a parent may consider taking an occasional lesson himself—if only to boost his confidence. However, the most valuable factor in such an undertaking would be the indication of a real desire to share music with the child. Anything else must be a bonus.

I have been told that many young teachers will not know the answers to some of the questions I suggest they may be asked; that neither will they appreciate 'interfering parents' attending their lessons.

I do have a great deal of sympathy for such young teachers. It is quite true that they may not have been taught how to deal with real teaching problems, and nobody should blame them for that. But if the enquiries made of them are sincere, and tactfully put, and if they take their job seriously, they will want to find answers—not only now, but throughout their lives. This is the mark of a fine teacher—and more than anything, we need fine teachers.

Those who retain their curiosity and desire to learn alongside their pupils, will find each lesson becomes uniquely geared to the individual. In learning to understand whom they teach, they will find the way to tactfully discourage interference whilst positively welcoming help from a sympathetic source.

The criticisms that have been made of this book are real, and inevitable. Had I been able to do so, I would have rather written a dozen books—each

designed for a different market.

There is one criticism which caused me concern. It came from a serious and respected source, was made in the face of my title, 'Give Your Child Music', and after the (admittedly still sketchy) manuscript had been thoroughly perused. It was to the effect that some of the material would be of use only to parents of 'gifted' children.

Since it is the main purpose of my book to suggest that it is possible for mortals—as well as the Almighty—to bestow just such gifts, I feel that I must conclude by further strengthening my argument. Only by so doing can I hope to persuade readers that provision for excellence in the field should be a normal demand.

First, I must say that (most rarely) pronounced natural aptitudes are to be found mysteriously lurking in individual persons. Throughout the ages, infants have been marked out for favour by Divine Intervention—regardless of circumstances, heredity or IQ. Some have enjoyed their gifts; some (often manipulated by parents or managers) most emphatically have not; many never knew they had them. (For the most stunning recent, documented example of this phenomenon, the reader is referred to *Nadia, A case of extraordinary drawing ability in an autistic child* by Lorna Selfe, published by Academic Press.) Although such gifts usually begin to appear fairly early on, there are a few fields in which development can occur at such an early age that we encounter the phenomenon of the child prodigy. Music is one of these.

I should like to consider why this is so. For having established the nature of the common factors, we may then consider which (if any) may be open to the ordinary baby-in-the pram, with his parents' help, to develop and enjoy.

First, two basic observations.

1. In the Beginning man was allotted three main types of role to perform—for good or evil—on this earth: they may be termed IMITATIVE, INTERPRETATIVE and CREATIVE.

Aspects of these roles coexist in every child, but a bias towards one or another usually occurs either naturally, or as a result of environment. Time alone plays no part in the original endowment or subsequent inclination.

2. As an infant develops into an adult he acquires EXPERIENCE and PHYSICAL STRENGTH. He also learns a LANGUAGE; this gives him recourse to the accumulated experience of the ages, upon which he can build to his own level.

The fields in which these last attributes are required are not open to the infant prodigy, for they require a passing of time in which to emerge matured. Thus, for instance, is the young poet of genius not to be found much before the mid-teens, whereas it is possible for a talent (natural or encouraged) for chess, gymnastics, dancing, diving, skating, maths or music, etc. to emerge very early indeed.

To return to my original observation. The apparent wealth of 'prodigious' talent which fashion from time to time brings into the open, is very often of a merely imitative nature. All non-brain-damaged children can be taught to imitate—anything which their elders consider desirable. Thus, through constant use, is learned the difficult lesson of language itself. Parents understand that infants will make mistakes, and most will correct them in great good humour. The more pleasant the lesson is to learn, the easier it is found to be and the more successful the task. All children love the sense of achievement—especially when it brings forth a warm response from a loved parent. That children should experiment with vocal sounds is considered natural and desirable. They learn to *interpret* tones of voice and shades of meaning, and they produce their own versions. They *create* verbal rules for themselves, and invent picturesque terms of undeniable charm. All their natural abilities are hard at work.

It is not quite so easy however, when the task is seldom performed. Usually the parent/teacher will show his child how to do a specific task. If the child 'interprets' the instructions or 'invents' his own ways, he will be corrected, and shown once more. He learns to imitate, but failure to do so precisely as instructed can often result in condemnation.

Obviously there are some tasks—in particular those which may be dangerous if performed otherwise—which must be copied exactly. But there are many more which require an open mind and a willingness to experiment together. For real control comes with real understanding. And sharing, and enjoyment. Thus children may receive from their parents gifts for a lifetime, of the highest order.

So many fêted infant prodigies reach a dead end; they have not been allowed the privilege of failure—and cannot begin to find a place in their talent for their own growing personality.

Unless your child is quite obviously determined to dictate his own pace, outstripping your attempts to assist, he should not be persuaded into the uncomfortable role of a child prodigy. However, with the benefit of hindsight, several students of music, when asked, have said quite firmly that they wished their parents had 'made' them practise more when they were very young. Parents themselves, faced with the problems of their own children's development, commonly express the same sentiment. Yet they all know that a child cannot be 'made' to practise if he doesn't want to. The secret apparently lies in making the practice itself desirable. If this can be done, there would seem to be no limit to a child's progress. It is not so much explanation that is required as a willingness to share and experience difficulties as well as triumphs with the child. Concern should be active.

At times, children, like adults, seem to come to a standstill. They need time to readjust their personalities to constant change. Whilst remaining vigilant, and being prepared to reconsider arrangements which may have become outgrown, there is little but instinct to guide parental response.

I have, in process of writing this book, met many children who are generally, and correctly, considered to be 'gifted' musicians. But so far I have come across only three whose original motivation was entirely their own, and who may thus be termed 'naturally' gifted. This is not to say that their gifts are better—or even of greater promise than those of their friends. What it does mean is that (usually very early on) in most cases, somebody has decided to make up for a Divine lack of generosity, and has begun to share his personal pleasure in music with his child. Thus does music 'run in the family'.

Is a child who is encouraged thus to be automatically considered 'gifted'? And if so, does it matter whether the gift was from Heaven, or Granny?

Is the gift wanted? If not, will it be wanted later? These questions are important.

At one extreme, children who have been forced to become prodigies under a tyrannical parental influence, have eventually arrived at a passionate love/hate relationship with music itself, whilst totally rejecting the donor. At the other, there are numberless cases of opportunities lost and bitterly regretted.

Somehow one has to steer the best course. It is not easy. Strangely, I have never encountered anybody with an 'unwanted gift'; no matter how it was come by.

Given the right circumstances, I believe that all children (with the tragic exception of the aurally handicapped) can learn to enjoy music at their own peak level of attainment.

Music is a gift to mankind. It is there to be enjoyed. If it is given in good time, with sympathy and understanding, who knows what may result?

Even for those (parents?) who come late to the scene, much can be recovered. Motivated in turn by my own children, my playing improved. But best of all, my hearing has sharpened to include a completely unsuspected dimension of sound. The tables are completely turned. My children have learnt to play; I have learnt to listen.

I can think of no more truly divine sequel than that the Gift of Music should prove to be mutual.

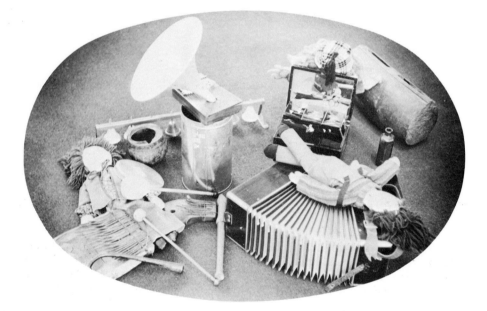

GLOSSARY

bar: measure of time used in western music; each bar consists of a given number of beats divided off on the staff (see below) by bar-lines.

chamber ensemble: a small group of players, generally between three and seven in number, who meet to play *chamber music*, which is designed for intimate performance in a room or small hall.

clef: the 'key' to a staff (see below). By fixing the position of one note all others within given compass may be located. The two clefs most commonly encountered are:

Treble or G clef, which fixes the G above middle C on the second line (used by instruments and voices with high compass).

Bass or F clef, which fixes the F below middle C on the fourth line (used by instruments and voices with low compass).

Kodaly Method: a most carefully graded method devised by the Hungarian composer and educator Zoltan Kodaly (pronounced *Kòdd-eye*), 1882–1967, which uses singing from the very earliest to the most advanced stages, as the basis of a general education. Widely used in Hungary and increasingly throughout the world.

madrigal: a composition for several voices in which each has an independent line. Madrigals were written in the sixteenth and early seventeenth centuries and were particularly popular in Italy and in England.

notation: the writing down of music. Common forms include *staff notation* (music written on a staff) and *tonic sol-fa* (doh, ray, me, etc.); recent developments include *prose notation* (comprising verbal instructions for performance, which may or may not be precise) and *graphic notation* (non-verbal material generally to be employed as a basis for improvisation).

Orff Schulwerk: Five graded volumes of material designed to be used daily by teachers with larger and smaller groups of children towards the creation of their own music and dancing. For use with associated tuned and untuned percussion. Devised by the German composer and educator Carl Orff (b. 1895).

percussive: pertaining to sounds made by the striking of one object by another.

staff or *stave*: the five horizontal lines on which western music is generally written.

transposing instrument: an instrument for which music has to be transposed (written at a pitch other than that sounded). The reason for this is to maintain a constant system of fingering on all related instruments. For example, a clarinettist is expected to play three differently sized instruments; when he reads (and fingers) middle C, his C clarinet sounds middle C, but his B flat clarinet sounds B flat and his A clarinet A. Therefore a composer must write or transpose his notation according to the range and timbre of the instrument he requires.

BOOKLIST

(Publishers are in London except where otherwise stated)

Chapter 1: LEARNING TO CONTROL SOUND

Begin Making Music by Richard Addison: Holmes McDougall, Edinburgh.
Fun to Make Music by Anthony Kemp: Hamlyn.
Lively Craft Cards: Mills & Boon.
Make Music Fun by Avril Dankworth: The Dryad Press.
Making Musical Apparatus and Instruments by Kathleen Blocksidge: Nursery
  School Association, 89 Stamford St, London SE1.
Making Musical Instruments by Peter Williams: Set 2.
Music and Language with Young Children by K. M. Chacksfield, P.A. Binns and
  V. M. Robins: Blackwell, Oxford.
Musical Games with Young Children by Jean Gilbert: Ward Lock Educational.
The Musical Instrument Recipe Book by Emily Romney: Penguin Education.
Resonant Rubbish by John A. Brune: English Folk Dance and Song Society, Cecil
  Sharp House, 2 Regents Park Rd, London NW1.

Chapter 2: TEACHING YOUR CHILD TO READ MUSIC

The Kodaly Way to Music, adapted for English schools by Cecilia Vajda: Boosey &
  Hawkes.
Nursery Rhymes by Zoltan Kodaly: Boosey & Hawkes.

Chapter 3: HOW TO CHOOSE AN INSTRUMENT: OR, FIRST FIND YOUR
  TEACHER

Music Education Handbook edited by Arthur Jacob: Bowker.
Music Year Book: Macmillan.
Play Time: Longman First Recorder Course, Stages One, Two and Three by Margo
  Fagan: Longman.
The Violin Family by Sheila Nelson: Dobson.

Chapter 4: HOW NOT TO BUY AN INSTRUMENT

The Persistent Pianist by E. D. Robilliard: Oxford University Press.
Orchestral Percussion Techniques by James Blades, Oxford University Press.
So You Want to be in the Music Business by Tony Hatch: Everest.

Chapter 5: THE FIRST LESSON: SOME NECESSARY QUESTIONS

Nurtured by Love by Shinichi Suzuki: Bosworth.

Chapter 7: MAKING AND LISTENING TO MUSIC TOGETHER

The Book of Music: Macdonald.
Class in Concert, kits 1, 2 and 3: Middle Eight Music Ltd, 7 Garrick St, London WC2.
Enjoying Music Book 1 by Roy Bennett: Longman.
Instruments of the Middle Ages and Renaissance by David Munrow: Oxford University Press.
The Larousse Encyclopaedia of Music edited by Geoffrey Hindley: Hamlyn.
Listening to Music by Keith R. Newson: Warne.

Chapter 8: MUSIC IN SCHOOLS: WHERE CAN IT BE FOUND?

Music Education Handbook edited by Arthur Jacob: Bowker.

LIST OF USEFUL ADDRESSES

Arts Council of Great Britain, 105 Piccadilly, London W1. (A list of Competitions, Awards and Scholarships for Music Students may be obtained free on request; the standard expected is usually extremely high.)

Blüthner Pianos Ltd, 47 Conduit Street, London W1; tel. 01 734 5945.

Boosey & Hawkes Ltd, 295 Regent Street, London W1; tel. 01 580 2060.

British Federation of Music Festivals, 106 Gloucester Place, London W1; tel. 01 935 6371.

British Institute of Recorded Sound, 29 Exhibition Road, London SW7; tel. 01 589 6603.

Central Music Library, 160 Buckingham Palace Road, London SW1; tel. 01 730 8921.

Chetham's Hospital School of Music, Long Millgate, Manchester 3; tel. 061 8349644.

Choir Schools Association, The Cathedral Choir School, Ripon, Yorks; tel. 0765 2134.

Cramer (J.B.) & Co. Ltd, 99 St Martins Lane, London WC2; tel. 01 240 1612/3/4.

Emerson (June), Wind Music, Ampleforth, York; tel. 04393 324.

Incorporated Society of Musicians, 18 Gloucester Place, London W1; tel. 01 935 9791.

London Music Shop, 218 Great Portland Street, London W1; tel. 01 387 0854.

Morley Galleries, 4 Belmont Hill, Lewisham, London SE13; tel. 01 852 6151. (For all good makes of pianos, harpsichords and other keyboard instruments.)

Music Teachers' Association, 106 Gloucester Place, London W1; tel. 01 935 6371.

National Music Library for the Blind, Royal National Institute for the Blind, 224–8 Great Portland Street, London W1; tel. 01 387 5251/5171. (Braille music library.)

Piano Advisory Service, 11th Floor, 30 Eastbourne Terrace, London W2; tel. 01 723 0105.

Purcell School, Mount Park Road, Harrow, Middlesex; tel. 01 422 1284.

St Mary's School, Manor Place, Edinburgh 3; tel. 031 225 1831.

Samuel Jaques Pianos, 142 Edgware Road, London W2; tel. 01 723 8818.

Schott & Co. Ltd., 48 Great Marlborough Street, London W1; tel. 01 437 1246.

Steinway & Sons, Piano Makers, 1 St George Street, London W1; tel. 01 629 6641.

Truman & Knightley Educational Trust Ltd, 78 Notting Hill Gate, London W11; tel. 01 727 1242.

United Kingdom Harpists Association: Hon. Sec. Isabel Frayling-Cork, 83 West Side, Clapham Common, London SW4.

Wells Cathedral School, Wells, Somerset; tel. Wells 72839.

Yehudi Menuhin School of Music, Stoke d'Abernon, Cobham, Surrey; tel. Cobham 4739.

Deeper than

Indigo

Tracing Thomas Machell,
forgotten explorer

Deeper than Indigo
Tracing Thomas Machell, forgotten explorer

Published by
Medina Publishing Ltd
310 Ewell Road
Surbiton
Surrey KT6 7AL
medinapublishing.com

Design & Layout: Richard Wood

ISBN 978-1-909339-53-8 hardback
ISBN 978-1-909339-56-9 paperback

Printed and bound by
Toppan Leefung Printing Ltd
China

Deeper
than
Indigo

Tracing Thomas Machell,
forgotten explorer

Jenny Balfour Paul

Medina Publishing

Writing on water

Single white goose quill
what are you writing
drifting gently on
water's silk surface
making your mark
between liquid and air
leaving behind you
an imprint of movement
the hint of a message?
there's more to writing
than words.

JBP

To the late Thomas Machell of Crackenthorpe and his wider family
and to my own immediate family,
my late husband Glencairn, children Finella and Hamish
and grandchild Felix Glencairn

JBP's sketchmap of the Indian Subcontinent showing places mentioned in the text

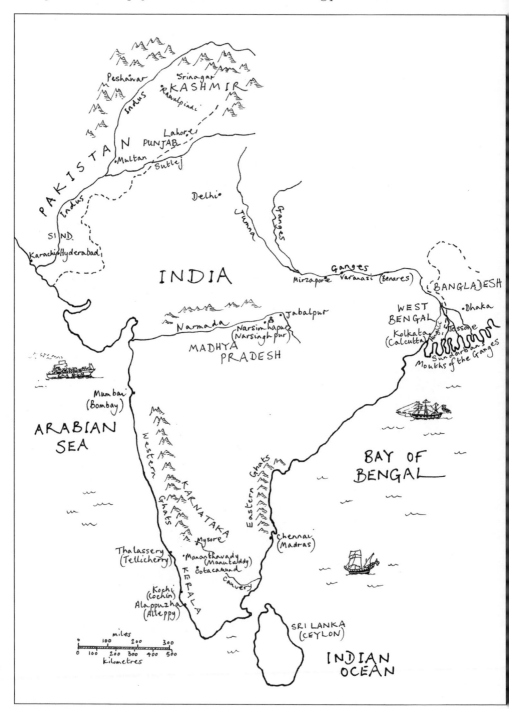

Contents

1.	Meeting Thomas	9
2.	Running Away from Home	20
3.	Passages to India	26
4.	Exotic Landfalls	37
5.	Opium Wars	41
6.	Going Home	51
7.	Rendezvous at the Rectory	55
8.	Coals to Nuku Hiva	67
9.	Marquesan Magic	72
10.	Guano and Missions to Patagonia	85
11.	The Ghosts of Crackenthorpe	92
12.	Into the Eye of the Wind	106
13.	Singing the Blues	109
14.	Kissing the Crescent and the Cross	119
15.	Limbo	139
16.	Memories of Indigo	150
17.	Suspended between Two Magnets	173
18.	'Further Travels and Adventures of a Vagrant Son' – up the Indus	183
19.	Coffee Time	191
20.	Closing the Gap	205
21.	Between the Known and the Unknown	216
22.	Beginning of the End	218
23.	Rowing into Eternity	228
24.	Into the New World	233
25.	Back to the Beginning	241
26.	Moments of Epiphany	249
27.	Eureka!	266
28.	Machells Reunited	284
29.	Pirates of the Arabian Seas	291
30.	Come Back Yesterday	303
31.	Twist in the Tale	307

Sketchmap of the Indian Subcontinent	6
Sketchmap of Bengal	152
Acknowledgements	312
Picture Credits	314
Chronology	316
Family Tree	318
Glossary	320

Thomas's self-portrait in Arab dress. He assumed the alias Sheikh Abdullah el Hajji while travelling with Arab merchants for five months from Calcutta to Cairo. His father, the Revd Robert Machell, endorsed the picture as being a true likeness.

1. Meeting Thomas

Let your life lightly dance on the edges of Time
like dew on the tip of a leaf.

(Rabindranath Tagore)

I first met Thomas at the very end of the 20th century. The attraction was instant and when I parted from him in London I felt physically sick.

Back home in the West Country I immersed myself in preparations for the last Christmas of the century. I made mince pies, wrapped presents, and dangled over the fireplace my great-great-grandmother's quaint Victorian fairies, almost succeeding in putting Thomas out of my mind. Almost, but not quite; every so often I caught myself thinking about him. The pungent spices of mulled wine transported me back not only to the East Indies but also to the lingering flavours of our meeting. I recalled his hints of exotic travels in far-off lands, and his longing for someone to heed his words before the century was over. I had no need of a new man in my life, but I sensed such yearning beneath his spirited tone and adventurous tales that it seemed heartless to turn my back on him without giving him a second chance.

Thomas was 129 years old the day I was born, and 175 when we met. But he will remain forever younger than me, since he died at 39, whereas I am still going strong. The fact that he is dead is no bar to his speaking to me, or to anyone else for that matter. He made sure of this during his lifetime by treating his personal Journals as his 'Talking Papers'. And talk they certainly do – in five volumes totalling almost 3,000 pages, sprinkled with whimsical watercolours.

These extraordinary Journals came my way by serendipity. An acquaintance from Devon, a librarian, while attending a meeting at the

British Library in the spring of 1999, had happened to notice a manuscript volume in a showcase. It was open at a page with an amusing watercolour entitled 'Indigo planters after tiffin'. He had glanced at the label. It described the volume as written by a Victorian, Thomas Machell, 'midshipman in the merchant navy and indigo planter'. The word 'indigo' sparked the librarian because he had previously supplied me with books for my indigo studies.

So indigo was the bait that lured me to Thomas, though he waited long enough to reel me in. I had been hooked by indigo one summer's day when, in the granite courtyard of an old Devon farmhouse, I fed a white cloth deep into an indigo dye-vat, pulled it out minutes later and watched its colour transform in the air from yellow through turquoise to midnight blue. I resolved there and then to discover more about this magical and most universal dyestuff, unaware that the hook was in for life and that I would pursue indigo all over the world until Thomas caught me and took over. Then I had to pursue him all over the world.

I cradle Thomas's life in my hands as I carry his Journals from the Issue desk and place them on a large library table. For some reason I'm drawn to Volume Two. I ease the bound book from its case, feeling its density in my palms before opening it at random. As I start to decipher the slanting script with its wayward punctuation my breath changes rhythm. The modern readers around me fade away and I join Thomas on his lonely veranda in the Bengali jungle on a night of steamy heat in the 1850s. Peering over his shoulder, I watch his hand move to and fro as he dips his quill into the inkpot to transfer his thoughts onto the paper. He is smoking his meerschaum, which keeps a halo of insects at bay. Their incessant buzzing joins the sounds of the quill's scratch and the harsh sawing of crickets. Thomas pauses and stares unseeing into the invisible, suffocating vegetation. He is brooding on his life and, out of the thousands of passages I might have read first, I have chanced across him just when he is musing on the unexpected way that indigo is shaping his life.

I lay aside this volume and try another (Four). The very next passage I read, again chosen at random, also hits home. It is dated the first day of April 1851 and Thomas has illuminated the letter 'A' and added a quotation from Byron:

>*'Tis strange, the shortest letter that man uses*
>*Instead of speech, may form a lasting link*

Of ages; to what straits old Time reduces
Frail man, when paper – even a rag like this –
Survives himself, his tomb and all that's his.

Just so. Thomas continues: 'Yes I think it very probable that like my more learned namesake Thomas Machell of Carlisle I shall leave behind me some seven volumes of manuscript papers… and mayhap the words carelessly written at Rooderpore factory will be lighted upon in some musty library in the 20th century and quoted by some descendant who has heard that such volumes exist somewhere.'

That passage, like the indigo one, seems to target me. After all, I did indeed hear that such volumes existed in a library, as Thomas anticipated – and though the new British Library isn't 'musty', the old one where they first landed certainly was. I am fulfilling Thomas's forecast of their being 'lighted upon' in the twentieth century but have cut things pretty fine by finding them just weeks before the century ends. I can also see that in the future I might find occasion to quote them, though I am not a 'descendant' as far as I know. It is odd to be holding five volumes rather than Thomas's predicted seven, though he voiced his forecast in Volume Four when very much alive, so how could he possibly have known that he would leave behind even five volumes, let alone seven? Strange. There is just time to look for clues at the end of the last volume before the library shuts.

This one transports me to the Malabar hills of southern India, where I also join my former self, since I stayed there in 1970. Both Jennys, past and present, savour the sweet coffee blossom with Thomas, but are thankful to be spared the rats that plagued him: '16th July 1856. The house is overrun with rats made traps for the unwary and squashed three.' Together we experience the relentless monsoon weather. 'The wind howls and whistles through the chinks and crannies of the old Bungalow, then suddenly it dies away and the heavy pattering of rain is heard faster and faster through the long hours of the dreary night.' Two months later dense clouds still envelop both jungle and Thomas himself as he pens his final entry: 'I have no longer the buoyant spirits and unbroken health of younger days… at thirty-two I feel older than many I have seen with ten more years on their shoulders.' He adds enigmatically: 'Who shall mark the line between perseverance and rebellion, who shall tell where the resignation of a Christian or the fatalism of an Oriental begins or ends.' Who indeed? I turn the page to find his very last sentence: 'I grope in darkness Light of the World. Grant to me that I may receive my sight.'

The lively young man of the earlier volumes now sounds utterly depressed. I assume he was on the point of death when he wrote those words in his rat-filled Bungalow.

The library is closing. The Journals are recalled to the Issue desk and I am recalled to the present, feeling disturbed and queasy.

At the time I was preparing to deliver the first lecture of the new millennium at London's Royal Geographical Society, its subject being 'Travels in Pursuit of Indigo'. I couldn't resist replacing two images of mine that I had previously selected with two watercolours from the Journals, thus giving Thomas his very first public airing in that Society's historic lecture hall, where such famous explorers as Shackleton have lectured. How proud and amazed Thomas would have been to see projected on a huge screen that comical sketch 'Indigo planters after tiffin'. The other projection was his hand-drawn 1846 map of 'part of Bengal showing stations or towns, and indigo and sugar factories'. His old map seemed just the thing in such a setting. I pointed to indigo estates and towns that were just hours apart by horseback in Thomas's day but now lay several days from each other, modern transport notwithstanding, due to the frontier that had divided Bengal between India and Bangladesh since 1971.

Having assumed that Thomas died suddenly aged 32 after writing the entry in southern India that concludes Volume Five, I contacted the organisations in London dedicated to recording British deaths and burials in India to establish when and where he had been buried. Their investigations showed no Thomas Machell to have died in India, though burials of other Machells were on their lists. This was surprising. It made me wonder whether a sickly Thomas had struggled on board ship intent on returning home to convalesce (as he tells us he has done before) but had died en route and been buried in some alien port, or perhaps at sea, echoing a scenario he had himself foreshadowed:

> *2nd December 1850.* Let us take a look at the living freight of this 'Budgerow' boat coming down from the Upper Provinces. On a low couch surrounded by a few dark faced servants an emaciated European is lying, gasping painfully for air whilst one of his attendants waves the hand punkah over his fevered head, see he sleeps and sleeping dreams of home. Disturb him not poor fellow, he is going home on sick certificate, sleeping he dreams he is there, hears the chime of the village bells, and sees again the loved faces, from whom he has long been absent, but let

him sleep on; for sleeping he dreams of that home which he is destined never to reach, for he will be shipped on board to die ere he reach the Line and add to the many thousands who lie under those dark blue waves.

I conducted a lengthy computer search. What would a Victorian make of someone sitting in a study in England's Devonshire countryside making contact electronically with city institutions all over the world at the tap of a keyboard? I tried the obvious sources first and drew blanks, and then a link took me to the Mormon archives in Salt Lake City. The Mormons (founded when Thomas was six) record as many deaths worldwide as possible in order to convert deceased souls to Mormonism. How Thomas's clergymen ancestors would splutter in their graves if they knew this. Of course Thomas's own name didn't appear on the computer screen – nothing was ever as straightforward as that – but the Mormon records directed me to a chapter, entitled 'Machells of Crackenthorpe', in an 1884 volume of a British publication with the cumbersome title of *Transactions of the Cumberland and Westmorland Antiquarian and Archaeological Society*.

I went next morning to my local university (Exeter) to submit a loan request, hoping the publication could be tracked down somewhere. Imagine my astonishment when I found the university's own library had a copy of this obscure book on its shelves. I wasn't so surprised to find that it had last been issued to a reader over 40 years earlier.

The chapter provides a short history of the family up to Thomas's generation, but gives no information about Thomas other than noting that 'the late Mr T. Machell' (which I deduce is him) with his father and elder brother helped the author to collate the chapter I am reading. The text itself therefore doesn't solve my mystery, but stuck into the back of the book I find a bulky sheet of folded paper. Gingerly I ease open the brittle folds and find an extensive family tree headed 'Pedigree of Machell of Crackenthorpe'. It traces the family from Saxon times to the late 19th century and holds the vital key. At the top of the sheet I find trios of greyhounds leaping above emblazoned shields, and ancient names like Umfridus. I recognise these greyhounds: they also prance around Thomas's Journals. My eyes zigzag down the centuries, encountering such names as Lancelot, Hugh and Robert. Important people have annotations summarising their achievements. The first Thomas on the tree dates to the 12th century, his entry stating simply that he 'confirms grants of land in Crackenthorpe received from his father'. However, his 17th century namesake, 'Thomas the Antiquary', has a lengthy description of his distinguished career. The tree broadens out to the generation I seek, which stretches right across the page, near the bottom. Here I find, among Thomas's siblings, an illustrious older brother who is a Canon of York, and an Army Captain younger brother decorated for bravery. Sandwiched between them is a stark entry for my Thomas:

THOMAS M.
b. 12 Nov 1824, at
Beverley, d. unm., 14,
bur. 16 Dec. 1862, at
Nursingpore, E. Indies
M.I. there and at Et
ton; Will 29 Dec.,
1861

The entry can hardly be briefer – no annotation for this Thomas – but here is the information that has eluded me for months. And it has been in my own university library all the time.

So my conjectures were wrong. I had failed to heed Thomas's own prophecy. A decade before his death, he wrote: 'I am like Muhammed's coffin suspended between two Magnets. Duty points to India as the place of my pilgrimage and most probably as the resting place of my bones when my destiny is accomplished. Affection draws me towards home the pole star of my wanderings.' So his hunch about where he would die was correct. From now on I learnt to listen to him.

The reason Thomas's death in India didn't feature in the registers was later pointed out to me. It seems that individuals in humble positions were sidelined by the Establishment, their burials not considered noteworthy. This explains why other Machell deaths feature in the official lists, but not Thomas's. Lancelot, his younger brother, apparently served with distinction in the Bengal Horse Artillery, as well as being the 'second best polo player in India' (who was the best, one wonders?). He could hardly have been more *pukka* therefore, whereas Thomas clearly wasn't, which made me warm to him more. Lancelot was buried in a famous military hill station in the North-West Provinces, but where on earth was Nursingpore, where Thomas was said to be buried?

I consulted a Victorian atlas and found that British mapmakers of that period often settled for approximate transliterations of Indian place names. Thus, for example, Manantavady, the town nearest to Thomas's coffee estate, appears as Manutoddy – in this case somewhat appropriately since much alcoholic toddy was made in the area. The old atlas showed two small towns anglicised to Nursingpore, both of them far from the coffee estates of Kerala where I assumed Thomas was still working when he died. Even on modern maps both towns, now spelt Narsinghpur and Narasinghpur, are remote. During British Raj times they were a world away from smart Calcutta with its famous Park Street cemetery. Trust Thomas, I thought, to make things more of a challenge.

I had at least established that he died a lonely death in a mysterious outpost far from his family anchor and that he had neither wife nor (recorded) children of his own. And he had reached the ripe old age of thirty-nine, having survived a further six years after the last Journal entry in the British Library. His lifespan was now only six years short of the European average at that time, not bad going considering his physical weaknesses as a child and his sometimes tumultuous life in the tropics that includes war, several bouts of near-fatal diseases, and other physical dangers that felled men far stronger than him. His ability to cheat death, like the proverbial cat with nine lives, was a source of surprise to Thomas. In April 1851 he writes: 'What can one think when one sees puny fellows like me knocking about by land and by sea now wet to the skin now sleeping for weeks like a vagrant in the open air and never a bit the worse for it whilst hale hearty looking fellows with the strength of a giant just drop off with a cold.'

What, in any case, is a lifetime? Virginia Woolf observed that 'the true length of a person's life, whatever the DNB may say, is always a matter of dispute,' and the biographer Richard Holmes concluded an article about Shelley's death with the following: 'Certainly human time is not divided into equal chapters. Nor is the "death scene" the true end of any significant human story. We need to be aware that many lives change their shape as we look back on them. The dead may always have more life, more time, to give us.'

Thomas, through his Journals, was clearly yearning to give us more life, more time. But of the different chapters in his life, the final one, covering six literal years (though goodness knows how many figurative ones) was now the most mysterious and open-ended, since written records appeared to be lacking. How was I going to find out what he had been up to during the most traumatic period of India's colonial history? 'I shall leave behind me some seven volumes of manuscript papers,' he emphasised. Since each of the five volumes now in the British Library covers approximately three years, the last six years of his life would indeed have produced two more volumes, bringing the total to seven, as he predicted. How could he have foreseen so accurately, over a decade before his death, that he would have written seven volumes of Journals by the time he died? And did the missing volumes actually exist somewhere waiting to be discovered? If not, had they vanished for good, or never been written? Thomas was clearly a compulsive writer. Could I unearth the ghostly two-volumes' worth of lost years that left such a gap in his story?

As Thomas gradually replaced indigo as the main passion in my life, friends took to greeting me with, 'How's your chap?' The more I got involved with his Journals, the more I thought of them as 'mine'. Once, a year after I had discovered them, I phoned the library to order them in advance of a visit. To my horror I was told they were checked out to another reader. Only then did I realise just how possessive of these Journals I was becoming (or were they possessing me?) since they are available to any reader in the world's most public of libraries. 'Who has taken them out?' I demanded, meaning: 'Who has had the audacity to take out my Journals?' 'Someone called Jenny Balfour Paul,' came the reply. What a relief it was to learn that after my last visit the Journals had remained in error on the shelves of the Reading Room, still reserved for me.

Thomas's family had settled into their adoptive home towns, Yorkshire's Beverley and the nearby port of Hull, by the time he entered the world. He passed his first decade in Beverley, but once his father took up the livings of the nearby parishes of Leconfield and Etton, the Tudor rectory of the latter became Thomas's lifelong lodestone. A delicate baby, with a 'birth defect' that dogged his life and puzzled me for years, Thomas – or Tom as his family often called him (and as I found myself doing later when I got to know him better) – surprised his parents by surviving potentially fatal childhood ailments and staging a rebellion at the age of twelve. And in 1840, the year young Queen Victoria wed her beloved Albert, Thomas slipped off to sea and a lifetime of foreign adventures.

The great spy writer John le Carré declared in a radio interview that 'the purpose of life is to make sure our origins are not our destinies'. Though vaguely aware myself from a young age of the importance of this belief, it had not made an impact until Thomas came along to point it out. I must be a slow learner; Thomas understood such ideas at a far younger age than I did. Or was it that when the average lifespan was half that of today, people had to learn, understand and act twice as quickly? It often seems like that when you read what numerous Victorians achieved in the time it takes many people nowadays to even get going. It is salutary to wander around a Victorian graveyard – especially in the tropics. Today such graveyards are of sociological interest, but Victorians had to confront the death in them head on, as 25-year-old Thomas himself points out:

> *31st August 1850.* Go to the churchyards or even my factory garden and read the ages of your fellow wanderers who fell so thickly around you, age 24, aged 19, aged 26 and so on. Count how many are under 30 and calculate your own chances, the odds against yourself, and the chances of those who make home dear to you surviving to welcome your return.

One can see that having the spirit of mortality forever whispering in one's ear was the best motivation for getting going. My generation and the next are inclined to let life slip by, incentives to action further diluted by comfort and machines.

On the other hand, old Journals remind one of the benefits of modern life, not least in the field of dentistry. Take these Thomas passages: '21st August 1850. Had such a violent toothache I was half wild with pain.' He endures five more days of agony before 'treatment', i.e. 'Had the enemy [tooth] pulled out, it was terrible work for Dr Palmer had to make two attempts and change his instruments before he succeeded.' Sometimes Thomas turned amateur dentist himself: 'That wretched man with the toothache underwent the torture this morning,' he writes on board a cargo ship in October 1849, having used tools from his portable carpentry box to yank out the tooth.

By dying midway in his century (1862) Thomas was balanced on the cusp of momentous innovations, just witnessing but rarely benefiting from their impact. The telegraph was just being launched and photography likewise. (His likeness was only captured by pencil whereas soon after his death his brothers could be immortalised in celluloid.) Later in the century came long-distance steam shipping and rail travel, and electricity. These inventions would have revolutionised Thomas's life, as would such medical discoveries as anaesthetics and the cause of cholera, which in his time killed thousands in Britain and the East, and very nearly killed him too. In the later 20th century came organ transplants, antibiotics, the discovery of man's genetic code and the extraordinary digital revolution. My generation and the next have embraced these discoveries and inventions, as would Thomas were he alive today – but then there would have been no Journals. Instead, the Journals are his equivalent of phone calls, letters, emails and

Facebook, diaries and photographs rolled into one, covering an era of stability at home, emanating from the self-assurance of Empire and the Industrial Revolution, counterbalanced by conflict and danger abroad. By driving himself overseas, with spells at home, Thomas experienced both aspects. The historian A N Wilson, in his *The Victorians*, memorably describes the British imperialist imposing Empire 'with his bible and his self-belief', confident of both technological and moral superiority over the natives. Thomas, however, with ironic detachment and a sense of the absurd, was well aware of the dangers both of bible and of self-belief.

Though Thomas chose to live thousands of miles away, he yearned to share his experiences with his adored father back home, in expanded letters that became the Journals. From the end of 1999 I joined Thomas's father to eavesdrop on his son's 16 chronicle of 'hopes, fears, expectations and disappointments'. 'I feel as if I am having a conversation with you,' he writes, 'though the talk is all on one side… each day I feel quite reluctant to put my talking papers back into my writing box.' In April 1851 he explains: 'It is just the thing to sit down with pipe in mouth and scribble without regard to the quantity of paper used, in a letter one is obliged to be concise but in a journal one can fire away as long as the *Cacoethes Scribendi* [the itch for scribbling] remains.' His character emerges while he meanders between news, opinions and moods in a stream of consciousness: 'I have got into another line altogether. But so it is in our thoughts, on paper we can trace the connecting link and I would not wish to be more formal here than I should be were I blowing a cloud with you at home.'

Thomas is surprisingly frank in his Journals considering both the *mores* of the time and the fact that he is conversing with a country clergyman who is passing his days in the conventional to and fro of English country parish life. However, at times the restraints can be almost tangible; he will launch into personal matters only to break off abruptly and change the subject. For example, in 1851 his boss's wife, with whom he is clearly smitten, leaves India. '*April 30th*. Mrs Forlong preparing to leave for England much to my regret… I shall never go to her house without feeling the loss of its lively mistress… I never thought I should have made so intimate a friendship in this blessed country nor was I aware how strong it was until the moment when I found it was to be ended. I will not however enlarge upon my feelings.'

The nature of Journals, even the most private ones, always raises the question of how much more lies between the lines, of what the writer chooses to reveal or conceal. In Thomas's case his Journals, though personal, were never fully private, and my challenge was to find out at what point he was applying the brakes. The things he left unsaid seemed to hover between the lines, as if written in invisible ink, waiting to be revealed to a future reader able to share his experiences and empathise with his sorrows and joys.

My young man defied stereotypes, fitting neither the image of the colonial Victorian Briton abroad, nor that of the Englishman 'gone native' – nor indeed that of a 19th century hippy. I had to let him set the pace. He seemed to dance enticingly just beyond my field of vision. All I could do was to follow in his teasing steps, waiting until he chose to show me a little more. Sometimes I sensed his exasperation when I proved a clumsy partner, but over the ten years we spent together we learnt to tango in time with each other. Slowly and magically the whole choreography emerged.

In July 1852, when in his late twenties, Thomas actually wrote: 'I have been meditating lately about writing a novel in the form of an autobiography.' Death prevented him from fulfilling his ambition during his lifetime, but clearly I was the one destined to complete the dance. Together we would bring his dream to life.

Illuminated letter 'I' for the preface to Thomas's hand-written volumes on the Machell family history, an updated version of those compiled by his 17th century namesake Thomas, known as 'the Antiquary'.

2. Running Away from Home

Life must be lived forwards but can only be understood backwards.

(Kierkegaard)

I was born on the 12th November 1824 at the Minster Parsonage, Beverley. Owing to an unhappy defect and a more quiet demeanour than the rest of my brothers, it was intended that as I was unfit to enter any of the professions I should be a home bird and be placed as a clerk in some mercantile house or something of that sort.

I was but little satisfied with this indefinite something in a family of Military and Naval aspirants, and after many a wild day dream secretly indulged in to the manifest prejudice of my Latin and Greek, I divulged my speculations to my younger brother Lancelot and declared my intention of sallying forth to seek my own fortune.

One thing I had not calculated on. Master Lancelot had no sooner heard of my design than he also determined on accompanying me. In vain I remonstrated – he would either let out the secret or go with me. As we both slept in the same room there was nothing else for it. So early one fine morning we got out of our window and left home to seek our fortunes.

This is how Thomas summarised his first adventure in his 'Rough Sketch of My Life and my brother Lancelot's written for the History of the Machell family'. He included the whole summary as an appendix to Volume Three of his Journals.

I picture the scene. Two small boys, hearts thumping, climb over their bedroom sill one summer's dawn in 1837. Twelve-year old Thomas, a 'puny' child (to use his own description), clings with thin legs to a rope borrowed from the stable and slides down onto the terrace below. Squirming above him comes Lance, his maddening younger brother recently turned eight. Lance, a sturdy little fellow, has the kind of foolhardy courage that marks him out as military fodder. After landing on the rectory terrace with flushed faces, the brothers sneak into the stable yard, pick up small calico bags they've hidden beneath a pile of hay in the store and set out to cross England from north to south on foot.

They have prepared for this journey by hoarding useful things in their hiding place: pocket knife, string, dirty kerchiefs, an old cork, tin flask, candles, flints, spare shirts and stockings, hand-drawn maps copied out at school, stubs of pencil, paper, and Lance's favourite wooden toy soldier. It has been easy in such a large household to hoodwink housekeeper Annie and purloin biscuits, dried meat and preserved fruit from the kitchen. The previous day Lance kept a lookout as Thomas pilfered fresh ham, cheese and bread from the pantry. There were whisperings, arguments and tense giggles at teatime before they went to bed.

The first day is thrilling. Both boys are excited to be taking part in a real life adventure. Once they have covered the first few miles, creeping through woods and alongside hedges to hide from early-morning farm labourers who might recognise them, they continue more boldly along deserted green lanes and over rough ground away from main thoroughfares. Birds sing. The sun burns off a slight mist. Hedgerows smell of cow parsley and honeysuckle. The brothers have ample food and stamina, and nothing seems more exciting than sneaking into a lonely barn that evening and snuggling into nests they hollow in the loose straw. They quickly fall asleep, exhausted by the long walk, not thinking of the weeks ahead dodging stagecoaches, angry farmers and dogs. Not thinking either of the mayhem they are causing in the Yorkshire village they've left behind.

That morning devoted Annie has entered their room to find empty beds and a rope trailing from Thomas's iron bedstead across the floor and over the sill of the open window. She has hurried downstairs to alert her master, the Reverend Robert, not wishing to alarm the boys' mother Eliza, who is at a delicate stage of her eighth pregnancy. Robert is not too worried because the family is used to Lance's japes and the boys will surely turn up by lunchtime. But as the day wears on with no sign of the young rascals, worry turns to concern, and concern to alarm when they don't return for supper.

The Reverend goes grim-faced to the farmer next door while Annie soothes Eliza and administers a glass of her famous hot malt tonic. Word soon spreads around Etton parish, from maid to groom to farmer to innkeeper. Parishioners appear at the door, offering help to their popular vicar and his wife. Retired army and naval officers join the farmers setting off around the parish, their dogs zigzagging ahead, noses down, tails circling in excitement. When dusk falls, lanterns are lit and held high as the searchers spread out to look in barns, haystacks, streams and ditches, calling and calling – 'Tom, Lance – Lance, Tom – where are you, where are you?'

No one sleeps that night and next morning the news spreads further afield when Robert rides the four miles into Beverley town to inform his relatives and the constabulary. He calls too on James Hogg, parliamentary member for the town and a family acquaintance, seeking his assistance in alerting magistrates and dispatching letters hither and thither to widen the search.

As the days wear on it is hard to remain calm in the parsonage, but Annie does her best for the sake of Eliza as well as the little ones. She tells the maids to dry their eyes as they bustle round dispensing tea and cakes to relatives and parishioners who drop by to comfort their priest, his gentle wife, and their expanding family. Hugh Devon, a difficult child, is six years old, Henry and Robert Scott just toddlers. Richard, the sensible older brother, upset at Tom's betrayal, helps Mother and Father by reading and playing with his siblings.

The family's grief increases daily when no news arrives of the errant boys.

Thomas and Lance, meanwhile, are making their weary way down the byways of England. The initial excitement has long since worn off. Their legs ache, their feet are blistered, and they are frequently lost. When it rains their soaking serge trousers cling to their thighs and refuse to dry. They are dreaming of Annie's nourishing stews and ginger cake. When food and pennies run out they dodge fierce dogs to steal fruit from orchards and, worse still, they mingle with crowds in village markets to snatch buns off stalls when the owners aren't looking. This pricks Thomas's conscience but not Lance's, for he is made of sterner stuff. The brothers are as unalike as war and peace. There are plenty of arguments as to who is to blame for the escapade. Lance tells Thomas it was a stupid idea, while Thomas reminds

Lance that he didn't want him to come in the first place. Each tries hard not to cry in front of the other. 'We endured considerable hardships,' wrote Thomas, in retrospect.

In the 19th century unaccompanied children were a common sight, working the land and daily walking miles from hovel or farm to village, market or school.

When the boys finally reach the south coast, they are hungry and missing home. From the cliff top they hear distant cries of seagulls rising on the summer breeze. They look across the English Channel and see a host of ships tacking to and fro on urgent errands on a choppy jade green sea, the far horizon smudging into the skyline. Down below in Portsmouth's harbour a lumbering man-of-war and merchant ships of all types and sizes ride at anchor, surrounded by busy little rowing boats and fishing craft. The sight fills Thomas's heart with a strange yearning, but hampered by little Lance he won't after all be able to seek employment or stow away on one of those merchant ships.

The scamps scramble down the cliff and take the road into the harbour, invigorated by the sight and smell of the sea. The bustle is intoxicating. They settle on a dirty coil of rope and breathe in mingled smells of tar, salt, horse dung and putrid fish as they watch the melée around them: barrels, chests and dirty calico bales of all sizes are being slung from laden carts hauled by steaming horses and then hoisted on thick ropes over the ships' greasy sides. Sailors with straining muscles stow the cargo or straddle the rigging, all yelling in an incomprehensible slang that competes with the screaming seagulls. Before them along the quay pass straight-backed officers in uniforms with bright brass buttons, cocksure midshipmen and scavenging dogs and cats.

And what happened next? 'The adventure ended as such Adventures generally end,' notes Thomas with resignation in his summary. 'We walked three hundred miles and endured considerable hardships before we discovered that we had left our good fortune behind us and that we had better go back and look for it. So having by that time wandered from Etton to London from London to Portsmouth and from Portsmouth to Brighton we sought out a friend who resided there by whom we were kindly taken in and in due time we were forwarded to our anxious parents.'

Imagine the joy in the old rectory and the neighbourhood when the skinny prodigals returned at last. No wonder they were welcomed with open arms rather than a scolding. Thomas recalls: 'I do not think we were very penitent after all but our dear Father was so kind and forgiving that for my part [not Lance's, one can't help noting] I regretted extremely having given him so much anxiety and requested that he would send me off to Australia at once where I secretly determined to amass an immense fortune and bring it all home to him.'

It is clear from Thomas's 'Rough Sketch' summary that the influential James Hogg was impressed by young Lance's stamina (never mind that it was Thomas's idea to run away): 'Launcelot Machell was early destined for the military profession and entered on the list of Sir H Vivian. But Sir James Hogg, an East India Director and member for Beverley, offered an appointment to Addiscombe Military Academy, it was accepted and he was sent first to a preparatory school at Edmonton in 1842. Having previously been educated by his father he soon rose in the schools...' Lance even forwent the final two years at Addiscombe (the Sandhurst of its day for the Indian Military) in order to serve his country, and was soon noted for bravery, setting the tone for the rest of his life.

As I grew to know the family better, I discovered it was characteristic of Lance to steal his older brother's thunder. One can feel the hurt years later in an 1851 Journal passage. 'Being especially ill today,' writes Thomas, 'I have been amusing myself with looking over a vast collection of old letters not opened for years, what a variety of emotions have they called up... here are your hopes for my future prospects, here are Richard's details of his hopes, fears and pleasures mingled with good wishes for my own success, letters all but unintelligible close written and crossed from Aunt Matilda, interspersed with few and far between straggling scrawls from Lance. One alludes to his share in the wonderful expedition to Koti Kangra and after a few short sentences ends with, "I believe I have nothing to tell you". This is the longest I ever had from him, while those you received when I was at home were most voluminous epistles.' Both brothers were living in India when this was written, and still were in August 1854, when Thomas only learnt at third hand of Lance's marriage, his boss having heard the news from an officer at a party. The officer, reports Thomas through gritted teeth, had related anecdotes 'to shew that Lance had been distinguished both in the field as an officer, on the Turf as a Sportsman and in the station as a Billiard player, among engineers as a first rate mathematician and what would have been little expected from such materials not only a successful lover but a steady one.' Thomas adds forlornly: 'I almost expect to hear from them shortly for I wrote soon after leaving Calcutta but Lance is an eccentric fellow and has remained so long silent that I have only very faint hopes.'

And what was the result of the escapade on young Thomas's future? Quite simply, it altered the whole course of his life – and much of mine too, a century and a half later. It was clearly considered astonishing that the retiring son, who rarely spoke and usually had his face in a book, had it in him to be so daring. An undemanding child with physical problems could easily get overlooked in a busy Victorian rectory.

Thomas's melodramatic gesture to get himself noticed achieved its objective. 'My dear Father saw that the spirit of adventure had gained complete possession of me and having already had proof of my capabilities of endurance and energy of disposition he resolved to give me a preparatory trial at sea before he decided on my future course. Accordingly he obtained a berth for me as Guinea Pig on board of an East India Trader and before long I was launched into the world to rough it out and test my spirit of enterprise.'

3. Passages to India

Avec ses quatre dromadaires
Don Pedro d'Alfaroubeira
Courut le monde et l'admira
Il fit ce que je voudrais faire
Si j'avais quatre dromadaires.

Four dromedaries carried you
Don Pedro d'Alfaroubeira
Round the great world with Oh and Ah
What you did is what I should do
Had I four dromedaries too.

(Apollinaire, translated by Oliver Bernard)

I was two years older than Thomas when I launched myself into the world to test my own spirit of enterprise, but I chose the same destination. On the winter night of my eighteenth birthday I was in a rackety Land Rover crossing the English Channel and heading for India. My companions were six hippies I had met in the underground car park of London's Paddington Station a few hours earlier. In the winter of 1840 Thomas was also in the Channel, but meeting his new companions aboard a three-masted East Indiaman called the *Worcester*. He was as little impressed with her as I was with the old jeep: 'She was a low sneaking-looking barque with her black figurehead and long hull, looking gloomy and formidable on the dull sluggish river.' He began his first journal with a sketch of the ship and the words: 'A memorable day in my life, for on this day I commenced a new era and entered into the busy scenes of seafaring life.'

Though Thomas beat me by leaving home at 16, I beat him in another way by travelling to India overland, something he planned but didn't, as far as I knew, achieve in his lifetime. On board a *dhow* in the Arabian Sea in 1848 he wrote: 'I intend if circumstances allow it to return to India by way of Persia and thus increase my experience.' Circumstances allowed it neither then nor six years later, when, he says, 'the young artist Mr Noakes and I made an agreement to travel northward in company, then to pass through Cabul and so to Persia and thence to Constantinople. it would be a fine expedition and would afford material for a very interesting book which he thinks I am able to write and I am certain he would be able to illustrate cleverly.' A century and a half later I would read that passage and realise that by fulfilling journeys of Thomas's dreams as well as his real ones, our combined visions are affording the material for his book.

While I swam with the tide towards the edge of India's net, innocently optimistic, Thomas was flung towards it out of his depth, as he recalls later:

January 17th 1851, Rooderpore Estate, Bengal. Is it possible that it is only eleven years since I was a dreamy schoolboy? Has all the whirl and bustle of my life only extended over so short a period? Why it seems as if it was oh so so long ago that this battered old letter was put into my hand that I feel as if it had occurred in some previous existence. I was writing at the long school table at Pockthorpe, the snow was falling in a sort of lazy indifferent way... Mr Keeling the schoolmaster sat at his desk winding up some accounts, two or three boys were whispering together by the fireside telling their plans for the approaching Xmas holiday, Lance was filing a key to make into a cannon... when in comes the servant, "Please a man come for the Mitchells," with Mrs Keeling holding in her hands the very bit of paper I am now perusing. Then followed the bustle which never seemed to cease. I went whirring away to London, my first lonely journey in a Railway train. In London the noise continued, the outfitters shop was strange... and the street was full and the rattle of carts and carriages whirled my poor head and the hot grog which the old lady made me drink did the rest. Stupified I went to bed and stupified I arose and then came the trip to Gravesend all steam clatter and confusion.

It was a lot to take in at 16, the age when my own transition to adulthood also took an unexpected turn, though much less harsh. I was chafing at the petty restraints of a minor girls' public school, the final straw being when the headmistress complained to my parents of my 'truculence', because I had refused to be confirmed into the Church of England with my peer group. Like Thomas, I recall the day a letter arrived that changed my course. It was from the headmaster of Marlborough College, announcing his bold experiment of admitting a few girls into the sixth form. Until then boys' English public schools were as unbreachable by the female sex as billiard clubs or cathedral choirs. Like Thomas, I was aware my upbringing was too conventional to be satisfying. Becoming one of Marlborough's 'First Fifteen' – as we were inevitably dubbed – provided a chance to play a tiny part in shaking up an outdated male institution.

Incredible as it seems today, the experiment made the headlines and attracted the paparazzi. The notes I made in the last year of my teenage five-year diary give a flavour of the surreal first week. '*Marlborough College, 9th September 1968*. We've been plagued by photographers and reporters from *The Mirror, The Daily Mail* and *The Times*, though we're not allowed to answer questions, and were even mentioned on Radio 1 and TV – honestly! The boys were very friendly and helped us with our timetables.' '*11th September*. Pestered today by a journalist from *The Sunday Telegraph*. We had a meeting about what the girls should do on Wednesday afternoons while the boys do CCF and Corps' [Military service training]. '*12th September*. Had my first fencing lesson today, it's rather a thrill using a foil… Horrid write-up in *The Mirror*, nice ones in *The Times* and *The Wiltshire Gazette*.' After several more days of hounding by the press a truce was reached and they took an embarrassing official photograph of the fifteen of us lined up outside the school chapel (skirts first measured with a ruler by the headmaster's wife, six inches above the knee when kneeling on the floor being the permitted limit).

By the end of the first week I had clearly settled in, since I noted: 'four of us went to a pub with four of the boys, which is strictly out of bounds'. Twenty-five years later the *Daily Mail* ran a feature entitled 'Where are they now?', which traced the careers of us First Fifteen. None had achieved anything outstanding. They sent one of the local paparazzi to snap me in our Devon garden. He told me he was pursuing a certain James Hewitt, who was having an affair with the married Princess Diana and soon the whole world would know about it. Now there was a real scoop – but at the time I didn't believe him.

Marlborough was stimulating, but like Thomas I was dreaming of my next move. Within a year I managed to ride into university on the back of E M Forster's *A Passage to India*. The university interviewer didn't get a word in edgeways while I expressed my passion to find my own passage to India. But it surely takes more than good books to compel some people to travel overseas while others are content to stay at home. Thomas often muses on this and what 'peculiar disposition of the individual' converts childhood dreams into real experiences. Of his own childhood dreams he writes: 'My thoughts were visionary enough I confess, but they led to action, and then followed the roving life by sea and land equalling in extent the visions of my boyhood, in results only differing.' Indeed, the results never turn out as anticipated.

Thomas was educated when the pink blush of the British Empire was spreading across maps of the world, but neither physically nor temperamentally was he Empire material. His career prospects were limited. Had he not chosen his own path, the option open to him was, as he has told us, boring work as an office clerk. After his running away escapade to prove his grit, he marked time at his Yorkshire school until the family could wave him off overseas and turn their attention to Richard, Lance, and the seven siblings born in the seven years before Thomas's departure. Richard filled his father's shoes by being ordained as a priest. Lance was born Empire-shaped and fulfilled his destiny of keeping the Empire in order, not least during the 'Indian Mutiny' (now known as the 'Sepoy Uprising'), by serving until his death in the Bengal Horse Artillery and its successor the Royal Artillery. Four of the younger brothers who survived to adulthood also entered the Services, two of them following Lance to India when British rule expanded there.

I struck lucky being young in the so-called 'swinging sixties' when everything seemed possible. As students we campaigned against the Vietnam War, Apartheid and Cold War nuclear arsenals, most of us unaffected by their realities. Back in 1968 I was more preoccupied with packing my rucksack with jeans and tee-shirts and choosing the best books to take with me to India.

'Never travel faster than the speed of a camel lest you leave your soul behind,' warned the mediaeval explorer Ibn Battuta. All my life I have known he was right and whenever I fly anywhere it takes weeks for my soul to catch up, if it ever does. I'm longing to tell Ibn Battuta, when I meet him in a Travellers' Afterlife, that nearly everyone travels faster than the speed of camels these days, but that souls retain a speedometer of their own and refuse to be hurried.

Thomas's first voyage to India under sail lasted almost six months; Ibn Battuta would surely approve. I failed to find a camel to take me there, but at least the overland journey took six weeks in that decrepit jeep.

To save money and beat the February cold we drove day and night across Europe, via Communist Yugoslavia and Bulgaria in all their grimness, reaching the gateway to the East, Istanbul – or Constantinople to Thomas – in six days. A typical diary entry from my first week reads: 'It's 2 a.m. and we're battling through a blizzard towards the Austrian border. We often have to push the Land Rover up hills, then we skid down the other side. It's absolutely freezing in the back but we keep cheerful with out-of-tune songs (my guitar) and try to sleep on the seats with icebergs as toes.' This was better than a sailors' job of scouring the decks of a merchant ship in winter. Within two days of his departure Thomas reported: 'We had a round of scrubbing, and holystoning the decks, this job can be protracted to any length of time, and in the month of December it was mighty pleasant to be dabbing and splashing about with sand, holy stones and water, on your knees, for four or five mortal hours, scrubbing away for dear life; till the end of ones nose and the tips of ones toes were numbed and senseless with cold.' Cold is a recurrent theme in both our first travel Journals. Wait until Thomas later sails around the fearsome Cape Horn.

As for the effect of bitter weather on the internal combustion engine, I wonder how many people have crossed the Turkish border into Iran thanks to feeding their vehicle with fresh eggs. On 8th March 1970 I wrote: 'Camping in the desert somewhere in Iran. Up at 5 a.m. to an icy haze. We hadn't gone more than two hundred yards when the radiator boiled and/or froze (I'm not good at such technicalities). Anyway, what I do know is that we all froze. Impatient to get on, we tried lighting fires beneath the engine and did move a few more yards, but the result was disastrous – four large holes in the radiator. The situation grew more and more ridiculous when we were feeding the Land Rover with about three gallons of water a minute. Then someone had a brainwave – why not use eggs to block up the holes? So a trek to the nearest house and the purchase of half a dozen eggs that were cracked into the radiator to poach into the holes at three thousand revs

The Land Rover Jenny travelled in overland from London on the hippy trail to India; somewhere in the Persian desert, with Tristan Thwaites, March 1970.

– and the leaks almost ceased. This evening we were still relying entirely on the six poached eggs.'

In Kabul we visited, as a Victorian traveller would have done, mosques, palaces and the thriving camel caravanserai. And on Easter Saturday we set out on a pilgrimage to Bamiyan valley. '*28th March 1970*. Left Kabul in a basin of mist at 4.30 a.m. and by 8 a.m. had hit the dirt track. The scenery all day was spectacular as we followed a deeply incised canyon beside a tumbling mountain river in the Hindu Kush. On either side a strip of fertile land with mud villages, barley fields and white blossom. We passed many burnt-faced Afghans on horseback, all dark beards and shining teeth. Then up over the Shyber Pass into barren mountains with chameleon colours in the setting sun, and through the snow line before camping on a stony plateau beside the river.' Next morning I was worshipping at the feet of a stone Buddha 175 foot tall, carved out of the mountainside over a millennium and a half earlier and originally coated in gold leaf. All overland travellers to the East passed that way – including Thomas in his dreams. A scramble up a rough mountain path and along dark winding rock tunnels took us to the top of the Great Buddha's head, framed by a halo of frescoes on the surrounding alcove. From there I gazed over Bamiyan to take in 'brown folded hills, great shadows cast by the sun and white peaks behind, all beneath a deep blue sky'. The fate awaiting this wonder of the world was as inconceivable to me in the later 20th century as it would have been to travellers in centuries past.

In *Four Quartets* T S Eliot writes: 'We had the experience but missed the meaning/And approach to the meaning restores the experience/ In a different form'. I've had many experiences without grasping their meaning, but even as a teenager was moved by these extraordinary statues. However, their meaning was overlaid by the terrifying political and religious developments that followed my visit. Damage to the faces of the Buddhas by the hordes of Genghis Khan in the 13th century seemed desecration enough, but in 2001, while on board an old cargo ship in the middle of the Pacific Ocean (sent there by Thomas, needless to say), I heard that the Taliban of Afghanistan had blown the Buddhas to pieces with dynamite. Only then could I fully appreciate how privileged I had been to experience those marvels of the ancient world, that I too can now only visit in my dreams.

More recently I sat in my warm kitchen listening on the radio to an old Afghani talking about his life. One of millions of penniless refugees displaced like garbage by incomprehensible ideological warfare, he was now sheltering in a cold cave in Bamiyan. 'When we lived in our village,' he said, 'we had a cow, we had a sheep – life was good.' Then he began to sing: 'Hold the poor gently in your arms. Careful, careful foreigners, you may go to Hell.'

'I think the Wanderlust has entered my blood,' I noted cheerfully on day three of my teenage journey, adding 'time is non-existent, life is chaotic – and I've never been happier.' Thomas, on the other hand, regretted his Wanderlust from the outset. The reality of life aboard a merchant sailing ship was a cruel shock to this unprepared, ill-suited new midshipman. Nevertheless, from the start he was making notes for his first piece of descriptive writing, closely observing his companions and his own reactions. The ship rolled as he lay squashed in a locker or a hammock. Later Journals were written *in situ* but the first ones at sea had to be copied out later.

December 20th 1840. As we neared the ship at Gravesend I felt my courage evaporating but a moment more, and we were alongside; I scrambled on board and looked around me despondingly, the deck was a puddle of dirt and snow, and a great bloated old fellow on the poop who, I afterwards learnt, was Reece the River Pilot, was cursing and swearing at a sailor who was evidently drunk. At last the pilot turned to me, 'Hello! Youngster! what do you want, are you come to join? Here! Mr Roberts, here's another of your Lord's sons come to join – Look at him as he stands, chest and all complete as a Captain. I say Youngster! take a fool's advice and go ashore, you'll get more kicks than halfpence here, You're like a young bear with all your troubles to come, get away home,

Thomas's sketch of the Worcester, *the East Indiaman he sailed in as a midshipman from December 1840 to July 1843.*

or if they won't keep you at home, go and hang yourself.' After delivering this eloquent oration from the break of the poop, my fat friend dived below to refresh himself with another nip at the bottle, leaving me to the tender mercies of the Chief-mate, Mr Roberts. This Gentleman I took an invincible dislike to the moment I saw him.

(Within a few months Thomas would write: 'Though an overbearing bully, Roberts was an arrant coward in his heart, and, young as I was, I could see that very plain.')

Christmas day. This morning we turned out at usual, and set to work Holystoning the decks until eleven o'clock when the mate went ashore… In the afternoon we were invited to dine with Mr Gabb in the Cabin, and after dinner there was a feeble attempt to make a jolly evening, but it did not answer and all except third officer Mason broke down badly – Night came at last and with it my watch, I went on deck, and listened to the church bells ringing on shore. It was bitter cold and dark, and as I leant against the mizen mast, saw the lights on shore, and thought of the happy firesides and many parties now enjoying themselves, I felt a choking in my throat, and the tears blinding my eyes, and trickling down to freeze in little icicles on my rough coat. In a little time I became more composed and walked up and down on the poop thinking that in ten or eleven months it would be all over, and perhaps next Christmas I should be at home again, amongst friends seated by a blazing fire, and relating all the wonders of those distant lands which I was now about to visit. So passed the last fleeting hours of Christmas day, eighteen hundred and forty – Strike the bell eight, and call the watch, Christmas Day is past.

Since it was literally a case of sink or swim, Thomas had to learn fast how to handle the sails as well as Captain and crew of the *Worcester*. It's 27th December 1840:

"Reeve the manropes! Get a rope ready for the boat! Call the Boatswain!" Presently the boat came alongside, the three officers and two midshipmen came to the Gangway. Scream, scream, scream, went the whistle, and lo! up came the great man. Off went our caps to the dread sovereign of our little craft… What a little man for a Captain, thought I, and yet Mr Roberts who blusters so terribly, and bullies all the crew, looks as if he were afraid of him. "Look at Bully Roberts," said Shears [the other midshipman, but not a novice] giving me a dig in the ribs. "Just look how mild he's drawing it with the old skipper, he looks as if Butter wouldn't melt in his mouth." "What's he frightened of?" said I, very innocently. Shears laughed, "Why you see, the Captain rules the roost here, he is Lord High Admiral, Commander in Chief, Lord Chancellor, and Lord knows what he is not, in this bit of a hookah... as you'll learn in time." "Why," said the Boatswain standing by, "If the Lord High Admiral and her Britannic Majesty were to come on board this here craft, they wouldn't be half such great people as Captain George Waugh. Cause he's Captain, and owner, of this here ship and once in blue water, he will do as he likes with her, and all on board of her."

Next day they were heading for blue water. The Hull-built *Worcester*, according to Lloyds Shipping Register, was brand new and, at 521 tons, large for a barque. Before long Thomas would appreciate the ingenious design of her sails, with top-gallant and main royal square-rigged to catch the wind, while the mizzenmast near the stern was rigged 'fore and aft' for manoeuvrability. And within days sailing terms were rolling with relish off his tongue and down his quill.

What a bustle, what a variety of orders – sheet home, clap on your topsail haulyards, run up the jib, stand by to let fall, hoist away my sons, cast the Gaskets off the yard arms, Hook the Cat! – what is to be made of it all? The men ran this way and that, ropes were let go, others hauled taught and belayed, as for myself I was lost, and knocked, shoved, and pushed about... "Come up on the poop here youngster," sang out the Mate, "and see if you can make yourself useful here".

At last we were fairly off, all sail set with a stiff Easterly wind nearly right aft, and the land grew more and more distant and undefineable, until the night closed in and thus I had seen the last of my own dear country.

We had about thirty passengers on board, bound for Madras and Calcutta, there were four Ladies, the rest were Gentlemen in the Civil and Military Service of the Honorable East India Company – Chiefly young cadets and Assistant Surgeons.

On we bowled with a stiff breeze and a week later were in sight of the Island of Madeira. At ten in the morning the hands were called aft to celebrate divine service for the first time on the Quarter deck of the *Worcester*... though I doubt very much whether all hands understood the service, for we had a strange motley crew, and there were some Dutchmen on board, who could hardly speak two words of English. These men, abominably ill treated by our bully mate, proved to be the best men on board, and our own countrymen in the good ship were decidedly the greatest scoundrels.

I now began to feel more settled, if indeed you can call that settled which was a continued life of misery and discomfort, indeed so much did it tell upon my appearance that I got the name of Smike, and being a Yorkshireman they used to chaff me about Mr Squeers and ask me if I came from Dotheboy's Hall etc.

By the time the *Worcester* crossed the Line and reached Capetown, Thomas had surely crossed the Line between Innocence and Experience.

In 1970, having opted to return home by sea from India, I intersected with Thomas at South Africa's Cape, without of course knowing it. Here I am on board an old Italian passenger ship in June: 'Having seen flying fish for the first time a few days ago I had an even greater excitement today when I saw my first albatross. It swooped over the water with wings curved downwards and looked huge even in the distance – when it flew within five feet of me I was really quite frightened... of course I thought of the Ancient Mariner.' Now here's Thomas in the same place in 1841: 'As we neared the Cape we saw numbers of Albatrosses and Cape Pigeons which we used to catch with a hook and line, and the young cadets found constant amusement at this work, as also in fishing for shark. Shooting was also the order of the day, but this was put a stop to by the Captain for one of the guns went off by accident, went through the deck and lodged in a Gentleman's leg.'

> *26th March.* I was standing near the lee quarter when I saw the Boy Nunn struggling and gasping in the water, I turned sick and almost senseless as I gazed on the terrible agonising expression on the boy's face. No cry escaped his lips, his whole face seemed convulsed into an expression of anguish, and dismay. The waters closed over him and I saw him no more, but in the dark night watch, as I paced the silent deck whilst the mate lay slumbering on the hen coops and the Helmsman dozed over the wheel, I called to mind the face of that drowning man.

How his poor mother will weep when she finds her son returns no more from his first voyage and his last.

How easily this might have been Thomas's fate had he stolen away to sea at twelve.

4. Exotic Landfalls

So the sea-journey goes on, and who knows where!
Just to be held by the ocean is the best luck
We could have. It's a total waking up!

(*Buoyancy,* Rumi 1207-1273)

Young Thomas's first sight of the Orient was Madras at dawn, the *Worcester* having dropped anchor in the roadstead overnight: 'Well this, thought I as I looked about me whilst out on the yard arm furling sails, this is indeed a foreign looking port… with its white houses, lofty palm trees and a clear hot sky above all.' He watched a bevy of rafts and rowing boats approach, bringing on board a crowd of men with 'black faces and white dresses', who 'arranged quite a little bazaar all along the ship's waist. Here was a shoemaker, there Tailor, next sat a fruit seller, here a man with a basket of eggs, there a curiosity vendor, whilst parrots, monkeys, squirrels, mongooses etc had their respective positions along the booms.' He was also fascinated by the large Masoulah boats (rowed by up to 20 men) whose planks were sewn together with bamboo strips to give them flexibility in high surf.

In Delhi I unfurled my sleeping sheet on a rooftop along with my companions, changed money on the black market, ran barefoot through the streets in the small hours to listen to the great sitar player Ravi Shankar performing in a vast tent, and managed to touch fingertips with my arms encircling backwards around the magical Hindu iron pillar at the Mogul Qutb Minar complex to ensure good luck for the next hundred years. Four days later I cast away the safety net of familiar faces and launched off alone like Thomas, defiantly heading south because in 1970 every other young Western traveller was being lured east by the intoxicating magnet of Kathmandu.

Within a week of leaving Delhi I was staying on a coffee plantation in the Western Ghats above the Malabar Coast. Oh where has she gone, that naïve long-haired hippy who jettisoned her rucksack in Delhi and travelled onwards, I noted then, 'just with my belongings packed around my guitar in its case and my bedroll strapped to the outside'? I know she is tucked somewhere inside this shorter-haired older woman who has lost the art of travelling light, but sometimes I seem to have more in common with Thomas than with my own former self.

Back in 1970 I left the divine scent of coffee blossom to the delirious bees and set my sights next on Madras. After his first glimpse of Madras from the sea in 1840, Thomas would twice return to the city. On the second occasion he took advantage of a brand new railway. It was July 6th 1856: 'Went down to the station and with some difficulty obtained tickets. Crush of natives tremendous, train late in consequence. Got off at last at 3.45 pm and arrived at Arcot 7 p.m. 65 miles, only a single line of rail with loop lines at the stations. On landing at Arcot Railway Station found I had five miles to walk in heavy rain and no conveyance for my traps'. Thomas was soaked through when he reached a travellers' bungalow, where the loan by a kindly officer of a dry shirt and mattress saved him from a recurrence of the fever that had almost finished him off the previous week. He covered the next few hundred miles in the standard way using relays of bullock and pony carts and walking.

I could do the whole journey, in the reverse direction, on a train that went marginally faster than a bullock cart. But Thomas couldn't have watched a contact lens drop down a lavatory hole onto the railway track, nor note that three astronauts who had been walking on the moon had landed safely back on earth.

In the days of sail Calcutta was a dangerous port to enter. Notorious sandbanks lurked at the entrance to the Hughli River, waiting to sink the unwary. An escort by pilot was essential. '*24th May, 1841.* After a tedious passage with very bad squally weather,' writes Thomas, 'we arrived at Sandheads, at the entrance to the river, where we found upwards of thirty sail beating off and on. Luckily we got to windward, and so managed to get a pilot... when we arrived in Calcutta we moored off Baboo's *ghat.*'

I had to wait a long time before I could join Thomas on the steps of Baboo's ghat. Though I had twice been to India by the time I met him, I had never thought of visiting Bengal. Since meeting him I've been four times, and arriving there feels like a homecoming. I've never had his kind of greeting though.

'It was the birthday of Queen Victoria so the very first sound to greet me was the band on shore playing 'God Save the Queen!'

Everything seems new to young Thomas. When he sees his first body floating downstream being picked at by screaming vultures he says: 'This is a common custom of the Hindoos but I must confess I was a little startled.' Another 'strange sight that struck me as remarkable he adds, 'is the sight of pious "Musulmen" prostrating themselves at sundown.'

'We were actively employed discharging cargo,' he writes, 'and I now hoped soon to see the homeward bound goods coming on board. But alas! no such luck happened, for the Captain informed us he had tendered the ship to the Honorable East India Company and we were taken up to convey troops and stores to China. We therefore had little time to look about us but moving down to the Company's moorings off Cooly Bazaar we proceeded in all haste to ship Commissariat stores and to fit up the ship for receiving troops.

> Nearly all our crew left us, as also Mr Gabb our second officer, who remarked that though we were only taken up for three months, we might very likely be three years... but what can express my delight when I found that my inveterate tormentor Shears was also to leave us. I was nevertheless most anxious to return home and tried hard to get away, but I was too young and green and no one cared to have me to work my passage home, though I was in hopes of getting on board a Hull ship called the Richards... I returned heavy-hearted to continue my cruise in the Worcester.

I had exactly the same experience on my first trip to India. After four months on the move, I too was ready to return home and planning to work my passage to England by sea, in my case from Bombay (now Mumbai). I was broke because in my naivety I had lent my last fiver to a smooth-talking bearded member of Sinn Fein I had met on a beach in Sri Lanka. (I had no idea what the organisation was, it just sounded quite jolly.) He was called Sean and was the only man ever to hit me. I reached Bombay in June 1970 and headed straight for the docks where, echoing Thomas in the same month in 1841, I traipsed (or rather, limped on an infected foot) in and out of merchant shipping offices pleading for work on a homebound ship. Like him I was young and green, and the experience was as dampening as the monsoon rains that accompanied it.

> *Calcutta, 4th June 1841.* Hardly was the old ship's company dispersed than another crew came on board, but how different from the former. Our English crew consisted of Large-framed men, whose weather beaten faces showed deep marks of many hardships and reckless and debauched lives… Even before we left the port we heard that many of them had fallen victim to outrageous intemperance. But our second crew were slight active intelligent looking fellows, with strange gestures and even stranger speech; their light copper coloured limbs, dark faces and bright gleaming eyes in strong contrast to our former crew… I learnt from my shipmates who remained of the old crew that these native Lascars were to be treated as an inferior class, little better than dogs; and yet when sunset came all of these inferior animals bowed in adoration to the supreme being, whilst we Christians looked on and scoffed in proud superiority.

In India in 1970 letters from Britain took two weeks to Thomas's six. Internet, emails and mobile phones were unimaginable. But I could make a long-distance telephone call and have money transferred from UK to a Bombay bank so I could buy a passage home by sea.

> *24th June 1841.* All was ready and the steamer came alongside with a detachment of H.M. 49th regiment commanded by Captain MacAndrews… and now all things being ready we got under weigh and exactly one month from the day of our arrival were now bound for China.

5. Opium Wars

War transforms men into devils.

(Thomas Machell)

Calcutta to Singapore took a month under sail. Thomas toyed with the idea of escaping the 'wretched ship' and playing Robinson Crusoe on a luscious island of the South China Seas, but was deterred by reports of ruthless pirates who also inhabited them. And still do, by the way.

It was just as dangerous on board: a deadly fever swept the ship and many sailors succumbed. Thomas was shocked to see the first deaths and funerals, blaming 'the great heat and foul smell in the Fore peak, caused by the Provision casks which were stowed there, and the old Doctor who was brutal and careless.'

The *Worcester* weathered a typhoon before dropping anchor in Hong Kong in mid August, where a large British wartime fleet was gathering. At this point Thomas expected to be home by the end of the year, since, as he says, 'the *Worcester's* agreement was now fulfilled', troops and supplies having been safely delivered. However, it was not to be because 'as we feared and the Captain hoped, we were taken up to continue in the present service.' But more confident by then, he admits:

> … now that we were fairly in for it I was not sorry, but hoped to see a little more of the country, and what was going on. My situation was now much more endurable. With a native crew I was no longer required to put my hand to dirty work, but was employed in charge of the boats, and in some sort treated as a junior officer, and had it not been for the overbearing conduct of our Chief mate, I should have been

comparatively happy... The Captain himself never took any notice of me... and yet notwithstanding his quiet manner, I feared him much more than I did Bully Roberts.

September 7th 1841. At last everything was ready. We sailed with the fleet under the command of Sir William Parker – Rear Admiral of the Red and one of 'Nelson's Captains' – who hoisted his flag on board the Wellesley and after a pleasant run of six days arrived off the harbour of Amoy, hoisted our ensigns and ran in. The entrance of the harbour is very narrow and was flanked by strong fortifications and a tremendous grim looking battery a mile in length. Our work lay before us as we prepared to land troops the next day.

Thomas was about to see military action for the first time. Meanwhile, he sketched the harbour packed with the British fleet. With his Victorian viewpoint he called what later became known as the First Opium War 'a necessary but cruel war'. I shall quote his account of the first day; others saw it differently no doubt. Notice how he mentions the famous *Nemesis*, the first iron steamship to double the Cape. 'Nevermiss', as the British sailors nicknamed her, played a vital role in the Opium War and became a British

Thomas's sketch of the British fleet in the harbour of Amoy (present day Xiamen) on the Taiwan Strait, on the eve of a major battle with the Chinese in September 1841.

icon to the supremacy of steam. The Chinese soldiers were terrified by this armed paddle-steamer that could tow sailing ships far up river, use her shallow draft to land troops directly on shore, and open fire near land. They called steamships 'devil ships'.

> Early in the morning the whole fleet was in commotion, and everybody in prodigious bustle… Officers busy as monkeys, examining their swords and pistols, parading the men and overhauling their accoutrements. The sailors… grinding their cutlasses and Chaffing the Red Coats. Whilst we were all in suspense waiting for the signal from the Commander-in-Chief, we saw a little boat shove off from the shore and run alongside the Wellesley carrying the white flag, but the old Admiral refused to take any notice. Ten minutes later up ran the signal 'Prepare to disembark troops'.

> We filled the boats, and dropping astern waited for the little Steamer Nemesis to come and pick us up. Presently she ran down to us and taking the boats in tow and the rest of the troops on board, we steamed off. It sounded rather queer when we ran in shore and heard the roar of artillery and the whiz of shot for the first time fired in right good earnest with considerable smoke and noise, though with poor effect on either side. However we were soon in shore and landed without accident, and took the batteries without opposition worth mentioning, and the same night the city was deserted. So fell the city of Amoy.

Following the easy defeat of Amoy, the fleet headed for Chusan Island in such foul weather most of it got separated, though the *Worcester* kept with the *Wellesley*. Captain Waugh's skills were not necessarily a good thing because the *Worcester* was chosen to lead the fleet, taking two new regiments on board, one being the Madras Artillery. 'The Chow Chow swept us under fire as we put round to pick out a good berth for anchorage, but the old Captain was not a bit put out but worked his ship with as much coolness as if the salute was rather gratifying than otherwise!'

> Early on 1st of October the signal was made to 'Land Troops', and shortly after a steamer came alongside and took our troops on board; we hooked on to her stern, and away she steamed, cram full of soldiers, with a long tail of boats full also of red coats and blue jackets. However, just as we got under the line of fire, there was a sudden stoppage, and

the steamer stuck fast in the mud. Splash wish dash came the shot, scattering the water about and sprinkling us over in fine style, and we were so jammed for room that it was some time before we could get the oars out. However we managed at last to get the boats ashore and land the men with fewer accidents than we might have expected since the guns exactly bore upon us and made a precious peppering.

By dusk Chusan was back in British hands but this time, unlike the last with its shameful looting, Thomas reports that 'private property was respected and the garrison of troops left in charge was quartered in the public buildings'.

The next battle was the capture of fortified Ningpo, defended by thousands of Chinese, as well as Tartar soldiers. This is where Thomas really saw the evils of war:

The dreadful line of muskets from the impenetrable compact bodies of the British regiments as they marched steadily on fell battery after battery, and the Chinese troops, unable to make the slightest stand against the terrible invaders, retreated in confusion to the river, our troops driving them steadily on and every now and then thinning their confused mass by regular salves of musketry. It was truly fearful work for the poor Chinese driven down to the river's edge, overwhelmed by a merciless rain of bullets. They fell in heaps or met death in the river while attempting to swim across… To the credit of officers I must relate that they used every effort to stop the work of Butchery, but the call of the bugle was long unattended by our excited and bloodthirsty troops. well may it be said that war transforms men into devils; between four and five thousand men were slain on this bloody day.

After this bloodletting it is hardly surprising that Ningpo, despite its population of 'six hundred thousand' (underlined by Thomas), fell unopposed.

Winter dragged on, cold and wet, and many of the crew were astonished to see snow for the first time. Thomas spent a second Christmas on board, joining with gusto in drunken singing in the carpenter's tiny cabin. More intoxication followed with riotous New Year's Eve revels when 'the whole Harbour was illuminated, guns and fireworks blazing in all directions. Bells were ringing, gongs beating and men cheering… this is a common practice among the Merchant men and is called ringing the old year out and the new one in.'

Before the winter was over the *Worcester* was dispatched with stores to Chinghae. 'With unwilling hearts we departed from our snug berth writes Thomas. 'The Indian sailors did not like it at all, for you may imagine how much they felt the cold, badly clothed and ill fed as they were. I pitied them with their bare feet in the freezing water at the bottom of the boat, but what could be done? We had no spare clothing and the Nebudda which was to have brought winter clothing etc for the Lascars was cast away on her voyage and the crew falling into the hands of the enemy were ruthlessly murdered.' Thomas was hardly in luxury himself. 'My bones were quite sore' he says, 'for I and my bed had long since parted company. I gave it or rather lent it to a soldier who suffered from the Rheumatism and he quite forgot to return it so I took the lid off my chest and it answered very well.'

On leaving Chinghae, where Thomas witnessed brutality too horrible to describe − 'let's draw a veil over it,' he says − he nearly met his end by shipwreck:

> The next day was another I shall never forget. We weighed and made sail for Chusan, Mr Thomas [Captain of another ship] again taking charge of us and again running us ashore. We had on board, beside our crew, upwards of five hundred soldiers and fifteen officers so our little craft was crammed full.

> As soon as we got off the bank, Mr Thomas, fearful of getting into another scrape, made all haste to leave us for the wind was light and the tide was sweeping us toward the rocks which form the passage called the Deadmans. there were two passages through this way into the open water which forms the anchorage of Just-in-the-Way, the outer passage through which ships generally pass and the inner, which is so narrow that few ships have ever attempted it, for the tide is so strong that it sweeps through with fearfull violence forming what is called Chow-chow water − this works like a Cauldron of boiling water and forms numerous whirlpools so strong they have been known to spin around large boats and dash them to pieces on the rocks. Whilst we were at Chinghae the Chief Officer of the Eagle on his way to Chusan with a large boat full of stores and money was compelled by the tide to take

the inner passage and lost everything, barely escaping with his life. Such was the inner passage which it now became uppermost we must take or strike on the rocks as the tide was sweeping us rapidly towards them and it was evidently impossible for us to weather the island to run through the outer passage. Every man on board now became aware of our imminent danger and every eye was therefore fixed on our little Captain. There he was, walking up and down the poop with a glass under his arm, his lips compressed and a stern hard smile wrinkling his face as he watched the ship closely and occasionally motioned to the Helmsman. "Steady – luff you may – Dice – no higher – steady so". Now was the crisis. Would she forge ahead sufficiently to clear the point and shoot through the passage, or would she touch and roll over? I looked up – our Studdingsail booms were all but touching the rocks; on one side we could not have had two fathoms and on the other there was no bottom at eighty so that had we touched we must to a dead certainty have rolled over and gone down with every soul on board and no chance of escape.

Every one looked dismayed and even the officers looked pale and whispered as they glanced at the sternly contracted features of the Old Captain who paced the decks with resolute self possession, had he lost it for a moment the fate of the ship and all on board would have been sealed. The mate had completely lost his self possession and jumped down on the quarter deck giving orders no one attended to – all felt who was the master now. Suddenly the old Captain stopped pacing and in a voice I shall never forget called "Silence". You might have heard a pin drop, even the Portuguese cook who was dragging his chest about the deck ready to jump overboard with fear stopp'd to wipe his face and open his large goggle eyes. "Now men," said the Captain with stern coolness, "stand by the head braces, make no noise and hard round when I tell you – Steady so." We now heard the waters rushing, boiling and hissing about us in an awful manner and we felt the ship bobbing like a cockle shell in a pot of boiling water. Once more I looked at the Captain, what a change was shown in his usually immoveable thoughtful face, now his lips were so closely compressed only a blue line showed his stern mouth, his eyebrows large and bushy met in a deep scowl and his eyes flashed with preternatural brightness as he closely watched the progress of the ship. She had just enough way on her for his purpose, the helm was put down and the ship luffed up. "Now!" he roared, "up with the helm, Brace round the head yards, box her aft." Round swung the yards, the ship's head pointed fair for the centre of the narrow slit, and she darted through like a frightened racer, cleared the point and was safe in the open.

"Now Mr Roberts, fill on her and trim the yards," and the Captain was himself again. The officers all came together and in a manner that shewed how little they expected to have got through safe congratulated each other on their escape and complimented the Captain, lauding him to the skies, but the Old man merely nodded with his usual grim smile and went below to his own berth.

Anchored back in Chusan's inner harbour the next excitement was in late February when a night alarm called out 'Fire Rafts'. 'We tumbled up in all haste,' writes Thomas, 'and there was a glorious sight, the whole harbour illuminated by dozens of flaming fire rafts floating down upon us on the tide and lighting up the busy scene in the crowded harbour. Our boats were away in a moment and we hooked on to the blazing rafts to tow them clear of the ships. Owing to the promptitude of all employed not one accident happened and the rafts were sent floating away among the islands or tow'd ashore to burn out on the beach.'

This turned out to be part of widespread Chinese counter-attacks, resisted by the British army with 'pitiless brutality' (Thomas's words) and deadly modern weaponry, not unlike the American/British 2003 Iraq war with its killings caused by superior fire-power ('shock and awe'). Thomas records, for example, an occasion when General Gough pursued the enemy up river 'where with one thousand men he routed the enemy of eight thousand with great slaughter'.

During the ensuing summer hostilities Thomas experienced numerous battles and new horrors. The *Worcester* was carrying artillery and rocket brigades when the fleet attacked the town of Cha-po. This time, instead of transporting troops on shore and watching from a distance, Thomas joined crew carrying rockets uphill to the army. He watched soldiers of both sides being hacked to pieces, and hundreds of Tartars blown up by rockets when taking refuge in a temple.

Tartar soldiers met us so fiercely they actually seized hold of our bayonets and tried to wrench them off. The garrison contained two thousand three hundred desperate men fighting madly for their houses and families, but what could their courage do against the disciplined unbroken lines of British Bayonets? Three hours were our men fighting with these desperate fellows ere they could force their way from gate to gate. At length they succeeded in seeing its heavy doors blown in and the storming part of the third division bound forward through the smoke followed by the unbroken ranks of the veteran Grenadiers. A dead silence, fearful and most horrible had we known its import, succeeded this explosion. Then followed the last desperate rally of the Tartar soldiers, madly they rushed on no longer seeking victory but death, and those who found it not in this last desperate rally continued to rise and attack us throughout the night.

What then meant that dread and ominous silence before the last desperate rally? Hush, I will tell you – They were murdering their wives and children... We saw scenes so distressing it is still painful to recall them. Whole families laying dead or dying, women and children stabbed, strangled or poisoned by their own frantic relatives, more cruel in their frenzied fear than the enemies storming their town. On every side we came upon fresh objects of Horror, little children lying with dislocated spines, mothers and daughters hanging with blackened and distorted features or with fearful gaping wounds. Oh it was horrible. On rich couches and rude benches, in gorgeous beds and humble pallets, on marble pavements and earthen floors, in Grottos and Gardens, in orchards and meadows they lay strewn about, a ghastly spectacle. There lay rich and poor, old and young, beautiful and beloved, all that rendered life dear to those desperate men who had sought death on the points of our bayonets and who now lay still warm in hundreds about us, cut off in the full strength of life.

After this battle General Gough wrote home: 'I am sick at heart of war and its fearful consequences.' At least he had chosen an army career, unlike young Thomas who was forced into the horror.

Whilst the Worcester lay here she became a hospital ship and almost every morning we had one or two burials. Everybody fell sick with Fevers, Agues and Dyssentary and our tween decks presented a melancholy spectacle. The greater part of the fleet went up to Nanking on the eighth but on the tenth orders came down for the Worcester to bring up the Flank company of H.M. 55th regiment and we were not a little gratified as we should now see Nanking and get rid of our sick and wounded. The next day accordingly we made fast to the steam frigate Sesostris and brought up off the city of Nanking. A portion of the troops were landed and the necessary preliminaries arranged for attacking the City when despatches and ambassadors arrived from the court to arrange a Treaty of Peace.

Thus it fell out that on 29th August 1842 I found myself a witness to the conclusion of the long War in China with the signing of the famous Treaty of Nanking, in which a lasting peace was declared between our two empires.

Thomas, a minor character at a major event, lists the treaty's terms, the main Chinese concessions being the opening to British trade of five ports, including Shanghai and Amoy, and the cessation of Hong Kong to Britain.

I trace my own fascination with China to family games of Mah Jong as a child, by a log fire on winter's evenings. On the faded green felt top of a collapsible card table we sorted exotic tiles of ivory and bamboo, silky to the touch and patterned with intriguing ideograms and colourful symbols. We arranged them into walls, and I longed to break through my Western wall and travel to China. Indigo research took me in 1993 to remote areas of Ghuizhou province in south-west China when parts of it were still mysteriously 'closed' to foreigners and some villages only reachable by river. I fell in love with the region and was at an early stage of my passion for Thomas when I received an invitation to participate in a UNESCO meeting being held in Yunnan in June, 2000. Here was a chance both to return to a fascinating part of China and also to tack on a peculiar foray into Thomas territory.

I couldn't follow in Thomas's wake up the rivers to all those southern Chinese ports he talked of, most of which have exploded into huge modern cities, but I was especially intrigued by Amoy, Xiamen today, since I couldn't find anyone who had ever been there. In Thomas's day Amoy became well known in the West as one of those five Treaty Ports, but nowadays the name only conjures up a type of sauce.

There were no ferries to Xiamen so I had to fly there from Hong Kong. The soulless commercial city of modern Xiamen only attracts foreign businessmen, but Chinese tourists like to take the ferry across the strait to explore the strange little cut-off island of Gylangya. I decided to join them.

I held up Thomas's sketches and squinted to see the British fleet in 1841 cramming the harbour, and Chinese fortifications where skyscrapers now rise.

I spent a week on Gylangya. I noted that 'the whole place is in a time-warp, like Thomas and me'. I couldn't converse with anyone since I had no Chinese and found no one who spoke English, and I was out of touch with home. In stifling humidity I ambled repeatedly up and down the same quiet streets – there were no motorised vehicles – past former mansions of colonial merchants and consuls, the sound of piano playing drifting out of their shuttered windows. I was the only guest in an enormous former colonial residence, spooked by sinister overgrown trees tapping against my bedroom windows, and deafened by cicadas. My diary states: 'President Nixon stayed here thirty years ago but clearly nothing's been done since, and it's as silent as a morgue.' The furniture in the public rooms was embalmed in dustsheets, dried leaves had blown up the wide front steps and scattered like burnt litter across the hall floor, there were no staff and there was nowhere to eat in the hotel. The only person I could communicate with was Thomas, who had at least been there. In my self-imposed loneliness I wrote him some letters. 'It's a gloomy place to be alone in,' I wrote in one, 'except I'm sort of not alone as I'm having a running dialogue with you… at least being alone makes us more observant, and gives us the compulsion to portray our experiences in words and sketches (and, in my case, in photographs too). Where does this compulsion come from? You tell me.'

On my last day on the island, when I was still pondering on what madness had sent me there, I lunched in a restaurant near the rubble of the recently demolished former British Consulate. The wall-to-wall fish tanks inside the restaurant were crammed with oversized doomed fish gulping in shallow murky water. They undermined my appetite, despite the menu's recommendation, amongst other 'colourful dollops', to sample 'sea-worm with its special tongue touch that stays for a little long while and refleshes the brain greatly'. 'I feel closer to the fish enclosed within see-through layers,' I noted, 'than to the diners around me picking at crab and eel flesh.' Maybe my brain did need refreshing with sea-worm.

After lunch I toiled in the heat up a hill named 'Gambling the Mooncakes', where, thanks to my Western height and clothing, I was 'borrowed' several times by Chinese tourists in yellow caps, to be immortalised in holiday snapshots. Like Alice-in-Wonderland after she downed the 'Drink-me' potion, I had entered a bizarre world where nothing was quite what it seemed.

6. Going Home

My chief knowledge of civilised life consisted in handling the murderous weapons with which our civilised troops had murdered whole hosts of flying Tartars and Chinese.

(Thomas Machell)

Thomas, now heading west, was glad to be alive. Following the Peace Treaty, many more crew died on board from what he calls 'ague and fever' and he succumbed to both at once. Reduced to crawling around the deck, he only survived thanks to the ministrations of an Apothecary. No wonder his mood grew jauntier as each nautical mile brought him closer to home.

The *Worcester* dropped anchor back in Hong Kong at the end of November 1842.

When we arrived in the harbour we were astonished at the altered appearance. When we were here last there were only a few miserable fishing huts but now – less than eighteen months after the British flag began to wave over the island – as if by magic its whole appearance had changed. Houses had sprung up in all directions, gardens been laid out, there was a broad street of shops and Pothouses, large barracks for the soldiers on the hill above the harbour, beautiful bungalows prettily dotted about the residences of the Merchants who had come to build and settle here under the protection of the British Government. Everything betokened a thriving and rapidly increasing settlement. The rising and setting sun was daily saluted with the roll of British Drums and the restless Hum of British traffic – Men-of-war and Merchantmen from many far distant countries – arose from the crowded harbour. No pen can do justice to the countless variety of Foreigners in the bustling town, not one of whom had most likely heard of the insignificant Island of Hong Kong before it had become enrolled in the mighty list of British Colonial Settlements.

Hong Kong's dramatic transformation was kick-started by the Scottish merchants Jardine and Matheson, who were establishing their headquarters there in a fortressed stone godown while the fleet was waging war for them along the Chinese coast. Along with others involved in East India trade (notably the East India Company) Jardine and Matheson directors had persuaded the British government to confront the Chinese authorities because their trade balance relied on exporting vast quantities of opium to China in defiance of the country's official ban on the damaging drug. 'The use of opium is not a curse, but a comfort and benefit to the hard-working Chinese' is how a press release justified the Second Opium War in the next decade! (No wonder the Chinese felt patronised and humiliated.) Since Hong Kong became an international mercantile centre in less than two years, it is hardly surprising that by the time Britain returned the territory to China in 1997 it had buildings enough to house over seven million people, and trade enough for thousands of Jardine and Matheson look-alikes. What on earth would Thomas make of today's extraordinary collection of skyscrapers and garish neon lights flashing round the clock? My own first impressions of the city were that it was 'an irresistibly exciting nightmare, and a god to consumerism.'

On that first visit of mine in 1993 the city was at the fag end of British rule, and I noted that 'it feels so Chinese that the stamps with our Queen's head on them seem curiously out of place'. Like Thomas I was fascinated by the cosmopolitan mix and the active harbour, now seething with burly container ships, passenger ferries, large fishing trawlers, and jetfoils skimming over to Macao across the Pearl River, with little sampans scattered amongst them like punctuation marks. Long since gone are the sleek opium clippers designed for swift getaways. At sunset the river lives up to its name, but by day, I wrote, 'it is far from pearly, more the colour of tarnished copper, thanks to factories up-river'. Modern transport notwithstanding, typhoons remain a threat; when I flew out of the city in one in July 2000 I wondered whether it was more frightening to be trapped in an aeroplane or in a sailing ship in such a buffeting.

The weather was fair when the *Worcester* sailed out of Hong Kong harbour late in 1842. Thomas saw his next New Year's Eve celebrated in Singapore harbour as noisily and drunkenly as the last in Chusan. On New Year's Day 1843 his dreams of home as he wandered around the deck were interrupted when he almost tripped over the corpse of a sailor who had died in the night. Such incidents had become commonplace.

Back in Calcutta a month later it was back to a normal merchant seaman's life:

> We landed our troops, bidding adieu to our agreeable friends, but there was no rest for us. We worked night and day to get rid of our cargo of stores and coals, and when all was cleared out we took the ship into dry dock to be overhauled and new Coppered... When she was floated out we commenced loading for home. Bags of Saltpetre came tumbling into the hold like fun. Then came Sugar, then Indigo and Jute, then Bales of Silk. All our crew had left us when we arrived and we worked like lumpers. But now that all was ready on came our new ship's company, most of them very drunk indeed.

> 'In spite of my delight in being homeward bound I was – shall I confess it – yes, I was in tears,' admits Thomas. 'My old Shipmate and kind-hearted friend Mason had just left the ship for good. He had determined to remain in the Eastern Seas in the hope of more prosperous employment than he would obtain in England... most likely we should never meet again.'

> "Goodbye Calcutta," said I as we glided down Garden reach. "Goodbye City of Palaces. You look right gay and lovely this fine morning, with your beautiful gardens and pleasant Houses, but I have no wish to return to you or walk over your dusty roads again. There is no land that can tempt me to forget my native country and no place like home. Farewell then Calcutta – a long farewell.

All focus was on home as the *Worcester* in 1843 sailed west with two defiant and high-spirited young midshipmen, Thomas and his friend Fraser. The boys were still in high spirits when, after more than two and a half eventful years on board the *Worcester*, the port of Dungeness in Kent was sighted at last.

Thomas's 1843 sketch of his childhood home, the rectory at Etton village four miles from Beverley, county town of the East Riding of Yorkshire in northern England.

Etton village rectory, 2000.

7. Rendezvous at the Rectory

I have been here before
But when or how I cannot tell:
I know the grass beyond the door,
The sweet keen smell,
The sighing sound, the lights around the shore.

('*Sudden Light*', Dante Gabriel Rossetti)

Thomas and I converged on the old rectory at Etton. Less than a year after we first met, it would alter our relationship. Thomas approached the village from the east on foot in 1843; I came from the west by car in 2000.

When I first read of Thomas's connection with Etton I had no idea whether or not his old childhood home still existed. A friend in York, Bruce Wannell, established that the rectory was still standing, but had passed into secular hands in the mid-1960s. He joined me, my husband Glencairn and our hostess Isa Denyer, on an outing of exploration.

Mediaeval Etton is one of the textbook villages that have settled over the centuries into the cleavages of the east Yorkshire wolds. We followed the long main street past the old coaching inn and the church and swerved around four Muscovy ducks wobbling across the road to their pond, before reaching the bend that curves the houses back into open country. Isa parked on the verge beside the hunt kennels and I jumped from the car and crossed the road ahead of the others.

'*North Bar Without, Beverley, Friday, 29th October 2000, evening*. As I began to walk slowly up the drive this morning I felt strangely choked up. The house was still hidden behind trees. Then suddenly I glimpsed it through a gap in the trees and, absolutely unexpectedly, the very moment I saw it I was engulfed by such an overwhelming depth of feeling that I found myself sobbing uncontrollably. It's hard to describe, but the emotion seemed to come from somewhere else, as if my reaction on seeing that house – almost "returning" to it – wasn't mine. It was much more than a sensation of sadness, it was an overpowering sense of loss such as I have never experienced in my own lifetime. Glencairn came up behind me, alarmed by my sobbing. He says my reaction was as if I had just heard the most terrible news about one of our children. When Isa and Bruce caught us up I tried to dry my eyes, but felt shaken and embarrassed. Then we all followed a little path in the woods that led towards the front of the house. The moment the whole façade came into view I pointed to the upper right-hand window and out of my mouth came the words, 'That was Thomas's bedroom – he climbed out of that window when he ran away.'

I was dabbing at mascara stains and still feeling shaky and rather stupid after my bizarre outburst, when a car came up the drive. The driver turned out to be the rectory's previous owner, Valerie Rambaut. Once we had explained our lurking presence in the private driveway she welcomed us into her new home, built in the Victorian walled garden where the Machell vegetables had grown. Rising by instinct to the occasion, she offered sherry rather than coffee. The bittersweet taste of that mid-morning alcohol on my tongue will, like Proust's Madeleine, forever summon up for me that mysterious mutation in my relationship with Thomas.

Valerie, who had happily brought up her own family in the former rectory, showed us records dating from Tudor times that included the layout of the house when the Machells lived there. She regretted no pictures existed to show what the house looked like before extensive alterations were made by the Machells' successors. Imagine, then, her astonishment when, like a conjuror, I produced a watercolour copy out of my bag. It was the house as depicted by Thomas at the foot of the Journal page recalling his desolate homesickness on his first Christmas away from home.

After all this there was no time to visit the church because I had an appointment at the East Riding Archives Office in Beverley. In the archives Glencairn and I found the Reverend Robert Machell's own Etton register of births, marriages and deaths, the last reading like a litany. I visualised a procession of tiny coffins of all the babies and toddlers who died in infancy, and gave thanks for Thomas's own narrow escape. Most poignant of all is the page dated August 19th 1841 that records, in Robert's hand, the death of his wife, Thomas's mother. Beside it is the only marginal note in the entire register. It states: 'Eliza Mary Machell, my dear dear wife, died three weeks after giving birth to her twelfth child, leaving ten children to lament their loss. Here closes a period of rather more than twenty years of happy union.' An additional line 'for those who come after' declares that 'the vault is seven feet by nine and will include my own bones if the Fates come in accordance with my wishes'. On the facing page Robert entered the death just six weeks later of his baby daughter Rosamund, Thomas's youngest sister, 'this child of sorrow' as he calls her.

With babies in mind we set off to explore the town, stopping first at Beverley's majestic Minster, which looks down Highgate. Having just read of Thomas's baptism there on 15th November 1824 I pictured him as a frail baby, three days old, being held over the enormous font whose carved wooden cover is so heavy it has to be manoeuvred by winch. The register revealed that Thomas was born across the road in the Minster Parsonage, where the family was lodging at the time, Robert giving his profession then as 'Gentleman'. Brazenly I rang the front door bell and the owners, nonplussed, offered to show us around, telling us the Machells shared the house with a famous Minster vicar, the religious reformer Joseph Coltman. There could have been no greater contrast with tiny Thomas, for Coltman was a great man in more than one sense, weighing thirty-eight stone. Records show that doors had to be widened and ceilings reinforced before he could take up residence in the Parsonage where Thomas was born.

It was almost dark when we left the Parsonage and we needed lodgings. We chose, at random, an old coaching inn on the Etton road just outside Beverley's gateway known as 'North Bar'. Our bedroom window faced the street. When I opened the curtains in the morning and looked across the road I saw an intriguing, elegant Georgian three-storey house, set back from the brick buildings on either side. Along the pavement in front of it a small boy was skipping beside his mother on his way to school in autumn sunshine. Later that morning a trail of phone calls led us to David and Susan Neave, local historians familiar with certain Machell relatives (but not Thomas) whose names were cropping up in diaries they were researching. They consulted their notes and told us Thomas's family lived for several years in a large Georgian house called 'The Elms' on North Bar Without – Thomas's mother, Eliza (née Zealey) having inherited it in 1826 from her childless godmother Mary Sterne (a relation by marriage to the writer

Laurence Sterne). I might have guessed that Thomas had lived in the house directly facing our bedroom window, and that it was when he was the age of that boy we had watched skipping in sunshine.

Our inn lay close to Beverley's other magnificent church, St Mary's. We stepped inside to admire its mediaeval carvings and in the south transept my eye was caught by sunlight filtering through an enormous stained glass window, turning grey paving slabs into precious jewels. The window was clearly Victorian, so I crossed to the wall beside it to read a brass plaque fixed there. What did I find? That the window was erected by nearly two hundred subscribers to commemorate the life of none other than Christopher Scott Machell, Thomas's uncle.

We walked up Hengate to North Bar Within to take money out of Barclays Bank. This turned out to be the former Machell bank (Thomas's uncles Christopher Scott and John Thomas being two of the founders). A photograph shows this bank then named Messrs Machell, Pease and Hoare, with Christopher Scott standing proudly beside the door – in top hat of course. The photograph was taken in 1861, the year before Thomas's death.

The more I shadowed Thomas in his home area, the more I understood what he had rejected by choosing to live on the edge. He could have led

Family crest of the Machells of Crackenthorpe with three greyhounds.

a safe and comfortable bourgeois life by working in the family bank, and posed beside his uncle for the photo, wearing top hat and waistcoat.

On Sunday we returned to Etton and the church, whose warm stonework defied the drab Yorkshire sky. Inside, a smell of beeswax sweetened the mustiness. We sat in the chancel where week after week throughout the Reverend Robert Machell's twenty-year incumbency his family took its place, its size expanding with births and contracting with deaths and departures. Young Thomas, legs dangling, wriggles between housekeeper Annie, Mother, Lance and sturdy James. Adult Thomas, hardened by war, buoyed by love, weakened by disease.

The Reverend Robert adored his Norman church; he planned improvements, later carried out by his successor, and made copious records invaluable for today's local historians, notably Gail White, who in 1992 used many of them in her publication about the village and its church. He integrated his family into the fabric of the building. The large East window shedding coloured light onto the altar remains his lasting memorial to his beloved wife. The family greyhounds leap over the crest in its apex, and in that of the large south window, which otherwise has clear glass. Why? I learnt later that this window was also formerly filled with coloured glass by Robert as a memorial to Thomas's fourth brother, Hugh Devon, but that the glass had shattered during an air raid on Hull in World War II. 'Many tears this poor Boy cost me,' notes Robert enigmatically in the parish register record of Hugh Devon's death at sixteen, in September 1850. The news of this death took three months to reach Thomas in Bengal.

Thomas had a hand in the design of both windows, referring to them in a passage written during a voyage to India in 1854 by cargo ship, the *Gloriosa*, after a convalescence at home: '*Saturday, six weeks from London* … I have been rather successful I flatter myself in drawing the painted windows in Etton Church from memory they are just about half the size of those I painted for your quarto Volume.' I was intrigued to read of a 'quarto Volume'. Did it still exist, I wondered, and if so, what else might it contain? Might I one day track it down and bring to light Hugh's lost window and other family treasures? All these hints were turning me into a greyhound, scenting a trail to unlikely places.

When the service was over and the smell of smoke from the extinguished candles still lingered in the chancel, I crossed to the wall where I had spotted a tarnished brass memorial. During the service I had prayed it would be the memorial inscription I had been longing to find ever since I unfolded the family tree. It was. But it turned out to commemorate not just Thomas but four other family members too. It confirmed that Thomas was 'buried at Nursingpore', 'MI there and at Etton,' says the family tree. Well, I had now found the memorial at Etton. Did the other one still exist in remotest Narsinghpur? I focused on the other four names. Three commemorate Thomas's younger brothers Henry Lancelot, Lancelot and Hugh Devon – but the fourth is the Reverend Robert himself. This was puzzling. Why did his name feature on a plaque put up for family members not buried at Etton? I had read, in his own hand in the parish register, his instructions for his bones to join his wife's in the churchyard outside. It didn't make sense. It was time to go and hunt for the grave.

The couple's double tombstone should have been easy to find in Etton's modest churchyard because Robert had provided its measurements. Glencairn joined me in zig-zagging amongst the gravestones in front of the church but we found nothing to match the description. We tried the back and also drew a blank. I was disappointed and ready to give up but made a final foray in unkempt grass near the row of leaning yews that border the graveyard. This time I literally stumbled upon a wide horizontal stone at ground level, almost entirely smothered by grass and ivy that had crawled across it over the years. Could this be it?

I dropped to my knees and began to tear at chunks of foliage and soil, and, as I did so, flowery letters forming a long inscription appeared, as in a child's magic painting. The words, blurred by lichens, were still legible, and when I had cleared the right-hand side of the slab I could make out a dedication in Latin verse to Eliza Machell by her husband Robert. It ended with:

> *Ecce sub hoc conjux mater dilecta sepulchra*
> *Intempestivo funere rapta jacet...*
> *At quum nostra tuis parita sopita quiescant*
> *Corda sub optato contumulata solo*
> *Sit mihi sit tecum sedes intrare piorum*
> *Tecum. Nam sine te gaudia nulla juvant.*

It was useful being married to a Classics scholar. Glencairn translated the touching inscription:

> *See, beneath this tomb there lies a beloved wife and mother,*
> *snatched away by untimely death...*
> *But when my heart is put to sleep and rests like yours,*

sharing the grave beneath the longed-for earth, let it, let it be
mine to enter with you the abode of the faithful – with you,
for without you there is no joy.

I immediately attacked the foliage covering the other half of the tombstone, expecting a similar eulogy to Robert from his sons. To my astonishment this half was blank. Did this mean Robert was cheated of his desire to be reunited with his beloved Eliza in the tomb he had himself prepared? The thought saddened me. Here was another conundrum to sort out. I wondered too why the tiny grave of Thomas's nephew Guy (who died before he was three months old, in the year Thomas died) was lying close to his grandmother's tomb rather than in the churchyard of the parish where his father was rector when he died.

Rewind to a summer's day in 1843. Who is this young sailor approaching the rectory from the Beverley direction, arms weighed down by traps gripped by coarsened hands? Can this really be the puny child who left Etton on a dismal November day three years earlier in a state of innocent bewilderment? Thin he may still be, but he is taller and swarthy and the realities of warfare have propelled him prematurely from boyhood into manhood. When he sees the rectory he stands transfixed, gazing across the forlorn garden and up the slope to the homely brick façade where smoke rises from huge kitchen chimneys. He seems overcome with emotion. After several minutes he walks slowly on, turns into the muddy lane that divides the rectory from its church, and hesitates beside a door in the garden wall. Then he opens the door and places his traps inside. He crosses the lane and goes through the lych-gate framing the path leading into the churchyard. He doesn't enter the church but instead wanders slowly among the surrounding gravestones, head bowed, clearly seeking something. Then, behind the church, he comes across a new tombstone at ground level and stops dead. He stares down at it. The damp stone is sharply chiselled, and petals from a bunch of pink roses placed at its head have scattered to stick onto the inscription like pressed flowers. Tenderly, his sunburnt fingers roll them away and he mouths the words:

In the vault beneath Lieth the Body of ELIZA MARY MACHELL wife of the REVd ROBERT MACHELL Curate of Etton and Incumbant of Leckonfield Aged 39 Years, Three weeks after giving birth to her Twelfth Child leaving Seven Sons and Three Daughters This record is here placed by her Husband in Memory of twenty years made happy by her hand and heart …

He begins to sob, falling to his knees and covering his face with his hands.

Confronted by the reality of his mother's tomb, Thomas, the returning wanderer, is facing the finality of her death two years after the rest of his family. They have already stowed away the black crèpe and black-edged writing paper until next time, whereas Thomas's period of mourning is just beginning.

Thomas wipes his eyes with the coarse woollen sleeve of his jacket, rises to his feet, and walks slowly towards the old church, sadness at his heels. It is the first time he has set foot in a church since leaving home. He slips into the family pew and hears his own breathing in the silence as memories file through his mind and he mourns his mother and thanks the Lord for his own safe return.

When Thomas pushes open the rectory's familiar back door he smells baking and laundry starch. He greets the delighted household one by one. Who is the first to know he's back? Perhaps it's Old Blucher, the family dog, named after the Prussian Field Marshall who saved the day for Wellington at Waterloo. Thomas frequently mentions this dog; he made a sketch of him which hung over the fireplace of his Bengal study. In 1854 he took one of Blucher's puppies, with the same name, out to India where five months later, finding himself still unemployed and homeless (a 'vagrant' as he calls himself) he gave it to his former boss, Mr Forlong. Traces of Blucher's genes are no doubt sprinkled among many pi-dogs in today's Bengal.

Thomas had his old room to himself because Lance, now fourteen, was away distinguishing himself at Addiscombe. Six years had passed since the pair climbed out of the window that summer's morning, bent on seeking their fortunes. Thomas spent many weeks creating what would form the first part of Volume One of his Journals from those memoranda made aboard the *Worcester*. While he leant over his childhood desk, his quill scratching page after page and his brush adding colour to his sketches and illuminated title pages, the house was full of activity downstairs. The 1841 census records five women servants indoors, one of whom was Ann Kirby, the faithful housekeeper they called Annie. She was busy caring for all the boys and toddlers now that her mistress was dead. And what of those children so much changed since Thomas last saw them?

The responsible eldest, Richard, now 20, was deep in the study of Hebrew verbs, preparing for his ordination. Thomas always looked up to him. Richard had his stuffy side, apparent in his letters and sermons, but frequently bailed out the feckless family members and got little credit for it. The four surviving younger boys were awkward Hugh Devon, just ten (with six more years to live), Henry eight, Robert a year younger, and rumbustious James. Henry (or Harry) would become the family's black sheep, whereas James (the baby in Eliza's womb when Thomas ran away from home) would use his daredevil streak to restore lost family pride. Next came Mary Matilda, whose arrival in the world after nine successive sons must have delighted her parents. She was two when Thomas left home. Baby Kathleen Annie, born a year after Mary Mathilda, had died at two months, and Kathleen had come along the following year, just months before Thomas's departure. Finally, while Thomas was involved in a war on the far side of the world, Rosamund had echoed her sister Kathleen Annie by also coming and going within two months. Maybe Rosamund wasn't the cause of her mother's death so much as was the accumulated strain for Eliza of producing a baby a year over seven years. How the two surviving little motherless sisters in their smocks and starched pinafores would have been spoiled by the whole household, not least by Thomas, who tells us he loved children.

Annie's name dots the Journals. Housekeepers, who inhabited that twilight zone reserved for governesses and certain nannies, were an integral part of a family's life yet never of it; they were doomed to channel their maternal affection into children not their own. Thomas's Annie died aged 76 in 1859. Her gravestone still stands sentinel close by her mistress's tomb.

It so happens that my own childhood revolved, like Thomas's, around a comforting woman also called Annie. She was Ann Hallam, a short-term maternity nurse who stayed on for a lifetime when my maternal grandmother died weeks after giving birth to my Uncle. An almost constant, nurturing presence in my own childhood as well as my mother's, I found her status bewildering but I loved her unconditionally. She seemed forever in the kitchen, rolling pastry, making sponge puddings or shelling peas shiny as marbles. But each evening she faded away like a ghost. Born in 1876, she was one of thousands of women whose spinsterhood was sealed by World War I and she remained forever in a time warp, like a wartime egg preserved in isinglass. Year round she wore straight tweed skirts, blouses buttoned to the neck, brown hand-knitted cardigans with collars, and flat lace-up shoes. Kirby-grips pinioned her hair, her false teeth clacked when she ate, and she had the sweetest smile in the world. She was born just 14 years after Thomas's death, but died when I was the age at which Thomas was caught up in the Opium Wars, an age when my generation was smoking pot and making love, not war. Years after Annie's death I realised to my shame that I knew next to nothing about her past.

Parishioners also welcomed Thomas back to the village. Their good wishes, passed on by Robert in letters, are often acknowledged in the Journals and it's clear that the curiosities, not least the cured animals Thomas regularly sent home, greatly entertained them. One wonders what the servants made of Thomas's collection, let alone the postman who had to deliver them. 'I hope to make my old room at Etton a museum worth visiting,' he notes after a typical entry in Bengal mentioning the preservation of an adjutant bird and a vulture to dispatch home by the next ship. 'I found curing these brutes rather disgusting nevertheless they were too necessary for our collection to be neglected so I held my nose, smoked my pipe and worked away if they reach home safe virtue will be rewarded,' he writes. Two days later he risks his life to preserve a hooded cobra: 'I did not wish to spoil him by giving him a coup de grace, so I got him into a bottle alive and corked him down much to his surprise and here he is on the table before me waiting for the arrival of the Bengali shrub (a Rice spirit) which is to finish him off and preserve him on his journey to England'. Also in this consignment is an iguana cornered by Thomas's dogs: 'I consider this a great addition to the collection and I think it will astonish the natives of Etton even more than the albatross.' The albatross, incidentally, was despatched home in 1849 from the *Rajah* to join, says Thomas, 'the porpoise I brought home last voyage and which is yet I daresay hanging under the apple tree in the back garden.'

Besides the parishioners and the Beverley relatives to call on there was a certain young lady to woo. Thomas drops tantalising hints. When he meets a very different kind of love the following year he compares the two: 'gay and merry is thy ringing laugh [this is the new lady] but the smile of her I will not name is dearer to me than thy merriest peal'. (He soon proves rather fickle). Seven years later he will write in Bengal: 'Last night I was sitting dreamily over the fire taking long steady pulls at the hookah and thinking of – well never mind who I was thinking of but though at Rooderpore I was not in mind far distant from York… ' And four years later still, in a passage about his love for women, and just visible beneath a heavy deletion, is a reference to 'others I could name in England'.

Life was dull. By New Year 1844 Thomas, now 19, was planning his next move: 'I was no longer a visionary boy dreaming of amassing huge fortunes in Australia but a bronzed weather-beaten youngster not over-enamoured of seafaring life but preferring it infinitely before the idea of quill driving in an office.'

When we left the churchyard we made for the old rectory, where the current owners, the Wilsons, welcomed us into the flag-stoned kitchen with mugs of coffee.

Sally Wilson showed us all over the still large house, though it is smaller since the east wing seen in Thomas's sketch was demolished in the 1960s. The interior was furnished to perfection for a modern nuclear family and much changed since Thomas's day, but the warmth of a cherished family home remained. The main rooms overlooked a well-tended garden created by Eliza. As we mounted the stairs I felt a little strange but dismissed the feeling when we were shown around the various family bedrooms. The last in the tour was the one I had 'identified' as Thomas's two days earlier. Imagine, therefore, how I started when I saw a plate screwed onto its door declaring it to be 'Tom's Room'! It turned out that the Wilson's son, another Thomas, chose that room for himself. Just a coincidence then.

We entered the room together, still clutching our coffee mugs. I gravitated to the window that faced the garden, the one I was sure Thomas climbed out of when he and Lance ran away. Then I turned round, and was chatting to Sally about Eliza and her garden when suddenly, as before in the driveway, I was taken over by a visceral sense of grief, and burst into uncontrollable tears. This was getting ridiculous. 'Whatever's happened,' I assured Glencairn when I recovered, 'will surely be out of my system if we ever return here.' When we made our apologies and farewells the Wilsons were clearly relieved to see the back of me and I didn't blame them. I didn't understand my behaviour either. I told Thomas about it in a note that evening: 'It took me utterly by surprise; it was a bright morning and I was talking to a stranger and in no way "psyched up" to feel as I did. It's almost as if I was paying a final visit on your behalf. It was very embarrassing and Sally Wilson retreated downstairs while I sobbed again on poor Glencairn's shoulder.'

When the Wilsons unexpectedly put the house on the market two years after my first visit I had a daft notion of buying it, even though it was far too expensive and far too big. I dragged long-suffering Glencairn up and down the length of England by train one wet Sunday just to view it. I even briefly fantasised about writing this book in the very room where Thomas had grown up and put together his various Journals.

On his 19th birthday, 12th November 1843, when he completed the fair copy of his first Journal account, he added a covering letter, later bound in as a frontispiece: 'I have at last completed for your amusement a rough sketch of my adventures during the last three years, and I hope I have written enough to enable you to picture to yourself the life I led during that time. I cannot say much for my attempt but I have endeavoured to do my best… Should it not be my lot to return to my family, but should my last breath be drawn in a foreign land, or my last resting place be the sailor's grave, far from home, you will I am sure look on this with a double interest.' For some reason this letter was addressed not to Father but to 'Richard Beverley Machell of Crackenthorpe, Westmorland'.

I had no idea why Thomas mentioned the name Crackenthorpe so often in his Journals, nor whether this mysterious place still existed.

8. Coals to Nuku Hiva

Still must I on; for I am as a weed,
Flung from the rock, on Ocean's foam to sail
Where'er the surge may sweep, the tempest's breath prevail.

(Canto III of *Childe Harold's Pilgrimage*,
Byron, quoted by Thomas)

While the family back home in 1844 was enjoying midsummer warmth in Eliza's rose garden, Thomas was frozen to the rigging of a barque as it battled to round Cape Horn, taking coals from Newcastle halfway around the world.

With the first of July commenced our mid-winter month off Cape Horn with its accompaniments of Rain and Hail, Fogs and Squalls, Boisterous winds and raging seas, vivid lightening and awfully pealing thunder. A thick fog surrounded us all day, followed by a tremendous heavy gale. What work we had to get our sail taken in. I thought we should freeze on the yards, or get so numbed with cold that the violent rolling and pitching of the ship might send us flying into the dark waters that raged and rolled beneath us. It is truly an awful sight to look from the Topsail yard whilst close-reefing the sail during a dark squally night off the Horn. To see the roaring mountains of water heaving and rearing with their white crests curling proudly above them rolling black and awful towards the little vessel, but as you gaze with awe on the terrible wall of water which seems about to swallow you the Giant wave sinks with a rush and a roar and hurries away like a disappointed Daemon in its ever restless course.

Ever and anon the little ship rolls and trembles, sinks creaking and groaning into the black abyss and rises, dipping her saucy bows in the wild waters and shaking a flood over her low decks like a wild Albatross disporting in her element. The snow and hail fell heavily that first week, the cold was intense and our barque was shipping heavy seas for she was so laden that she did not work so lively as she would have done had she been lighter in the water.

On the 10th of July we sighted Statin Island. It was blowing stiff and we were under double-reefed topsails. The next day it moderated and we were at last in sight of Cape Horn. What a wild and desolate country it appeared, bleak mountains and rugged Rocks varied here and there with the smoking summit of a slumbering Volcano.

Sad signs floated past us – the topmast and head of a lower mast twisted sharp off with all its hamper floated silently over the stormy water telling its tale of shipwreck and loss of life as plain as a newspaper advertisement.

We had a fresh leading wind when we sighted the Horn and fully expected to have cleared it before night. But we were not to double the Cape so easy as all that. Early in the afternoon the wind shifted and came switching over the waters, blowing as if it intended to send us round the world and back again. However, there was no help for it so we took in one sail after another, reef upon reef, until once again we lay to under a close-reefed main Topsail. As we lay out on the yards to furl a reef the Hail came so heavy it was impossible to face it, and for some time after my face was considerably swelled.

After two days the weather began to moderate but the sea was running awfully high. Sometimes our little Hooker would roll gunnel under, but she weathered it gallantly. What is remarkable, notwithstanding the violent straining she had to encounter, nothing was carried away, though sometimes the sea would fly halfway up the leach of our topsails.

The 16th was the coldest day we had yet experienced. The ice was half an inch thick round the jib guys and pendants and hung down in long thick Icicles, whilst the lower rigging was completely cased with ice and we had to beat it off the ropes before we could attempt to haul them. On the 18th we found ourselves again in the Longitude of the Horn, having been driven back to the eastward of Statin Island.

Only on the 20th were we at last clear of the Horn. "Hurrah" thought I "now I can give in without fear of being considered a skulk." In fact I was worn out and really unable to do my work, but so long as all hands are required in weather like this no seaman will give in untill he can no longer hold up – for with a small ship's company one man or even a boy is missed when all hands are required to work the ship. I was not long on the sick list, the second day I was again on deck and keeping my watch for the valiant Ganges was again labouring with close-reefed Topsails.

At last we were blessed with a fair wind and pleasant weather and bowled away for the Latitude of Valparaiso.

Four months earlier, in Newcastle's port of South Shields, Thomas had boarded the 317-ton collier, its name resonant of his previous adventures in the East. The *Ganges* was, he writes, 'bound for the Marquesas laden with coals for the French steamers plying the South Seas.' The outward passage took almost six months. The revolutionary era of iron-hulled long-distance steamships was still around the corner but small short-haul steamers, often built *in situ* from kits, were already proving their worth for western powers intent on imposing their authority locally. Thomas had seen the effect of a British steamship in the late China War, and would soon witness the French overwhelming a brand new Polynesian colony thanks to coal brought under sail all the way from Britain.

29th March, 1844. Well, she's a smart little craft for a collier thought I [she was built at Govan two years earlier] as I step'd over the side and saluted the Mate, a Raw looking young Red-haired Scotsman. As soon as I had got my chests below I found time to examine more closely my future companions. The Captain James Gibson appeared to be a smart middle-aged man of slight build and dark weather beaten complexion, a man apparently well used to his profession and capable of being a good master. However there is no telling what a Captain may be untill a ship is on blue water and the Lord of the Plank shows himself in his true colours.

The Mate was a relation of the owners... a person never much liked on board a ship either by the Captain or the men. The second officer was a stout fellow strong as Hercules. Four apprentices, five men and the old Cook completed our ship's company.

The first few months of the outward passage, in the wake of *The Beagle* with Charles Darwin aboard a decade earlier, were uneventful. Then, Thomas tells us: 'The men began to talk about Cape Horn as the weather gradually became colder and the Whale, the Large Albatross and the Cape Pidgeon more numerous.' Even today sailors brace themselves to navigate the world's most dangerous shipping passage – known as 'the sailors' graveyard' – with its icebergs and Himalayan waves up to thirty metres high.

On the evening of 10th of August we sighted the welcome light of Valparaiso. Next morning we pulled the Captain ashore and I took the opportunity of having a look at the town which is built in straggling rows. I was much struck with the appearance of the place and the strange medley of people from all parts of the Western World who fill the streets; dark Chileans and Spaniards in gay dresses with endless cigaretto in their mouths, Germans, French, English and American... It is curious to walk down the streets and observe the shops, taverns etc and their respective owners. The French keep the best Coffee Houses and Perfume shops, Italians own the Chemists and Druggists, the Spaniards and French are the linnen drapers, the Germans are the Watchmakers whilst the shoemakers and lowest class of drinking shop are kept by English or American vagrants who are generally from Sydney or some such equally respectable port which they had been obliged to leave finding the place too hot to hold them. The better sort of Shipchandlers and general store keepers are also either American or English... Churches and religious houses are plentiful and the sound of holy bells perpetually tinkling reminds you that you are now in a truly Spanish country.

Having filled up our water and sent ashore what bales we had for this port we left Valparaiso on the 15th of August... We looked forward to discharging our cargo on the islands of the Marquesas with anything but pleasant feelings especially as we had heard we were to be on salt food all the time, and the chief pleasure in harbour is to have good fresh meat and soft bread. Salt beef and pork such as are served on board ship are anything but luxuries and barely sufficient to support life. In fact the salt beef, or junk as they call it, is generally believed to be not the flesh of bulls or oxen and such like fatted beasts but neither more nor less than old horse.

9. Marquesan Magic

Lovely indeed is the fair Island of Nookahiva
and lovelier still are the dark daughters of that Sea girt Isle.

(Thomas Machell)

Adonis stood on the quayside, naked apart from a pair of flowered shorts. Indigo blue warrior tattoos defined his magnificent gleaming torso and his long black hair was tied back at the nape of his neck. I watched entranced from the ship's rails as with strength and grace he manoeuvred nets of cargo swaying inches above him, suspended from the end of the ship's crane. Several times I caught my breath when it seemed a precarious load must knock him over, but each time, with the precision of a ballet dancer, he performed a practised *pas de deux* with the cargo.

He glanced up at the ship's railings, met my gaze and flashed a knockout smile. Pure white teeth contrasted with his bronzed skin like a virgin conker shell newly sprung. I was smitten. It was pure Mills and Boon. Now I understood how easily Thomas lost his heart to a young beauty on Nuku Hiva Island. I was doing the same thing, on my first day in Polynesia, ready to make a proper fool of myself.

And who wouldn't be attracted by a place that doesn't have the word 'work' in its vocabulary, the word 'dance' being used instead?

Two thousand years before Thomas a group of people undertook what has been described as the most remarkable voyage of discovery in human history. This group, navigating by intuition and by 'way-finding' (i.e. with no instruments) covered almost seven thousand kilometres by canoe north-east from the western Pacific before they came across the world's most remote archipelago at the eastern limit of all the islands. No wonder the new settlers named the islands Fenua'enata, 'The Land of the People'. Beyond these high islands lie almost six thousand kilometres of uninterrupted ocean eastwards to South America, yet descendants of these intrepid people later covered more vast distances northwest and south-east by canoe to colonise Hawaii, Easter Island and New Zealand, spreading stone carving and tattooing traditions, knowledge and language.

The islanders' first contact with foreigners came in 1595 when the Spanish chanced upon the southern island group, renaming them Marquesas after the viceroy of Peru, a Marquis. Next was Captain Cook, almost two centuries later in 1774, on his second voyage to the Pacific. He admired the handsome natives and many of their customs, and his sailors took the art of tattooing (and the neologism) back to Europe. Marquesan tattoos were the most elaborate in the world, a vital element of local culture banned by French colonisers and missionaries. Cook was right to express concern, in his last journal, about the impact of contact with the West. The rot set in after the northern group was 'discovered' in the 1770s by traders seeking sandalwood, and by various French, Russian, American and British sea-captains. Together with whalers' crews, the intruders brought weapons, alcohol and disease, rapidly reducing the 80,000 population to fifty thousand. It had dropped to 20,000 by the time Admiral Dupetit-Thouars claimed the Marquesas for the French Empire in 1842 for purely strategic reasons. This was the situation when Tom arrived two years later. (The population was 8,000 by the time I got there, at least an advance on the lowest point of well under 2,000 in the 1920s.)

After the long sail from Valparaiso, here's how Thomas describes his first sight of the islands:

"Land Ho!" cried a man from the topsail yard. I looked ahead and there loomed the faint blue outline hardly distinguishable from the light blue of the horizon but clear enough for the experienced eye to discover the high land of the Marquesas Islands... as our little craft neared the land... we could at length trace the undulations of hill and valley that decorate the lovely island of Nookahiva. As we approached the horseshoe harbour a canoe full of wild looking creatures waved us to go round the other side of the Island but the Captain determined to pay no attention to them and we held on our course. Well was it for us that we did so for we afterwards learnt that a brig some time previously had been decoyed into the wrong bay and then plundered by these wretches who swam out and boarded her in hundreds.

When we opened the harbour which is a lovely bay and beautiful anchorage we found a French Corvette, an American Whaler and a Jersey ship laying at anchor. Presently a white whale boat darted out from the shore and an Englishman rowed by natives boarded us… and proceeded to pilot us to our place of anchorage. He was not so steady as he repeatedly desired our Helmsman to be, nor did the stiff Norwester of Rum and water which he had just imbibed in the Captain's State room make him more so. In sober truth I may say that our good friend was tipsy when he came on board and drunk when he went ashore.

The French found him here on their arrival and made him Pilot for the harbour. He appeared to have been once a respectable man and a Yorkshireman. Some said he had been an officer in the Royal Navy but I hope for the credit of our service that was not the case.

Two years earlier the whaling ship that included future novelist Herman Melville in its crew was piloted by the same renegade, then too, in that writer's words, 'in that interesting state of intoxication when a man is amiable and helpless, and a lot else besides.' When Thomas was visiting the Marquesas Melville was in America writing the blockbuster, *Typee*, which would make his name. Melville used many sources to turn the month he spent in the Marquesas in 1842, after deserting his whaling ship, into a romantic part-fiction. Readers loved the resulting tale of a bloodthirsty cannibal Typee tribe and liaison with the dusky Fayaway, woven into vivid descriptions of island life. Since Thomas's trip came so soon after Melville's, it is not surprising he had similar experiences, but he must have been surprised when he later read *Typee*, published in 1846, to find how much the two young men had in common. Both deplored the way Christian missionaries distorted the truth when portraying the natives. Melville gained fame for his controversial questioning of the superiority of 'civilised men' over 'savages'. He wrote: 'Thrice happy are they who, inhabiting some yet undiscovered island in the midst of the ocean, have never been brought into contaminating contact with the white man,' while Thomas also raged against European colonisation in his 1845 Journal. 'What can be a more melancholy sight in a savage country than to see our own countrymen greater savages than those whom we call Cannibals and Gross Idolaters?' he complains.

Thomas's rant against colonial and religious arrogance, globally as well as in Polynesia, covers many pages. One can also see here his lifelong struggle to retain his Christian faith, not least for his family's sake. This is a young man working out, on the page, his views on life's big questions, as inconsistently as the rest of us as we tack back and forth between bewildering complexities.

Though Thomas concludes that 'the White man is not the regenerator but the annihilator of the uncivilised races, he brings no blessing to the savage', he makes an exception for the 'savage' to whom perhaps he did bring a little blessing – as she certainly did to him by initiating him into the joys of unfettered love. One wonders what the family made of the following passage:

The Anchor was no sooner gone than we were up the rigging and lying out on the yards to furl sails... and now we found time to take a squint round us. "Hello," said one of the men, "What do you call that? They're not fish making all that bobbery in the water there – they must be porpoises." "More like sharks or Alligators so near shore as that," growled an old salt, "when did you ever see Porpoises tumbling in breakers, eh?" "Why," said I, "they look more like men than fish," calling to mind the hundreds of bathers I had seen in Calcutta's River Hoogley. "Men," growled old sulky, "when did you ever see men swimming half a mile from shore – ain't there no women there too Mr Smart-eye?"

Nearer came the splashing leaping swimmers and now we could hear merry cries and hearty peals of laughter as they came darting through the water and boarded the ship. There followed a scene that beggars all description. The good old ship was boarded on all quarters by dusky forms of such graceful shapes as would have led us to suppose that the fables of nymphs of the sea were realised. They clung round our rough iron cables with tender limbs and laughing shook back their long black hair showing sparkling eyes and ivory teeth gleaming with wanton gaiety. They scrambled up our fore main and mizzen Chains and sat wringing the water from their long curls like sirens or mermaids. My dreams of all that was wild and lovely were realised in the hundred graceful forms that now took possession of the Ganges – and I'll wager not even the daughters of that holy Indian river who daily bare their dark forms in her waters could excel in charms these nut brown maidens of the Sea.

I felt as if all I saw must be a fantastic dream, but was roused from my trance by the touch of a delicate brown hand on my sleeve, and raising my eyes from the decks I encountered the laughing gaze of a pair of brilliant dark eyes whose glance darted through my whole frame like an electric shock. "Ti ho," said the little Gypsy laughing in my troubled face, "Ti ho Whyheva moutakee?" And again laid her delicate tattooed hand on my arm. What could I do? From that moment I was the slave of the dark-eyed Whyheva, daughter of a savage Chief.

You may laugh at the idea of falling in love with a little savage girl, daughter of a cannibal. But in good earnest such was the case and who with half such a tender heart as I possess but would have done the same?

Our ship didn't swarm with naked dusky maidens when we entered the horseshoe bay but the general scene hadn't changed much. Taiohae has fewer than two thousand inhabitants and, in 2001, was free of supermarkets and internet cafés, though not satellite dishes. The remains of the French fort still overlook the east of the bay, near a tiny prison where the few prisoners come and go at will. A huge open-sided Catholic church, built in the 1970s on top of a traditional sacred site, dominates the bay's centre. Beyond the little capital, unscaled pinnacles were playing hide-and-seek with sudden cloudbursts and teasing dawn clouds. 'Papeete,' I had noted on our arrival there by plane from Los Angeles, 'smells of traffic and flowers.' Taiohae, however, just smelt of flowers, as did its beautiful women, who stud their hair with sweet-smelling gardenias and rub fragrant oils into their skin.

We began to unload our cargo of mattresses, frozen chickens, livestock and road-building machines on loan from Tahiti and load up hessian sacks of copra (fermented coconut meat). This was easy enough at Taiohae's wharf, one of only three on all the islands. Elsewhere crew and passengers scrambled down ladders into sturdy wooden whaling boats to get near the land and then had to leap into pounding surf to wade ashore, just as in Tom's day. Even in heavy swells and sudden downpours the Polynesian crew can, by floodlight, unload onto treacherous barren cliffs swaying nets holding heavy oil drums needed to refuel the Tahiti plane that flies to Nuku Hiva's tiny airstrip.

When the waves were exceptionally high, lucky Glencairn, being an older passenger, was carried in the muscular arms of Adonis.

Thomas wasn't built like these swarthy Polynesians. He found it tough work unloading the tainted cargo of the *Ganges* in Taoihae's harbour. It can't have helped knowing that coal from his native Yorkshire mines was fuelling France's brutal suppression of the islanders. 'From 5 am to 6 pm we worked with little intermission… discharging Black diamonds into the boats of the French Corvette… '

How he longed for the evenings, when, he writes, 'we swept the decks and plunged into the clear blue water alongside to wash off the thick coat of coal dust… and here whilst splashing about we were joined by our merry friends from the shore like a shoal of dolphins.' He then went ashore and stole away hand in hand with his near-naked lover.

'Whyheva led me far up the secluded valley which led to her father's house,' Tom writes. I followed them a century and a half later, through a lush valley filled with wild bananas, oranges, lemons, coconuts, ylang-ylang and breadfruit with glossy leaves the size and shape of giants' hands, and up a stone path deep into the hills, occasionally coming face to face with the enormous eyes of a *tiki*, huge carved stone figure of an ancestral god, staring mournfully out from another age through dank undergrowth. Whyheva would have averted her gaze, for such sacred objects and places were *tapu* (taboo) for women in her day. The path still leads to a traditional assembly site, with its ceremonial banyan tree where skulls of tribal enemies are said to have been interred in the roots (after gruesome 'fishing' expeditions), but the buildings described and sketched by Thomas are all reconstructions. In his day the Marquesans jousted on decorated stilts, sang and played conches and tall drums. Men in grass skirts danced with spears while girls imitated the sinuous flights of swooping frigate birds. (Today's tourist displays are sad imitations of these practices that were being exterminated in Thomas's day by prudish missionaries and the foreign invaders. Watching such displays made us feel like hypocritical voyeurs.)

It was brave of Thomas to call on a cannibal chief who hated white men, French soldiers having just murdered his three sons and wounded him. Fortunately for Thomas the chief's tribe was the comparatively peaceful Happar, the one Melville was seeking when he hacked his way over a steep ridge and entered, by mistake, the neighbouring valley, home of the feared Typee tribe. Thomas says he was 'uncertain how to behave'. Indeed, what is the etiquette for greeting a cannibal chief?

When I first approached the Chief's hut Whyheva accompanied me and we entered together. The hut was a long shed, the entrance on the lower side. Mats were spread the whole length of the room close to the high side with the long trunks of the cocoa nut tree to serve as head and foot boards Along the roof were triced up the spears and other implements of war, fishing and boating also the neatly ornamented nose flute and many other articles peculiar to the inhabitants of the south sea Islands. Seated on a pile of mats was a figure who immediately fixed my whole attention. It was the chief himself. A slight piece of Tappa [bark] cloth encircled his waist and his whole body was covered with tattoos, his face was stern and fierce and the strange blue patterns traced completely over Eyes nose and mouth could hardly divert the attention for a moment from the fixed gaze of his unwavering eye.

I bowed to the grave figure which looked more like an Indian warrior god than a living man, and uttered the words 'Tiho' (friend) which was the full amount of my knowledge of the language at that time. The chief nodded his stern head and repeated the words, at the same time pouring forth a long speech of which the only words I could make out were French and English, and I saw he was working himself up into a violent state of excitement against the cursed invaders of his country and destroyers of his people. It was a fearful sight in that dark hut to see this savage creature with terrible energies cursing as the wild man only can curse, and looking in the dim uncertain light like a dark spirit of another world, swaying to and fro, his wild eyes gleaming with fury as he raved in impotent rage against his all powerful enemy and subduer.

At last he became more calm, for knowing well the contempt a savage has for any expression of alarm I kept a steady countenance and gazed unshaken on his passionate face. Presently he recovered and gravely and most courteously pointed to a seat beside him and filling his pipe he lighted and presented it to me, all the time speaking in a calm unbroken manner as if it never occurred to him that I did not understand a word he said. I offered him a cigar which he accepted with the air of a Prince. Truly these savages are born gentlemen, never did I see him in a passion except when by any accident the French were named and then all his pent up rage would burst out again in mad fury and he would show his wounds and rave like one possessed.'

Would the English cottager invite a foreigner into his house... and invite him to share his food, his pipe, his dance, his every enjoyment?

Would an English clod give even to a stranger of their own country the courtly reception which I have received in the house of every savage I have visited?

He seems to have made a hit with the tattooed chief who might have become his father-in-law. It is hard to imagine the average British sailor sharing an evening pipe deep in the jungle with a cannibal chief, and learning his language, as Thomas did. Meanwhile, the chief's daughter was showing Thomas the joys of sexual union, something far removed from his experiences of the sailors' lust for young shipmates and whores.

In Victorian Britain women were clothed from top to toe. On this South Sea Island Thomas, hampered at home not only by social *mores* but also by his sense of physical inferiority, could freely indulge his teenage hormones. He is defiant. 'Do you blame me,' he proclaims, 'for those feelings, young wild and ardent as I was? Ah, the inhabitants of a country dwelling constantly in the circle of civilised life can have little sympathy with the half wild romantic spirit of a wandering sailor boy.'

Glencairn's ancestor, Robert Louis Balfour Stevenson, sailed his schooner into Anaho bay, a rare lagoon on Nuku Hiva Island, en route from California to Samoa in 1888. Glencairn and I bounced along in his wake by speedboat.

Knowing the island's reputation for cannibalism, RLS was horrified when apparently hostile natives over-ran the *Casco* as soon as she dropped anchor. However, the Stevensons soon fell under the island's singular spell, like Thomas before them and me in the future. Perhaps they reminded RLS of his native land, as they would his fellow Scot, Gavin Bell, who compares them with the Hebrides in his *In Search of Tusitala*, including frequent complaints about the weather. ('How long has it been raining?' he asks one inhabitant. 'About one year,' is the reply. My own diary has such entries as 'needless to say, there was a deluge as we began our walk'.) Typically, RLS soon befriended the locals and explored the island's interior. 'The interest has been incredible,' he wrote to a friend, 'I did not dream there were such races or such places.' His doughty widowed mother, who hailed from Edinburgh's genteel streets, relaxed so much that she discarded her serge stockings and shoes to promenade along the beach by moonlight with a tattooed native dressed in a 'single handkerchief' (as RLS's wife Fanny described it to the writer Henry James). Mrs Stevenson never, however, gave up wearing her starched white organza cap. That would have been going too far.

Mrs Stevenson, a pillar of the Missionary Societies in Edinburgh, changed her mind in Polynesia, writing of the Marquesans to her sister that 'their conduct to each other and to strangers, so far as kindness and courtesy are concerned, is much more Christ-like than that of many professing Christians'. Thomas would agree.

Like the Stevensons, Glencairn and I anchored in Anaho's turquoise bay and waded ashore. Depopulation has vanquished the villages and we had the curving white beach to ourselves – not that we could lie on it, for it teemed with the island's vicious biting flies known locally as nonos (white ones on the beaches, black ones inland, what better tourist repellent?). But the lagoon is still classically fringed with coconut palms, 'those giraffes of vegetables' as RLS called them. Their stiff leaves crackle in the breeze and the water's movement rolls their great orange fruits ceaselessly up and down the sand in a lazy game of boules. The ghosts of the barefoot Edinburgh matron and her near-naked escort seemed as fabled as the owl and the pussy cat who also danced hand in hand on the edge of the sand, by the light of the moon, the moon, the moon.

Other artists were drawn by the islands' mystery and 'savage element' to quote Gauguin, who found Tahiti tame and bourgeois and had run out of willing models there. He retreated to Hiva Oa Island, in the southern Marquesan group, where he painted his last works in his 'House of Pleasure', baited the local Catholic priest by exposing his hypocrisy, and died in his fifties in 1903. In the 1970s the Belgian singer Jacques Brel also sought refuge on Hiva Oa. His aeroplane remains there, and his grave lies beside those of Gauguin and the priest, beneath frangipani trees in a cemetery overlooking the ocean.

My own favourite island, Fatu Hiva, also in the southern group, is so remote that the *Aranui* is the only lifeline to the outside world for the six hundred islanders who live in two villages separated by a long ride in an outrigger canoe or a day's hike over high mountains on the island's only track. Even Gauguin changed his mind about settling on what our guidebook called 'a semi-wild paradise'. It also turned out to be the home of my Adonis, Moana.

We first spoke (in French) on our second day at sea. 'Which part of Polynesia do you come from?' I asked, knowing the crew came from many different island groups. 'The Marquesas,' he announced with pride. Thomas's influence may have led me to be attracted to the only Marquesan among the crew, but he was also the tallest and most handsome and I wasn't the only female on board to fall for him. When I learnt that Moana was the ancient Polynesian word for the Great Ocean and its colour, indigo blue, it seemed too good to be true; on the other hand, the further I travelled down Thomas's path the less anything surprised me.

'What does the name Whyheva mean?' I asked Moana next. 'It means a child from far away,' he replied. That also seemed spot on.

I leant on the ship's rails beside Moana. 'What does the word *mana* mean, that keeps cropping up in conversation?' I asked him. He described it as a kind of divine or creative power, a spiritual otherness. 'It's hard to put into words,' he said, his dark eyes soulful, 'but tomorrow, on Fatu Hiva, you will feel it yourself and then you will understand'.

We reached the island just before dawn. I climbed sleepily on deck to find Moana already there. Together, in silence, we watched sheer jagged cliffs slide past, silhouetted black against the rising sun, until we came to anchor in the Bay of Omoa. Whaleboats lowered, we were ferried through high surf to wade ashore and walk to the village to see a demonstration of the ancient Polynesian art of bark cloth manufacture. In 1937 Thor Heyerdahl and his young bride spent an uncomfortable year living outside the village for fear of catching elephantiasis and other diseases prevalent then. They studied skulls and other remains, forming the theory (since disproved by DNA science) that Polynesians originated from Peru – hence their Kon Tiki expedition. They even met the last old islander to have witnessed cannibalism.

A few passengers opted for the long mountain walk to Hanavave village and headed off together. I had a perfect excuse not to join them because I needed to linger in Omoa to make notes on its bark cloth and select examples to join Captain Cook's Polynesian collection in my local museum of Exeter. When I did leave the village I climbed for several hours in rare and total solitude. The dirt track curved higher and higher between luxuriant trees, including wild mango heavy with sensual fruit smelling of honey. The air, unpolluted, was luminous. Deep inland lay a mythical landscape, while far out to sea the *Aranui* was a tiny white creature sliding across the lapis ocean. The only sound was birdsong, and the island was even free of *nonos*. Life's moments of pure joy are usually fleeting; I had never before experienced such sustained joy as I did that day, alone on the mountains of Fatu Hiva. Notwithstanding its sinister ghosts, it felt like Eden before the Fall.

I eventually descended into Hanavave's gloomy valley, overhung by towering stone ridges sculpted by nature into angular faces that bear a striking resemblance to the famous Easter Island statues. The canyon plunges down to the Baie des Vierges, said to be the world's most spectacular bay. Originally named Baie des Verges – phalli – from the shape of the surrounding crags, missionaries bowdlerised it into the pointless 'Bay of Virgins'. I scrambled aboard the last whaler to leave, manned by Moana, whose head was now crowned by a garland woven from palm fronds. On board I found our pillows strewn with scented flowers to celebrate Valentine's Day. The *Aranui* remained at anchor so that passengers could watch an amber sunset spotlight the bay and dusk descend. On the night dedicated to love, beneath the stars, there can be nowhere on earth more faraway or romantic. Moana was right, on Fatu Hiva Island I understood the meaning of *mana*.

Thomas could hardly bear to leave the islands. I knew the feeling. In fact we both almost didn't leave.

For Thomas it was after the coal was discharged and, having no return cargo to collect, the ship was being filled with ballast. 'This was the hardest of all our work,' he writes.

Our longboat was moored outside the surf and we had each to wade backwards and forwards with the stones on our heads. When the surf ran at all high it was cruel work as each wave could roll right over us and we soon found such constant buffeting in the waves filled our eyes with sand and completely deafened some of us. For my own part I was at last obliged to give in for on two occasions my life was near lost beneath the waves.

The first time was a day when the surf ran so high it swamped our boat, hurting some of us and nearly drowning others. Whyheva was on the beach and saw my danger. The merry girl dragged me out almost insensible. She then addressed some of the natives, they immediately set to work, cleared and helped to beach the boat, which had a hole in her bottom large enough for a boy to walk through.

Next time I was near drowning whilst fetching off water from the well at the fort. I had swum off to the boat for a line and as there was a bit of a swell on and the tide was going out, being dressed I was unable to get back and should have sunk had not the boy Charley swum to my assistance with an oar just as I was going down the third time. When I rose again and got hold of the oar I saw our gallant little Skipper in his best clothes [he had been dining with the Governor] rushing into the surf to save me.

There was no gallant Captain to pluck *me* from the surf when I inadvertently copied Thomas on our last afternoon on the islands. Within minutes of swimming out of my depth a vicious undertow dragged me out to sea. I battled across the current towards the tip of a rocky outcrop where it met the ocean, managing just in time to haul myself up its sharp rocks. As I lay on them, gasping for breath, clinging on with bleeding hands and surrounded by giant black crabs, I reflected that following in another's footsteps can sometimes get too close for comfort.

The thought of Civilisation and the pallid, corseted young ladies of Beverley had no appeal to Thomas after two months with Whyheva. How he longed to stay behind with her.

> The temptation was indeed very great [he admits]. In my last visit to the chief he proposed that I should leave my ship and accompany him over the ridge of Hills beyond which no French can go, far into the valley of Happar Long and earnestly did the chief speak and at last calling Whyheva she came and laying her little hand on my shoulder she gazed laughing and persuasively in my troubled eyes Oh how I longed at that moment to throw aside the chains of civilised life, to leave the ship where I had to toil from morn til night. But through all this one consideration kept me from becoming another outcast from the pale of civilisation. It was the recollection of a grey haired old man in the downhill of life who would wonder what evil had befallen his wandering son and how would my conscience have let me rest had I neglected him to wander in the sunny Islands of the Pacific.

> Alas my poor Whyheva, you must seek another lover amongst your own people from the tattooed warriors of your Father's tribe if indeed your stern invaders will leave you one to chose from for alas... a few years more and there will be but few left in this lovely Island and those like many hundreds already will soon waste away victim to the vices and cruelties of their European masters.

I hope Tom never learnt the fate of Whyheva the year after he left. She and her sisters were incarcerated in the fort and raped by soldiers, while her father was executed by firing squad at Taiohae for killing six French soldiers to avenge the murder of his sons.

I lay on deck with eyes closed as the islands melted into the horizon and into memories, lulled into the hypnotic, timeless in-between world induced by water and by music. I joined Thomas alone on his deck in the small hours, the ship's boards creaking rhythmically beneath him as he gazed at the Southern Cross. The parting from his first true love was painful and when in later life he recalled this love it sharpened his intense loneliness. Memories of his time with Whyheva washed over him as he wondered what he might have left behind with his heart on those islands. He pictured a love child splashing in the surf, and on his deathbed he would see this child as a young man the age he was when he landed on the islands. The young man, like Moana, had long black hair and oiled limbs and was tattooed from head to foot.

Robert Louis Stevenson, on his own departure from the islands, wrote: 'The first love, the first sunrise, the first South Seas island, are memories apart and touch a virginity of sense.'

Jenny's sketch of Moana Vong on the prow of a whaling boat laden with sacks of copra collected from Ua Huka island, Marquesas, Polynesia, 2001.

10. Guano and Missions to Patagonia

Those who do not move do not notice their chains

(Rosa Luxemburg)

Sentimentality and nostalgia. Thomas and I share a tendency to wallow.

The night of our departure from Nookahiva [he writes] saw me walking up and down the waist smoking a short clay pipe as the ship bowled away with all her light canvas spread. I looked up at the glorious stars shining as brightly as the sparkling eyes of my lost Whyheva. I was indulging in a sentimental reverie when I was joined by two of my shipmates. "Well," said one, "what cheer? Give us a draw. So we're once more afloat, well I'm glad of it and now for Valparaiso and real fun and frolic at the Foretop [a notorious public house] Savages and Cannibals is all well enough but there's nothing like civilization with lots of fiddling and dancing and Grog to the mast head. That's civilisation that is, none of your Cannibal Teatotalium for me and I hope we may never have to lay another couple of months in harbour without no grog nor fresh meat nor yet any soft Tommy [bread] except that breadfruit which is no better nor a soft sweet potato."

The *Ganges* passed Pitcairn Island in mid-November, when Thomas had just turned 20, and took on water in Valparaiso a month later. 'We were soon off for Pacya the place where we had to take in our cargo for home,' he writes.

'This place was as wretched as Cobija... the very gloomiest bay I ever saw.'

And why were they anchored in this ghastly place? A jingle, said to be Tennyson's but more likely coined by a member of the Gibbs family, sums it up:

Mr Gibbs
Made his dibs
In foreign birds'
Turds.

Yes indeed, seabirds' droppings, known as guano, were like gold in those days. Rich in nitrogen, phosphate and other vital elements, guano's use as a fertiliser underpinned the Inca empire but was unknown in North America and Europe before the 1840s, when word of its miraculous properties spread fast (it was said to be 35 times more potent than farmyard manure). This was a time when farmland productivity in North America and parts of Europe was declining and progressive farmers were desperate for a remedy. British trials with the first import of Peruvian guano in 1841 were so encouraging they triggered a guano rush that created fortunes, though, like indigo, it was a volatile commodity attracting over-speculation. In 1842 the Peruvian government nationalised guano reserves and created a monopoly that included the English firm Anthony Gibbs and Son. Within two years this firm had sole control of the British and North American markets and dominated the international guano trade until the early 1860s. The year Thomas was involved, 14,000 tons were already being imported into Britain, but this rose to a 100,000 tons in 1858, forming 80 percent of Peru's exports. It also made William Gibbs one of the wealthiest men in the West Country. Guano gold financed his extravagant Gothic mansion near Bristol, called Tyntesfield, that has survived intact to this day.

But all that glitters isn't gold, especially when it's birds' turds. Many agriculturalists consider that a rot literally set in with the import of quick-fix guano, the 19th century equivalent of modern industrial fertilisers that damage the earth's natural fertility and remove its healthy nutrients. Politically, too, the effect of the guano rush was far-reaching and de-stabilising. In 1865-66 the Spanish waged a guano war with Peru dubbed the 'Chincha Islands War', and Chile attacked both Peru and Bolivia in the 1879-84 'War of the Pacific', a battle for control of both guano and mineral nitrates. Bolivia still grieves for the resulting loss of her Atacama coastline; landlocked for well over a century, she nevertheless retains a 5,000 strong navy and a yearning for the sea. Guano imperialism also drove the USA to seize nearly a hundred islands and rocks to ensure direct supplies of the fertiliser for her own citizens. But the guano rush was as short-lived as a gold rush and after fifty years Peru's principal export was depleted and the country had squandered most of her profits on waging war. In the 20th century desert nitrates and artificial fertilisers took over, but sustainable supplies of sea bird and bat guano are back on the market today.

Thomas tells us what it was like for the workers:

> The guano filled up a large chasm in the mountains and though thousands of tons had been taken away there seemed to have been little impression made on the vast quarry. Two hundred Spaniards were constantly employed working at this bed of fine dust and filling it into bags which were then sent on board... Christmas Day came and as the Spaniards did not work we were set to lighten the ship by discharging the ballast of stones... On New Years day also the Spaniards did not work but we did and precious hard work it was too sending the guano aft to the men... Only fancy a strong fine powder like Scotch snuff getting into your eyes nose and mouth and you working in the dark hold of the ship the hatchways blocked up and the thermometer at 150 farenheit. We did all we could to exclude the powder from our mouths and noses by tying them up but then it was so hot we could hardly breathe and what with perspiration and guano dust we looked like red men.

> On 14th January 1845, heavy laden with four hundred tons of Guano, we unmoored and left Pacya and now hurrah we're homeward bound.

In Valparaiso Thomas narrowly avoided death by stabbing when caught up in a drunken riot, but there were further dangers ahead.

> The weather grew colder [he writes] and we learnt it was the Captains intention to take the ship through the Straights of Magellan as, from her heavy lading and leaky state, she was considered too cranky to stand the Cape gales.

They entered the Straits on the 13th of March, had a brief exchange with a boatful of Tierra del Fuegans, and after battling yet more gales and hailstorms reached Port Famine, with its colony of Chileans 'sent there', writes Thomas, 'to protect stray seamen wrecked on that wild coast, the southernmost point of South America. The Chileans live in a fort on the top of a hill in a most wretched state and in constant fear of the wild Patagonians or Horse Indians as they call them.' The *Ganges* ran aground in a gale several times before managing to anchor off the port, and all hands were relieved when next morning they got away intact and 'turned the corner from the west to the east side of South America.

'When we got to Cape Gregory,' writes Thomas, 'the Captain went ashore to bargain with the Patagonians for some skins. However as soon as the boat touched shore two English missionaries came down to meet us and asked the Captain to give them a passage to England as they stated their lives were in danger from the natives and the Chilean Government had ordered them to leave the coast.' At risk to their own lives, Thomas and other crew ferried the missionaries in turbulent seas and got them aboard the *Ganges*, only to be almost wrecked on a reef thanks to misguided advice by one of the missionaries, a retired naval captain.

> Our two passengers [writes Thomas] were Captain Gardiner R N and Mr Hunt. The first an old invalid looking man who merely accompanied Mr Hunt to see him settled, whilst the latter was as little suited for the arduous undertaking he had been sent out for as it was possible to be. Had he been sent to the South Seas he might have lived and dreamt of conversion and written home glowing accounts of his labours.
>
> After we had left the Straights little occurred to vary our daily routine of employment. When we crossed the Line we fell in with a Glasgow ship laden with Guano and as she sailed faster than us Captain Gardiner went on board of her leaving Mr Hunt to remain with us.

And there Thomas thought he had taken leave for good of Gardiner, naval captain turned missionary. But not only did he hear news of him by chance years later, but so did I even more surprisingly over a century and a half later.

In Thomas's case the news came seven years after this voyage. He added a marginal note to the 1845 Journal entry quoted above. It reads: 'The melancholy fate of this enthusiast Captain will he found mentioned in my journal of 1852. He made a second expedition to establish a mission in the same neighbourhood and the whole party perish'd miserably by starvation.' Turn to the 1852 Journal and you find Thomas commenting on an article he has just read when the ship he's travelling in from Calcutta to London is given some out-of-date newspapers by a passing ship:

July 6th 1852. The first newspaper that I took up was the Times of April 29th and my eye was caught by a column headed 'The Patagonian Mission'. Glancing down I saw something about Captain A. Gardiner R.N. – this old gentleman was one of the two miserable fellows we picked up on our way through the Straits of Megellan, they having found themselves in such danger from the natives and the climate that they were glad to get away at any price even though they had to rough it out on the guano. I should have thought their experience would have cooled their ardour most effectively... but it appears there is no fool like an old fool for I find that Captain Gardiner with six companions landed on Picton Island about the close of the year 1850. From the first they were worried by the natives who chased them backward and forward from the little island to that of Tierra del Fuego. About the middle of April Captain G begins notes in his journal that the provisions are getting low... the scurvy breaks out, they are half drowned in a cave by the rising of the tide and after a succession of disasters while day after lingering day they look out for the arrival of an expected provision ship that never comes one after the other dies from starvation. The Captain was the last to die, on September 6th according to a faint note in his journal that was discovered in the cave by a ship that finally came that way four months later. They say the old man showed great devotion to the cause and fill up the columns of the Times with praise. But what think you of the misdirected zeal of an old man who leaves his family to go on such an expedition? Could he find no scope for his energetic philanthropy in the length and breadth of Great Britain or in the Colonies or our great Indian Empire? But alas such missions are dull, for the missionaries there never serve as side dishes in a cannibal feast or die of starvation in Patagonia.

Glencairn ran up the stairs to my study one morning in 2003. 'You won't believe what's just come in the post' he declared. It was a long letter from the former vicar of our local church, Tony Gardiner. He and his wife Nancy had become friends of ours during his tenure there, before they retired to New Zealand. The letter said: 'We thought you might be interested in our recent trip to South America where we were thrilled to accomplish our aim of getting to Spaniard Harbour, east of the Beagle Channel in Tierra del Fuego, where my great-great-grandfather, Captain Allen Gardiner, died as a missionary'. Not just interested, we were amazed by another coincidence. The letter described how local coastguards took Tony and Nancy on board the *Canal Beagle* through rough seas to seek out the cave where Tony's ancestor had secreted his diary on a ledge above the corpses of his companions before dying on the rocky seashore. The coastguards had managed to locate the actual cave and the Gardiners had had time to wade in and out of it before, typically, a storm closed in.

Imagine Tony's astonishment when I told him that not only did I know about the exploits of his foolhardy ancestor, but that I had a firsthand account of his dramatic rescue on his previous madcap mission. After he read Thomas's story this was Tony's comment: 'I think Thomas would not have had much in common with Allen Gardiner except a love of the sea. AG was not of the same tolerant disposition being a zealous Evangelical with his mind fixed on saving souls... I am not at all offended by Thomas's opinions – in fact I enjoyed them!'

Tony suggested I seek out a rare book by E. Lucas Bridges called *Uttermost Part of the Earth*. It turned out that Glencairn had bought the book in Chile in the 1950s and still had his copy. One can only wonder – in the 21st century – at the blinkered piety of 19th century missionaries. The author, son of a missionary, declares: 'Captain Gardiner's plans were followed as closely as possible through trials and disasters to a successful conclusion. Though I am well aware that within less than a century the Fuegians as a race have become almost extinct, I deliberately use the word "successful".' I wonder if Darwin would have considered the extinction of a people for the sake of religion to be 'successful'.

The following year I met the explorer Robin Hanbury-Tenison. Over dinner he happened to relate how a single remark in a lecture on Patagonia, given jointly at the Royal Geographical Society by Bruce Chatwin and Paul Theroux, had sent him rushing to the British Museum. Chatwin had mentioned that the way of life of the now extinct Fuegian race was poignantly evoked in their language, preserved in a single hand-written document, a Yamana – English Dictionary. (The Yamana, or Yaghans, were the Fuegian group whose territory included all the southern islands as far as Cape Horn.) It had been compiled by Bridges' father in the 1870s, and later been lost twice in Europe in each of the two World Wars. Yet twice it had miraculously resurfaced, the second time long after the family had given up all hope of its survival. It had been hidden in a kitchen cupboard during the blitzing of Hamburg. The dictionary finally reached the British Museum, where Robin (a founder of the charity 'Survival International', dedicated to supporting threatened peoples) had been moved to hold in his hands the fragile testimony to a vanished race.

Reading the rich language of over 32,000 words spoken by these 'savages', who were flourishing at the most southerly extreme of the globe when Thomas passed that way, conjures fragments of their lives. They had, for example, at least five different words each for 'snow' and for 'beach', but single words for such activities as: 'coming on a hard substance when eating something soft' (e.g. a pearl in a mussel); 'to be lying down picking over mussels'; 'to get out of one canoe and into another while on the water'; and even 'to pay a formal visit as a wizard'.

11. The Ghosts of Crackenthorpe

I am like a tree,
From my top boughs I can see
The footprints that led up to me.

(*Here*, R S Thomas)

'Last night I dreamt I went to Crackenthorpe again.'

With growing excitement Glencairn and I travelled through the hills and dales of Yorkshire into present-day Cumbria, until we could see the Lake District mountains pastel blue in the distance. I had located the tiny village called Crackenthorpe, but headed first to nearby Appleby-in-Westmorland, an ancient royal borough and county town of Westmorland until Cumbria swallowed up the county in 1974. Staff at the information office advised me to contact the local genealogist to find out about Crackenthorpe's big house and its former inhabitants. I returned to our car and dialled the number they had just given me. The phone was answered at once: 'Fiona Thwaytes here,' said the voice. I briefly outlined my mission. She corrected me at once. 'You mean Machell,' (pronounced 'Maychell') she said. Until then I had been mispronouncing the name, which I had never come across in the south, to rhyme with 'satchel'. 'The house and family have a fascinating history,' she continued, 'that I happen to be researching at the moment because of a recent Will that's being contested. I'm going out shortly but could see you now if you're able to come at once.' When I asked for directions her flat turned out to be directly above the bay we were parked in; looking up, I could see her at her window talking to me on the phone. This was a good start. A minute later we were shaking hands with Fiona Thwaytes and her husband, called Lance, like Thomas's brother. They led us to a table that, like a miracle, was covered in 'Machell of Crackenthorpe' documents and family trees, and filled us in on background to the family, the house and its recent owners.

Crackenthorpe village, two miles from Appleby, lies north of the A66, a hectic main road whose construction severed the umbilical cord that previously linked the village with its big house to the south, Crackenthorpe Hall. The Hall now lurks in isolation, its drive leading off the defunct original road. Letting curiosity overcome courtesy I opened the peeling white-painted gate and drove slowly between forlorn stone pillars, down the drive and down the centuries. Stately copper beech, limes and evergreen oaks guarded the house. Bushes were overgrown, dozens of rabbits lolloped across unmown lawns, and when we pulled up in front of the neglected façade of the oldest part of the house and stepped from the car the raucous cawing of the crows that gave it its name (krakr, a crow, thorp, a hamlet) matched the eerie atmosphere. (I later learnt that they are in fact rooks and their noisy rookery expands each year.)

The owners appeared from a wing of the house and I allayed their suspicion of our intrusion by explaining my unusual quest, though it would take further visits over the years to gain their trust and become friends. It was quite a surprise to learn we almost shared the surname, Balfour (Glencairn's

Jenny outside Crackenthorpe Hall, the Machell ancestral home near Appleby-in-Westmorland in Cumbria in northern England, 2002.

family name before the Paul was tacked on). A reclusive couple, they told us they had bought the house because it was remote and neglected.

We were not invited inside the house, but the Balfours let us wander through the old Georgian stable yard with its weeds and cobbles, and down through dank overgrown woodland to the lazy brown river below. The stillness was so dense the house and its grounds seemed encased in cotton wool.

We were hemmed in by Machell ghosts from more than a thousand years, so no wonder the air was crowded. The pedigree of Machells of Crackenthorpe stretches back in an unbroken line as far as almost any in Britain. It seems fitting that the first on the family tree, Halthe le Machel, chose a wife called Eve to share his meadows on the banks of the Eden. This was in the 12th century, during the reign of Henry the First. Today the Eden remains a Paradise, with fish rising and oystercatchers swooping low over the water as it curves gently downstream between the fells of the Lake District to meld with other rivers in Solway Firth.

It wasn't so peaceful in the Middle Ages when the Scots kept launching raids from the north. This explains the fortified pele towers and castles that dot the area. The Emperor Hadrian had already built his wall for the same reason and his soldiers made camps at Crackenthorpe, leaving traces both tangible and intangible. This is why our Thomas's namesake known as Thomas 'The Antiquary' (born in 1647) – Thomas A from now on – and other family members plausibly believed the Machells to be of Roman stock. Thomas A explains all this in his own hand in records now held in Carlisle, so the Thwaytes had told us.

Carlisle's archives are held in the town's splendid redstone mediaeval castle. When the librarian brought five fat volumes written by Thomas A to the table where Glencairn and I were waiting, our hearts both leapt and sank. The writing was close-packed and almost illegible. Too much genealogy can be indigestible, and Thomas A was a fanatic. He seemed to have left no reference unexamined in his determination to 'prove' that the mediaeval Machells (Mauchell/le Machel) were descended from a late Roman centurion called Malus Catalus who stayed at Kirkby Thore fort in the 5th century AD. If so, this also gave the family kinship with Richard the Lionheart's famous Vice-Chancellor, Roger Malus Catulus, who drowned with the royal seal around his neck in a shipwreck during the King's conquest of Cyprus in 1191.

We had already chosen a farmhouse at Bridge End near Kirkby Thore village, two miles west of Crackenthorpe, to lodge in that very first night of the ancestral search, almost a year after meeting Thomas. We knew the house was in the Machell's patch but not, as we soon discovered, that past Machells had actually lived in it. This is not so surprising though, since the family was based in the area for so many centuries.

On our second visit to the ancestral seat the following year, the Balfours showed us round both parts of the house. Already mentioned in Domesday, the old manor evolved over the centuries with major Tudor remodelling of the mediaeval house in 1685 and subsequent Restoration and Georgian alterations. With the construction of the Victorian half of the house the entire building became known as Crackenthorpe Hall. Both houses have links to royalty as well as numerous ghosts, one a legendary troublemaker.

The Tudor house, with its stucco and red sandstone façade crumbling at the seams, has an air of mystery reinforced by two main windows being boarded up. Of its earlier manifestations, at least one house was burnt in a Scottish raid. The present bricks and mortar owe much to Thomas A's avant-garde designs for his elder brother, some of which feature in his Carlisle manuscript. Thomas A made sure the Machell coat of arms in the north gable wall was framed between two Roman altarpieces. Entering the dark Jacobean entrance hall we see another reminder of his obsession: the words Malus Catulus carved in stone in a fireplace surround, accompanied, of course, by the eternally prancing greyhounds. A memorial stained glass window by the front door reminds us that while Roman forebears died on England's foreign soil, a millennium and a half later English Machells lost their lives on Europe's soil.

The wide staircase made of ancient black bog oak leads up to a narrow one where you find the wooden beams and irregular walls of the older mediaeval house. On the third floor we join the former maids. Think of all the Machells and their servants who climbed up and down these old staircases over the centuries, the women and children soft in dainty shoes, men noisy in heavy leather boots.

I picture Thomas at Etton's polished rectory table, so engrossed in his family's history that the old manor appears in his dreams, sometimes sunlit and filled with people, at others swathed in mist, its restless ghosts in the half-lit trees beckoning him to follow them into the woods.

The worn boards of the manor's dark corridor on its main bedroom floor hold a patina of family tales, including those of the most famous guest, King Henry VI. The Machells gave him refuge following the Lancastrian defeat by the Yorkists in the Wars of the Roses battle of Hexham in 1464.

The panelled main bedroom is still known as the King's Bedchamber. Naturally it has a four-poster bed, but its famous carved Elizabethan one, still called the 'Crackenthorpe bed' and one of Britain's finest, now belongs to London's Victoria and Albert Museum. It is on loan to 16th century Oakwell Hall in West Yorkshire, a house immortalised as Fieldhead in Charlotte Bronte's novel *Shirley*.

One window in the gloomy King's Bedchamber overlooks a sad, fern-filled sunken garden known as the 'King's Garden' ever since Henry VI was disguised as a gardener while in hiding. The facing window, however, is one of the two blocked by a false wall, the other being on the floor below. Why were these windows boarded up? This is where the ghost comes in – or doesn't.

The ghost is of Peg (Elizabeth) Sleddal, who married Thomas's great-great-great-great grandfather Lancelot to become mistress of Crackenthorpe Manor during Cromwell's time. The Machells were determined Royalists and Lancelot caused a stir by refusing to become Mayor of Appleby until the restoration of the monarchy, when his first public act was to cut to pieces Cromwell's town charter. Lancelot died peacefully in 1681 but his Will

A 17th century manuscript of family history written by Thomas Machell, known as 'The Antiquary'.

caused havoc. It is said that its terms upset Peg so much that after her own death nearly two decades later her vengeful ghost began to haunt both house and family. The 'Grey Lady of Crackenthorpe', as her apparition became known, grew so troublesome that her corpse was exhumed from its grave in the churchyard's consecrated ground and reburied in the River Eden below the Manor when water levels were low. The Catholic priests recruited to conduct the exorcism, because Latin was considered most effective, decreed that Peg should remain in her watery grave for nine hundred and ninety-nine years and only be allowed to roam once a year. The new burial was covered by a large granite boulder, still known as Peg's Stone, hauled there all the way from Shap in the Lake District. Since then there have been many sightings of the Grey Lady, risen from the riverbed to haunt the King's Bedchamber or to weep beneath an old oak tree known as Sleddle's oak, her tears said to predict misfortune for the Machell household, notably the deaths of family heads. Sometimes, when the September Helm winds blow down from the Pennines, she appears on the old Crackenthorpe road in her carriage pulled by six black horses. At the end of the 18th century Brockham Dick of the Elephant Inn, keeper of the tollgate, reported seeing not just the carriage and horses galloping right through the closed gates but also the coachman in a three-cornered hat and large black boots, with shrieking attendants on horseback. A much later sighting (and there have been others since) was by a convalescent soldier during World War I who saw Peg's ghostly carriage career down the road with torches ablaze before it plunged into the woods near the house. This spot is marked on local maps as Peg Sleddle's Trough. Some older residents of Crackenthorpe village still refer to the autumnal howling of the Helm winds as Peg having a tantrum.

So this is why no one has removed the false walls said to have been put up to prevent Peg's ghost from entering those rooms, though I thought that a characteristic of ghosts was that they could pass through walls. Even the Balfours, who dared to remove the block from the top floor (it would surely be beneath Peg to haunt a maid's bedroom) left the main ones in place, just in case.

It was in Kirkby Thore's 12th century church of St Michael's that Thomas A left the biggest legacy, apart from his dense tomes in Carlisle. The parish was lucky to have him as Rector from 1677, when he turned 30. An Oxford College Dean and Chaplain to both King Charles II and James II, he was following in the footsteps of an earlier Machell, known as 'the Divine', who was Chaplain to James I. Thomas A, a Fellow of the Royal Society as well as a keen artist, antiquarian and historian, was the most famous incumbent of what was then a large and lively parish. Today Kirkby Thore village is dead quiet. When you enter the churchyard nothing stirs save rabbits nibbling around tilting gravestones shaded by huge trees that almost block the views of Westmorland's distant hills and dales in their faded mauves and fawns. Alas, the church doors are now locked against vandals, sending a visitor on a hunt for keys. Once inside, the first thing to see, in the main aisle beneath the splendid early 16th century ceiling, is the large stone font donated by Thomas A. Around its sides prance the three greyhounds in the family shield. Thomas A also provided the richly carved dark oak pulpit, probably the altar, and certainly the altar rail, whose inscription is an act of defiance more durable than his father's destruction of Cromwell's charter. The Latin reads, in translation: 'Given in the thirty-fifth year of Charles II.' The monarch didn't reign that long, but Thomas A airbrushed the Commonwealth years and counted the King's reign from the execution of Charles I. In 1698 Thomas A was buried in the church chancel. We do not know what he thought of his mother Peg's fury over the Will, and as she died after him he didn't have to deal with her difficult ghost. His own ghost seems happy to stay put. Or was it waiting benignly for the last visit I paid to the village before I completed this book?

This time, another September nine years after my first visit with Glencairn, I was travelling with my mother to visit Glencairn's brother in Scotland. We made a detour past Crackenthorpe and still had miles to go before we slept. I filled the car with fuel and re-joined the rush hour traffic on the busy main road linking the east and west motorways of northern England. After a minute I saw a sign to Kirkby Thore and said to my mother: 'I'll just make a quick loop through the village to show you Thomas Machell Senior's church.'

I turned right through a gap between speeding lorries. Seconds later the car stalled in the middle of the empty road entering the village. The engine was dead and I realised I had filled its near-empty tank with petrol instead of diesel. Luckily I could freewheel the car back to the kerb. I tried to ring for help but there was no mobile phone signal. So I followed an alleyway and chose to knock on the door of the fifth cottage, where the owners, just back from holiday, let us use their phone and later fixed for us to spend the night in the holiday cottage next door. When the rescue man arrived after dark and heard how we would have come to a sudden halt on the notorious main road had I not impulsively turned off to the village, he said to me: 'Someone was looking after you this evening'. 'I know,' I replied.

Next morning I paid a visit to the familiar church in hazy sunshine, the fells beyond blurring into sky. All was quiet, save crows circling above like a subset of those down the road at Crackenthorpe. I walked up the rough path to the porch in the footsteps of Thomas A, and 'my' Thomas. Inside the church, empty of the living, soft sunlight was grazing the pews. I sank to my knees and said out aloud to the silence: 'Thank you, thank you, Thomases both.'

I soon gave up hunting for older gravestones, the friability of the local pink sandstone having made the inscriptions unreadable, rendering the occupants twice ghostly. Sometimes a few words are legible if you squint at them sideways, which sounds like a metaphor for my search for Thomas's final years.

Some Machell gravestones are in Appleby-in-Westmorland, whose famous castle on a hill above a loop in the Eden is glimpsed from the manor's bedroom windows. Thomas's forbears walked or rode the two miles to town through the river's water meadows. Many Machells were Appleby mayors, or involved in church affairs there. The town is so little changed that it is easy to imagine them strolling up its broad main street, stopping to chat with local townsfolk about fishing and markets, taxes, wars and the weather. Easy, too, to imagine the thrill of market days and the annual horse fair, one of Europe's largest. Gypsies since 1685 have been gathering at Appleby to barter horses washed in the river near the town's ancient bridge and hold trotting races on the old Roman road. All this would have formed Thomas's childhood memories had the family fortunes not gone haywire by the time he came along. He would have gone to Appleby's school, championed by Thomas A, and fidgeted and shivered through services in the 12th century church of St Lawrence at the bottom of town, where the road makes a right angle to cross the river by the bowling green. The church has the oldest working organ in England but its stained glass window with Machell arms has vanished.

Climb up the town's steep pavements, in autumn enjoying the hiss of brittle leaves crumbling underfoot, and you will pass former coaching inns and almshouses en route to St Michael's mediaeval church near the top, where the east window also contained Machell arms. Though the church is now deconsecrated, the sight of chancel windows hung with lacy curtains and a four-by-four vehicle parked near the porch looks surreal. Its gravestones are ignominiously propped up against the walls, the Machell ones presumably among them, but unreadable.

Five miles of country lanes with expansive northern views lead to the village of Great Asby. Here too the Machell gravestones are indecipherable in St Peter's churchyard, but if you cross the dry stream bed, known as a 'gill', that divides the village you can raise a glass to the Machells in the village pub, named 'The Three Greyhounds' after their family arms. You cannot miss the three large painted models of hounds guarding its entrance.

A single night at the gambling table shattered the family in 1786. Is it axiomatic that all posh families have one bad penny who squanders all the family pennies? For the Machells it was one of their Lancelots. This one was born in 1741. He lost a bet to Lord Lonsdale of nearby Lowther Castle and put the estate up for sale to pay it.

Christopher Machell, Thomas's grandfather, was far from Crackenthorpe on that catastrophic night. Imagine how devastated he felt when he broke the seal and read the letter brought to him by a relay of riders and runners. The letter announced that his bachelor elder brother was about to sell the entire ancestral estate to settle his gambling debts, with no right of refusal to Christopher, who was next in line and expecting to inherit it. Christopher wrote a desperate letter to Lancelot, offering to repurchase at least part of the property, but it was to no avail and the sale went ahead.

Christopher could hardly have been more different from the rakish Lancelot. Tall and valiant, he had served in the American Revolutionary War, losing his left arm in the Battle of Bunker's Hill. Later he became Lt Colonel of Hull Volunteers and deputy lieutenant of Yorkshire's East Riding. But he wasn't just a soldier and public servant. Like his great-grandfather Thomas A, he had many interests and talents, including art, music and botany. Having lost Crackenthorpe, he and his descendants were soon making new Machell imprints in Hull and Beverley. You would think there would be a mass of Machell offspring issuing from at least some of his seven siblings, but four died in infancy and the only other who married had no issue. So it was up to Christopher's own five sons to produce heirs. When the four eldest of these didn't marry he must have feared that the Crackenthorpe Machell lineage was fated to be lost like the estate. However, by the time he died in 1827, his last hope, Thomas's father Robert, had married and produced three sons, though one had died as a baby. This left Richard and Thomas, the latter, as we know, being considered a bit of a runt.

The first person you meet on entering Crackenthorpe's Victorian house is Grandfather Christopher. Admittedly he is only in a large self-portrait, but at least he is back where he belongs. He portrays himself with a book and spectacles on his lap, his armless sleeve pinned up just as we see in our own family pictures of Glencairn's father, who likewise lost his left arm in a foreign war.

The portrait of Christopher was put there by Thomas's little brother James, who was only three when Thomas left home and showed no signs in his youth of being the one who would restore the family pride. Indeed, how would any of Robert's children ever have that kind of wealth?

'So run that ye shall obtain': this biblical quotation (I Corinthians 9.24) is the Machell family motto. The preceding sentence is: 'Know ye not that they which run in a race run all, but one receiveth the prize'. James took the Apostle Paul's words more literally than intended, because it was by running horses and receiving the prize that he obtained what the family desired.

James Octavius was born in 1837, Robert and Eliza's eighth son, as the name reflects. By then they had surely despaired of having daughters, but in the next four years they managed four, though as we have seen, two of them died in infancy. Two boys also died in childhood, but James was tough and athletic, always up to pranks, coming home from sorties in the countryside with grazed knees, bruised elbows and a mouthful of fibs. Keen to follow in his grandfather's footsteps, he joined the army at sixteen, hoping to see active service in the Crimea. Had he done so, the fate of Crackenthorpe would have been very different.

James, disappointed to have missed the action, was posted to Ireland by the Army when almost 19. Penniless apart from his army pay, he soon discovered an exceptional talent for betting on almost anything, including jumping over billiard tables and onto mantelpieces, and he also developed an acute eye for horses. Betting gains enabled him to buy three horses that were soon winning Irish races. Leaving Ireland and the Army at 25 after a characteristic clash with his Colonel, he moved to Newmarket with three horses, only one of which was decent, and little cash. But that soon changed. The following year, 1864, he ran, as a nobody, his best horse in an important race, backing it at odds of 50 to 1, and beat all the favourites to earn £11,325 of winnings and prize money (almost a million pounds today).

Over the next decades horses owned, managed and/or trained by James (known in Newmarket as 'The Captain') won all the major races of the day. It was only when I sought him out in Newmarket and Aintree that I learnt just how significant he was to the racing fraternity. (At Aintree's racing museum James's name is the only one to feature four times on the mahogany board that names owners and trainers of Grand National winners.) Obituaries described him as a 'sporting celebrity', the most famous racehorse trainer and owner of his age. In 1877, aged 40, he used his fortune and influence to repurchase Crackenthorpe from the Lonsdales. It's ironic that this reversal of fortune was thanks to inheriting his great-uncle's gambling genes, and turning them to advantage against the Lonsdales themselves.

Restoring the Tudor house wasn't enough for James. He built onto its west side a grand Victorian house and an additional wing. Going into the large new entrance hall from the Tudor hall, as originally conceived, you would meet the Colonel centre stage. His portrait, incorporated into a large carved wooden fireplace surround, supervises the original billiard table that is lit from above by an oval glass dome. Turn left and you find the enormous drawing room, with its carved marble fireplace, ornate plaster friezes, chandeliers and a raised platform at the far end embraced by a large bay window. Next door is the dining room with Italianate embossed faux leather wall panels in red and gold. Climb up the elegant wide staircase with its carved oak banisters to the landing. From here you enter large airy bedrooms and bathrooms that still have roll top iron baths with claw feet and, in one case, a throne-like mahogany lavatory. Through the main bedroom window look down at the sandstone terraces designed for strolling and admiring views (since obscured by trees) over parkland and down to the river whose fishing rights go with the house.

All was well, and all manner of things would have been well, had it not been for World War I.

James never married. You would think having seven brothers would mean plenty of nephews and nieces; but of the brothers who reached adulthood, it seems that apart from Robert Scott, who had one son in New Zealand, only the eldest, Richard Beverley, had children. James selected his nephew, Percy Wilfred, Richard Beverley's fifth son, as his most worthy successor.

By the time Percy inherited the house he had had a distinguished career, including service in the Nile Expeditionary Force, much action as a *bimbashi* in Sudan in the 1880s and 90s, and almost ten years as adviser to the Egyptian Ministry of the Interior under Lord Cromer. His numerous medals and other memorabilia are now on display in the Carlisle military museum. In his forties he crowned his career by marrying royalty. This late love-match would have thrilled the Royalist Machell ghosts and astounded

Thomas. Percy's bride, the Princess and Countess (later Lady) Victoria Alice Leopoldine Ada Laura Gleichen, youngest daughter of Prince Victor of Hohenlohe-Langeburg and Lady Laura Wilhemina Seymour, was named after her great aunt and godmother, Queen Victoria (Prince Victor being the Queen's half nephew). So, having housed a King in the 15th century, the Machells of Crackenthorpe gained proper royal links by this perhaps unlikely marriage. The sumptuous wedding of Percy and Valda (as she was known) in 1905 was held in the royal chapel of St James' Palace and attended by the King, Edward VII, and numerous other royals, many German. The following year the couple's happiness seemed complete when, in her fortieth year, Valda gave birth to their only child, Roger.

The Countess, used to the sophisticated cities of Europe, took to Crackenthorpe because of her beloved Percy's devotion to what he described as 'the place I love most in the world'. When in residence, she imposed her aristocratic standards, insisting, for example, that the village maids changed her satin sheets daily. The house came alive with distinguished visitors, not least Valda's brother Lord Edward Gleichen and her talented artist sisters, Feodora and Helena. Valda herself, a singer and former pupil of Dolmetsch, filled the house with music. But in less than a decade the shadow of World War I descended dark as the Crackenthorpe crows over the soul of the family, the house and Britain itself.

In 1913 Percy was already in his fifties and had seen more than enough action to have earned his retirement as rural squire. However, loyalty to country prevailed when the fifth Earl Lonsdale, seven years older than Percy, persuaded him to join Kitchener's New Army and take command of a new battalion. On the Carlisle racecourse Percy turned a ragtag group of civilians into a disciplined border regiment of over a thousand soldiers. Leaving his German wife to manage Crackenthorpe, he marched the Lonsdales to France at the end of 1915 to fight the army of Valda's native country. His diaries record his pride in his men and his concern about conditions in the trenches. He knew their task at the Battle of the Somme on 1st July 1916 was ambitious. In his final instructions to his Officers that morning, he wrote: 'If it goes badly, I shall come up and see it through.' It did go badly, with many Lonsdales killed in the first push. Percy honoured his word and moved forward. He was shot in the head while leading his remaining men over the top into No-Man's Land. In that one day nearly two-thirds of the battalion and most of the officers were killed.

Valda was of course heartbroken. To commemorate Percy's violent death she privately published a full account of the actions of the Lonsdale regiment, based on his wartime records, personally inscribing almost two thousand copies and presenting one to every family with a member who had served under her late husband's command. Next to the front door of the Tudor manor she installed that memorial stained glass window. Offered a grace and favour residence in St James's Palace, next door to the Prince of Wales, she retreated with her grief to widowhood in London.

Little Roger, meanwhile, was often alone, aged eight, at Crackenthorpe in the 'care' of a nanny who turned out to be cruel. Just imagine being a fatherless solitary child incarcerated in the nursery wing of a shuttered, cold and melancholy house in an echo of *Turn of the Screw*. Dispatch to Eton was his eventual escape from those horrors.

In 1928 Valda sold the house and estate. On the family's forced departure in the late 18th century, the place fell asleep under the Lonsdale Earls of Lowther, who used the land for farming and sport but neglected the old manor. Since Valda sold the house there have been three owners, but it has often been left in charge of caretakers, used mainly for its farmland and fishing holidays – the Luxmores, owners before the Balfours, even called it their 'fishing cottage'. Their male guests would perch in the spartan house while their wives lodged in more comfortable local hotels.

The Balfours, who sold the house in 2014, didn't live in the main house either. In 1997 they found it little changed since World War I. The Georgian stable block was filled with paraphernalia from a lost age: mouldy carriage tack hooked over curved mahogany horse stalls, old hip baths, trunks with rusting hinges, and leaky cell batteries from the early days of electricity. Within the house paintwork was peeling back and wiring and plumbing dated to Machell occupation. The grounds were so overgrown that the summerhouse and greenhouses were buried in creepers and ivy, terraces and steps blanketed in grass, the King's sunken garden choked with ferns and the fountain dry-eyed. The Balfours slowly tamed the grounds and modernised the house enough to let out for holidays while still keeping its character. Were Thomas to visit today, he would feel at home in both the Tudor house and his young brother's flamboyant addition. The Balfours live in the nursery wing. Often empty and shuttered, the main house seems cheerless, devoid of families, laughter, tantrums and dogs. You can tell when a building is fully inhabited; it is like a person comfortable in his or her clothes. With only crows to disturb the peace, Crackenthorpe is still waiting.

Since Thomas was excluded from Crackenthorpe Manor during his lifetime and died before the Hall was built, I felt we were exploring the house together. I dreamt of sleeping under its roof and even of discovering mementos of Thomas in the network of attics beneath that roof. I imagined having a book launch there if I completed this book, but fretted that by then the house would no longer be available to rent, or my own circumstances would have changed. Then, early in 2002, I happened to ask the Balfours what kind of people rented the house. They mentioned various categories, ending with 'people with important birthdays such as fiftieth ones'. That was the trigger. I hired the manor and hall, which between them sleep thirty, for an extravagant weekend party with family and friends. My real birthday is in late winter so I copied the Queen and had an official one in mid-summer.

The weekend was magical. We seemed to cast a collective spell over Crackenthorpe Hall that weekend, as if resurrecting its Victorian heyday. The house embraced us when we returned from picnics and dawn outings to Hadrian's Wall. The click of billiard balls in the hall punctuated the murmur of conversation and passionate sounds of cello sonatas in the drawing room next door. One evening we dressed for dinner in an eccentric collection of Victorian costumes, the ladies taking hours fashioning ringlets and squeezing themselves into crinolines and taffeta gowns. All except me. I dressed as Thomas, of course, in floppy-sleeved shirt and shabby velvet breeches, wearing a wig beneath a ridiculous Colonial hat. After a dinner lit by ivy-wrapped purple candles, we entertained each other in the drawing room with readings of Tennyson and Walter Scott, drama performances and classical music. Valda had been the last singer to entertain guests there. That was before the First World War. When the Balfours entered the room they were spellbound to find it resonating with Schubert lieder as it would have been then, though this time the singer was nurseryman Graham Gough in frockcoat and sideburns fashioned from sheep's wool picked up on Hadrian's Wall.

At three in the morning we broke the Victorian spell by rolling up the enormous drawing room carpet so that my godson, Will Dalton, now dressed in street gear instead of scarlet military fancy dress, could dazzle us with a display of urban break-dancing backed by loud rap music on a modern ghetto-blaster. I doubt Grandfather Christopher Machell next door in the billiard hall approved of that. But I hope Thomas was laughing.

12. Into the Eye of the Wind

For no reason I can think of, I've wandered far astray.
And that is how I got to where I find myself today.

(*The Indispensable Calvin and Hobbes*, Bill Waterson)

Thomas, at home and unemployed, having abandoned his planned career in the Merchant Navy, had also messed up his love life and caused upset with his provocative opinions. When he embarked on his next voyage overseas I bet there was relief all round.

'September 13th 1845,' he writes, 'found me once again on board ship, but this time returning East, bound for Madras and Calcutta, on the good ship Earl of Hardwicke, Captn James Drew. But it was not until I had dressed and sprung on deck in answer to the well known Boatswain's pipe and hoarse cry of "All hands up anchor" that I remembered I was no longer a sailor but now a passenger.' The Earl of Hardwicke was a famous ship, designed for steam as well as for sail. However, when steam proved unsuccessful her paddle wheels were removed and she reverted to full sail. Thomas's sketch plan of the ship includes the defunct funnel. At a time when 1,000 tons was the maximum size of a ship, she was large at 852 tons. But what would Thomas think of my last voyage in his footsteps, on a 60 thousand ton vessel?

His journey had its share of tragedies – men overboard or injured in the rigging. There were plenty of storms too, both meteorological and of the argumentative kind that arise when too many people are confined with too little to do. 'A large ship is a little world full of envyings jalousies and groundless bickerings,' writes Thomas. He filled his days by sketching, writing and curing sea bird carcasses.

'The bells were ringing for church when I boarded the Worcester,' recalls Thomas of his first sea voyage, perhaps echoing Coleridge's famous poem, where the bells ring for marriage. Was Thomas, like the Ancient Mariner, destined for a restless wandering life and a compulsion to tell his tale, a mantle I would shoulder? His killing of an albatross seems shocking today, even if his motives were well intentioned, and he questions his hobby of preserving birds and animals for his home-made 'museum' when he is on his next voyage to India in 1849 and the ship is becalmed in blazing heat. He writes: 'I begin to think I am doomed like the Ancient Mariner who shot the albatross. The skins of my victims are all round me and the head of one with its mouth wide open hangs gasping over the edge of my cot as if reproaching me for bringing him from the stormy south to be frizzled to parchment in this terrible ocean.'

For now though, his wandering life is about to take a new direction. Remember how he vowed, as the *Worcester* sailed away from the Calcutta ghats in April 1843, never again to set foot in the city? Well now we find him, at New Year 1846, about to do just that, and even about to find a familiar face from the Opium War days that he thought he would never see again.

Thomas admitted back in 1843 to shedding a tear on saying goodbye to his friend Mason. I didn't tell you that he later added a note in the margin of that journal entry: 'Met Mason again in Calcutta when I went out in the Earl of Hardwicke. He was then master of the Barque Prince Regent.' Now, on 7th January 1846, you find a lively Journal account of the partying that celebrated this unforeseen reunion as soon as he arrived and found the Prince Regent lying off Chandpool Ghat. After much drinking and smoking of cheroots and manilas, Thomas stays on board 'to be worried almost out of my senses by Cockroaches and Mosquitoes,' he says, 'for like all ships in these hot lattitudes she was swarming with them and besides these I found she was also a nest of centipedes and scorpions. However,' he continues, 'I am one who has learnt to put up with such trifles and prefer a hearty welcome in poor quarters rather than the best of everything without a friendship.'

It is all very well to party on arrival, but there is a living to be earned. 'On landing in Calcutta,' writes Thomas, 'I intended to look for employment on board the country ships, but having a letter of introduction from Sir James Hogg to his brother I was by him introduced to the partners of Cockerall and Co House and expressing an interest in Indigo planting I was recommended to Mr James Forlong then Managing Superintendent of the Bengal Indigo Company. A fortnight passed before I received from him the long wished for order to proceed to my new destination, Patakabaree Factory, Moorshedabad, one of the Company's estates on the banks of the river Jellingee. I was about to quit seafaring life and try my hand at life in the jungle.'

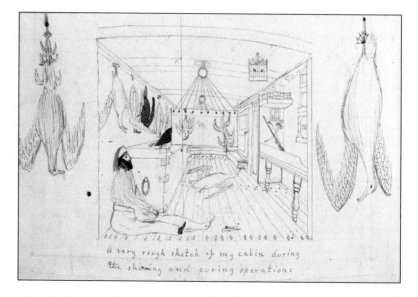

Thomas's sketch of himself in his cabin on the Rajah, *skinning and curing sea birds for his 'museum' in the family home at Etton village near Beverley. He was returning, as a passenger, to Calcutta from Liverpool in 1849.*

13. Singing the Blues

Me the Sea-captain loved, the River built,
Wealth sought and Kings adventured life to hold.
Hail England! I am Asia – Power on silt,
Death in my hands, but Gold!

(*The Song of the Cities (Calcutta)*, Kipling)

Thomas owes his indigo career to a letter from Sir James Hogg while I owe mine to a revered dyer and fabric hand-printer, the late Susan Bosence. She was already in her later sixties when I, still in my twenties, became her quasi apprentice. Looking back, I see she was mentor as well as friend and teacher. With a Quaker background, she achieved a 'work-life balance' long before 'lifestyle' concepts became magazine clichés. My life, on the other hand, usually borders on chaos barely held at bay. A perfectionist at work and a devoted mother of four, Susan nevertheless found time for letter writing, gardening, music and entertaining. Turn up for tea and you would be offered home-made bread, spread with a sweet emerald-coloured paste made from her own mint leaves; imagine the smell of yeast blended with fresh mint. Her husband, Bo, would enter the kitchen in a battered straw hat, music score in one hand and a trug of rare potatoes in the other, like an advert for the 'Good Life'. In summer the family retreated to a simple village house in the French Pyrenees long before the practise became *de rigueur* for the English bourgeoisie.

Susan relished nature's rich colours and soon infected me with her particular love for indigo. I inherited not only her habit of inviting friends to share summer indigo dyeing sessions, but also, later, her special indigo dye vat, in whose mysterious depths my journey had begun. (Though had fate not already led me to share my life with Glencairn, the indigo journey – which led to Thomas – would never have started.)

Susan had a collection of indigo-blue cloths from around the world that she fingered for inspiration, and when she learnt of indigo's demise in the Orient, she sent me there like her carrier pigeon, to gather information in places she couldn't visit herself.

The first place was Yemen in 1983. I had joined Glencairn when he travelled there to organise an unusual Exeter University conference on what was then a divided country, the Republican North and Marxist South. Few people travelled to this storybook land then and when we mentioned our destination to one friend, she asked, 'Is that somewhere in Wales?' Nowadays Yemen is often in the news, for the wrong reason.

During that first visit we saw few craft industries, but for the conference I displayed exhibits supplied by the Yemeni embassy, including an exotic dress of burnished indigo cloth embroidered with silver thread, and photographs of indigo dye shops, which I learnt had been common in many towns before north Yemen modernised after the 1964 Revolution. In the small town of Zabid, I was told, the number of indigo workshops had dwindled in 20 years from over a hundred to just two. As soon as I mentioned this to Susan when she came to see the show, she turned to me and said: 'You'll have to go back to Yemen as soon as possible and record its indigo traditions, Jenny.'

'But I know almost nothing either about indigo or about Yemen,' I protested.

'So who else do you know who's interested in indigo and has travelled in Yemen?' was her riposte. 'Such traditions need to be recorded – and if they aren't, there can never be revivals in the future.'

I could see the point of making historical records but could not envisage future revivals.

'Anyway, I can't afford to go back there,' I objected next.

'How about applying for a grant?' suggested Susan.

I laughed. 'Who on earth would give a grant to an unknown mother with young children who's doing textile dyeing in Devon? I don't even have a postgraduate degree.' (Not that that was a *sine qua non* back then.)

'How about writing to the Elmgrant Trust for funding?'

Within days I received a reply from the Chairman of the Trustees enclosing a cheque for the cost of carrying out indigo research in Yemen. I was astonished, and now had no choice but to go. I phoned Susan. 'That's wonderful – well done indeed she said. Many years later, after her death, I learnt that it was she who had advised the Elmgrant Trust to support me.

Maybe even Susan didn't know what a life path she was steering me into but her prediction of future revivals worldwide has proved spot on.

Later that year I flew back to Sana'a, Yemen's capital, fabled for its whitewashed mud brick buildings with honey-coloured alabaster windowpanes and archaic plumbing. Soon I was clutching the seat of a 'service taxi' as a driver high on masticated narcotic *qat* leaves drove erratically down seven thousand feet of hairpin bends to the Red Sea coastal Tihamah plain. In clammy heat in the ancient town of Zabid, I followed a narrow dirt alley between courtyard houses of brick patterned like fabric blocks, pushed open a carved wooden door and stepped into a fabulous forest of blue cloths dripping over huge clay pots filled with pungent indigo. A man in skullcap and stained loincloth was wringing out a length of newly dyed calico over one of the pots and from a dark corner I heard a sound of rhythmic pounding. Weaving towards it through dripping cloths I found two men naked to the waist, taut muscles gleaming like polished mahogany as they hammered away with heavy wooden mallets at folded lengths of dyed cloth. Beside them were the results of their labour; tall stacks of deep purplish-blue cloth with the same coppery sheen as on the dress that had magnetised me in the exhibition. I learnt that indigo production like this had been practised in Yemen since biblical times and that Bayt 'Abud was one of the last surviving workshops in southern Arabia. Hitherto nobody had made a record because the industry had been taken for granted, indigo-dyed garments having been as ubiquitous as today's blue jeans throughout Asia for hundreds of years, until well into the 20th century.

Spurred on by Susan and, to my surprise, by some historians of the Middle East, I was soon doing more fieldwork in the Arab world, often with Glencairn as translator and companion. We shared meals, stories and laughter with fellow dyers and their families in the mountains of Oman, Syrian Aleppo and Damascus, the eastern desert oases of Egypt, and east-west across North Africa and south to Mauritania. Back home I was still dyeing and teaching with no plans to write a book on indigo, unlike Thomas who was preparing his back in the 1850s: '27 November, 1854. At present I am gathering all my forces to write on Indigo planters,' he tells us. However, I somehow ended up doing a PhD that became a book on 'Indigo in the Arab World' and led to a commission by the British Museum Press for a book on Indigo worldwide. Now I had to travel further afield – what a hardship – to such places as south-west China, Tokushima Island in Japan, the Dogon cliffs of Mali near Timbuktu, and back to India for the first time since a teenager. Sometimes our children, Finella and Hamish, came along too. My long-suffering family overdosed on indigo. Friends who knew of my childhood yearning to travel off the beaten track assumed I had chosen indigo as an excuse. But in fact indigo had chosen me.

Though I was trying to move on from indigo when I met Thomas, it is too tightly woven into our joint lives ever to be disentangled.

It is February 1846 and Thomas is about to leave Calcutta and head for the first time into Bengal's jungles.

> I proceeded to hire a boat and lay in a stock of provisions and next morning my boat was alongside and the Captain and Doctor accompanied me on a cruise up the river to see the country and the Towns on the banks of the Hoogly. After three days I parted with my good friends and proceeded alone, soon entering the Jellingee River and passing Kishenaghur. After three more weary days we stuck fast on a sand bank three miles below Patakabaree, the factory to which I was going. Accordingly I unloaded the boat and sent my traps off in a hackery, or native bullock cart, and in the cool of the evening set off to walk along the river bank to Patakabaree. The whole country from the mouth of the river upwards has no variety at all – a dead level partly cultivated with rice tobacco and Indigo, some parts covered with low rank vegetation and some covered with swamp or 'bheels' as they are called, which are plentiful with Snipe, Florican, quails Teal ducks and other small game whilst the dry jungle is frequented by deer antelope Buffaloes wild Hogs jackals panthers and such like animals. Occasionally you see a great beast of an alligator lying on the mudbanks sunning himself until he is disturbed and scrambles off into the river. It is remarkable that the natives seem to have no fear of these brutes for every morning you see the banks lined with bathers who daily perform their ablutions. Nevertheless we occasionally hear of some unlucky creature being whipped off by these villainous brutes and from the first moment I saw one I swore to wage mortal war with the whole race.

'How do you Sair' said a sallow-faced gentleman with long black hair and snow-white dress as I walked up to the house at Patakabaree. 'How do you sair are you walk all way from Ballee? I did not knew you to have arrive till jost now or I should have moch plesaire to send you one orse for ride.' Monsieur Verplough the manager of Patakabaree was the gentleman who thus addressed me as, followed by a crowd of native servants, he advanced to welcome me to his house where I was to reside with him until initiated into the mysteries of Indigo planting. He was a Frenchman but had resided all his life in India and although he spoke Hindoostani and Bengali like a native he had seen so little European society that I doubt if his French was not as bad as his English.

We entered the house together and in a large Cool room sat down to an excellent dinner whilst the waving punkah kept a constant breeze over our heads. After dinner we lighted our cheroots and kept up a desultory conversation until nine o'clock when Mr Verplough showed me into a large comfortable bedroom and wished me goodnight. Two servants proceeded to offer their services to undress me which much to their surprise I declined... the newness of my situation the constant whirring and buzzing of insects the melancholy howl of the jackals and loud croaking of frogs kept me long watching and it seemed as if I had not dozed half an hour when I was roused by the dusky form of a servant by my bed with a cup of coffee in his hand. 'Saheb pauch budyah his Caffee lijah' (five o'clock Sir I have brought your coffee) – Mr Verplough is already up and away on horseback.

At nine Mr Verplough returned and after breakfast and a cigar the Factory clerks came to show their accounts, make their reports and receive orders. at noon we retir'd to bathe and change and at one met to Tiffin a very good meal similar to our hot luncheon after which we retired again to our rooms to doze read and pass the time until five when we sallied out for a stroll round the vats followed by a long tail of Factory clerks with whom Mr Verplough kept up a constant conversation in Bengali and Hindoostani. Occasionally he was met by some Ryot who had a complaint to lay before him this he soon settled and continued his stroll. At seven we went in and Mr Verlough played the Piano till eight... Then dinner came then another smoke till nine o'clock and then once more Goodnight.

Here comes the illustration on display in the British Library in 1999 whose short caption, which included the word 'indigo', led me to Thomas. Choosing the unusual perspective of the *punkah wallah*'s viewpoint, with the *punkah* rope bisecting the page, Thomas portrays himself and Verplough in profile, tilted back on their chairs with their legs crossed on the table top, and smoking cigars while the *punkah* swings over their heads. Verplough's music is propped on the square piano in the corner of the room. A century and a half later, I shall be looking for that room.

The organisation of the indigo industry that was so commercially important in Thomas's day was complicated. Around 500 planters in Lower Bengal, which produced the best quality dye, managed 143 'concerns'. Each 'concern' ran four or five 'factories', which in turn had several out-factories, all with indigo-producing units. A proprietor normally owned and managed just one or two 'concerns' but notable exceptions were Hills and White and the Bengal Indigo Company. The most influential managers in Lower Bengal, each responsible for thousands of workers and large investments in land and infrastructure, were James Forlong and Robert Larmour. The two men could hardly have differed more. Lamour was a more typical harsh master, whereas Forlong was known – and sometimes criticised – for his liberal attitudes and philanthropy. In 1832 he had started out as an assistant planter but within four years was running Mulnath (Hills and White in those days) with its forty thousand acres under indigo cultivation. He built a large mansion, surrounded by deer-filled parkland, which became Thomas's refuge, and also built the only hospital for miles around, free to all estate workers and run by an Indian doctor whose training he funded, as well as establishing English and Bengali schools in the main factories, financed by planters' subscriptions. Thomas lacked means and power to emulate Forlong, but when properly settled in Bengal he managed to establish a school before fate intervened and moved him on again.

Indigo, the world's only natural blue dye, has a unique and curious chemistry. Until it is processed, its colour is invisible in the green leaves of certain plant species in many different countries – woad and a particular knotweed, for example, in temperate climates, Indigofera in the heat of India and former colonial plantations. In mediaeval Europe, Japan and West Africa, composted leaves were supplied to dyers; but for durability and long-distance trade the dyestuff was extracted from the leaves by a process that involved soaking them and adding oxygen to the resulting liquid. This created a clay-like paste that dried into hard blocks of insoluble dye pigment. The chemical transformations are so extraordinary to witness they seem like alchemy. In Bengal they were carried out on a vast scale in a series of tanks, or vats as Thomas calls them. He was fascinated by the whole scene:

At last the preparations for the great indigo manufacturing business commenced at Patakabaree and everybody began to bestir himself. Labourers (or Coolies as we call them) came trooping into the factory, carts and boatswain were looked up in all quarters and put in order for the coming business. The vats were washed out the Chinese pumps were erected the pressing frames repaired and finally all the workmen having arrived a couple of goats were given to them with which they performed the ceremony of striking off their heads and sprinkling the blood on the Vats which were about to be opened. They then sat down and soon had the animals cut up dressed and eaten.

Presently we heard the creaking and the rumbling of the hackeries, loaded with indigo plants, the shouts and songs of the drivers, the shrill cries of the women and children and the restless clanking of the Chinese pumps. The whole factory presented a scene unlike anything I had ever seen before.

Women and children flung sheafs of green indigo plants into the vats which were carefully and quickly stowed by the noisy coolies the gratings spread over them and hove tight down by means of stout cross beams and iron pins and then as each vat was filled the reservoir sluice was opened and the water rushed in down narrow channels, but long before the last vat was filled the sun had disappeared in a red twilight glow. Illuminated by the light of many Torches, the busy night scene was truly beautiful, the dusky figures of the labourers and Torch bearers the groups of Women enveloped from head to foot in their white Cloths looking like groups of spectres gliding amongst the dark trees, whilst here and there were dotted about the tall figures of the Burkandanses with their crimson Turbans and sashes their swords under their arms and shields on their backs oxen carts with their vociferous drivers kept up a constant bustle, scattered in every direction were numerous little fires with dusky figures moving about them preparing the evening meal and at the end of the vats contemplating the busy scene stood the colossal figure of old Mooty the Elephant quietly fanning himself.

… as the first streaks of dawn appeared there was a sound of wooden mallets hammering at huge wooden plugs and then a rush of orange coloured water pouring in to the lower vats. It is from this fermented Indigo juice that the dye is made by the dark skinned sons of India – the dye which may colour the purple robes of royalty or the blue coat of the charity boy, the fair forms of our northern beauties or the dark uniforms of the British soldier. This is the dye for the sailors blue jacket and labourers Sunday coat – a tide golden to those who far from here know not and care not for the toil and groanings of the thousands whose lives are spent in one long struggle of want and toil for the benefit of those who know not even of their existence.

First the coolies flung out the plant from the steeping vats and then one after another dropped into the beating vats into which the golden water was let off from the steeping vats now commenced the work of the day for to and fro round and round those men up to their waists in liquid now dark green stir these pools with their sticks now they worked it into waves now it foamed like a huge washing tub full of lather again you looked and blue streaks were seen on that lather and so they worked on now in silence now breaking out into wild chants until the water turned to a dark inky blue – now the white plate was brought and we saw how the small indigo grains had formed… it was done and the purple skinned coolies emerged at last from their redolent bath. And so it goes on until the whole manufacturing season passes away when things are all put away pumps unrigg'd Vats clean'd and the manufacturing closed for the year.

It was during this busy season that we had the second visit of Mr Forlong the managing director and great was the adulation paid to this Burrah Saheb and I found he was well worthy of it for I have never met a more benevolent man. To the natives he was a kind and generous master and to the Europeans a hospitable and amiable friend.

After the indigo manufacturing was completed the river flooded the lands and the roads became almost impassable. During the rainy season the higher lands not flooded are much infested with snakes some of them very venomous especially the Cobra di Capello or hooded snake whose bite is certain death.

The monotony of my life at his time was only occasionally relieved by the visits we exchanged with our two neighbours but at best my residence at Patkabaree was a dull business and I longed for the time when I should be appointed to take charge of a Factory of my own. At last in October 1846 a Letter arrived from Mr Forlong desiring Mr Bush to move down to a factory on the Eshamuttee river called Bajainghant, Mr Snadden to be promoted to Ramnaghur and Mr Machell to take charge at Ballee!

Fellow planters sometimes dropped by Ballee factory and there were occasional trips to towns such as Jessore, today a backwater in Bangladesh but in Thomas's time a typical modest hub of Raj administration offering a racecourse, clubhouse, billiards, missionary societies and the rest. In between was solitude. Some planters went pig sticking, many turned to drink. Thomas wrote his Journal.

He tried to make the most of things, with his genuine curiosity and wish to entertain his reader, but admits to low moods: 'A Planter's life is not without its cares and troubles. Fancy me playing the magistrate at twenty two with fractious natives... there are anxieties about the indigo cultivation and manufacture, about lawsuits and private affairs and there are long weary days and nights passed for weeks and months utterly alone. A great deal of this misery I escaped by applying myself to studying Oriental languages and litterature but in spite of this there were many long hours passed when overcome by languor and ill health I was unable to fix my attention on my studies.'

Thomas expects to remain at Ballee for up to two years, but within months, just as he is unpacking the furniture he has bought at Christmas in Calcutta, he is posted to Babadanga, because a fellow planter has just died of drink. In his new post Thomas, now the old hand, oversees the sowing and subsequent manufacture of indigo in its twenty-four pairs of vats, and looks after a further three factories. His district of Nadia-Jessore produced the highest quality indigo. He appends to his Journal newspaper cuttings and information on the organisation and economics of the Bengal Indigo Company, its directors and shareholders (among them two members of the influential Tagore family), factories and their production. The textile industries of Europe and America were consuming vast quantities of indigo to dye the clothing of most working people (hence 'blue collar worker') and service uniforms, both military and civilian ('hospital blue', 'navy blue'). Even humble laundry needed 'washing blue', and all this dye came from cultivated indigo plants until its synthetic equivalent appeared on the market at the beginning of the 20th century. Synthetic indigo is mainly used today to meet the world's annual demand for over a billion pairs of blue jeans.

In the mid-19th century four-fifths of world supplies of indigo came from those hundreds of factories in Bengal that were established following

Robert Clive's victory at the 1757 Battle of Plassey (after which the East India Company virtually ruled India for the next century). Before long the Company was promoting indigo as a commercial product, using expertise gained on the slave plantations of the West Indies and southern States of America, whose own indigo trade was disrupted by the American Revolution (1775-83), Britain's loss of her colonies and the abolition of the slave trade. Bengal's fertile land provided the prefect replacement and there were plenty of workers to coerce. Though the Company handed direct control of the factories to private planters in 1802, most indigo exports were channelled through its 'agency houses'. By 1815 3,500 tons of Bengali indigo (valued then at six shillings a pound) were being exported annually through Calcutta but this had risen to several thousand tons, half the value of all the city's exports (raw cotton and the Company's vital monopoly of opium for its China trade being its main rivals) when Thomas became eye-witness during indigo's peak years (1834-47).

Indigo was, however, a volatile commodity, creating fortunes when demand was high and dramatic falls in profit when excessive speculation caused over-production. And, as Thomas often reminds us, the vagaries of the Monsoon season could also ruin a harvest. He went on leave at an opportune time.

14. Kissing the Crescent and the Cross

I always went the wrong way round the maypole as a kid.
'O why she says, 'did I not wait to see what others did?'
Lady, a poet married you because you danced there so.
Your own way round the maypole is the only way to go.

(*The Only Way*, Robert Nye, from *The Rain and the Glass*)

In January 1974 a teaching job I had lined up in Tokyo had just fallen through, and with it my plans to travel there on the trans-Siberian railway. I was desperately disappointed and wondering how to get east again when my father spotted a tiny advert in *The Times*: 'Interesting job in warm agreeable country. Applicant must be a graduate with wide interests and a driving licence'. Eighteen words that would change my life – quite a lot considering that a single word would later change it again. The intriguing advert turned out to have been placed by Her Majesty's widowed ambassador to Jordan, who later admitted to leaving out the country's name from the advert because Jordan had just suffered the '73 Arab-Israeli war and he thought this would put people off. The job was for 'Social Secretary'. I had no idea what it meant, which was just as well because I had no qualifications for it; I couldn't type, arrange flowers, do menus or make small talk, and knew nothing about foreign policy, Arab or otherwise. Furthermore, the idea of diplomatic life was anathema to a quasi hippy.

I dressed carefully for the interview, in a fashionable black trouser suit with scarlet flowery blouse and clumpy shoes. My long hair hung loose and I wore huge silver hoops in my ears. I thought I looked rather good. My future boss, Glencairn Balfour Paul, told me much later (as did my mother, 30 years too late) that he thought my outfit dreadful. What is more, when he visited my family home my African grey parrot, perched on his shoulder, defecated down the back of his Savile Row jacket and we were too cowardly to point it out. Yet despite all this, and my obvious lack of qualifications, he offered me the job, mainly because he admired my italic handwriting. I admired an ambassador who made me laugh.

Soon after my arrival in Amman I discovered Glencairn was a poet who could mesmerise a room with a lecture on Auden. What happened next? Reader, I married him, thereby attaining the preposterous position of youngest British ambassador's wife. I was no doubt considered a dreadful upstart in diplomatic circles but at the time youthful ignorance was indeed bliss.

In Thomas's life Arabia comes to him in late 1847. 'I think I hear you say what has a voyage from Calcutta to Muscat to do with coming home this I will proceed to explain' he says, anticipating our question. He has spent a week investigating English homebound ships, finding prices high due to freight loads, and is considering travelling back to England overland instead when he has a chance encounter:

> One morning as I was strolling down to the river side to look again at the English shipping a guttural voice sounded in my ears and I found myself addressed by an Arab shipmaster who imagined from my redundant beard that I must be one of the true Believers so we had some little conversation during which it struck me that by taking a passage in an Arab vessel I should have a good opportunity of becoming more intimately acquainted with the Language and manners of the Arabs and from some Arabian port I might succeed in getting on to Suez and thence by way of Alexandria to England No sooner had I settled this point than I acted on it and forthwith went on board some of the Arab vessels lying in the River.

> The Customs house Officer informed me that the Arab Barque Hamoody had just gone down the river and was then off Garden Reach. I accordingly set off for the house of Gokal Dhoss a wealthy Bamian, owner of the craft. After wandering through a long succession of narrow lanes in the native part of town I passed through a broken down archway into a large courtyard filled with Bales and goods of all description and found the Bamian seated in his office surrounded by Arab and Indian Sailors, Merchants, Nacodas, Captains, Jews, Persians, and Malabaris.

Thomas has to be quick, for the *Hamoody* is sailing on the next tide. It will be an adventure, so he books a passage on the spot and rushes off to pack his traps and say goodbye to his 'Anglo Indian friends'.

'Homeward bound once more, Farewell Calcutta,' writes Tom. As he is rowed downriver in an 'eight-oared Beaulio' towards the *Hamoody*, the sun sets red over the city. He watches the last rays 'with a parting glance gleam on the lofty spires and minarets, kissing at once the Crescent and the Cross'. A metaphor for him, but also for us.

Arabian *dhows* are not designed like British ships, but first impressions are good. Next morning, Tom writes:

> I came alongside the Hamoody off Diamond Harbour. She was a snug looking little craft about 400 tons with a poop and topgallant forecastle. I took possession of the Starboard after cabin and the Nacodah had the Larboard berth. As soon as I had slung my cot and stowed my chest I came on deck and found the Pilot Leadsman and Custom house Officer on board... We entered into conversation and all of them spoke Hindi fluently and were very friendly with the Arabs and the crew who were a set of cheerful manly looking young fellows... The night before our Pilot

Thomas's sketch of the crew of the Arab merchant dhow, Hamoody, *performing an Islamic devotional ceremony,* zikr, *on the deck at the start of the passage from Calcutta to Muscat in 1847.*

left us they performed the Zikr, a sort of sacred chant. The men ranged themselves along the deck with a basin of Frankincense burning before them and opposite to them knelt three or four crew who were leaders of the Chant... one of the wildest chants and most fearful scenes I have ever witnessed.'

His watercolour of this scene is a delight.

Tom will be travelling as an Arab merchant for the next five months, adopting the alias Sheikh Abdullah al Hajji, and taken by strangers for an Arab throughout the journey. His chosen outfit clearly went down much better than mine for the job interview.

'I had previously determined to go the whole hog as was necessary if I wished to become acquainted thoroughly with these people... I therefore laid aside the European dress and appear'd on deck to their great delight a la Mogul in an oriental dress; my beard had grown to the proper length and many were the highflown compliments of the Arabs on the improvement in my personal appearance.' Thomas, always conscious of his 'puny' physique, is enormously proud of his dark beard, an excellent attribute in Muslim company.

Being fair-haired and female, how I envy his ability to travel incognito all over the Islamic world – I would have to be imprisoned in a full burqa to do likewise, and to borrow his fluency in Arabic and Hindi.

While the *Hamoody* makes her lumbering way south down the Coromandel Coast, Thomas passes the time sketching his shipmates. Over the bubbling, 'Gunjar' filled hookah, there's much exchange of views on religion. 'The Arabic Bible that Uncle Christopher gave me is now in great use,' he writes. 'The Arabs who take us for a set of Kafirs or infidels were quite surprised when I show'd it to them as our Koran and evince much curiosity about it. One of the party reads it and the rest sit round him and occasionally interrupt with interesting remarks which are on the whole far from unfavourable.'

They were much surprised when it came out that I drank no wine for their ideas of the English Character are taken only from the Sailors and other loose characters they see rolling about the streets of Calcutta...

Thomas has to defend Christian habits deplored by his shipmates, such as eating pork and not performing devotions. 'You may now form some idea of how I get on with these people,' he tells us. 'I never attack their religion on the contrary I always express a desire to become better acquainted with it. I do not think a missionary could do any good with these sort of men for the mere knowledge that a man is a missionary is enough to raise suspicion and close the hearts of the people against him... I am not at all desirous of making converts (though the old man is trying to convert me to the Deir el Islam) but I think a little information on our Religion Habits and Customs must serve to enlighten them and convey a more favourable opinion of our nation.'

Thomas is negotiating the Koran while the *Hamoody* negotiates treacherous waters around Ceylon's Point Galle to swing north up the Malabar Coast. She makes first landfall since leaving Calcutta at Alleppy (Aleppuhza today), south of Cochin.

> The Old Nacoda asked me to go ashore with him. At first I was reluctant as I did not feel inclined to show off my strange attire however my desire to see the place determined me and so tightening my Cummerbund slinging my sabre and adjusting my turban I got over the side into the boat and away we went... As soon as we landed on the sandy beach an Old Arab dressed in a long red gown advanced and welcomed me in the Persian Language supposing me to be a Mogul and the Supercargo of the ship... We all proceeded up to the town. I felt rather bashful as I passed the first English gentleman I had seen since I assumed the Oriental dress but was relieved to hear him remark that I was a fierce looking dog.

Thomas describes the town, from the inland waterways knows as 'backwaters' that famously link the Keralan hinterland, to the variety of products made from coconut trees. As always, in the bazaar he is 'much delighted by the costumes and particularities of many varieties of the Oriental race including Bamian merchants in crimson turbans whose descendents, many with the surname of Patel, I would later meet. Among the almost cartoon-like sketches in the Journal's margins we find a 'Portuguese Dandy' and a 'Ben Israeli'. He spends the night in the agent's house with 'a party of merchants and officers from other Arab ships in the harbour.' 'I did not speak much,' says Tom, 'because I was indulging my fancy of observing the countenances and characteristics of the group who surrounded me.' He sketches the house, lamps, hookah and even himself asleep, a lump under a rug on a veranda beneath the stars.

When the *Hamoody* sails away again Tom writes: 'The mountains visible from the sea cannot be very far distant and must afford a delightful retreat for the panting European during the hot season.' In a future century one panting European would venture into those hills just because of him.

Troops of elephants were hauling away at timbers when Thomas was in Alleppy and were still doing so in 2001 when Glencairn and I arrived there by ubiquitous Ambassador taxi. When we walked up the dusty main street in midday torpor it had the stifled feel of a ghost town. Like most of these spice ports, it has slunk into obscurity like a dog into shade, today being known only for the manufacture of umbrellas. Tom's narrow 'backwater' still runs beside the main street, though 'run' is a misnomer since it is so clogged with water hyacinth you can almost walk on it.

I crossed a small bridge over a side canal and came to a sudden standstill. There in front of me was the merchant's house where Thomas stayed, hardly changed since his day, its roof still tiled in terracotta and the latticed wooden shutters in place, though askew. My sweat tingled as I stared at it in the heat, testing the centuries, unable to move. Then I followed Thomas up onto the shady veranda and down into the deserted dark interior jammed with coir mats and ropes, sacks of ginger and pepper, grimy packets of sugar, hanging lamps and rusty tins of coconut oil. It even smelt of 1847.

Thomas considered Cochin harbour one of the finest he had seen and went sightseeing in the town. In the same month as him I absorbed echoes and atmosphere lingering on in this still exotic spice town, whose activity he lyrically depicts, not least when he makes a sortie by canoe, passing through the shipyards in 'the Wapping of this harbour' and the great Bazaar until he reaches 'Jewstown'. Here he finds 'a long street neatly whitewashed illuminated from one end to the other with hundreds of little lights set in niches in the walls and in front a door is open from which issues a stream of brilliant light and strong Hebrew voices chanting the service of the synagogue.'

All was quiet when Glencairn and I approached the whitewashed porch of this Cochin synagogue. There could be no chanting congregation because only one Jewish family remained. But the interior, care-taken by a Hindu family, was exactly as Thomas describes, with porcelain blue and white tiled floor, brass chandeliers and a 'venetianed' gallery for the women. Indeed the entire whitewashed street, though too quiet, felt ageless.

Close your eyes in the nearby market and breathe the spices of India into your nostrils. Then open them, peer into old warehouse courtyards and you will see pyramids of peppercorns and coir sacks stuffed with spices piled onto the large square platforms of antique scales. Ignore the mopeds, go to Fort Cochin and back-pedal several centuries to the churchyard where Vasco da Gama was originally buried, his remains later taken home to Portugal (the tombstone is now inside the old church, where heavy satin punkahs still fan the pews). Continue up the street to see the last of the Chinese fishing nets rise and fall in the water's edge like giant praying mantises. They are leftovers from the days when the great Chinese fleet of 1421 'discovered' and mapped the world almost a century before European explorers got there. We can connect with all these pasts as well as with Thomas.

At last, on 22nd December, the Arabian headland of Ras el Hed is sighted, but the ship is becalmed and off-course. Tom is grumpy on Christmas Eve but at last a breeze springs up and the *Hamoody* makes Muscat harbour. During the long voyage from Calcutta he has got on well with the crew, but grown sick of the skipper and is ready for a change. He has, however become close friends with Razumea, the First Mate.

Once ashore, Thomas keeps up his oriental disguise, enjoying an English officer's surprise when this long-bearded Arab suddenly addresses him in perfect English. Thomas is impressed by Muscat, sketching the harbour around three sides of a page. When I went there myself I wrote: 'Muscat must have been enchanting in the past but the old buildings are being bulldozed and replaced in a wink by hideous concrete villas.' 'I wandered about the place,' writes Tom, 'took a peep into the palace diwan where the Imam's son was holding court, had a look at the dilapidated forts and the place down which they pitch their criminals which smashes them to pieces, a Portuguese invention.' He notes the popularity of the Imam, 'who lives mainly in Zanzibar,' the well stocked bazaar and the importance of the port with its 'continual interchange of goods – Cloths, Rice and Spices from India and China Coffee Dates and Salt from Arabia Silks carpets tobacco and spices from Persia and also a great abundance of pearls from the Persian Gulf and slaves from the coast of Africa.'

I too enjoyed Oman and its people, and Thomas would be amused to hear why and how I was smuggled into Muscat in 1995. Keen to record Oman's last indigo dyers, I couldn't get the obligatory 'No Objection Certificate' to enter the country because I was a woman and my reason weird. However, I hitched a lift to next-door Sharjah when its Ruler's private plane flew to UK to fetch various Exeter University figures, including Glencairn, for a fund-raising trip to Oman. From Sharjah five members of the party got permission to enter Oman, and when they set off for Muscat, again on the Ruler's plane, I sneaked on board as stowaway. On arrival in Muscat I hung back in dark corners of the airport while the party whizzed off in shiny cars to see the Finance Minister. However, their meeting ended in a row, so the party retreated in a huff back to the waiting plane and immediately took off for Sharjah, abandoning me as a lost cause, which suited me fine. Though penniless, I found my way into Muscat city, cadged some funds, and made contact with Gigi Crocker, a weaver, living in Salalah, with whom I had been corresponding. She drove six hundred miles in her jeep to meet me in Nizwa oasis and we had a splendid adventure in the central desert and its Eden-like date gardens, with Gigi's Bedouin friends, Oman's last indigo dyers (one of whom has since staged a revival, Thomas and Susan Bosence please note) and of course the local djinns. I eventually returned to UK having borrowed money for the airfare from a trusting Omani banker. Tom would have applauded the reason for the trip and looking back the whole escapade had a Thomas-like edge.

He leaves Muscat on New Year's Eve 1847 in self-imposed discomfort. On learning that the wind is in the wrong direction for sailing north up the Persian Gulf he has decided instead 'to go round by the Red Sea'. He writes: 'I suppose we shall get to Suez in about two months "Inshallah". It will be a very interesting trip and I shall have a good opportunity to improve my Arabic.' He has just boarded a *baghla* type of *dhow* that he describes as 'a vile high-sterned antique looking craft that appeared to have been built on the model of everything that should be avoided.' He continues: 'The mosquitoes were very troublesome thanks to the dates with which the Futel Khair was partly loaded the rest of her cargo consisting of Tobacco from Shiraz and rugs and beautiful carpets from Bushire. She was so lumber'd up that there was not space for a fisherman's walk which as all the world knows is only "three strides and overboard". I moved my traps as close aft as possible (there was no place for me below decks) and as the night closed in I rolled myself up in my horse blanket and with my weapons at hand I lay down to sleep with one eye open and the other shut.'

On New Year's Day Thomas reflects prosily (for Father's benefit?) on the Eternal Verities, reminds Father how much he relies on their 'one-sided' conversations and reiterates his belief in the value of travel and exchange of views between European and Oriental to demolish prejudice and intolerance on both sides. Over the next few weeks, while the *dhow* is frequently becalmed off the desolate coastlines of southern Arabia, he has ample time to practice his Arabic and exchange ideas, though he admits to being baffled by certain Islamic beliefs.

He toasts Richard's birthday with a 'thimbleful of genuine Mocha' and says he is fishing and playing doctor with the only medicine he has with him. 'You would be much amused to see the gravity with which I examine my patients' tongues and feel their pulses looking very solemnly at my watch which doesn't go,' he writes. The next day's entry simply reads: 'fair wind and plenty of it and nothing to say.' This is unusual for our Thomas with his garrulous inner voice. Perhaps he's joined his shipmates whose 'general pastime,' he says, 'is sleep'.

The crew does rouse itself for a ceremony when at last the Bab el Mandeb Strait at the entrance to the Red Sea is spotted. By this time they have hugged the coasts of southern Arabia for weeks, by-passing such ports as Aden. Recently annexed by the British and nicknamed 'Gibraltar of the East', Thomas likens its forbidding fortifications to 'a clean row of teeth'. They didn't prevent the British being expelled in 1967.

Thomas didn't take to the Yemenis: 'The people appear to be a wild warlike race and are much dreaded by the Muscat Arabs,' he writes. My own trips to Yemen also had scary undertones never felt in Oman, not helped by car steerage as wayward as the *dhow*'s navigation. 'I am getting tired of this clumsy craft,' complains Thomas in mid January. 'My good friends get rather frightened as the wind and swell increases. The Arabs are smart fine-weather sailors but they don't like rough weather at all and their vessels will not stand it We had a jolly night of it and my drenched and shivering shipmates are all huddled together like a pack of sheep At daylight we hauled up for Mocha but the wind blew so stiff and the sea has risen so high that we missed it and are scudding away under a triangular sail now in hopes of catching Hodeida. I however hope we may miss it and run straight on to Jeddah.'

They don't miss it though, and on 18th January anchor off the town to find it in turmoil, the Sultan of Yemen waging civil war against its governor. Nevertheless, inquisitive Thomas arms himself and goes ashore, posing as a 'Persian durwish'. He is as unimpressed as we would later be. 'They tell me the interior is much better. I am well satisfied it cannot be worse,' he writes, and I annotated my copy of his journal with the comment: 'Hodeidah no nicer in 1989.' We spent a comfortless night there after visiting Zabid further down the coast, where the children had sped around its dusty streets on the back of a young man's motorbike while Glencairn and I talked indigo with the dyers. Hodeidah has none of Zabid's dozy charm. 'I returned to the boat glad to be clear of Hodeida,' writes Tom, and we felt the same as the local bus left the port to swing uphill to Sana'a around bend after bend, stopping at intervals so we could be sick in roadside bushes. My diary note says: 'Not an Easter Day to go down in the records.'

Tom goes on lurching up the coast of Yemen with alarms I can match with my own.

> Having left Hodeidah on 19th, we coasted to the Island of Kameran as Hodeidah is in such a disturbed state we could not take in water there. The island is a miserable place... with a fort to protect the pearl fisheries which they say are very plentiful here... Lightened the Bogolah at Loheia, a miserable town worse than Hodeidah, by sending ashore some bales of Canvas and Tobacco.

The Serang is knocked overboard but survives and many of the crew are ill. 'As for myself,' writes Tom, 'I am as well as ever and sleep as sound with my rug wrapped around me on the bare planks as many a man in England who luxuriates in clean sheets and a feather bed.' Famous last words, as the saying goes.

> *26th January*. Last night we had some very suspicious characters on board.

Thomas goes on to describe an encounter with pirates off Yemen's coast; the notion of pirates crossing my own path seemed unimaginable when I read this passage. After this the crew grapple the *Futel Khair* up the Red Sea for another fortnight to reach Jeddah. Thomas draws charts for the Navigator, swaps stories with his shipmates, and listens to the crew chanting Koranic stanzas for hours on end. Meanwhile the Nacoda fears the Turkish authorities might commandeer his *dhow*, since everyone is talking of war.

There are so many guns in Yemen today you would think it was still at war. Thomas finds them the main items of commerce, so there is no change there. The symbol of Yemeni virility, a horn-handled silver dagger flashing at the waist, is now paired with a Kalashnikov rifle slung over the shoulder. And a Kalashnikov bullet very nearly finished me off during an indigo research trip too far, both literally and metaphorically.

This was just after we had visited the hospitable dyers of Zabid. Assuming then that we would never reach South Yemen's Bayhan, we decided to visit

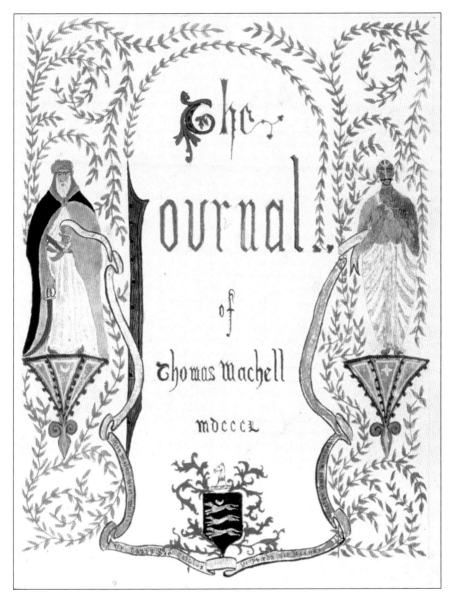

Illuminated frontispiece to Volume Two of Thomas's 1850 Journal. The Machell family crest with three greyhounds features at the bottom of the page.

On the hippy trail to India in 1970, attracting a crowd in the Persian desert.

Looking up at the the great statue of Buddha at Bamiyan, on the old silk road in the Hindu Kush mountains of Afghanistan. Created in 554 AD, it was the tallest standing Buddah statue in the world before it was blown up by the Taliban in 2001.

View over Bamiyan valley from the top of the head of the great Buddha statue.

Left: John Thomas (1795-1827), Lieut 8th Hussars, who fought in the Napoleonic battles of the Siege of Badajos and Waterloo.

Right: Christopher Machell (1747-1869) Thomas's grandfather, Major in the 15th Regiment of Foot, who lost his left arm at the battle of Bunker's Hill in the American Revolutionary War.

Left: Richard Beverley Machell (1823-1898) Thomas's elder brother, who was vicar of Barrow-on-Humber in North Lincolnshire and Canon of York, England.

Centre: Portrait of James Octavius Machell (1837-1902) in the County Gentleman magazine, May 29th 1880. Youngest of Thomas's brothers, he was a celebrated racehorse trainer and owner and repurchased the ancestral home of Crackenthorpe Manor in 1877, adding its grand new Hall.

Right: Lancelot (1829-64) one of Thomas's younger brothers, Captain in the Bengal Horse Artillery, who served with distinction in the Punjab and 'Indian Mutiny'.

Moana Vong, Tokoragi Maihea (right) and Papa Noeve (below) relaxing after a long day shifting cargo.

Three sad tikis *(powerful spirit statues) in Tahiti museum, far from their Marquesan* me'ae *(sacred ceremonial site) where their* mana *(spiritual power) remains.*

Jean-Claude Pahuatini, crane driver, on watch.

Jenny's sketches of members of the crew of Aranui II, *the cargo ship that sailed from Tahiti via the Tuamotu atolls to drop off and collect cargo in the Marquesas Islands, February 2001.*

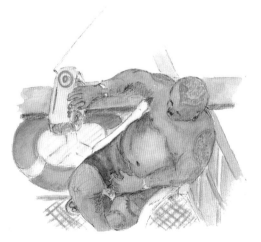

Papa Noeve taking a break after two weeks loading and unloading cargo in the Marquesas Islands.

Moana Vong from Fatu Hiva island, the only Marquesan among the Polynesian crew. He has warrior tattoos.

A handsome tattooed local man on the
Marquesan island of Ua Poa, Polynesia in 2001.

Jenny looking down over the bay of Taihoe on Nuku Hiva, main island of the northern group of the Marquesas in Polynesia. Thomas and Jenny both disembarked here from their respective cargo ships. Behind Jenny is the valley of the Tai Pi, formerly feared cannibals dramatised in Herman Melvilles' book Typee *(1846).*

Aranui II *rides at anchor while whaleboats unload drums of oil and collect copra (fermented coconut) in the Tuamoto Atolls en route to the Marquesas Islands in 2001. Moana Vong, crew member, is in the foreground.*

Illuminated letter 'P' painted by Thomas for the preface to his updated Volumes of Machell family history (inherited by David Wheeler from Roger Machell in the 1980s).

Thomas's painting of the south stained glass window installed in Etton church by his father Revd Robert Machell as a memorial to his fifth son Hugh Devon, who died at seventeen in 1850.

Thomas's Uncle Christopher Scott on the right, outside the family bank of Messrs Machell, Pease and Hoare in Beverley, East Riding of Yorkshire in northern England, shortly before it was rebuilt in 1861. In 1930 it became Barclay's bank.

Jenny revealing the double tombstone, covered over by grass in 2000, over the vault where Eliza Machell, Thomas's mother was interred.

Left: An undated sketch, in the family history compiled by Thomas, of the church at Great Asby, near Appleby-in-Westmorland in Cumbria, northern England, where members of the Machell family were vicars and were buried. The village pub still bears the name 'The Three Greyhounds', symbol of the Machells of Crackenthorpe.

Right: Great Asby church in 2002.

Left 1843 sketch, in the Machell family papers, of the north side of Etton Church near Beverley in the East Riding of Yorkshire, northern England, showing railings around the double tombstone covering the vault intended for Thomas's parents Eliza and Robert Machell, but in fact only used for Eliza's burial (and her teenaged son Hugh Devon and babies Kathleen Annie and Rosamund, according to a note in the family book).

Right: South side of Etton church in 2005.

An 18th century painting, in the family history compiled by Thomas, of the garden view of 'The Elms', the Georgian house – on North Bar Without, Beverley in the East Riding of Yorkshire – where Thomas spent his early childhood before the family moved to Etton village four miles away.

The front of 'The Elms', 2000.

*Thomas's sketches of men and women in indigo
clothing in southeast China, 1841–42.*

*Jenny's sketches of men and women in indigo
clothing in southwest China, 1993.*

Jenny's skecthes of small riverboats in southeast China, 1993.

Center: Thomas's sketch of a river boat in southern China, 1841.

Bottom: One of many sketches Thomas did of river boats in Bengal, 1850.

Jenny's sketch of Nanputuo Buddhist temple, founded in the Tang dynasty (618-907 AD), in Xiamen (formerly Amoy), China, 2000.

Abuse
Ruins Life
吸毒毁一生

$3.10 中國香港
HONG KONG, CHINA

Thomas Macheli esq,
% H. G. Balfour - Paul esq,
Uppincott Barton
Shobrooke
Crediton
DEVON   EX17   1BE
ENGLAND)

A postcard written to Thomas by Jenny in Hong Kong, 2000.

Xiamen (formerly Amoy) harbour on Taiwan Strait in 2000, taken by Jenny near the place where Thomas made a sketch in 1841 (see page 42) on the eve of battle in the 'First Opium War'.

Lieut-Colonel Percy Wilfred Machell (1908-1916) C.M.G., D.S.O, when Commanding officer of the XIth (Service) Battalion Border Regiment, departing from Cumbria in northern England for the trenches of World War One. His son Roger Victor (1908-1983) stands, in a replica uniform, on the step below his father. Roger was the last in the long line of Machells of Crackenthorpe in UK.

Crackenthorpe Hall near Appleby-in-Westmorland, Cumbria, in 2001, forlorn and unloved after Valda and Roger Machell sold the house in 1928.

The central hall and drawing room of Crackenthorpe Hall, painted by the late Anthony Harrison in 2002.

the remote border town of al-Baydah, where some Bayhani dyers were said to be practising their trade. To approach al-Baydah from the west meant a long drive though harsh mountains. Here is my bad-tempered report from al-Baydah jail:

Al Baydah dump, 8th Dec 1983. Glencairn and I are locked into a squalid cell at the top of the prison overlooking the main mosque in the middle of this surly town. It's in North Yemen at present but there's no proper border here, even on maps, and the town's changed sides several times. Took the early morning bus from Taiz to Dhamar, then squashed into a shared taxi for the rough five-hour slog here, where the road ends in a network of mountain tracks. Inter-country, inter-tribal and inter-family feuding is continuous round here, with many shoot-outs. When we stopped for a loo break I wasn't thrilled when one of the passengers shouldered his huge gun and aimed straight at me. My heart missed several beats when he pulled the trigger and hit a large boulder just beside me, shattering it to pieces. It was a relief to see the villain disarmed by the army on the outskirts of Al-Baydah. The Government guesthouse was full, but a hoary old man with a mouthful of gold teeth said we would be much safer lodging in this squalid jail. He

Thomas's sketch of himself in April 1848 embarking by camel from Suez to Cairo having spent over four months travelling with Muslim merchants aboard dhows *from Calcutta.*

may be right, because the young men here are overbearingly arrogant and we were pelted with stones and tin cans by a crowd of shouting children as we scrambled downhill to the dyers' houses. However, the dyers were welcoming and behind the scenes the women were, as always, jolly in their togetherness, rocking their babies and busy decorating their arms from shoulder to fingertip with henna and antimony.

With hindsight, my determination to visit every last indigo dyer in the Arab world seems absurdly obsessive, and an inner voice frequently whispered 'irresponsible mother'. On 10th December I admitted it was a relief to leave al-Baydah on the morning bus. Had Glencairn not come along as chaperone I might not have survived that trip.

However, I didn't die then and neither will Thomas on his Arabian jaunt, though he will soon think he is going to. Here he is in Jeddah at last. '*7th February 1848.* We anchored at sunset and early next morning I was guided up the Bazaar to call on the British Consul, Mr Ogilvie.' For the next ten days Thomas lodges on the floor of his humble house in the suq. Ogilvie, gone native after ten years in the country, has taken to the bottle, 'much to the horror of the pious Mohammedans who themselves get daily muddled with opium or hashish,' comments Tom, waspishly.

> Juddah is a notable town in Arabia [he writes] and has considerable trade with the various Red Sea and Persian ports and with India and China. It is governed or rather misgoverned by a Turkish basha and is the utmost limit of the Turkish empire in this direction. People from all parts of the Moslem world throng the market and on account of being the seaport of Mecca it is yearly filled with pilgrims during the months of Hajj and Mohurram. There is no toleration for people of other religions and great is the squabbling amongst the worthy sects of their own religion.

Thomas is revolted by 'honour' killings, carried out in public, and against women. Shall we tell him that 'honour' killings are still being carried out in our century and that women in many countries are still brutally suppressed by men (often in the name of religion)? I doubt he will believe us. But he won't be surprised to hear who was behind the attack on New York in 2001, for he warns us about distorted extremes of puritanical Wahabism. 'The Wahabis,' he tells us, 'are a hostile and warlike arab tribe – many of the men in the Hamoody showed me scars received in fighting the Wahabis and even the peaceable old Skipper assured me he had received fourteen wounds in encounters with them.'

While in Jeddah Tom secures a passage on another uncomfortable *baghla*, bound for Suez. He nearly dies on board. So much for boasting how well he feels.

> The second day after leaving Jeddah I was taken severely ill and fully expected to end my journey abruptly in the Red Sea,' he reports. I made every arrangement in case of death and resigned myself to my fate. However thank God I was spared. On the 1st of March after nine days of severe suffering my distemper abated and though reduced to a pitiable state of weakness I felt I was recovering. I had no medicine with me but by feeding only on Rice water and taking a little opium supplied by my fellow passengers I succeeded in stopping the rapid progress of that painful disease which in the east sweeps off hundreds.

> *12th March.* Four months today since I left Sandheads and no knowing yet how long it may be before we arrive at Suez. I am daily getting better and making acquaintance with one or two men on board My fellow passenger who shares my den under the poop is a very agreeable man a chief of the Kurdish race.'

Tom also befriends the 'Arabian effendi' who takes a lively interest in his Arabic Bible and is surprised by Tom's studies of other religions.

For the rest of the month the *baghla* labours northwards, and just escapes being wrecked on a reef in a terrible storm. When at last the mountains of Sinai come into view supplies are running out:

> I have only eaten one small fish and one still smaller fowl for the past fortnight and the sea is breaking over us so I cannot get my miserable cake of flour and water baked… anyone looking in upon us in this dark hole in a dense fog of tobacco smoke would take us for a set of pirates, unwashed uncombed untrimmed surrounded with guns pistols and sabres, a heap of tin pots and basins and piles of Persian carpets.

> Yesterday my Kurdish friend proposed that we should get a couple of camels from the Bedoo camp ashore and push on overland. I agreed and we made all haste to land and try our fortune in the desert.

So we meet again unknowingly, Thomas, this time on camelback in Sinai's mauve mountains in the same month. It is during our stay in Egypt in 1989, when, thanks to a Greek contact, we're privileged to be guests within St Catherine's monastery: 'Left crowded Cairo early, crossed underneath the Suez Canal a few hours later and drove down the Gulf of Suez before turning inland towards Sinai's sandpapered crags... St Catherine's monastery is like a fragile egg in the nest of a deep valley, its gardens bright with translucent pink almond blossom, silver olives and bottle-green cypresses against orange granite. Rode camels to the mountain top. The monastery has a patina of great age and is completely peaceful; ten-year old Hamish remarked that 'the silence here is not the usual kind – it's a silence that makes you think of nice things.' Then he asked, 'Is it only people with beards who can become monks?'

On 3rd April Thomas dispatches his Journal from Suez, which is just as well or he would have lost it. The covering letter still exists, bearing an Alexandria frank six days later and a note recording its arrival at Etton three weeks later, via Southampton port. The postal system seems to have been efficient then; I wouldn't risk a precious journal in the post these days.

Thomas dislikes Suez and is glad to leave, crossing the desert ridges to Cairo, the camels pacing beside the new telegraph line and then the Nile. Three days later, it's in through the Gateway of Grand Cairo. Here he has a shock. When his Kurdish friend lets slip Thomas's true identity he is thrown out of the caravanserai, but by this time he's so used to Arab company that he dreads lodging with 'queer looking Christians' and is unable to sleep in a bed after months on bare boards. Forced to return to his own kind he visits the Consul's Office, only to be asked if he can read and write English by insolent staff members who take him for an 'East Indian Creole'. The evening is no better. He dines at the English Hotel but the men are condescending and his swarthy appearance frightens the ladies. Returning to his cheap lodgings he admits to weeping from 'a deep feeling of sadness... the most grievous hardship a wanderer feels, the sense of utter loneliness, a stranger in a foreign land desolate amidst a crowd of fellow creatures.'

He cheers up next day when he explores the city, reassuring us he will not describe the hackneyed sights that 'have already worn out every scribbling passenger with the transit company to India'. He finds Cairo crowded, so just imagine what he would think of the metropolis now. It was bad enough in the late 1980s when we took our children out of school and based ourselves there on the pretext of my indigo research but actually to give them some real education. The population had already risen in just fifty years from half a million to fifteen million. Despite the crowds, Hamish remarked after a couple of days, 'everyone is so friendly that we'll have to be more friendly too.' He also wondered whether the Egyptians 'not only write backwards but think backwards too.' I think it's more likely me who thinks backwards. We rode stallions to the pyramids, whereas Tom went by donkey. Planted on the top of Cheops' pyramid, Tom is proud to be taken for a genuine 'Persian derwish' by his Egyptian guide.

Leaving Cairo, both Thomas and I were disappointed by much of the journey to Alexandria, though for different reasons. I viewed the slums through a dirty train window whereas Thomas was in a native boat full of labourers: 'We passed some pretty places on the banks of the river... but you see no crowds of people bathing and washing clothes as you do in India,' he writes, adding that Egyptian peasants are 'ground down by their masters the Turks and in worse condition than slaves.' To compound his mouldy impression, two days downriver disaster hit. His writing box was stolen. It contained not only many precious souvenirs of his trip but also the last of his money. He reported the theft at once to the Turkish authorities, who searched the boat but failed to find the thief, so he had to travel on with, he tells us, 'the most brutal set of boatmen I had ever met with'. On arrival in Alexandria he hadn't eaten for nearly two days and the final straw came when the boat men seize his Arab cloak as payment for the passage. 'Thus Friendless Hungry and penniless I entered the town.'

When Tom went to the British consulate to report the theft to his fellow countrymen 'they did not care a pin,' he says about this destitute Englishman who landed on their doorstep like a feckless hippy. The owner of the English hotel likewise turned him away, but an Italian hotelier's Maltese wife took him in. 'God bless her and all her sex,' he writes in relief, 'who is there among the many wanderers over the face of the earth who does not remember many instances of kindness received at the hands of females?' Hear, hear, say I, though I might be biased.

Now he has lodgings, Thomas can explore Alexandria while he waits for the mail. He has sent home for money just as I did when penniless in Bombay. He enjoys the cosmopolitan city and makes several friends there. I see that my descriptions of 1980s Alexandria closely match his, though concrete monstrosities were already doing their homogenising worst. 'The mixture of races and religions... makes Exeter seem awfully dull by comparison,' I wrote. We also had friends in the city, notably John and Clara Semple, who introduced us to Hussein Cherine, grandson of King Fuad, a direct descendant of the first Ottoman ruler, Muhammed Ali. Hussein's spade-shaped chin, china-blue eyes and cartoon handlebar moustache above thin lips come from those Circassian Turks who were ruling – or 'misruling' as Tom puts it – the country when Thomas was there.

On 4th August, three years after he left her shores, Tom catches sight of England:

> It came on thick, rainy and cold as charity, however who cares we are near home. The land looks lovely green fields and hedgerows villages Churches and scattered houses are a pleasant sight to the eyes which have long been unaccustomed to look on such things. This is Sunday too and this evening we shall hear the sound of Church bells… .but here we are entering the river so I must conclude my Lay and once more set feet on Father Land.

> So ends the journal of the wanderings of Sheikh Abdullah el Hajji alias Thomas Machell the son of Robert Machell.

Tom also renders the last sentence in Arabic script, appends a self-portrait in Arab dress with impressive beard and gets Father to endorse it: 'Thomas Machell after his return from India through Arabia – and very like him it is – Robert Machell.'

Sheikh Abdullah el Hajji's efforts at rapprochement seem forlorn in light of what was to come. Despite millions sharing his liberal religious views, in recent decades religion has been highjacked by fundamentalists and politicians, for numerous reasons, not least unresolved Middle Eastern conflicts. Neo-conservative Christian and ultra-Orthodox Jewish fundamentalists are facing their nemesis in 'Islamist' extremists, dragging us all into unforeseen conflicts that make the Crusades look paltry.

Of course the catalyst was when Osama bin Laden's suicide bombers blew up New York's twin-towers on 11th September 2001 and the world's united sympathy afterwards was squandered by a disastrous pairing of 'leaders', Bush and Blair, who chose war over peace.

Glencairn and I were staying in a tranquil mediaeval village in France when it was becoming clear that, having failed to capture bin Laden in Afghanistan, the US would kick oil-rich Iraq instead – just as Imperial Britain assuaged her humiliating defeat in the First Afghan War by kicking the weaker neighbour (in that case Sind and Punjab, with, of course, an eye on their trade).

20th March, 2003. Caunes, Minervois. Just after reading Thomas's account of the Opium Wars I turned on the television and saw the first bombs dropping on Baghdad. God help all the citizens in the wrong place. I can only repeat Tom's reaction to the slaughter one day of 5000 Chinese troops by British soldiers with superior weaponry: 'Well may it be said that war transforms men into devils.' Glencairn, with his direct experience of Iraq's Sunni/Shia sectarianism, has just said to me: 'This folly will lead to civil war in Iraq and sectarian violence in other parts of the region.'

It did. Uncounted thousands of Iraqi civilians have died, not only at western hands because American and British troops were stuck in Iraq for years, but also from sectarian Islamist attacks, and civil war has since spread beyond Iraq's borders. Predictably and depressingly, war has also played into the hands of those whose views echo the most extreme of Thomas's shipmates, who warned him back in 1848 that: 'because the English have by treachery gained possession of India from a set of miserable Hindoos they think they are strong enough for the Arabs but wait a little. The day is not far distant when all Christians will fall under the sword of the Moslems and the followers of el deir el Islam will reign triumphant.' Even fearsome Western industrial armies are finding they cannot defeat martyrdom by sexually frustrated suicide bombers who imagine virgins await them in Paradise.

Here is Thomas in 1850: 'At almost every table you sit down to in every house you enter you hear creeds discussed… and yet how little do you see of the spirit of true religion. People argue and mistake their heat for zeal whereas they are only angry at being contradicted… are we in our vain turbulent squabbles losing sight of the pure fountain gushing forth from the rock of ages.'

We are indeed. Despite many lovely rituals and buildings, the heart of religion often seems crushed by dogmatism, by an obsession with sex, and by sectarianism. Thomas in his puzzlement was groping towards a religious one-ness; the eastern beliefs that he admired would later also influence his nephew Reginald, whose spiritual path affected future Machells and even took me on an unexpected voyage of discovery. Here is Thomas again, sounding very New Age for 1852: 'It seems to me that each of the varied religions of the earth contains some portion of divine truth… what is more beautiful than the notion so simply expressed, God encompasses us? The

Arab seems to have no difficulty in comprehending the perfect power of soul over matter, and the Hindu religion is stigmatised as the vilest of all inventions of the evil one and why? Because a Hindu sees god in the beasts of the field and in the stars of the heaven, in the whole system of the world he sees and feels that god encompasses us, that all is resolvable into that mysterious 'om'.'

Einstein had similar ideas, predicting that: 'The religion of the future will be a cosmic religion. It should transcend a personal God and avoid dogmas and theology… it should be based on a religious sense arising from the experience of all things, natural and spiritual, and a meaningful unity. Buddhism answers this description.' The Buddhist Dalai Lama (who has a deep interest in science) has, however, gone even further: 'The reality of the world today is that grounding ethics in religion is no longer adequate. This is why I believe the time has come to find a way of thinking about spirituality and ethics that is beyond religion.'

But for now religious sectarianism and its overspill into politics seem more entrenched than ever, balanced by the equally absurd stridency of evangelical atheists. Surely truth is ineffable, which is why Buddhists, Sufis and Hindus naturally embrace the mystical. Have I caught these ideas from Thomas, like 'flu?

Within a single hour on television in August 2005 I heard the following three statements being made by representatives of different faiths:

1. 'Be assured of the supremacy of Islam over Jews and Christians' – a British Muslim mullah.
2. 'God gave us this land for we are the Chosen People' – Zionist settlers being removed from occupied territory in Palestinian Gaza.
3. 'I implore you to cast aside other forms of Christianity and follow the True Church' – the Pope.

Quod erat demonstrandum, as Thomas would say.

My own religious upbringing had been a flaccid, unquestioning Church of England until the term when our headmistress taught 'World Religions'. Each lesson, covering a major belief, began with a single word on the blackboard written in her looping script – Allah, Buddha etc. The course was a revelation. Suddenly I saw that my own professed religion wasn't based on ultimate truth but on cultural belief and background and on society's structure; it dawned on me for the first time that had I been born in Saudi Arabia I would have been raised a Muslim, in Japan a Buddhist, in Israel a Jew etc. So how could anyone claim their own faith was more valid than any other? It didn't make sense then and still doesn't.

In the last lesson of this course our headmistress wrote three words on the blackboard: GOD IS LOVE. Now that made sense.

Jenny's sketch of a group in converstation in the Tuareg oasis city of Djanet, on the edge of the Tassili n' Ajjer mountain range in Southeast Algeria, 1976.

MDCCCL

بسم الله الرحمن الرحيم

And some are gret, and some are smalle
Some ryse to good, some from good torture falle
Some wyse men and some fules we calle
Figures alacke of speeche syth Destinie plais alle

he cannon of Fort William boomed forth their sullen wellcome to the New Year, as I knocked the ashes out of my old meerschaum and replenished it for the, I dont know how many eth time, well well thought I here beginneth the year 1850 – God bless all at home and give them a happy new year, I was with them last year, when shall I be next? What will have been my fortune in this fresh start? Too long have I been drifting about, but I trust that he who hath thus far protected me still watches over me. And in the words of the Psalmist I will also say "Yea though I walk through the Valley of the shadow of death "I will fear no evil thy rod & thy staff shall comfort me."

Thomas's illuminated 'T' for the title page of Volume Two of his Journal, New Year, 1850.

15. Limbo

'There's a divinity who shapes our ends
Rough hew them how we will'

(*Hamlet,* Shakespeare; lines quoted by both Thomas
and me in our respective diaries, at the same age)

Towards the end of 1849, after his extended leave in England, Thomas
takes a passage back to Bengal, though he has no idea what to do next.
In an age when most of his contemporaries had pre-ordained lives (often
literally since many entered the Church) Tom's haphazard career path
sounds rather modern.

The opening entry of what became Volume Two of the Journal is
characteristically illuminated like a mediaeval manuscript and Thomas
writes: 'The cannon of Fort William boomed forth their sullen welcome
to the New Year as I knocked the ashes out of my old meerschaum and
replenished it for the I don't know how manyeth time. Well well thought I
here begineth the year 1850 – god bless all at home and give them a happy
new year. I was with them last year, where shall I be next? What will have
been my fortune in this fresh start? Too long have I been drifting about.'

Throughout the year Thomas touches base with Calcutta. On arrival
this time he finds the city buzzing with talk about construction of the railway
that will transform travel throughout the vast sub-continent of India. Other
topics of conversation he noted in this volume include the annexation of
Burma, the danger of war between Britain and Russia, the governance of
India by Lord Dalhousie and the death in 1850 of former Prime Minister
Sir Robert Peel (Thomas despised the former man and admired the latter).

Expatriate social life in the city was no more Tom's cup of tea than was diplomatic life for me; Glencairn described the activities expected of an ambassador's wife as 'a sequence of trivialities'. Many such social trivialities were denied Thomas, however, because most British doors were closed to him, what with his lowly (or non-existent) jobs and his friendship with native Indians and with the Howards. The latter were social outcasts both because they were 'box-wallahs', i.e. in trade, and because Mrs Howard was of mixed English-Indian blood. What is more, they were hospitable to anyone in need, regardless of social background. Thomas considered them, along with his former boss Mr Forlong, among the kindest people he knew and he had a permanent home-from-home in their modest Calcutta houses – the first of which they shared with another family near the new cathedral at the bottom of Chowringee.

Thomas visits his Arab merchant friends in the city and fills the subsequent weeks and months with meanders around Bengal's hinterland, relishing, through his young Victorian eyes, a landscape he grew to love almost as much as his native Yorkshire. As he travels on horseback or by boat between familiar indigo estates, visits towns and sugar factories, and plans new adventures, he strains to convey in words the sublime fecundity of the jungle 'unpolluted by the step of man'. With so much time for observation, he fills two hundred pages with descriptions, thoughts and social gossip, adorning the margins with watercolours, many of them comical. We find Indian puppeteers, musicians and villagers; Hindu holy men and Rajput athletes. The *dak wallah* (postman) is shown resting beneath a tree and one can almost hear lizards rustling in the leaves around his feet and the choir of mynahs overhead. Thomas also sketches native and colonial buildings, shrines and the various types of boats found on Bengal's waterway (being him, he even imagines the thoughts of those aboard). He admits his failings as an artist but his sketches entertain his friends and 'will I hope some day amuse you he says. And indeed they do, whether the 'you' is his beloved father or his besotted admirer in the 21st century.

In the New Year he travels with his friend Charley Sage to the vast estuarine mangrove forest of Sundarban in the Ganges delta and later in the month stays with him at the remote and modest indigo factory of Rooderpore. Here he feels at home and even nostalgic for his old indigo life. Like the other factories in its orbit, Rooderpore was sited beside the Ichamati River that flows into the Ganges Delta east of the Hughli. Tom would be saddened to know that this idyllic river, whose name means 'God's Earth', would later acquire negative associations due both to colonial oppression and to its position as a major crossing point for resistance fighters against West Pakistan in the 1971 war of Independence, when what is now Bangladesh was East Pakistan. His magical river, which now forms much of the border between India and Bangladesh, is dangerous once again because criminal gangs smuggle cows (considered sacred in Hindu India) across it to Muslim Bangladesh to sell for meat. Meanwhile, the Ganges delta – described by Thomas as 'god's earth sacred to the preservation of the wild beasts which he has created' – is now a world heritage site trying to protect the remaining wildlife, not least the Royal Bengal tiger population.

Thomas here includes in his Journal a sketch of Rooderpore's bungalow; a low square house surrounded by a balcony shaded by calico blinds, and an extra room on the roof. He admits he copied the drawing from a professional British artist, Colesworthy Grant, and would be surprised if he knew that Grant later chose this simple house to feature on the front cover of his *Rural Life in Bengal* (published the year Tom died). Colesworthy Grant inspires Thomas's own attempts at sketching and provides one of only two existing pencil portraits of him.

In February Thomas visits Jessore, that town nearest to Rooderpore where planters sought relief from the visceral loneliness of their rural plantations by mingling there with magistrates, doctors, clergyman, soldiers and officers. Thomas arranges with the Commander of a passing regiment to join their march to Calcutta later in the month and then accompanies Charley to an out-factory at nearby Benapol. Typically he's busy measuring the girth of a giant cotton tree when the postman appears with a letter from Father. Its seal has melted in the heat. 'Seated under the spreading branches,' he writes, 'I read the news of home it was your Christmas letter telling of snow and bitter cold... though I was in light clothing perspiring profusely for a few moments I was by your fireside and the present was forgotten in the memory of the past. Distance is like death I often fancy, the body may be taken away, but the soul still remains hovering around those it loves until they also have made the journey... and once more they are united.'

When Thomas was out of the country the indigo industry was jolted by the 1847 collapse of Calcutta's joint British and Indian Union Bank, bringing thirty agency houses down with it (including Cockerall and Co. House). This banking crisis was echoed in the West in 2008, though in Bengal the unsustainable lending was for indigo planting rather than for mortgages.

Tom was lucky to leap-frog the crisis, but the financial volatility of indigo during his absence, and continuing setbacks in the industry, may explain his wish to find different employment. Or perhaps he was just seeking fresh adventures and new colleagues.

He was certainly fed up with unscrupulous private planters who tarnished the whole indigo planting community. They had direct control of their indigo factories and many of them were notorious for their brutal treatment of the workforce and for their wheeler-dealing. 'I would not like to chronicle the many grievous instances of oppression and abuse of power which I daily hear of,' he writes, though he does give plenty of examples. One is that of Scottish planter McKenzie, 'reputed the greatest scoundrel in the country' who even managed to increase his fortune during the slump. 'We may conclude,' writes Thomas, 'that he followed the old Scotsmans advice to his son – Make money Sandy, honestly if you can, but at all events make money.' Thomas later visits one of the grandest indigo houses and finds it ruined 'thanks to McKenzie's villainy' and the former native employees so bitter that they 'have sworn to skin him if they catch him'. Charley Sage's cousin, by contrast, though 'ruined by the failure in Calcutta has accepted with good grace his indigo losses and his resulting 'inferior situation'.

When accompanying that regimental march carrying 'treasure', Thomas drops in on one of his own former indigo out-factories and finds it a dilapidated testament to the industry's decline, its grounds reverted to jungle. He writes his journal account in its ruined house, sitting on a pile of straw with his writing box on his knees. On reaching the Howards' house in Calcutta he expects to secure a job in the travelling retinue of a Nepalese Rajah but McLeod, another former (Scottish!) planter, has grabbed it first, to Tom's disgust. Paintings in his Journals of Nepalese officials in elaborate turbans, copied from Colesworthy Grant, reflect his fascination with the Himalayan kingdoms. Within a fortnight of, as he puts it, 'meeting with most grievous mortifications and disappointments', he returns to the countryside, still pursuing work with Rajahs, but now also considering another job in the North-West provinces where Lance is stationed, not that he's at all close to his young brother. He gets frequent reports at second hand, usually from army officers, of Lance's all-round successes. One evening he arrives at Rooderpore exhausted after a long trek and before he even has time to wash another visitor, a Sage relation, engages him in conversation. 'Frederick of the 11th' is fresh from the N-W Provinces where of course he has come across Tom's wonderful brother: 'He asked me if I was related to Lance and told me that Lance was considered a very smart fellow, that he had been mentioned twice in the despatches, that he was a gallant fellow some inches taller than myself and was considered one of the best riders in the Punjab.' Oh dear – poor Tom.

While waiting for confirmation of the job near Lahore, Thomas plans his route there by horseback and moves restlessly between indigo factories he thinks he will never see again, meeting up with old friends and new acquaintances such as Yule of the Bengal Civil Service, whose family was renowned for Oriental scholarship as well as for colonial administration. He also has an unexpected visitor when he finds his former *khansamah* (manservant) on Sage's doorstep: 'The old fellow was affected to tears on seeing me again,' he tells us. 'He had been in my service all the time I was in India last and though he was in service when he heard I had returned he immediately left his place and travelled over a hundred and fifty miles on foot to find his old master although he knew I paid less wages than he was receiving.'. This instance of devotion sparks a rant in the Journal against the patronising attitude of many British – not least members of the Anglican clergy – who often, he complains, 'treat the natives of India worse than dogs.'

In April Thomas makes another trip downriver to Calcutta, which he now dubs 'the City of Palefaces' for its snootiness, saying 'City of Palaces' is a misnomer. He sketches the simple green-shuttered house of the Howards and the more upmarket versions of their neighbours. Did he ever wonder whether someone in the future might use his sketches and maps to track down locations that meant so much to him? And I wonder if he knew how unusual it was for an Englishman to explore the alleyways of what the British referred to then as 'Black' Calcutta and take the trouble, as he did, to sketch the ornate interior courtyard of a rich Indian's residence there.

By May, the heat has become overbearing and Thomas has reached page 100 in this Volume. He wonders if this is a bit overbearing too, but I'm glad he is too 'prosy' at times, the detail draws me in. The next few pages, for example, describe, with illustrations, a local wedding Tom chances upon while his friends are all off pig-sticking again.

Now we've reached June and over the next two steamy monsoon months he often seeks refuge at Mulnath estate, still the headquarters of Mr Forlong, friend, mentor and father figure. Forlong, unlike the Howards, is well born and a respected member of British Society; he is, however, rare among indigo planters in inspiring loyalty in his Indian workers. Tom provides a recent example: 'When Forlong met with an unfortunate wound

1850 sketch by Thomas of Mulnath house, Bengal Headquaters of his boss James Forlong, indigo factory manager. This sketch may have been inspired by those of writer and artist Colesworthy Grant, author of Rural Life in Bengal *(1862) and founder of the Calcutta Society for Prevention of Cruelty to Animals.*

and his life was despaired of, Hindoos and Moslems offered prayers and made poojah for his recovery... when Mckenzie was seriously ill they made poojah for his death.' (Even the nationalist newspaper the *Hindoo Patriot* later described Forlong as 'a white sheep in a black flock', in an article about the 1859 violent uprising of indigo workers against their masters, including McKenzie and even Charley Sage. This rebellion, later dubbed the 'Blue Mutiny', followed so closely on the heels of the widespread 1857-58 'Indian Mutiny'/'Sepoy Rebellion' that Viceroy Canning in Delhi feared a renewed catastrophe across India. However, shocking as they were, the troubles were confined to Bengal.)

Thomas selects his drawing of Forlong's Mulnath house to be the frontispiece to his Journal volume. It's a building designed for the monsoon heat, with a cooling basement, screened verandas and large airy rooms whose windows have slatted shutters and 'glazed doors to keep out the damp hot air'. The *punkah*, he tells us, 'is kept in constant motion night and day at this time of year'. On his floor plans he marks one room 'the bedroom in which I am writing this'. He finds the surrounding gardens and parkland sadly rundown since he was last there. Forlong had brought his first young bride, then only 17, to Mulnath during indigo's boom years; when she died six years later, leaving behind a two year old daughter, he could afford then to create a lavish memorial garden around her tomb. We don't know what Mrs Forlong the second thought of this constant reminder both of youthful mortality and of the saintly virtues of her predecessor.

The second Mrs Forlong, Constance, also a minor when Forlong, 20 years her senior, married her, sounds feisty rather than saintly. Thomas calls her 'a very lively young woman' and admires her spiky wit. She stars in this volume of his Journal and he seems to grow fonder of her than he's quite prepared to admit. Hampered by his lack of money and settled job as well as by the 'defect' he often mentions, he has little chance of finding a wife of his own, so it's not surprising he falls for other people's. When Forlong goes off to prepare his indigo factories for the new manufacturing season, Tom and Forlong's wife alleviate each other's loneliness. Forlong may be glad to have his wife distracted because the son and heir, Henry Gilbert Michell, she had given birth to in 1847 had died from a fever a year later. (Today his tiny grave lies double buried beneath a blanket of weeds and rubbish in the 'Scottish and Dissenters' cemetery in Calcutta.) When important company turns up at Mulnath Tom feels 'patronised and uncomfortable', but alone with Constance he revels in their 'tête-à-têtes', flirtatious banter (nothing more?) and discussions on such favourite topics as religious bigotry, the latest books, and irritating guests, the worst being Colesworthy Grant who always overstays his welcome. His 'antediluvian jokes and everlasting stories' give the pair the giggles.

Thomas's empathy and admiration for women extends beyond the expatriate community. We don't know if he takes any local Bengalis to his bed or not, but he lovingly sketched a village beauty called Seeta and mentions the temptation for solitary planters to 'transgress'. He certainly worries about the daily grind of poor rural women and makes plans to improve their lot with employment in textile crafts and education if he gets a chance. He is also full of ideas for political reform but no one takes any notice. He criticises the nepotism, corruption and inefficiency endemic in the hierarchy of both Indian and British officials, all of whom exploit the toiling *ryot* 'whose doom is sealed'. Meanwhile he has visits from 'a Brahmin and Pundit with shaven head and face coated with Ganges mud' and from a Muslim scholar. He is amused that both men have heard of his interest in Oriental languages, literature and beliefs and travelled far to meet him. These visits sully Tom's reputation with his fellow 'Sahebs', not that he cares.

Here's how Thomas signs off an entry after labouring over a map: 'I must leave off for the night, the Rain has filled the house with insects, I am covered with them and with grasshoppers of all sizes and colours which are swarming over my paper, hopping on my pen, filling my nose and eyes, worrying in my hair and whiskers – so go to bed Tom.' It is hard to be neat, he sighs, when 'the insects get into the inkpot and cause you to blot your paper when they are brought out impaled on the end of your pen.' Sometimes he signs off in despair with such notes as: 'the mosquitoes are biting furiously so good night', or 'got bitten by black ants on my little finger and my hand swelled down to the wrist for two days, but I forgive them their bite for the great benefit they bring in destroying the omnivorous white ants who work away at the timbers of the house.' At this time of year his pages risk destruction by mould as well as by insects: 'Do you remark how greasy this paper looks,' he complains, 'I can hardly get the ink to hold.' Extreme humidity affects his music-making that month too: 'My poor old Violin unable to stand the climate has dropped to pieces from the sheer dampness and heat no glue will hold in weather like this. I am horribly disgusted and to make matters worse a mouse has found its way into the case and taken a nibble at one of the 'f's.'

Still he ploughs on, partly to counter the solitude, which he nevertheless often chooses, not being a great 'joiner'. He again admits that busyness keeps at bay his incipient bouts of depression – or 'miserable thoughts' and 'desponding feelings' as he calls them.

It's now August and with indigo manufacture at full throttle Thomas is reminded of his status as hanger-on. But the month starts well with letters from home. 'I am so glad you like the Journal,' he writes to both Father and brother Richard, 'for it encourages me to hope that you will be still more pleased with this one as there is more variety in it and I have taken more pains to make it interesting to you… ' Tom finds he has written an average of a page a day for the past two hundred and twenty-five days and again reviews the function of the Journals. 'How many pipes have I smoked over this Journal how many hours that would have been sad and lonely enough have I spent in writing these pages… it is so like having a chat with you after dinner that though I have so little to say for myself I always feel sorry to leave off.'

Next month the end of the indigo manufacturing season brings a round of visitors: a 'graceless set of noisy sugar men' and 'an invasion of three boats full of planters'. 'I can't say I like this sort of society,' Tom complains, '… with few inclined to any pursuit but field sports but I must not abuse them for they are very hospitable and I shall most probably have to spend the rest of my life amongst them.' No wonder so many planters took to the bottle in those isolated out-factories, as Tom had soon discovered; many took no leave for a decade, if they survived that long, and knew they would probably die alone and unmourned, deservedly so if they had been harsh masters. 'No native Moslem or Hindoo will touch the dead body of an Englishman,' writes Thomas, 'they are rated as carrion and if the European dies in his factory before he can get removed to a station his neighbour must perform the last offices for him and lay him decently under the turf.' These words would haunt me when I found some of these planters' graves still *in situ.*

In October Tom joins a group of planters going to Calcutta, where to his delight he finds moored at the ghats both the *Rajah*, the ship he returned to India in, and the *Hamoody*. Tom visits his 'old Arab and Banian friends... all jolly fine fellows redolent of rose water and more savoury, he says, than many of his own compatriots. When the *Rajah* sets sail for England she founders on that dreaded 'James and Mary' sandbank and nearly sinks with her cargo, which includes a chest of Tom's containing his specimens and the latest precious Journal volume.

Back in the countryside in perfect autumn weather, Thomas stays at Hanskalle Factory with its proprietor, 'old Mr White the great indigo planter... a man of liberal views' and watches the packing of indigo chests for dispatch down river. He drops in and out of Khalbolyah, the grand headquarters twinned with Mulnath, and the local station of Kishenaghur, 'which,' he writes, 'has a pleasing variety of strongly contrasted opinions and as much petty squabbling as any town in England.' He laughs both at the sectarian 'split religious causing such petty quarrels as whether the church should have a cockerel or a cross on top, and the 'split civil' with its equally ridiculous divisions by social class or occupation among 'Company John's' civil servants and the wider expatriate community. All his sketches are useful for me later and so is the portrait of him done just before his twenty-sixth birthday by Major Laing, Superintendent of Rivers. Tom's large dark eyes stare into the middle distance as he tries to look relaxed, one arm draped over the back of his chair and hands loosely clasped. A floppy cravat is tied at the neck and his jacket falls open at his narrow shoulders, revealing a pale waistcoat buttoned across his thin torso. Thomas says it's considered a good likeness and dispatches it to Father with the comment: 'Not having any fair friend to whom I can send a tender memorial of myself to make endpapers of I send the pictures of myself to you, who I know will put them carefully away with the rest of my voluminous correspondence and doubtless if I ever return to Etton I shall find them all sealed up in the little closet with the rest of the family correspondence.' By the time I came along it wasn't as simple as that.

(I often peered at Thomas in this and Grant's sketch, willing him to turn his head and tell me about the unnamed 'unhappy defect' that coloured his life. But he always remained silent. Did he think, 'I've given you a lot – try harder and work out the rest for yourself'? Or was he just saying, 'Be patient'? With no help forthcoming, I would close my eyes and think my way into his body. Neither sketch shows any sign of a hunchback, withered arm, or hand or facial deformity. I ruled out ailments such as TB (though he may have had it) as that wouldn't be a 'defect' visible at birth. I wondered therefore if he had a problem with his foot that made him limp and therefore 'unfit for any of the military professions expected instead by friends and family to remain a 'home bird'. I speculated on his 'quiet demeanour' and lifelong sense of being an observer on the edge of things – which probably led to the existence of the Journals themselves. We know he was largely educated at home by Father, unlike his more robust brothers, was bullied on his first ship and shunned balls and hunting expeditions. All this would fit a person blighted by an awkward gait, who was nevertheless determined to overcome it and travel. But I was guessing.)

On his birthday on 12th November, after nearly a year of drifting, Thomas finally gets a job, and it's back in indigo after all. Charley Sage is moving on and Forlong offers Thomas first refusal of Rooderpore, 'the berth' that already feels like home. He has grown even fonder of Bengal and the informality of country life, saying: 'the longer I remain in this part of the world the more I like it ... there's no occasion here to swelter under the uncomfortable weight and tightness of European dress nor to confine yourself to a house for want of a conveyance. No town luxuries can compensate for the loss of the liberty you enjoy in the country.' Never mind that his conventional elder brother considers his adoption of local dress makes him a 'thorough sloven'.

So of course Thomas decides to stay, and a trip to Lahore will have to wait. As master of Rooderpore his first job is overseeing the packing of indigo in its eight out-factories, including Benapol. 'Busy weighing Indigo boxes and marking them according to colour – that is superintending for I do nothing but saunter about smoking all day he writes. It's a novelty to be rooted in a home where he can hang his pictures and cultivate a potager. How long will fate give him here?

What would Thomas have thought of the partition of India in 1947? He could reach his indigo factories and other Bengali haunts by horse or by boat within hours, whereas Glencairn and I faced far longer and more complicated journeys between two countries to search for them, assuming we could even get the visas.

The date is 13th February 2000, and I'm flying with Glencairn from London to Calcutta on a hazy mission to a country that didn't exist in Tom's day, trusting to Thomas-luck, with plans as fluid as his usually were when he landed there. I only met him a few months earlier so I don't know him very well, but a rapport is already evident and my marriage to Glencairn now seems to include a third person.

The plane touches down at Amman. On my 22nd birthday in 1974 I arrived at this same airport knowing nothing of the Arab world and unaware my life was about to be steered off course. Glencairn, as the country's ambassador, flew first class while I, his lowly employee, slummed it back in economy. I would have dismissed as completely mad any notion of becoming his wife (and an ambassadress!) before the year ended. Jordan was supposed to be for me that staging post to India and independent adventures, matrimony the last thing I was seeking. But surely it's the unpredictability of life that saves us from despair.

And now we're back again at Amman airport, travelling side by side in economy class, married for 26 years and launching on a new adventure. In the transit lounge I take my new diary out of my rucksack. How shall I start it? First sentences are always hard, but especially the first entry of a new millennium, and the first since meeting Thomas. I turn to his pages for guidance.

They give me the answer. The reason his writing is so immediate is because he is talking to his father – as we know, he calls his Journals his 'talking papers'. He describes 19th century Bengal to Father, but the person who would most want to know what Bengal is like today would of course be Thomas himself. So the obvious thing is to address my new diary directly to him, as if he is still alive. (Later I shall even send him faxes, and the odd letter and postcard – daft but fun.) This way I shall have no option but to view the world in parallel timescales through two pairs of eyes.

16. Memories of Indigo

Of those so close beside me, which are you?
God bless the Ground! I shall walk softly there,
And learn by going where I have to go.

(from *The Waking*, Theodore Roethke)

CALCUTTA, 13th February 2000

Dear Thomas,

You would hardly believe how Glencairn and I travelled from London to Calcutta, and at what speed. It used to take you months. It took us one day! Do you know what? We flew here – don't laugh, it's true. And we don't use horses any more, except for recreation. Now we travel fast by motor vehicles invented towards the end of your century. Trains you know about. They haven't changed much since your day.

Our arrival in Calcutta wasn't a bit like yours. No gliding up the river as a band played 'God Save the Queen' to herald the New Year. Instead, a long drive into central Calcutta, a maelstrom beyond your imagining of traffic, noise, rickshaws and, above all, people. Fort William's still there though, and the Maidan remains a great open space, where young men in white flannels were playing cricket among the litter, the bosom of Queen Victoria's vulgar monument rising beyond them through smog as dense as London's when you were there.

We finally reached our lodgings in sleazy Suddar Street, where Jewish trading families lived in your day. One of their homes became an eccentric hotel called Fairlawn. Its owners, Violet and Ted Smith, stayed on after the British left in 1947 and are as fixed in the past as is their hotel. Though Armenian they couldn't be more old-style British. The hotel's an oasis of green plants and careworn chintz; in every corner a glass case crammed with memorabilia, most of it ghastly, the walls a collage of old photographs, posters and framed reviews of the hotel, not all favourable. A gong summons you to the dining room, where you sit where you're told and grumpy waiters in turbans and over-wide cummerbunds serve tepid old-fashioned English food on dirty plates. You're not allowed to drink tea after lunch or dinner, but only at teatime, when you're unlikely to be in.

Our stomachs leaden with mashed potato and treacle pudding, we set off (or 'sallied forth' as you would say) for our first foray into Calcutta's crowded streets. Swarms and swarms of people everywhere make it hard to walk. Such a mass you're in danger of not seeing humans as individuals. You skirt around lifeless bundles of people sleeping under thin blankets, and I must have stepped over at least six dogs today that had just curled up and died. How do people survive such chaos and squalor? It makes our western lives seem unbelievably clinical and separate... and how can you have an enjoyable 'holiday' in a country where the poor can be so desperate that to earn money a beggar will amputate his own leg on a railway line?

We consulted your hand-painted map of 1850. You'll be delighted to hear we found it useful and discovered we were lodged just ten minutes walk from your familiar Wellesley Street (recently renamed Rafi Ahmed Kidwai Road), now a noisy, squalid main road. My heart was in my mouth, as they say, as we walked its length, hoping to find intact No 45, the modest house where you so often stayed with your friends the Howards. It wasn't there. It's been demolished and replaced by a concrete building with a shop selling 'videos'. Videos and suchlike would astonish you, as would most of the technical inventions of the late 20th century. Though your Number 45 has gone, beyond it on Park Street, and up the road at Number 47, the last relics of the Raj houses you sketched are dying in unkempt grounds shaded by old trees. Now split into many dwellings, their rotting green shutters cling on at angles, moulded columns are patched with sloshed-on cement, front entrances have nasty shiny tiles, and across the façades run tangles of cables like long black snakes. Soon these houses, tangible links to the city you never liked, will be demolished too. But I've already connected with you on our first day in your City of Palefaces. Most of the palefaces around today, however, are degenerate tourists like us, or missionaries who are, I hope, an improvement on the species you grew to despise.

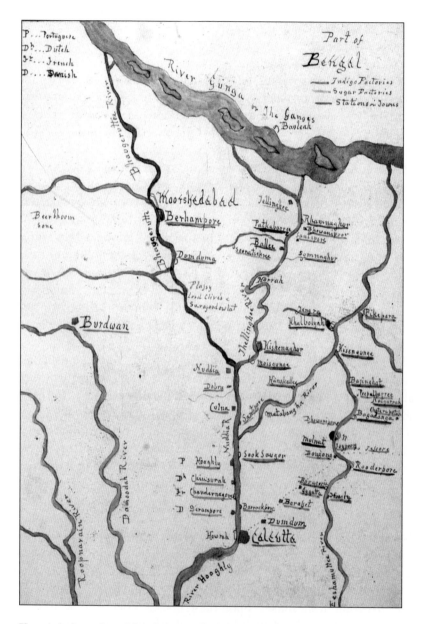

Thomas's sketchmap of part of Bengal (eastern section being in Bangladesh today) showing indigo and sugar plantations and 'stations' and towns.

Let me tell you about an extraordinary coincidence, Thomas. Before I found your Journals I'd never heard of the small town called Jessore you often mention, nor had anyone else I asked. But when I decided to pursue you in your old indigo haunts it was obvious I'd have to try to reach the Jessore area, now in Bangladesh. Then, with brilliant timing, a Christmas card arrived from Liz Wickett, a friend from our Cairo days, who later married Stephen Brichieri-Colombi. Both work overseas in what we call 'development projects'. This was her surprising news: 'We're currently living in Bangladesh where Stephen's working on a water project near a small town called Jessore.' Talk about serendipity! I contacted Liz at once to outline our mad plans, and she said they had just rented a flat near Jessore for a few months and could meet us there if we managed to get overland visas at short notice. What are the odds not only of finding friends living in this obscurest of towns but also just for a short spell that coincides with our strange wish to go there ourselves?

To compound the coincidence, just after this exchange Liz was in Dhaka, Bangladesh's capital, and wandered into a shop called Aranya (meaning 'forest') on a day when its founder, Ruby Ghuznavi, happened to be there. I've never met Ruby, but we corresponded about indigo in the 1980s after I learnt she'd had the foresight and persistence to revive natural indigo in her country, despite resistance caused by its tainted history. (Residual memories of an indigo rebellion in Bengal in your time had been reinforced more than half a century later by Mahatma Gandhi, a famous Indian who harnessed the discontent of indigo labourers in Bihar for his first act of peaceful rebellion against colonial rule on India's path to Independence.)

Ruby and Liz got talking about natural dyes and when my name came up, thanks of course to indigo, Liz told Ruby about my quest to hunt for your old indigo factories, *nilkuthies*, around Jessore. Apparently Ruby, having no idea that remains might still exist, was so excited she's cleared her diary so she can join us in Jessore if we manage to get there.

It was too late to fix Bangladesh visas in London, so we had to rely on the Deputy High Commissioner here in Calcutta. The meleé on the pavement around the visa window of the office was so discouraging that we told a lie and got an interview with the Deputy High Commissioner himself. It started badly. He despises all former ruling powers, he told us, and was a freedom fighter for his country's independence. He glared with suspicion at us palefaces beyond his huge desk, saying: 'It is not usual to issue overland visas to foreigners in Calcutta – why are you not planning to travel to Dhaka by air like everybody else?' (Everybody who can afford it, he meant.) 'We don't want to visit the capital,' I explained, 'because I'm looking for a young man who lived near Jessore in the mid-19th century'. My quest sounded bizarre and it took some time to convince him it was valid. Finally agreeing to our request with great reluctance, he imposed one strict condition. 'If I provide you with visas,' he said, 'can you promise not to venture anywhere near the border areas, which are dangerous for foreigners?' 'Oh absolutely,' we confirmed, over-vigorously, 'we quite understand and of course shall steer clear of those areas.' Inside my head was that map of yours showing all your indigo places dotted both sides of the 'dangerous' modern border.

We retreated to South Park cemetery, which you knew well, since most of the graves are eighteenth century and some are of 19th century indigo planters. Distracted by crows dropping large twigs on my head, I did a bad sketch of the famous monument to Rose Whitworth Aylmer, poet Walter Savage Landor's beloved, who in 1800 died from cholera, aged twenty.

17th February. What a huge contrast there is between the former British and Indian parts of this city, both of which you knew so well. The buildings your contemporaries built to administer the Empire are certainly grandiose in their Victorian, mock-Gothic way, but I see why you considered many of them 'ugly and ungainly', including Bishop Wilson's new 'toy' i.e. his cathedral that you rudely call a 'tawdry gingerbread absurdity'. The esplanade you strolled along, lined by warehouses, is run down and now separated from Dalhousie Square by a grimy railway line. In northern 'Black Calcutta' we found surviving buildings like the one you sketched, where rich Indians lived. I love the surprising inner courtyards with their pillars, carved wood and plasterwork and raised platforms holding shrines to the 'House God'. Apparently such houses, known as *thukurdalan*, are owned by extended families plus the god, so can never be divided or sold. Therefore they decay. How complicated everything is in India, with convoluted layers of meaning incomprehensible to an outsider.

Boys on barrows squeezing sugarcane, women pumping water from street pumps, old men leaning from windows, curious children everywhere. Familiar? Not so familiar the hammer and sickle graffiti on the walls, since Communist beliefs would hold no meaning for you. But how about the long street full of young men making *pandels*, straw figures of goddesses and animals that are coated in clay and painted in vivid colours? You sketched a group of these, and even sent one back to UK, fragile as they are. These marvellous models, used fleetingly at festivals, are ceremonially immersed in sacred rivers where they float like corpses – or like as not among actual decomposing corpses in your day – before lodging in eddies and ditches to disintegrate back into their elements.

Several were doing just that in the stagnant puddles edging the Hughli River where yesterday morning we paid homage to *ghats* you often mention, among them Babu Ghat where you landed after many weeks at sea. The ghats now reek of human shit since many poor have to live in slums beside the railway line, washing themselves and their clothes in the filthy river and defecating on its slimy banks. (Half the world starves while the other half gets fat and ill from over-eating, but I suppose it was like that in your day too, not least in London.) In homage to you we found a dinghy like one you sketched and were rowed into the river's centre where old-fashioned steamers and ships freighted with rice floated like ghosts through the haze of pollution.

We later took an underground train (imagine that) to see the Tollygunge Club, now a smart club but formerly the wealthy Johnson family's home, built from profits from their indigo plantation. In 1807 a Johnson husband, wife and child died in a cholera epidemic, which wouldn't surprise you. We found their graves mouldering within dark shrubbery in the grounds.

Our last call yesterday was on Anjan and Amrita Mukerji, thanks to a contact passed on just before we left UK. Amrita was delighted to share her passion for textiles and when we told her of our proposed *nilkuthie* hunt her eyes sparkled.

18th February. Long gone are the days of stepping aboard a river boat with your traps to be rowed upstream to your indigo plantations, or even taking a relay of horses. You boast of covering the fifty miles between Rooderpore and Calcutta this way in four hours, much quicker than our journey. It took two hours in a car just to pass though Calcutta's indistinguishable suburbs, dodging motorbikes, battered lorries and buses vomiting fumes, all the time deafened by a cacophony of horns and hooters. Oh for the freedom to travel that you had.

At the scruffy border of Benapol you read letters from home in the spot that's now a taxi park. We took hours leaving India and entering Bangladesh. On the Indian side there was only one gloomy official to deal with all non-Indian travellers going in either direction. He copied all our passport details very slowly into four separate ledgers. A group of Thais who had no intelligible language to communicate in had already been in the queue for three days.

All this palaver because of what happened after two World Wars in the first half of the 20th century. India got rid of the Raj in 1947 but her Independence sliced your Bengal in two; the mainly Hindu western half stayed in India but the Muslim eastern side was joined to the new West Pakistan, miles away on the other side of India. After much turbulence and suffering, East Pakistan broke free from the domineering West Pakistan in 1971 to become the new country of Bangladesh. So this is why your former indigo district now straddles two countries (and the two religions that interested you), why we needed permits to enter both and why it has become so complicated to get around.

Liz and Stephen were waiting patiently in Bangladesh to drive us through your territory, which is now all cultivated. The population of Bangladesh alone is nearly a hundred and thirty million, and growing fast. And did I mention that the population of Calcutta and its suburbs is over fifteen million? Truly.

Ruby joined us later, so thanks to you we've met at last. Elegant and energetic, she campaigns for natural dyes and the betterment of women's lives through education and employment in textile arts, preoccupations you share. She and her husband Farhad have held four nationalities in their lifetimes; British, Indian, East Pakistani and Bangladeshi.

We headed off to find Khalishpore, a house Ruby had heard was still intact. We'd been warned that most old planters' houses have either collapsed into jungle or were occupied or plundered for their stone by refugees after Partition, so we didn't expect too much.

However, nearing sundown, we saw Khalishpore's colonnaded façade intact across pink water. Crossing a bridge to reach it, we found the adjacent ground being used as a market, with hundreds of long-horned cattle milling around, circled by painted trucks. On the far side of the house was a tented camp of Bangladeshi soldiers. We feared they might prevent us from poking around but they showed no interest whatsoever.

Though the house is run down we found the main room occupied by a solitary tax collector seated at a table filling in forms. The walls still have original pale indigo paint, and hand painted floral designs. Even the lavatory with its long drop is still there. Beyond the front porch, on a terrace beside the river, are fixed stone seats curved around a table. I sat there and looked across to dense jungle on the far side. Khalishpore is not a name I've come across in the Journal, yet I had a strong feeling you had sat on that seat before me, also admiring back-to-back crescents of bamboo fishing boats reflected in the water.

(When I read your later volumes back in UK this hunch was confirmed, for I found that you had indeed visited Khalishpore before me. It was when your old friend Charley Sage was in residence and you went to say farewell before you left Bengal for new work elsewhere. So my backside did sit on the same bench as yours and we must have used the same lavatory too!)

19th February. Today we had an unexpected jaunt. You mention the influential Tagore family as shareholders in the Bengal Indigo Company, but three years before you died one of them, Rabindranath, was born who later became world famous. You remarked that educated Bengalis are natural 'sages, poets and philosophers' and he was an outstanding example in all those fields. Among many other things, he founded Shantiniketan University near Calcutta, which had close ties with Devon's Dartington art college and education centre where Susan Bosence and I both taught indigo dyeing. What I didn't know until today was that for years Rabindranath managed his family ancestral estates at Shilaidaha, which are in Kushtia, in your day part of the famous Nadia indigo district (though Nadia town itself is now in West Bengal). Few Westerners get to this remote house today, so we were lucky. Rabindranath wrote some famous works here and we were delighted to find original manuscripts on display, as well as many of his paintings. My own watercolour of his terracotta coloured house is rather modest but I'm quite pleased with it.

We also found an isolated former indigo estate at Amjupi, where vats, offices and storerooms remain. Someone said a locked building might contain remnants of its indigo past. Peering through its dense window dust I could just make out a dark room with an iron chest embedded in its dirt floor. We managed to prise open the window where the woodwork was damaged.

You should have seen me, pushed from behind, squeezing through the gap head first in semi-darkness, landing on a smelly morass of rat and bat droppings while everyone outside was shouting 'watch out for snakes!' Actually I was more alarmed by aerial attack because I disturbed a colony of giant bats and they were diving around my head in a frenzy. 'There has been an awful stink in this house for the flying foxes have taken up their abode in the roof' you once wrote, so you know what the smell's like. At a planter's party at dusk you wrote: 'The bats are out and the ladies are in' – but in my case the bats came out when the lady went in.

The iron chest was crammed with ancient tax returns, chewed and soiled by rats and bats. I noticed a side room and went inside. Guess what? It was lined on three sides with wooden racks that, incredibly, still had blocks of indigo piled on them after all this time. Think of all your notes saying 'busy packing indigo today'. Here was indigo awaiting packing until the end of time. I knew I would never see such a sight again so I took lots of photographs while the angry bats performed acrobatics overhead. 'Whizz swoop,' in your words.

20th. Into your familiar town of Jessore today, Thomas. Nothing left of the social whirl you avoided whenever possible. Almost feels like a ghost town, dusty and forlorn. That's why so many old Raj buildings still stand, not least the enormous Court building where those endless cases went on and on. Is this where you sat 'playing the magistrate as you called it, amazed to find yourself in such a position in your early twenties?

Of course the *nilkuthie* I most hoped to find today was your home, Rooderpore. While driving around in circles looking for it we spotted an intriguing building that I recognised. 'Tom sketched this,' I told everyone. Here's your comment on 25th July 1850: 'The last few days we have been at Chandoria indigo factory... I took the accompanying sketch of a ruined Mandel or temple once dedicated to Siva.' Built in 1703, it's much more ruined now and the top has collapsed, but we actually found restorers at work. 'When did you arrive in Bangladesh?' they asked us. We told them we'd just arrived, and asked how they planned to reconstruct the building. 'We are not knowing what it was like before so we are having to guess,' was the reply. 'I know exactly what it was like before it collapsed,' I announced, which puzzled them since I'd just told them I'd never been in their country before. Imagine their astonishment when I handed them the copy of your drawing; they can now restore it as it was, thanks to you.

It was only a mile and a half to Rooderpore, the pinnacle of my explorations. Excitement increased when a passer-by told us we were almost there. And we continued to be 'almost' there after we'd reached the place called Rooperpore. Because what did we find from your time? Nothing at all! We drove back and forth between flat green fields, searching for a sign, a mound in the earth perhaps, or the edge of a tank, or a pile of stones where your factory chimney had collapsed. We had, after all, this morning found ruins of an insignificant sugar factory you mention in your Journals. I know your house and estate were modest, but I did expect something. And if not tangible remains, at least a memory from an old farmer who had heard talk of the far-off indigo days. But everyone we asked just shrugged or stared, as if we were crazy.

I left the car, followed a path into a rice paddy and suddenly found myself following you into your past. People talk about the spirit of a place but here I found your spirit in the place. When I unfolded your sketch plan marking your home and plantation there it all was in my mind's eye. I saw you in your loose shirt, smoking away, followed by your manservant trying to keep at bay a crowd of villagers. I smelt the flowers in your little garden and picked a lettuce in that vegetable plot you were so proud of, tasting the dust on its leaves. I heard servants sweeping your veranda and, in the distance, shouts of children in the innumerable villages scattered among the bamboo jungle. As far as the inner eye could see stretched your four thousand acres of indigo fields, almost ready to harvest. And there was the set of twelve vats draining into the Ichamati River flowing lazily below the house on the course it used to take when you were there.

I also pictured children running bright-faced out of the school you were so proud of. As Colesworthy Grant wrote in *Rural Life in Bengal*: 'Rooderpore has changed hands, and my friend Mr Machell… following the example of Mulnath, has established a school for the education of the poor lads around – upwards of one hundred and fifty have already put themselves under Mr M's tuition. He models his little academy on… the Lancastrian system,' (whatever that is).

You disappeared into the interior of your house. 'How I wish you could look in upon me now,' you wrote at the end of 1850, 'and see Tom at home sitting in this Library (one may as well give the place a fine name)… … would that you could join me… my happiness would be complete.' So is your happiness complete now you know that someone does join you when looking at this sketch and reading those words? You wrote them after spending your self-inflicted lonely Christmas at Rooderpore, having refused an invitation to spend it with sugar boilers from those very factories we poked around in earlier today. You didn't expect to find yourself still at Rooderpore for a second Christmas did you? 'As the year comes to a close I find myself more frequently wondering where I shall be next year at this time such has been the uncertainty of my life… I am fond of Rooderpore and though lonely enough at times I feel it is better suited to my disposition, my defect and consequent dislike to society… Great hopes I have no grounds for but I still have room for great wishes. How ridiculous!' In fact you were there for another Christmas, giving you time to make that modest mark with your school.

On New Year's Eve 1850 you reiterated the way your strings of words, though sometimes 'stupid' or 'prosy', prevented your mind from becoming 'rusty'. Defying convention, you had your friends the Hindu Pundit and Muslim Mullah to talk to, as well as Mulnath's Indian doctor who 'owing to the prejudices of the country,' you wrote, 'is never able to socialize with Europeans'. Even more defiantly you have your old shipmate from the *Hamoody*, Razumea, staying with you 'as Moonshee and companion... much to the surprise of the natives who have never before seen a saheb on such familiar terms with a dark skinned Indian.'

'It always strikes me as very strange that I never met an European who speaks well of Bengal except Mr Forlong, for my own part... I think this country the finest in the world though the steamy heat of the rainy months is death amid a bed of flowers... I like the country and the people and the language and above all my present employment,' you wrote. Throughout 1851 your enjoyment of settled indigo work in the place you had grown to love was only marred by your recurrent bouts of fever, the extreme summer heat, Mrs Forlong's departure for England, and your dismay at the oppression of the poor by 'Native Landlords and Landowners' as well as by the majority of your fellow planters, Forlong being the notable exception. You reckoned that unrest at Khalbolyah and elsewhere were only a taste of things to come (you were right) and you had a personal dilemma of whether to leave on principle, or stay to 'mitigate the consequence of impolitic commands'. You considered native policing 'rotten to the core', Britain's justice system 'vile, absurd and a heartless monopoly for the employment of Directors sons and such like people', and Parliament's neglect of India deplorable.

Your volume overflows with descriptions of, and comments on, every aspect of local life, interspersed with thoughts and aspirations from your busy brain. Letters this year include family excitement – 'I little thought the arrival of my box of oddments would have caused such a sensation' – national excitement at the opening of the Great Exhibition in London's Crystal Palace, and such international news as '4th August His Majesty the King of Siam is dead! alas!'

You even described Rooderpore's ghosts. According to your servants, the night cries you heard were of two planter's children whose graves were on your estate. But this didn't frighten you, because you believed a person's spirit returns 'to watch the progress of those kindred souls to which it is bound by the previous ties of love and sympathy.' 'When I hear men ridiculing such fancies,' you continued, 'it seems to me a kind of sacrilege, communication with the dead would be more perhaps than man could bear... but still we may have an instinctive knowledge of their presence about us.'

You often had intuitions didn't you Thomas? On your birthday in November you wrote: 'Barque Thomas Machell Launched 1824 outward bound, cargo sundries, twenty seven days out middling rough passage but no damages what's your longitude?' In your first entry in 1852 you called Rooderpore your favourite place in India and were busy painting it, building extra bookshelves, hanging a newly arrived portrait of Father, planning to extend your school and repairing a dwelling for Razumea and his family, who were about to arrive from Calcutta. But you wrote: 'I am daily growing fonder of this place and when I have to leave it will be with no small regret, I have many pleasing associations with this part of the country and hope I shall have many more before I leave it, but why should I think of leaving at all... a change seems to have come over the spirit of my dream... I have a presentiment that I am not to remain long and perhaps it is that fear of a speedy removal that makes me like the place so much more.'

How did you sense that you would soon have a speedy removal? You were right, but it was almost a speedy removal from life itself.

You were in high spirits when you visited Forlong at Mulnath at New Year, laughing with pretty young women, Forlong's father-in-law, a man 'as witty and improper as our relation Old Laurence Sterne and a stranger, Captain Smyth of the Bengal Artillery, 'a very clever engineer who superintends the revenue surveys of Bengal'. This 'fat major' not only impressed and amused you but also later played a big part in your life. And on 8th January you had a soldier visitor who, typically, extolled Lance's energy and all-round brilliance and also brought rumours of his latest success i.e. his imminent marriage. This was news to you.

Two weeks after this came your first blow. '*24th January.* A day of bitterness and heavy sorrow little did I think when I rose this morning and went to hasten the completion of Razamea's house that I should never see my poor friend again... but I received a note from Howard telling me he had died on the evening of the 22nd of cholera. Howard sent forthwith to recover the money which I had advanced Razumea but he little knows what my feelings are towards the moonshee I loved as my own brother... and so far from wishing to recover anything from his unhappy widdow I sent her some more money and would fain do all in my power to help her in this deep distress... all day I wandered about seeing on every side things to remind me of my lost companion... I feel once more desolate and alone.'

Then it was your turn to succumb. Here's how you described the onset: '*8th February.* Hullo whats this. *9th.* Wrote to the Mulnath Doctor touch of

Dysentery. *10th.* Very ill took strong dose of Laudenham and set off in a Palankeen for Mulnath.'

Five weeks later you were back in Rooderpore, but only to pack up your belongings and take leave of the only house that felt like home, other than Etton's rectory:

> *17th March.* I felt very much inclined to cry as I went down to the boat but as all my servants household and factory were salaaming me off I bottled up my sentiment and uncork'd my dignity and so farewell to Rooderpore. Tonight I shall pass alone at Mulnath.

21st February. Today it was my turn to look for you in Mulnath, a century and a half after your hasty departure from Rooderpore.

I had your maps marking Mulnath within striking distance of Benapol, but rivers have changed course and tracks have disappeared. When we had asked around no one recognised the name. No modern map mentions it either. What's more we had to cross the border more quickly than last time to have any hope of searching for Mulnath and reaching Calcutta by nightfall.

Ruby and the Wicketts stayed in Bangladesh and Glencairn and I braced ourselves for the border. To our surprise we were able to bypass dispiriting queues of lorry-drivers bringing huge bales of jute into India and were back on Indian soil in good time.

We hired a tatty taxi through the ostensibly reliable Sheikh Travel Office housed in an open tin shack. Extra to go upstream first to look for Mulnath. No problem, smiles all round.

It would have been much easier by boat or palanquin. The road, full of potholes, soon narrowed to a rough track that snaked through a string of scruffy villages, with crowded markets and food stalls frying delicacies stained bright orange. At least we found, at last, someone who actually recognised the name Mulnath. More than an hour later we ground to a halt on the shore of a wide river, which must be your Echamuttee/Ichamati. Mulnath, we were told, was on the far side. Luckily there was an old wooden ferry, still crossing where you marked it on Grant's map. We made a strange procession squeezing aboard, the driver and his mate swinging our case between them because they refused to leave it in the locked car boot, a large group of villagers and bicycles, and Glencairn and me with rucksacks on our backs.

Once across we attracted the attention of the entire Mulnath village (descendants of your indigo labourers) as we walked like pied pipers the half mile or so to the site of the estate. Of the mansion and its deer park there was no trace, but two office buildings remain and beyond them in the jungle we were led to an enormous rectangular tank, still plaster-lined. How many times did you walk along the same paths to watch indigo being whisked to a turquoise froth in this tank, or amble along them in the quiet season laughing with Mrs F?

> *7th March 1851.* Mrs Forlong… is a curiously tempered woman sharp and clever enough with… a mind perpetually wavering between the sublime and ridiculous… she is a most agreeable companion and I have a great regard for her She has all the virtues and thank heaven she is another man's wife I have been teaching her the Latin grammar we have not got as far as amo yet: but I find her a very apt pupil – in the grammar I mean.

Oh yes, Thomas? Amo, amas, amat indeed.

Then you would go inside the mansion with Mrs F – cooled by marble floors, venetians and the basement with its arched windows – and write what Father and I would later read.

In December 1851 you talk of dismounting at Mulnath's office to check the colours of indigo samples with Mr Forlong. You couldn't know Glencairn and I would get into trouble at the very same spot, many decades later. And neither could I when I read your words in the safety of the British Library a couple of months ago. But picture us today in what is now remotest jungle, the wrong side of the river and no one knowing we were there. The driver suddenly turned nasty and demanded an outrageous amount of money. We realised how vulnerable we were. The atmosphere darkened. How quickly a crowd can turn. We had got ourselves trapped in the kind of way one reads of in a newspaper and thinks 'those travellers were foolish to let themselves get into that situation.' It was not the first time that I alone, and Glencairn and I jointly, had done it. Incidents in Afghanistan and Yemen sprang to mind. Help. This time it was partly your fault. Just think, it could have been us joining the first Mrs Forlong in the Mulnath graveyard, instead of you who very nearly did.

Right beside the old indigo office the driver threatened to abandon us and ordered his companion to drop our case. Glencairn and I picked it up but, luckily, the companion had a word with the driver and to our relief beckoned us to follow him. So we all processed back to the river, where we queued again for the old ferry, with local villagers, bicycles and two enormous buffaloes.

The driver was surly all the way back to the border.

Benapol was the worse place you led us to but we had already chosen to ignore the High Commissioner's warning, let alone your own foreshadowing. In your day it was just a village near an indigo out-factory but that didn't stop you almost dying there, and the spirit of the place continues to be shady for more than its tall trees. You make light of being attacked in the bazaar by a 'mad looking faqueer high on gunjah' when you describe it later, but admit that he had already broken a man's arm that week and 'would have pretty well done for me had not Charley jumped in and warded off the blow'. We could have done with Charley's protection ourselves.

At Sheikh Travel's shack we renegotiated the fare to Calcutta, anxious to be off, knowing the road is twice as dangerous after dusk. Then our driver suddenly announced that he'd changed his mind and his 'friend' would take us instead.

The 'friend' looked slimy and his sidekick slimier still. We were uneasy from the start but had no choice because our case had already been transferred and locked into the boot of the new taxi, the ropiest ever seen. So erratic and dangerous was the driving, even by Indian standards, that the normally phlegmatic Glencairn blanched at every near miss as we made figures of eight around thundering lorries and buses on the main road. The driver rarely glanced at the road ahead, instead he looked sideways at his mate who was counting wads of money and shining a torch onto the meter. Though we had hired the taxi privately, it picked up more passengers in the front, squeezing the driver so far over that he could barely reach the steering wheel. We were terrified.

Twice the taxi jolted to a halt, and the mate fiddled in the engine to get it going again. The third time it happened we were on a bend in the almost dark, traffic charging from behind and no light in the taxi. We thought it safer to get out this time, though instinct made us shoulder our rucksacks. The engine seemed dead and we thought we'd have to find another car, though we were far from any town. Then, in a flash, the mate slammed the bonnet, jumped into the front seat, and the engine sprang into life. I grabbed at the back door but the mate had already locked it and the taxi was driving off at amazing speed.

So there we were, stranded at nightfall on the edge of a forest notorious as a bandit hideout, watching our taxi vanish down the road with our case in its boot, the driver and mate laughing their heads off. We should have been laughing too, since our valuables were on our backs and the case mainly contained old clothes and shoes too big for an Indian. But inside were also copies of your journal pages, all my Bangladesh sketches and diaries addressed to you and my films taken in the neelbaris, including of those unique indigo racks. So a copy of your journal will now remain in Bengal where you wrote it, though in the hands of a rogue who's probably already chucked it into the bushes in disgust. I now know just how you felt when your writing box and clothing were stolen en route to Alexandria.

My birthday, 22nd February. We eventually managed to flag down a taxi that two hours later dropped us off at Calcutta's Police Station in the small hours. We'd realised things could have been much worse and have today been told many tales of druggings, physical attacks, kidnaps and loss of all possessions at that notorious overland border crossing. We were foolish to have ignored the warnings. The policemen, busy eating pizza (a worldwide staple today) refused to take a statement, telling us to drive back two hours and do it in the district where the crime had been committed. At this we announced our intention of complaining to the British High Commissioner (not that there is one in Calcutta). This did the trick. Finally we made our statement, got back to the Fairlawn hotel for a few hours' sleep, and awoke to restart my birthday.

It began anew with a call from Amrita. 'Great news!' she announced, 'I've hired a jeep and driver and I'm coming with you to look for indigo houses – it will be as much an adventure for me as for you as I've lost touch with my roots in the Bengali countryside. See you at five tomorrow morning.'

The evening brought a surprise birthday celebration. Through friends of a friend met in England we received an invitation to dine in the grandiose old Calcutta Club with the Maharajah of Burdwan, Danny, and his wife, Pussy(!). Leftovers from your era – remember watching the then Maharajah, Danny's ancestor, playing billiards when Smyth took you to meet him? Danny's father was the largest landowner in the British Empire, owning four thousand square miles, nine palaces and hundreds of temples. Disillusioned after Independence, he gave it all away, retaining only a few temples to Shiva. Danny, who did a London degree on 'Land ownership in Bengal', feels betrayed by the Communists who now rule Bengal and spends his days pursuing numerous court cases.

23rd February. Amrita arrived at dawn in a jeep with driver and a young woman, Monoleena Banerjee, from 'Weavers Studio' in Calcutta. Having crossed the border that divides your past to find you on the Bangladeshi side, I wonder what we'll find in this western half of Bengal?

We drove north for hours along crowded smelly roads. I showed Amrita your sketch of Hanskallee indigo factory, which you often visited. 'Let's see if we can find it,' she said. So we turned right off the main road and were soon passing through countryside little changed from your day, except for the throbbing sound of tube wells that irrigate fluorescent rice paddies. It was an auspicious wedding date, so in many villages men were pinning up shiny cloths and coloured lights. Cattle were being sold illicitly to smuggle for slaughter across the border to Bangladesh. That explains the cattle market we came across at Khalishpore.

We saw so much that fascinated you, such as triangular shaped bullock carts (*garoo-garee*) made of fat bamboo, tools for de-husking rice, the largest clay storage jars I have ever seen and models of a Hindu goddess being painted for a puja. A girl in the brightest pink sari, thick black hair snaking down her back, was plastering a tree trunk with cow dung patties while another beauty cooked round chapattis on a fire fuelled by dung sticks and rice husks. Her mother sliced up cabbage with a huge sickle held between her toes. On the roof of their house climbed a gourd of the type whose fruit are made into those musical instruments you and I both drew.

I wish you could have seen us stopping every few miles to show people a copy of your Hanskallee painting. Everyone recognised it but said it was a little further on. At last we turned off down a dirt track between banana groves and there it was, looking largely as in your painting, apart from extra trees. You will love the reason it's been preserved – it's become a shrine, lived in by priests called *mohantas*. 'These followers of Krishna are gentle and humble, unlike followers of Shiva or Kali who can be hot-blooded and even violent explained Monoleena.

As we walked towards the veranda you often sat on, out stepped a *mohanta* in a peach robe, with white daubs on his face. He was most intrigued by your painting, counting the veranda columns with his finger and beaming on discovering your accuracy. Though much is unchanged, a domed temple has been added to one end. Invited inside, we found the sitting room, still with fireplace and *punkah* pulley, now the priest's bedroom, and the dining room a cow shed. You would enjoy the gods in garish clothing and offerings of flowers and burnt substances on the temple shrine. By the way, the wooden shutters hang on, their cracked and peeling paint in that characteristic Raj green, a cross between pea and jade.

Glencairn, now dubbed our 'scout' by Amrita, went exploring in the bushes leading down to the river and found hidden in the foliage a tall stone column with elegantly carved numbers used by you planters to gauge the water height. It's astonishing how high the river rises in the wet season.

The river's heavenly isn't it? I stood on the bank thinking of you smoking your cheroot after a day's work, watching identical long low fishing boats with angled bamboo structures suspending nets, wooden ferries full of people gliding past, and flashes of iridescent kingfishers scooping up river.

I went off to inspect the remains of the office blocks while our 'scout' went to find the source of a 'clack-clack' sound you yourself describe. This led him to an open-sided shed where two women were weaving fine pink and orange jamdanis on a pit loom, a common enough sight for you. No wonder the Romans called this Bengali speciality 'woven air'.

Our next stop was Kishenagar town. Your account of the rivalry between different Christian sects made everyone laugh when I read it out loud. We passed the dilapidated gateway of the old palace and inside the stark church that you sketched we found paper streamers saying 'Happy New Millennium' slung between the columns, and marble memorials to missionary wives and planters you probably knew.

Driving to Baharampore for the night, there were strips of mist over rice paddys and strips of pollution over roads where lorries ground along, nose to tail.

24th February, Plassy House, Panighata. Well Thomas, this is a dream come true. After several days of indigo hunting, tonight we're actually staying in a former neelkuthie. You may even have stayed too in this house that belonged to British indigo planter before the Banerjee family bought it in the late 19th century. (You were impressed by Banerjees you met in Bengal – perhaps it's the same family?) Just as you describe, we're surrounded by flying insects, the odd cockroach and sounds of night life such as croaking frogs.

When we arrived at dusk after a long day's indigo hunting we tiffed on the veranda, watching a white owl flap slowly back and forth across the river. You'd recognise the house, though the 'satellite dish' would surprise you.

After exploring the remains of Domkal indigo factory and sight-seeing in Murshidabad (Bengal's capital for half a century, until the defeat of the Nawab by Clive at the 1757 battle of Plassey, pivotal for the British Empire, as you well know), we were right on your trail this afternoon, seeking Patakabarre, the first 'factory' you lived in, mapped and sketched. There's such a sense of excitement as we near sites of your former homes. Once again we had turned east towards the Bangladesh border, the road growing increasingly narrow and bumpy, the driver negotiating a stream of bicycles and buffalo carts, and an occasional flashy 'motorbike' driven by a young man in dark glasses.

Patakabare's pretty remote isn't it? We approached it up a long track, turned a bend and there before us was your first indigo house: 'an odd specimen of architecture, a very comfortable but ungainly building with its glistening white washed walls and Verandahs and contrasting green folding doors Venetianed from the top to the bottom to quote your first impression. It's now a ruin, but I followed your ghost up the wide curved steps to the main veranda and entered rooms filled with dirt and rubble, though fireplaces and ceiling bars remain. In the main room I could almost hear you playing your fiddle and see you sitting at the table with Monsieur Verplough in the sketch that drew me to you last year – the one you labelled 'indigo planters after tiffin'.

When we walked around the grounds looking at your old office blocks we were mobbed by hundreds of village men, the sight of white faces in such an isolated spot being very rare today, we were told. The mobbing was good-natured and we didn't quite suffocate to death.

By the time we'd finished exploring your factory dusk was approaching, but we drove on two kilometres to see the river. Alongside fishing boats curved like melon slices was a strange bamboo raft lying across two low-sided fishing boats. It turned out to be an improbable looking car ferry.

Glencairn, Monoleena and I were cowardly and all for taking the long road to Plassey House, but Amrita, who's fearless as well as fun, decided we should risk the ferry crossing as it was such a short cut. With total confidence she sat inside the heavy jeep like a Maharani while it was gingerly manoeuvred onto the precarious raft. Once the jeep was aboard, the rest of us leapt on and stood squashed outside it, poised to jump into the river when the raft sank. But we were all punted safely across the river by one elderly man.

So this is how we reached Plassey House by nightfall, to be greeted by the scent of a million flowers and write our Journals on this veranda where you yourself may have sat writing yours. Who knows, perhaps the ghost of a young man that's recently been seen walking on the balcony above us is you?

26th February. Yesterday we were up before dawn and as light crept up could see fishermen in palm tree dugouts on the river beyond the sloping garden. They were hauling in the night's catch, while above them swirled flocks of grey-backed herons.

Early mists were still rising off the river as we left, after poking around leftover indigo buildings and vats. We needed petrol but all the petrol stations were closed due to a strike. It looked as if the day would be a disaster (and I had a meeting arranged in Calcutta with the head of the company that formerly handled most of the indigo exports). However, we found a roadside shack with some illicit petrol, and Amrita persuaded them to sell us enough to get to Calcutta.

So off we went in high spirits, me dreaming of finding the handsome house of Khaboulyah you often stayed in. The journey was long and every time we asked directions we were told we had another twenty kilometres to go. From time to time random red patterns of flowers of the kapok (silk-cotton) tree, you will remember them, and scatters of bright bee-eaters. As we neared our destination the landscape grew junglier, closer to how it would have looked in your day, dense with palms, mangoes and huge rain trees. Suddenly we were at Kisengunge, a 'station' you often mention, and ten minutes later reached Khaboulyah, just short of the border. We wondered if any white person had ventured here in the past century.

To my disappointment this large mansion, a standing ruin just thirty years ago, was also victim to the refugee crisis. You describe it as 'next to Mulnath the finest house in this part of the country' but all that remains today are the curved veranda steps prominent in your drawing, and some old paving stones. The villagers told us they recently dug a well and found the soil stained blue with old indigo. It was odd to picture you here in October 1851, packing up the belongings for the manager, who was ill in Calcutta and returning to England. He was lucky not to die alone on the estate like so many others (you almost among them).

As we were leaving the little village, disappointed to have found so few traces, a group of older men told us there were two British graves in the distant paddy fields. It sounded unlikely so far from the house, but we turned around and followed a rough track until we had to leave the jeep and wobble our way along mud-built ridges edging the paddy. Each time we slipped into the mud the youngsters now following us had a good laugh. We stopped at an overgrown island of shrubs and creepers, untouched among the fields. Very cautiously one of the boys, wary of snakes, clawed back the undergrowth with a forked stick and after a while two large tombs were revealed. I wonder who last visited them? The inscription stones had been removed so we don't know which planter, or wife or child, were buried there so long ago, but they must have been an important family to have been living at Kahboulyah and warrant such large memorials. These untended tombs stand testament to the dangers and the remoteness of planters' lives in your day. No wonder there aren't more planters' graves in the Calcutta cemetery – in this heat and humidity bodies had to be disposed of quickly upcountry, as you describe.

So although Kahboulyah's mansion has gone, graves and memories linger on. And as for you, I have no idea how or where you died. Are you also lying in an unmarked and isolated grave, somewhere in southern India where you wrote your last Journal entry?

The main road was still miraculously quiet thanks to the petrol strike, lorries all parked along the roadside. While we tiffed in a shack on the milk of large coconuts, Amrita telephoned Calcutta (imagine that, mobile phone – new technology – just like the invention of the telegraph at the end of your life) and was told the meeting to see the documents had to be postponed as no one could find the key for the locked chest. However, during a random conversation back in the jeep Amrita told us her sister was married to Sandip, son of the late Satyajit Ray, who was India's most famous filmmaker and also a painter and writer. 'Would you like to visit the Rays' house now we have extra time?' asked Amrita. Thanks to that mobile phone a meeting was arranged in an instant.

At the Rays' large and gloomy house in a Calcutta suburb we were greeted by Amrita's sister, a gentle woman who led us straight into Ray's hallowed study, kept like a shrine. Books were two deep, wall to ceiling, on labelled shelves, and more books and film reels lay on tables. Ray had been fascinated by indigo and collected publications on its history, including *The Blue Mutiny*, which describes the indigo uprisings you foresaw. When I picked it up it fell open at a page on your boss James Forlong that confirms his exceptionally liberal attitudes.

After a while Ray's widow, a sweet-faced elderly woman, appeared. She told us that a collection of short stories by her late husband had recently been republished in an English translation and she had just received some copies. She bent down, took a book out of a cardboard box on the study floor and offered it to me. I looked down at the title and my heart missed a beat. Guess what it was? *INDIGO*, can you believe! Imagine being given that treasure in the very room where it had been written, and having it inscribed to me in a wobbly hand by Ray's widow.

That may sound uncanny, but now comes the spooky bit. Back at the Fairlawn I climbed into bed almost too tired to read, but thought I'd glance at a short story of Ray's, and chose the title story, 'Indigo'. Bear in mind I'd spent eight days tracking back through time to places as they were in your day, and while writing my diaries imagining you writing yours, sometimes even in the same place. I had read of your loneliness and near-death from disease, and had even heard through your ears the ghostly cries of two planter's children, buried at Rooderpore, rising from their graves to disturb your sleep.

Satyajit Ray's story is about a present day Indian, a part-time writer, who sets off on a trip into the Bengali countryside and gets stranded when his car breaks down in an isolated location. Seeking shelter, he spends the night in an old Raj planter's bungalow. Here, in the high-ceilinged old bedroom, he has a kind of waking dream and becomes a former occupant, a 19th century British indigo planter about the same age as you were at Rooderpore. He sees the room as it was then, and inhabits the planter's body, prematurely aged by a tough, disease ridden life. The planter is alone, his family having died and friends having returned to England to escape death from disease. Here are some excerpts from this story:

In spite of my surprise and terror, I suddenly felt a great urge to find out what I looked like.

I strode towards the bathroom, opened the door with a sharp push and went in... the thing I was looking for was right in front of me: an oval mirror fixed to a dressing table. I looked into it but the person reflected in it was not me. By some devilish trick I had turned into a 19th century Englishman...

I went closer and had a good look at 'my' face. As I looked a deep sigh rose from the depths of my heart.

The voice was not mine. The sigh, too, expressed not my feelings but those of the Englishman.

What followed made it clear that all my limbs were acting of their own volition. And yet it was surprising that I – Aniruddha Bose – was perfectly aware of the change in identity. But I didn't know if the change was permanent, or if there was any way to regain my lost self.

I came back into the bedroom.

Now I glanced at the table. Below the lamp was a notebook bound in leather. It was open at a blank page. Beside it was an inkwell with a quill pen dipped in it.

I walked over to the table. Some unseen force made me sit in the chair and pick up the pen with my right hand. The hand now moved towards the left-hand page of the notebook, and the silent room was filled with the noise of a quill scratching the blank page. This is what I wrote:

27 April 1868. Those fiendish mosquitoes are singing in my ears again. So that's how the son of a mighty empire had to meet his end – at the hands of a tiny insect... I will lay down my life on this alien soil. My place will be beside the graves of my wife and dear little son…

I could write no more. The hands were shaking. Not mine, the diarist's.

I put down the pen.

At this point in the story the planter/narrator pulls a revolver out of his desk drawer, goes onto his veranda, calls his dog and shoots it. The sound reaches the factory workers.

I came back into the bedroom, bolted the door and sat on the bed. The shouting drew near.

I placed the still hot muzzle of the pistol by my right ear.

That is all I remember.

Next thing it's morning and the narrator wakes up. *Will anyone believe me,* he writes, *when they hear of my experience on the night of the hundredth anniversary of the death of an English indigo planter?*

What do you make of this, at the end of a week spent shadowing your ghost, and on the *very day* when I had not only spent the previous night in a former indigo planter's house, but had also found two un-named and neglected British graves on an isolated old indigo plantation where you had stayed?

I dreamt last night of you and me and planters past.

Sketch of Thomas relaxing at Rooderpore indigo factory, near Jessore in Bangladesh (formerly Bengal) by writer and artist Colesworthy Grant, bound into the beginning of Volume Two of Thomas's Journal, 1850.

17. Suspended Between Two Magnets

Can the shadow go back on the dial..?

(*A Rector's Memory*, Rudyard Kipling)

On 8th April 1852 Thomas, weighing less than eight stone, is carried on board the 750 ton merchant sailing ship *Asia* by his cook and his faithful *khamsamah*. Cholera was a killer, and not just in India; thousands of Londoners were also dying in cholera epidemics at this time. It's amazing he is still alive.

He owes his life to Mr Forlong. By luck Forlong returned to Mulnath on 9th February after a trip away. Here he found a note, written that morning by Thomas, announcing he was suffering from dysentery. Forlong wrote back at once advising him to take a strong dose of Laudenham in brandy, and, if that didn't work, to come over to Mulnath at once – or send a note and Forlong would come to Rooderpore (Thomas bound this crucial letter into his Journal volume). The following day Thomas struggled into a palanquin and got himself to Mulnath. It was just as well. The 'touch of dysentery' turned out to be cholera.

Thomas just managed to summarise the drama, in an entry curiously dated 11th February:

> … from this day I loose count of time to the end of the month I only know that I am wandering in the valley of the shadow of death I see Mr Forlong's kind face bending over me by night and by day my old Khansamah too never leaves me Dr Archer comes over from Kishnaghur he is with me all night and there is talk of the crisis then

there is a terrible struggle for life and it is succeeded by a deep sleep of unconscious. Daylight broad daylight when I woke refreshed beams upon me the crisis is over and the Dr runs out of the room to bring in Mr Forlong and shows him the triumph of art – but still I cannot rise from my bed I am a mere skeleton and so the month ends the disease is banished but the patient reduced to an extreme of weakness the hot weather increases daily and I am condemned to loose my berth and leave the country too weak to work – what can I do but go home.

This is why Tom's return to Rooderpore the following month is so sad. He is still unable to walk unaided and is on a diet of bread and milk. Nevertheless, he manages some lively descriptions of local life so at least his sense of curiosity is returning. He also bottles two interesting snake specimens and indexes his collection of 'mythological pictures', which he can't wait to show to Father.

He stores his belongings at Mulnath because he hopes his frail body will recover and he will return to work in indigo, where he believes it is possible to do good: 'I think I have a vocation to fulfil a destiny to work out in this land of my pilgrimage.' But for now it's goodbye to his home, philanthropic dreams, friends and servants.

Down in Calcutta Thomas still feels 'even at the best very rickety indeed, looking like a churchyard disaster'. No wonder he cannot face the dentist, despite suffering a 'glorious toothache' for days. At least the Howards have come to the rescue again and he feels lucky to be part of the family and to have made good friends abroad: 'The hour has come at last when I have had to part with the best of my friends on this side of the world and truly I have done so with a very very sad heart… I have taken root in this soil deeper than I thought and with an unaccountable perversity of mind I feel myself drawn more toward the home I am leaving than to the home I have so long regretted.'

Howard has managed to secure for Thomas a passage to Britain on the only affordable ship to sail there that month. Thomas has already dispatched home by 'overland steamer', whatever that means, letters and his latest journal.

He starts a new chapter the day he boards the *Asia* and quotes the liberal Catholic writer Arthur O'Leary in its preface: 'Most men live as it were with one story of their lives… Their history consists of the development of early character… They fall in love, they marry, they grow old and they die. Each incident of their life bearing on that before and that after, like link upon link of some great chain. He however who throws himself like a plank upon the waters to be washed hither and thither, as wind or tide may drive him, has a very different experience. To him life is a succession of episodes each perfect in itself. The world is but a number of tableaux changing with climate and country. The past throws no shaddow on the future and his philosophy is to make the most of the present.'

As for actual tableaux, the one Thomas encounters as he boards the *Asia* – or 'floating jail' as he calls it – is dispiriting: 'An Old sow with a litter of piglets was blocking up one of the cabin doors and a drunken sailor the other.' To escape the 'disgusting' smell below deck he goes up on the poop for a smoke only to find 'the stench of Tar, decayed vegetables and confined fowls' enough to turn anyone's stomach, let alone a convalescent's. And of course the ship is over-run with rats. Thomas adds his own 'family', as he calls it, to the menagerie. He's taking home, for Father's aviary, three dozen Java sparrows and a pair of tame lorikeets that whistle, dance and 'speak Hindoostani'.

This peculiar Noah's Ark is far from harmonious. During storms the steward battles to keep the pigs, sheep, goat and goose out of the cabins, and throughout the voyage the Captain's vicious one-eyed 'scurvy tinker's dog' regularly bites most of the crew and the animals. Much to Tom's chagrin the dog attacks his bird cage and eats most of the sparrows, leaving the rest to escape. The beautiful lorikeets last a bit longer before dying from the vile food on board but at least Thomas can preserve their corpses for the Etton 'museum'. Not for long though; the dog soon sneaks into Tom's cabin and shreds those up too.

As for the humans on board, they are an equally odd mixture. The second cabin on this Clyde built cargo ship is taken by a Romish Priest called Sardi. He is also retreating west with a 'battered constitution', in his case after spending ten years as a missionary in China. Though both invalids 'enjoy bad health' from time to time, they perk up on the open seas and Tom gains weight. Common fare is salt ling and tripe supplemented by an occasional fresh fish or a glut of pork when a young pig is slaughtered. Drinking-water from an iron tank is at least an improvement on water from wooden casks which is often putrid, 'especially when an unfortunate rat or two chances to get drowned in it'. No wonder sailors frequently died on board, including one on this voyage.

Time is measured in Sundays, Trade winds, the Tropics, doubling the Cape and sightings of passing ships, islands, whales and birds of omen such as albatross and stormy petrels. To fill his 'busy idleness' Tom chats away on paper as usual, to the bemusement of his shipmates, who, he says, find his 'writing fever' absurd. He teaches chess to the Captain's sulky son and writing to the Steward but his favourite amusement is observing the old Skipper goading the misanthropic Sardi. The conceited priest mistakes Tom's loathing of 'cant' and dogma for atheism and pointlessly tries to convert him to Catholicism. He is wasting his breath of course, since Tom finds Sardi's views 'biggoted and bloody minded', not least in comparison with the 'abstract doctrines and gentleness of the sages on the banks of the Ganges'. As we know, Thomas considers truth to be beyond Faith, and salvation 'a free gift not only to the elect but to all'. Sardi, he writes, 'is quite disgusted with my freethinking as he calls my speculations.' Despite this they become friends, though the Catholic priest's misogyny infuriates Tom, who writes; 'female society tends more to soften and civilize our rude natures than all that monkery with its pious frauds and proud Humility.'

As he gradually recovers from cholera Thomas anticipates returning to Bengal after all, saying he would be content to spend the rest of his life there. He also muses on the way his 'distressing defect' spurred him on early in his life to choose a vagabond path 'the least suited to my circumstances', and on the way he has escaped death so often. He still hopes to do something of use in India.

Four months after leaving Calcutta the *Asia* at last enters the English Channel. Thomas reluctantly shaves off the big beard, which he thinks makes him look 'venerable'; 'without it I am simply ugly'. When Thomas looks alien with his beard and dark skin he is treated with contempt in his homeland: 'Why is it that the English are so prominent in their dislike to foreigners?' he asks. As always, he works out his ideas as he writes – in this case analysing both the best and worst characteristics of his fellow countrymen and discussing his native country and love of the countryside, villages and Devonshire beaches that both he and I played on as children.

With 'nervous excitement' he steps ashore at Gravesend, the port where he boarded the *Worcester* 12 years earlier. Though still in his twenties, so much has happened to him that he's surprised to be alive. 'Here I close my journal for the present with the heartfelt exclamation of every good Moslem – Praise be to God The Compassionate and Merciful.'

By early spring 1854 Tom has spent almost two years in England since leaving India at death's door.

Father has a new bride and has applied for another parish. Again he's married well. His new wife, a poetess whom Thomas calls Madre, is heiress to her father's wealth and also widow of Henry James Torre Holme, owner of the Paul Holme estate, in the Holme family from the late 13th century until 1921 when it was sold by the son of Thomas's stepbrother Bryan Holme. Today it's an atmospheric deserted mediaeval village near the Humber estuary west of Hull.

For Thomas each homecoming foreshadows difficult partings that may well be final, given the dangers and long years between visits. 'Nearly every time that I have returned home I have found one member of our family missing' he writes. This time, however, painful partings have been postponed while he regains his strength. But home comforts and his brush with death haven't extinguished his wanderlust and he's determined to return to Bengal and 'try again', as he puts it. He may be 'puny' but he won't give in.

So once again we find him packing and presenting bound copies of his Journals to Father, knowing he's probably saying a last goodbye to Etton.

Look thy last on all things lovely,
Every hour – let no night
Seal thy sense in deathly slumber
Till to delight
Thou hast paid thy utmost blessing;
Since that all things thou wouldst praise
Beauty took from those who loved them
In other days.

The last stanza of Walter de la Mare's poem, *Fare Well*, a favourite of Glencairn's, also runs constantly in my head as I get older. Had it been composed earlier in the century it would surely have replayed inside Thomas's head too every time he prepared to return overseas.

He remains torn between his two home lands of Yorkshire and Bengal and between the influential father figures in each. He describes Forlong to Father thus: 'Next to yourself he has been the kindest friend I have met with… no employer could have behaved more kindly and no friend more affectionately.' Nevertheless, Forlong isn't family and for a son it's a father's death that Freud called 'the most poignant loss of a man's life'. This is not true for everyone, but surely would be for unmarried Thomas who communicated daily with his father in his head via his Journals. 'My cheroot is finished and I fancy I see you also knocking the ashes out of your little meerschaum so good night my dear father and pleasing dreams and slumbers tight.'

In late March 1854 we find Thomas boarding a Calcutta-bound cargo ship, the *Gloriosa*, 'advertised as a Frigate it is a great lump of a ship adapted for carrying a heavy cargo.'

'It is the same story over again,' he sighs as the sailors prepare to warp out. 'A drunken crew came tumbling on as we hauled out of the Dock Gates... I found myself much to my satisfaction the only passenger with a large comfortable cabin on the Port side (Larboard is obsolete now) and a captain who seems likely to turn out a very decent fellow.'

A week later Thomas wryly remarks that 'whatever may be the sailing qualities of the ship her rolling power is indisputable... we have a good deal of Iron on board for the Indian Railways'. As the journey gets into rhythm he tends to his canaries and playful puppy, Blucher junior, plays chess and cribbage with the Captain, paints the heraldic motives and designs for the Etton church window that I would love to see now I have found those windows in situ, and reads everything from 'shilling novels' to Taylor's *History of Enthusiasm*, a Bengali grammar and a Surveyor's Manual.

By 16th April the *Gloriosa* approaches La Palma Island. 'Exchanged signals with the *Royal Albert* carrying troops to Madras... I wanted to ask if War had been declared with Russia but the Captain was so disgusted at having been outstrip'd that he would hoist no more signals so we saluted and parted company.'

By early May Tom is struggling again with ill health. 'Six weeks from London. Latitude 014'N. Longitude 24 13' West we have had a steamy time of it and I suffer a good deal... however I must grin and bear it.' At last, two weeks later, they get the news everyone has been fearing since hostilities have been escalating between various Empires (notably Ottoman Turkey, Britain and France against Russia): 'Exchanged signals with the *Ballarat*... we learnt that War was declared between England and Russia after we left London.' In the ensuing weeks several other ships, American clippers, French barques and British ships carrying emigrants to Sydney, fly past the cumbersome *Gloriosa*. All are anxious to share across the ocean waves the latest news from the Crimean front.

Three laborious months pass before the *Gloriosa* rounds the Cape, and she's soon floundering again in wild seas. 'The ship is too heavy laden and too weakly man'd to stand much of this,' writes Thomas. A fortnight later come new problems: 'I believe some of our hands are in for scurvy and the rest very bad with dirt.' In mid-July disaster strikes one night in a storm that sends the ship rolling gunnel under. 'And then,' writes an anguished Thomas, 'came the cry which once heard is never forgotten and which has too often rung in my ears "Man Overboard".' The skipper asks him to write and tell the young midshipman's mother the dreadful news that her last surviving child out of thirteen has died at sea.

On the 'nineteenth Saturday since leaving London docks' the *Gloriosa* at last reaches the estuary leading to Calcutta. As a steam tug tows her up the swollen brown river, Tom revels in the luxuriant beauty of the familiar Bengali landscape and guides us upstream to Calcutta's ghats, telling us to look left and then right and see it through his eyes. 'But enough of this,' he then says, 'we are in a hurry to arrive at Calcutta we drift up past the great fort and bring up at Bankshall Ghat and there on the left you see the great railway station looking like a huge ugly red barn and on the right the plaster-pillared houses and green venetians of the great city of oriental pale faces.'

Tom's bravado slips before the ship docks. 'I walk the deck at all hours, the mind speculates constantly on the uncertain future, it is long alas since I heard from home and the place where home was no longer exists I suppose. How many of my friends have migrated to New Zealand, how many to their homes in England and how many to the dust.' Letters come aboard and he receives confirmation of the news he dreads; Father has found a new living at Marton-in-Cleveland and has therefore left Etton for good. Despite knowing that Father will later read his words, he struggles to sound pleased. His cholera attack lost him his home in Bengal and while he's been in sea-limbo, his English taproot has also been severed. Now 'drifting about the world', he approaches Calcutta homeless, jobless, out of money and out of sorts.

> You can imagine my feelings as I prepared to land once more in Calcutta... a sickening feeling of doubt and uncertainty made me feel far from comfortable'.

It's as well his friends the Howards offer refuge once again.

Without them Thomas would be destitute in Calcutta. This time his pleasure at renewing old friendships is tempered by news of several deaths since he left the city, including, worst of all, the Howard's own two children. Despite this double tragedy the house remains a haven for the needy. 'I have met more characters in this the only house in Calcutta that is open to me,' Tom tells us, 'than I should have met in the whole course of my life had I lived quietly at home and taken what job I could get in England. Howard is always ready to open his house to people in difficulties and his own troubles seem only to have enlarged his heart. As for his wife... if ever an angel inhabited a human person here is one.' Tom drops hints from time to time about the womanly charms of Mrs Howard. It's clear he loves her and he gets close to admitting it. Indeed he seems to have actually spelt it out before thinking better of it because he deletes with heavy ink what he has just written on the last few pages. He rarely messes up his precious Journal like this and slams it shut after writing in frustration: 'I fancy I hear someone say Humph and pray what sort of touchstone or test do you call your particular friend. Well, if you haven't found out by this time it is of no use attempting further explanations so I'll wish you good night and close my journal.'

Tom cannot overstay his welcome at the Howards; he has a future to work out. His options sound vague but he puts 'business news' in letters rather than in the journal. These letters are lost. How I would love to creep my fingertips along the grimy base of a drawer in an old bureau smelling of dusty beeswax until I touch at the back a forgotten package labelled 'Correspondence of Thomas Machell esq, 1854'.

Over the next few months Thomas travels the 'beastly Hoogly River', his moods mirroring the ups and downs of the journeys themselves.

> There is a certain vagabond charm in the prospect of wandering far away from the beaten track of civilization and plunging into new scenes of travel and adventure... to succeed we must be either pioneers or the sons of influential men.

Money or influence – Thomas has neither. Despite glowing letters of reference from James Forlong, it's hard to stay buoyant, and he dips again on his birthday:

> *12th November 1854.* My thirtieth year is now completed. I have accomplished nothing. Indigo planting has ended in the same result as seafaring and I have had my full allowance of apprenticeship seven years to each. I have not lost heart but have altogether lost confidence.

While staying with Forlong at his new estate, Thomas befriends a German missionary called Schur and is inspired to revise his judgement on missionaries and get involved himself. Though he has often been critical of missionaries, he can see some merits and potential in their work. Accordingly he spends much time considering ideas for improving the lives of the peasants while at the same time making missionaries more effective. He's rather proud of his proposals and sends them to the zealous missionary Lord Shaftsbury. However, all his suggestions are dismissed and Tom's previous disillusionment is confirmed: 'Thank God that I learnt to comprehend something of the pure spirit of Xtianity before I met these men.' He has a good rant against Wilberforce, whose religious fervour, that helped to abolish the slave trade, was less savoury from the perspective of India, because evangelicals like Wilberforce considered colonial India a gift from God where missionaries could go and save heathen souls from Hinduism. With liberal views closer to those of 18th century Englishmen such as Warren Hastings and 'Hindu' Stuart, Thomas was struggling against the narrowing Imperialist mindset of mid-19th century India that was leading to disaster.

As he has long since abandoned seafaring, indigo is no longer an option now Forlong has left Mulnath, and the missionaries have let him down, Tom's decides to 'employ his pen' and become a freelance writer. He plans to complete his book on indigo and then write travel articles, starting in the Himalayas. Meanwhile he has a chance to go on an interesting little jaunt. '*24th November 1854*. A letter from Major Smyth of the Revenue Department inviting me to Burdwan. I shall go and see him for I like him very much and at the same time shall visit the Coal mines and travel by an Indian Railway.'

The new railway line that leads from Calcutta to the mines amazes the locals. It's brand new and the main station at Howrah is still under construction so Tom has to buy his ticket in a makeshift shed. He takes the train to the end of the line so far, which is 50 miles, then it's back to horse and bullock cart for the last five miles to Burdwan. The 630-mile journey from Calcutta to Allahabad on the Ganges took three weeks by carriage and ferry then, but within a few years the journey time shrank to just two days, thanks to the new 'iron horse'.

Thomas is delighted to meet up again with Major Smyth, whom he encountered just before cholera struck, but delight turns to embarrassment when, on arrival, he is taken ill yet again. However, he overcomes this latest bout of fever in time to join Smyth on a visit to the Maharajah of Burdwan: 'We got into the Rajah's carriage a sabre and a brace of double-barrels lay on his seat... the Rajah spoke English like an English Gentleman and Major Smyth informed him I belonged to one of the old English families. Indeed said he is your name in Burke? I have every new edition of the Peerage and Landed Gentry.' They tour the Burdwan estates and palaces, as well as the missionaries' comfortable houses and hideous new church. To learn that 'The Rajah contributed £500 to the building of this church though himself a Hindoo' confirms Tom's opinion that the well-educated Maharajah is far more open-minded than the missionaries.

Smyth's invitation to Burdwan is followed by a letter offering Thomas a job. European entrepreneurs like Smyth, worried by indigo's decline, were now pioneering coffee in southern India, aping Ceylon's recent coffee rush. The position is supervisor of Smyth's new coffee estates in the Malabar hills of south-west India. Thomas agrees to go on a recce with him and from there take the opportunity to sail up India's western coast and the Indus River for a fraternal reunion in the North-West Frontier.

18. 'Further Travels and Adventures of a Vagrant Son' – Up the Indus

December stillness, crossed by twilight roads,
Teach me to travel far and bear my loads

(Siegfied Sassoon 1886 - 1967)

A deadly bomb exploded in the marketplace of Peshawar in January 2007, just weeks before I was due to meet Thomas there. Foreigners were advised to stay away. The incident wouldn't have surprised Thomas. In 1855 he was in Peshawar with his brother Lance, who was overseeing the ordnance needed to keep the peace in this troublesome frontier town at the eastern end of the Khyber Pass, in what's now known as the North-West Frontier Province.

Thousands of foreign soldiers who served, in previous centuries, Alexander the Great, Genghis Khan and Babur the first Moghul, had crossed these gaunt mountains before soldiers of the British Raj took their turn. A century later degenerate hippies like me spluttered through in patchwork vans during a relatively peaceful spell, though bandits always prowl and we spent a memorable night in Kandahar's squalid jail avoiding them. All the years I've been writing this book, this lawless region of fluid borders has again been a crucible of terrorism.

It's such a cliché that history repeats itself, with variations, but Kipling's 'savage wars of peace' continue to be the 'White Man's burden'. Empires and allegiances may alter but the same battles are being fought by descendants of the same people in the same places; the main pieces of Kim's Great Game now shuffling round the board in Afghanistan and neighbouring Russia,

Iran, Pakistan and Kashmir as they were when young Machells were there.

Lance, a brilliant mathematician, nobly abandoned his final two years of engineering training just after his 16th birthday to rush east and serve the Empire. Tom's summary for the family book understates the reason: 'The war with the Afghans had thinned the ranks of the Artillary and the troubled state of the Punjab induced the government to increase the Arm of the Service and supply more Officers by giving direct employment to the best men at Addiscombe.' The 'thinning' of ranks was in fact the total slaughter of Britain's rag-tag 'Army of the Indus', a shock to the nation's amour propre in what was later labelled the First Afghan war. It occurred in 1842 while Tom was stuck in the (first) Opium War in China.

The 1842 fiasco was Afghan tribesmen's revenge on the British for deposing their popular ruler, Dost Mohammed, in 1839 and replacing him with the former Amir Shah Shujah, by then a weak and debauched puppet of the Empire – a classic case of regime change by bayonet that would backfire on the protagonists, who chose to ignore warnings from their experienced emissaries. Even true life accounts such as those of the formidable Lady Florentia Sale – 'the Grenadier in Petticoats' held captive for nine months, whose tombstone reads 'Under this stone reposes all that could die of Lady Sale' – read like the fictions they've inspired, such as the Flashman escapades. In a film it would seem over-dramatic for everyone to die save a single badly wounded survivor who struggled into the fort on a dying horse; but this is what actually happened. And he only survived thanks, he wrote, to 'a portion of Blackwoods Magazine' stuffed into his cap that saved enough of his skull from the slice of a scimitar; a most Victorian salvation, though it was usually the Bible in the breast pocket that did it.

To avenge her humiliating defeat and protect and extend her Indian empire, Britain sent a punitive Army of Retribution into Afghanistan and in 1843 conquered Sind (General Napier being convinced he was an instrument of God, which also sounds familiar). Two years later the British East India Company was fighting the Sikhs in the First Sikh war, which is where young Lance comes in, joining his regiment on a Punjabi battlefield in February 1846. The Second Sikh War, to finish the job, followed two years later. In 1849 the Punjab – and the Koh-i-noor diamond – were acquired for the British Crown in an act of vengeance likened by Hopkirk, in his wonderful book *The Great Game*, to that of a bully losing a street fight, going home and beating up his wife.

Lance distinguished himself in both Sikh wars, was commended several times in dispatches and promoted to First Lieutenant in the Horse Artillery before he turned 20. He also won all the horse races. ('Nothing has surprised me so much as the general acknowledgement of Lance's talent and gallant conduct' Thomas wrote in 1855. No wonder he felt inferior to his younger brother and no wonder Lance had little patience for weakness.)

Five years after the end of the Second Sikh War we find Lance on sick leave, issuing a rare invitation to Thomas to join him. It nearly doesn't happen because Thomas, having done his recce in southern India, loses another of his nine lives en route to Bombay. Again he suffers a near-fatal fever. He only survives thanks to having taken a last-minute passage in Cananore on a Jewish owned opium clipper whose solicitous Captain personally nurses him. Tom recovers just as the clipper reaches Bombay, where it will exchange its cargo of 'beautiful goods from the Celestial Empire' for opium.

Thomas finds Bombay 'dull dirty and disagreeable', comparing the city unfavourably with Alexandria, Cairo and Calcutta. Poet Laurie Lee later found wartime Bombay 'A nakedness of jewels and sores/Clutched with our guilt in her embrace', but I wonder what he and Thomas would make of modern Mumbai with its Bollywood film-stars flashing expensive mobile phones, shiny blocks of flats, and huge flyovers arcing over stinking slums. And how about the luxurious Taj hotel, where in my hippy days I unscrupulously took free meals off a lonely American businessman when myself lodging in a communal dormitory in a rough city hostel? Thomas makes excursions from Bombay to the Elephanta caves, samples the thirty-five miles of new railway line 'that leads to nowhere at present', and enjoys the Hindu theatre despised by his naval companions. The local papers are, he tells us, obsessed with the races, and the overland mail with the siege at Sebastopol. (This sounds like the early years of the 21st century if you substitute football for races, and Iraq and Afghanistan for the Crimea.)

Thomas reaches Karachi on Sunday 18th February 1855 and then travels up the Indus to Kashmir and the North-West Frontier by steamer and local boat, and on land by camel and horse or on foot. Much of the time he is feeling what he calls 'desperately seedy'. He describes a forty-four mile horse ride over rough ground in a day 'nothing for one in sound health but a heavy undertaking for an invalid'. He traces his attacks of 'ague and fever' back to his sickness in China, presumably malaria. But he usually rallies, determined, as he puts it, 'to be jolly under the circumstances', and I admire the way he keeps up his journal entries when unwell, though his handwriting betrays the effort.

On my birthday four days after Tom's arrival in Karachi, I canter beside him into the starlit desert before dawn to visit the famous hot wells of Muggur Peer, the alligator saint, returning to a Karachi army camp for a birthday breakfast. Two days later he boards the little Chenab steamer from the Indus flotilla, bound via Sind for Multan in Punjab. The steamer has a 'flat' in tow for transporting troops while Thomas has me in tow. As well as the usual army crowd, he meets Major Strange, head of the 'Astronomical Survey Department', and repeats his longing to consort with the intellectual elite of the Trigonometrical Society instead of working among 'vulgar and illiterate men'. It's too late though, he is on the wrong path.

The long anticipated reunion with Lance, after a 12 year gap, takes place in March 1855, at Dera Ghazi Khan halfway up the Indus. The day the brothers meet Thomas writes a few lines that are emphatically crossed out. We know he only messes up his passages in the Journal with such erasures when he's written something too personal; has his old sense of inferiority surfaced so quickly? His increasing isolation becomes clear enough over the next few months. He records no warm words from Lance, and expresses hurt when Lance cuts him out of his plans. What about Lance's plucky fair-haired new wife, Susey? At first she and Thomas get on fine, often riding together when Lance is occupied elsewhere or too unwell. Her energy often outstrips both men and she revels in being the first white woman ever seen in many of the settlements they pass through on their tough march up the Chenab and Jhelum rivers and over innumerable mountain passes into Kashmir.

En route they pass through Punjab where the landscape is equally bipolar. Thomas relishes great date plantations and riverside villages with 'neatly cultivated fields watered by the Persian wheel', while inland the scenery is 'as wild and desolate as anyone could wish to see'. But he enjoys the drama of these desolate hills, and is fascinated, for example, by the shapes and colours of the Great Salt Range when the party visit Maree's salt station. They camp by mountain streams or stop off at military outposts where Lance is well known. Bigger settlements such as Maree, founded four years earlier, were fast becoming social centres for the military and would soon be favoured Raj hill stations.

The route the little Machell group takes north-east to Kashmir via Rawalpindi is beautiful in late spring and Thomas revels in the trees, flowers and birds. One can almost smell with him the dog roses and juniper, see the flowering pomegranates, mulberries and opium poppies, and hear cuckoos singing across terraces of bright green corn. But the going is often hard. Sometimes they ride ponies while camels carry the baggage, but often they scramble on foot over steep stony ground through dense pine forests, keeping an eye out for bears.

In early June the party approaches the summer capital, Srinagar, by water. Thomas calls the landscapes of this Kashmir valley 'sublime' but there are drawbacks, not least the oversized mosquitoes. Srinagar also has two sides, summed up in Thomas's conclusion that 'it is one of most picturesque and filthiest cities under the sun.' He's as disappointed by the 'tumbledown' Royal palace as he is by the behaviour of his fellow countrymen when they pay court there to the Amir: 'Though rejoicing in the appellation of Officers and gentlemen they are apt to play the snob and confirm the general opinion of them entertained by the natives that they are drunkards and gluttons.' Not that he is any more impressed by the Amir, who, he says, oppresses and over-taxes his people, who are 'patient hard-working slaves resembling the Russian peasantry'.

While faithfully describing, with some lovely sketches, the outward sights and events on this long journey to Kashmir, Thomas sometimes allows us into his inner landscape too. One idyllic June day, for example, as they pass through 'a land of milk and honey', he is in despair. 'This day our journey has been through beautiful places – but the heart knoweth its own bitterness. Oh Lord my God, deliver me from these hours of darkness.' What has happened to his dreams of adventure? 'I remember the time when I read *Lallah Rookh*

Thomas's sketch of the boat, with detail of its carved woodern stern, in which he travelled down the Indus River in 1856.

and *Robinson Crusoe* and I almost wish those pleasant boyhood dreams had never been dispelled. the world is a very matter of fact place to me now I feel more like a postbook of roads and conveyances than a romance.'

The family heads north from Srinagar to rest at the shrine of Shah Saduk Calundan, on a hillside spur in a grove of willows and mulberries. Susey adopts native dress and goes bear-hunting alone, with a boldness that astonishes the locals and Thomas alike. On his first wedding anniversary Lance receives, thanks to visitors bringing letters and a newspaper, his official appointment to be in charge of Peshawar's Ordnance Dept, and they learn that Sebastopol is still holding out. Thomas is horrified to read of the death of James Forlong's adored daughter Charlotte at sixteen. 'The cloud deepens, my soul is wrapped in gloom and I cannot distinguish how much I owe to physical or how much I am a victim of mental disease.' Tom is ashamed of himself as he struggles to cling onto his aspiration to achieve something 'useful' in his lifetime.

In early August, when the Machell brothers are back in Srinagar, they read that their young brother Robert was among the two thousand English killed at Sebastopol. 'The very flower of our family, fallen in his first fight before his 21st birthday,' Thomas laments. 'This is a bitter sorrow to me but how much more so to our dear Father. Right willingly would I have taken that poor boy's place and substituted my life for his. Again the flower is taken and the weed remains.'

Within a couple of days comes anticipation of another loss to compound Tom's despair. 'Another parting from Lance who went off to Peshawar to join his appointment he is still very ill and I fear we may never meet again. Susan accompanied him as far as Baramula but she is to return and stay with me for a time until we hear of Lance's arrangements after which she goes to him and I turn my face southward.' Next day Thomas, though 'very far from well and very very sad and lonely', manages to visit a rundown Moghul mansion, sketch Kashmir's oldest Hindu temple, and buy a papier-mâché cover for his Journal. And the following day, to his great surprise, Lance and Susey return together, having decided to leave Kashmir for good.

So all three now set off for Peshawar, back through the Punjab via Rawalpindi. There were no roads and the return trek is particularly hard. No wonder the brothers remain ill; they're forever wading through muddy swamps, climbing over rainy mountain passes, or camping in frost. Incidents en route include Lance shooting an enormous porcupine. Tom writes that day's journal account with one of its quills.

Back in Muree, after three weeks on foot from Srinagar, things look up. There is a letter from home saying Bob is alive and in Ireland, having never been to Crimea, though Father had received an official letter of condolence from Lord Panmur. 'How they will laugh at our letters from Kashmir,' writes Tom.

In mid October the air has turned frosty, the leaves autumnal, and Tom and Susey turn towards Peshawar, to join Lance, who has now gone on ahead. The high route to Huzara district, in the North-West Frontier, takes them past many locals – 'a hardy and industrious race' – gathering tiny harvests on terraced fields. At Abbotabad station, in territory just as volatile today, General Cotton, 'one of the stiff old school,' reviews the troops and stages a mock battle, watched with amusement by Tom. (In 2011 Abbotabad would make the headlines when US President Barack Obama announced that American troops had killed there the world's most wanted man, Osama bin Laden. After a ten year search for him they discovered his final hideout near the city's military cantonments which were under construction when the Machells passed through.) Being foreigners, the Machells require a military escort to the Khyber Pass because the Amirs of Afghanistan and Punjab are at loggerheads over possession of Peshawar.

Thomas now withdraws into a place no one can reach. Up to his arrival in Peshawar on 29th October 1855 he has scribbled away even when ill, but over the next two months spent in the town's military cantonment he doesn't write a single description (that he's prepared to keep, that is). In bad health, plagued as always by his physical disability, unemployed and unsure of his future, he is the misfit side-lined and humiliated by Lance and Susey, who are now settled among their own kind. He never again refers to Susey by name, instead calling her 'Lance's wife' or 'Mrs Machell'. Hurt and inadequate (in modern jargon lacking self-esteem), he descends into a depression.

This appalling blackness is hinted at in notes buried in a mass of Journal appendices that include samples of Kashmiri cloth, pieces of birch bark and transcriptions of local songs. Three days after his arrival in Peshawar, he rides out of town and writes a near suicidal line: 'The temptations of death compass me round about and the pains of Hell gain hold of me.' He heads the second, undated note, 'the same old tale'. 'I am a lover of nature, admirer of beauty and have seen some of the noblest views in the world,' he writes, 'and I can bear fatigue and welcome privation but in all this the recollection of bitterness which must accompany me through life has preyed on me here; and neither the music of the shepherd… nor the mountain and forest have for one moment lightened the weight on my heart or enabled me to lose my own wretched identity.'

On New Year's Day 1856 Tom's mood lightens enough for him to resume writing. He starts with a description of the lively pageant held on Peshawar's parade ground to celebrate – at last – the Fall of Sebastopol. It is watched by 'thousands of natives mounted and on foot, and Ladies in Carriages or on horseback, including 'Mrs Machell with a staff of her own'. All the regiments march past the general to the roar of artillery, until Lance's Horse Artillery appear in a cloud of sand and dust. 'Such gallant looking men such splendid horses they seem the very pickd and chosen of the frontier army.' Irony may be the best defence against inner turmoil.

Next day Thomas can leave these darkest of days behind him. 'What I have so anxiously desired today came to pass Lance is to go home to England on medical certificate and we start tomorrow Thank God for my own part I leave Peshawar and the Punjab without regret and never wish to see it again.'

19. Coffee Time

What would the world be, once bereft
Of wet and wildness? Let them be left,
O let them be left, wildness and wet;
Long live the weeds and the wilderness yet.

(*Inversnaid*, Gerard Manley Hopkins)

My path criss-crossed so often with Thomas's in southern India that I couldn't tell whether I was stalking him or he was stalking me.

Near the end of 2000 Ratna Krishnakumar spotted a copy of my *Indigo* in a Mumbai bookshop window and bought it just before meeting up with her friend Ruby Ghuznavi, only to discover that I was the person whom Ruby had joined in Bangladesh to share escapades with Glencairn and a young man called Thomas. Ratna was intrigued to hear that my young man had also worked in coffee on her own home patch. She asked Ruby for my contact details.

I had a surprise call from Ratna, who introduced herself and said: 'I'm on a brief visit to UK and would love to meet you. Will you by any chance be in London this week?' I was going next day so we arranged a meeting. I was instantly entranced by her serenity and poise. Over a Keralan fish curry we talked and talked. 'Promise you'll let me know if you ever come to southern India to look for Thomas,' insisted Ratna when we parted. 'I'd love to help you with your search for him, and also show you my natural dye project with disabled children.'

This meeting sowed a seed (or in this case bean). I was even awarded a grant to pursue Thomas among the coffee bushes in the Western Ghats above the Malabar Coast.

Hitherto, trips to India had included scrums at railway stations, impenetrable officialdom and insalubrious hotels. Not this time though.

When Glencairn and I arrived at Mumbai airport in early March 2001 we were gathered up by a white-gloved chauffeur and driven straight to the Krishnakumar's luxury downtown flat, the start of a two-week magical mystery tour that would end with a bang. Ratna and her husband KK, who, we now learnt, was Managing Director of the famous Taj hotels group (having previously managed Tata's tea and coffee estates), were away but had left us a note. 'Make yourselves at home' it read. So we did.

Two days later we were back at the airport after a morning spent dodging rainbows of gaudy paint being chucked around the streets to celebrate the festival of Holi. The Krishnakumars had booked our flights to Banglalore and arranged for Bency Isaac, senior manager of Tata's coffee interests in Karnataka, to meet us at the airport and accompany us on our expedition.

My previous arrival in Karnataka over three decades earlier could hardly have been more different. On Thursday 9th April 1970 I had stepped down onto the platform of Mysore railway station after three days on the train. Back then, windows of third class railway carriages, where people crammed in like cattle, only had bars, so soot from the steam engine flew in and settled like black snow on everything in the carriage. I was as grubby as the Afghan carpetbag slung over my shoulder. (How do India's poor women manage to look so beautiful when surrounded by squalor – like exquisite butterflies dancing over cowpats?)

I was expecting to be met by my unknown host, John Morris. But he wasn't there. I later learnt he hadn't received my letter from Delhi. John Morris was southern India's very last British coffee planter. He and his wife, friends of friends of my parents, had invited me to stay, though busy packing up a lifetime's possessions prior to emigrating to Tasmania. Despite my ignorance of colonial history I was vaguely aware their departure marked the end of an era; an era launched, as I found out 30 years later, by Thomas and his fellow planters in the 1850s.

Picture the dirty me, standing outside Mysore's now deserted station, clutching my old guitar case and watching the last chattering family groups seep away like water down the plughole of my dream bath.

'Can I be helping you please miss?' asked a young Indian in a brilliant white shirt who materialised djinn-like by my side after I slumped onto my carpet bag to think out my next move. 'I don't think you can, thank you,' I replied, 'unless you happen to know a British coffee planter called Morris who lives somewhere in the hills over there near a place called Chamarajanagar'. 'I have never been hearing of him,' replied the youth, wobbling his head, 'but I am having the telephone number of another foreigner who lives in Mysore and who is also having a coffee estate somewhere abouts.' And on the spot he wrote out a name, address and phone number, just like that. I found a phone box, dialled the number and asked for the person written on the scrap of paper – a Mr Joubert Van Ingen, whose name meant nothing to me.

Joubert answered my phone call and I outlined my predicament. 'The Morrises are good friends of mine he said. 'Would you like to come to lunch?' Ten minutes later a battered jeep with canvas top appeared at the station and out jumped a 'lank and wrinkled man' (as seen through my teenage eyes) in long khaki shorts. 'Welcome to Mysore,' said Joubert Van Ingen, as he stretched out his bony hand and drew me into his history.

Over 30 years later, in 2003, an historian called Pat Morris would publish a book on the Van Ingens with these words in the introduction: 'Meeting Joubert Van Ingen I felt as Stanley must have done on his first encounter with Dr Livingstone. Here was a man whose name was internationally known, whose experience encompassed much that is now the stuff of history books… His outstretched hand was like a bridge to the past.' My first handshake with Joubert unknowingly spanned bridges to the future as well as to the past.

However, when I followed Joubert through his front door in 1970 I had no idea his family was famous, nor what it was famous for. So it was a shock to step into an immensely long and tall hallway resembling a macabre gallery in a Victorian natural history museum. Hundreds of pairs of eyes stared me out from either side; the walls were stacked floor to ceiling with mounted animal heads and cases of stuffed birds and fish, interspersed with sepia photographs of men in shorts and funny hats holding the day's catch, or standing with a heavy boot planted on the carcass of a tiger or elephant.

Over lunch I met Joubert's brothers, de Wet and Botha, and a picture, filled in later by the Morrises, began to emerge of my courteous hosts and their unusual profession. With names like that, the three brothers (and absent Kruger, not involved in the business) must surely be South African. But no – they were named after Boer War heroes, their parents cocking a snook at those in India who, after the Boer War, ostracised people with Dutch-sounding names. The family has deliberately glossed over its true origins, preferring to be considered 'Anglo-Indian' in the sense of Europeans long established in India, so no wonder I was puzzled back then, writing in a letter home: 'I'm not sure what nationality they are.' (A younger family member told me years later that they descended from 17th century Dutch traders in Ceylon, who later moved to India and took up hunting, shooting and fishing – and later taxidermy – to become more 'British'.)

I learnt that the taxidermy firm of Van Ingen and Van Ingen had been founded in the 1890s by my hosts' father and that, two decades later, the house, Bissel Munti, with its extraordinary gallery, was built near the enormous taxidermy sheds that covered an acre. The firm was world famous in the 20th century and examples of its products are still sought after and widely displayed today in museums, palaces and private homes. Many nobs were Van Ingen customers, game hunting being synonymous with colonial rule in British India. When Tom declares, 'I have no fancy for knocking over birds or animals for amusement,' he's out of kilter with the times, and he qualifies it with: 'at the same time I confess my tender heart is not in the way when I want to secure a specimen for my museum or to destroy a beast of prey.' Big game was so abundant then that villagers welcomed hunters who shot the tigers that menaced them. Europeans and Indian princes alike threw lavish hunting parties and wanted trophies to adorn their walls. The Van Ingen products were of exceptional quality, thanks largely to Joubert, who applied his sculptor's skills to trophy modelling from 1929 until the business closed.

Visitors to the factory over the years, apart from Maharajahs and Viceroys, included the Emperor of Ethiopia, the Shah of Persia, the King of Afghanistan and many famous Hollywood film stars. In post-colonial 1970 there was no sense of an end in sight, for trophy hunters worldwide were still dispatching hides to be stuffed and mounted. The huge main shed hummed with workers. I was fascinated by their narrow specialities, such as cleaning skulls with toothpicks and painting the insides of mouths. 'Highly skilled work but rather morbid' was my conclusion then. Soon after my visit the Kenyan and Indian governments banned big game hunting on conservation grounds, India also prohibiting the import of trophies from Africa, but the factory limped on until the end of the century, mainly working for zoos and museums.

My eccentric weather-beaten hosts seemed to be bachelors (though Botha did have an absent wife) and being around sixty years old – not much older than me as I write this – appeared as ancient as the surrounding hills. Their impression of the guitar-playing teenager who had landed like an alien in their midst can't have been all bad because they invited me to stay. Thus I got a bath that evening, the first since leaving London. It was a freestanding tin tub filled up by a 'boy' using buckets (do I sound like Dr Livingstone?) and it was heaven. Next morning I wrote in my diary: 'What luxury, yet the Van Ingens call it 'roughing it'. After the bath we had supper, waited on hand and foot, eating fish caught by a Rajasthani prince and duck shot by Joubert. Good gamey conversation [reminds me of Tom's comment at a dinner also near Mysore: 'made acquaintance with some hunters just in from a shooting expedition and of course I was a good listener']. After dinner listened to tapes of birdsong and animal sounds recorded in the forest around their coffee plantation. And a lovely sleep in a huge bed shrouded by a ghostly grey mosquito net.'

Thomas and Major Smyth leave Calcutta together by P and O steamer in 1854. Thomas satirises the week-long non-stop eating and drinking on board until they reach Madras, a city he compares favourably with Calcutta. Just before he left Calcutta he went with Howard to visit his children's tomb, and in Madras he accompanies Smyth to the grave of one of his children. Both men have accepted the family tragedies with the forbearance of the time, remaining generous to others rather than becoming embittered.

After two days of riding in horse- and bullock-drawn carriages and walking, the two Englishmen reach Bangalore, where, to their amusement, Tom is saluted as a military man because of his moustache and whiskers, while the clean-shaven major is ignored. The pair soon continue on towards Mysore, finding roads under repair and brand new travellers' bungalows constructed in preparation for an imminent visit by Governor General Lord Dalhousie, or, in Thomas's sarcastic description, 'the great Lord Sahib the Viceroy of all India from Cormorin to Peshawar.'

Nearing Mysore they stop at Seringapatam, site of the decisive battle between the future Duke of Wellington and the fearsome Tipu Sultan just over fifty years earlier. Tom finds the large fortified town a typical 'medley of magnificence dirt and decay'. Heading towards the hills, Tom and Smyth pass through cultivated land until they reach unhealthy dense jungle at the foot of the 'Nilgherries', the 'Blue Mountains'. The air grows fresher the higher they climb. Stopping to admire the view, Father is in Tom's thoughts, such is the yearning homesickness at the heart of his peripatetic life. 'I thought of our walks together when we used to sit down and call a prospect,' he writes that evening in a traveller's bungalow. 'I have written till the candles are out and Major Smyth asleep and so good night.'

Next day, Tom describes 'aborigines', whom I termed 'jungle tribes' when likewise dwelling on their singularities. They reach Ootacamund, the famed hill station loved by the British and even back in the 1850s nicknamed Ooty. Tom calls it an English village on top of the highest mountain in southern India. He and Smyth explore the town looking at potential retirement houses for Smyth's family, but alas, within two years Tom will have added a note in the margin of this page telling us Mrs Smyth died soon after arriving in Ooty and was buried in the churchyard. Perhaps someone will seek out her grave after reading this and place a nasturtium on it on behalf of Smyth and Tom.

Tom's jolly mood is short-lived. He soon tires of Ooty, which is sociable but snobbish and uninspiring. 'Only at home can I endure rest and then it is happiness,' he tells us, 'for I have all that I love around me but here I must have active employment or – Nay, I will not think of it, but if I die out here it will be for want of employment; but now I'll be off and smoke a cheroot for I feel as melancholy as a sick monkey.' Here's that hint again of suicidal thoughts. Tom is only happy at home yet cannot allow himself to live there. He must prove he can overcome his disability and make his way in the world.

Like Tom, I relished the cool mountain air, landscapes and lakes but soon grew bored with Ooty and find my 1970 notes to be rather unflattering. 'With its dreary shops it's as dead as an old gold mining town (apart from a brief summer racing season), a ghost that had a brief moment of glory.' With sharp relish I added: 'the Club where the men were once so snooty is now a place of past brilliance.' I described two people eating at separate tables in the huge dining room, a solitary elderly white woman with wispy hair sitting at the bar, and the enormous drawing room empty, though its scrapbooks were, I wrote, 'filled with photos of moustachioed hunting types and their horsey frivolous wives'. At the old Lovedale public school I met the young man who had beaten me to a teaching job there and was very glad he had done so.

Leaving Ooty in mid-December, Tom and Smyth hike, on foot and on pony, through near impenetrable jungle, covering the 84 miles to 'Manutoddy', the Wynaad (Wayanad) region's military cantonment cum planters' station. The best village name en route is Gunnapuddywattum, says Tom, who's amazed to be taking horses across the Manutoddy River on a bamboo raft.

Thomas is impressed by Manutoddy's setting but not by its English inhabitants. 'The Madras Presidency has not obtained the title of "the Benighted" for nothing,' he observes after his first evening with narrow-minded Wynaad planters who take no interest in their locality. Next day,

Christmas Eve, Smyth and Tom ride the eight miles to Smyth's new coffee estate of Bon Espoir.

> The bungalow is rather picturesquely situated on a hill overlooking the estate, the background filled up with steep hills crowned with dense jungle and all around is cleared land covered with coffee bushes at this season laden with red berries looking like Christmas holly in England. A blazing hot sun and sharp North-Easterly wind explains why fever is so common here.

25th December 1854 Christmas day. Blank enough.

The following pages are filled with descriptions of the local population, religious festivals and topography ('I know nothing about geology but I like to make a note of these things' he writes, with a Victorian's curiosity) and detailed discussions on all aspects of coffee cultivation and production. 'There's no place so well able to produce coffee as these Malabari hills, save perhaps Mocha or Coonoor,' he marvels. On these new estates even the steepest slopes were being cleared and planted with lines of bushes. Since virgin forest filled all the horizons then, Tom's sensitivity to their destruction is more than a century ahead of his time. Two days after Christmas, he writes: 'Walked some three or four miles this morning to look for a suitable site for the new estate which Major Smyth is intending to open and fixed upon a fine piece of woodland which will be as bare as axes and fire can make it before this time next year... one cannot help a feeling of regret that those splendid trees should be cut down and burnt like so many useless weeds and rubbish.' He then writes a prose passage so lyrical that Glencairn thought it was free verse when I read it out aloud to him. The last line of this moving elegy to each type of tree reads: 'High in the forest you may see the Sandalwood that... sheds a perfume upon the axe that fells it.'

These southern Indian hills were 'a sportsman's Elysium' for those so inclined. Elephant-shooting was especially popular (in 1850 alone eight thousand Indian elephants were shot to make British billiard balls). Thomas Bassano, a contemporary of Thomas, delighted by his Wynaad posting wrote to his brother: 'How happy I shall be there – plenty of shooting, tigers by the hundreds and wild Elephants by the scores,' whereas Thomas writes: 'Major Smyth said I vote that if we do see an elephant we let him alone ditto said I provided he lets us alone.' How I love them for defying the trend. Since their day, most of India's big game has been tortured to near extinction, often just for use in traditional Chinese medicine.

In March 2001 Glencairn, Bency and I wound up to the Western Ghats on a nightmare road of aggressive traffic. Had Thomas joined our party he would have felt reasonably at home because the Wayanad hills, part game reserve, remain unusually wild and wet. Peacocks stride fearlessly across roads, wild elephants still frighten people and monkeys leap among gigantic creepers 'drooping from huge branches like cables hanging out to dry' as Tom put it. I liked best the armies of giant bamboos that march up and down the hillsides.

First stop was, of course, the hill station of Mananthavady, Tom's 'Manutoddy', where I'd pinned my hopes of finding clues to his last years.

But now I was actually in Mananthavady what a let down it was. A typical scruffy town with house fronts swept clean but streets full of litter and whiffs of decay. Street stalls displayed plastic toys in shocking pink and lime green, admired by young girls with younger sisters in their arms, matted dusty hair, snotty faces, big eyes, sadness. Patient Bency had already entered into the spirit of the Thomas trail and was following its twists and turns, however absurd, with genuine interest as well as remarkable good humour and patience. He made enquiries for me in dingy offices where there were indeed, crammed inside and on top of Dickensian wooden cupboards, unopened mounds of folders tied in ribbons and coated in dust, as if dirty icing sugar had been sifted all over them. But that is old India, not romantic Victoriana. The chances of Tom's missing papers hanging around in India a century and half after they were written (if they ever were written) were, now I came to think of it, about one in five million.

'This is a waste of time, let's push on to Bramagiri,' I suggested. We bought fizzy orangeade in grimy glass bottles and a packet of stale biscuits, and set off for Tom's former home of Bon Espoir. Before leaving UK I had intended to hunt down old maps of the area but did not do because I had received an email from Ratna announcing that Bon Espoir had been located (as the present day Bramagiri).

Heading for Tom's estate should have been exciting, but I felt flat after visiting Manathavady, perhaps preparing myself for further disappointment. The journey shouldn't have taken long by car, seeing as Thomas did it on horseback, but we seemed to be going far too far, up and down through jungle bright with yellow cascades of laburnum, scarlet poinsettia and flashy parakeets. Endless roadside shacks offered palm liquor toddy. There was still no sign of Bramagiri. At last, after Bency had asked directions fifty times, we found a dirt track with a faded 'Bramagiri A' painted on a low wooden sign. We lurched down the track but I didn't feel as thrilled as I knew I should. I had absolutely no sense of recognition. 'Where are you Thomas?' I asked. 'Please don't desert me now, I've come all the way from Polynesia to find you in these remote jungles, and you seem to be vanishing.' I forced myself to feel something, but I didn't.

We passed through acres of floppy coffee bushes, with a few unsmiling bedraggled workers among them, until we reached a bungalow. It was in unappetising Raj style, roofed in fat clay tiles, and could well have been Tom's but I just knew it wasn't.

Unusually for India, the place seemed deserted. Bency called out in all directions while Glencairn and I peered into the stygian interior, which reminded me of Thomas's description of his bungalow. On his ground plan he labelled the rooms thus: 'damp bedroom always', 'dark and damp useless room', 'dressing room wet as a pond', 'useless room' and – a little more hopefully – 'dry bedroom sometimes'. Still trying to feel excited, I glared at a distant grass hill, willing it to be the one Tom sketched.

An old man in a filthy *dhoti* slid up from nowhere. He gabbled away to Bency, with much head wobbling and suspicious glances at us. Bency

Thomas's sketch of the bungalow on Bon Espoir coffee estate in the Wynaad (Wayanad) district of the Western Ghats, northeast Kerala, where he lived from 1855-56.

turned to me with surprising news. 'Guess what?' he declared, 'half of this estate belongs to Michael Van Ingen, son of Botha, one of the brothers you told me you stayed with thirty years ago!' I didn't know whether any Van Ingens were alive, let alone still living in India and growing coffee. Besides, the Morris's had claimed thirty years earlier to be the end of the Raj coffee planter line, but maybe they hadn't considered the Van Ingens to be British, given their mysterious Dutch origins.

'Let's go there,' I urged Bency. The old man, looking shifty, scratched his crotch through his *dhoti* as we returned to our jeep.

Continuing along the dirt track, we soon reached the gates of 'Bramagiri B'. The gates were locked. 'The workers are on strike and have been rioting,' explained Bency. He wanted to contact the local police in case of trouble, but there was no phone signal, so he couldn't. We decided to leave Glencairn, who was nursing a sore foot, with the jeep while we climbed over the gate and made a dash down the unkempt track. 'Come on, let's be off,' said Bency, looking round nervously. The place seemed deserted but no sooner had we set off than a surly man materialised from the coffee bushes with their rotting fruit and started to shadow us. Bency's nerves were contagious. I wished he hadn't just passed on the old man's account of the horrible fate of Mr Duncan, the owner of the estate before Botha bought it in 1934. Firstly Duncan's French wife went literally mad with loneliness, and then he himself was murdered by a worker, his body dragged into the bushes. The crime was discovered by chance when Botha visited the estate soon afterwards and a wild boar appeared from the bushes with Duncan's foot and shoe in its mouth. This had occurred on the track we were now walking along. It hadn't put Botha off the purchase.

'I had to lend my sword and pistol to a neighbour who is having trouble with his workers,' wrote Thomas at Bon Espoir. This sentence dropped into my head when I glanced behind me and found the evil-looking man still following us. Suddenly we heard a noise from the direction of the jeep. Bency tensed further. 'Let's go back,' he said.

We escaped to the safety of a nearby Vishnu temple, Thirunatti. In late afternoon sunshine women in pink saris, leading bony cows necklaced with huge rectangular wooden cow bells, jerkily descended steep worn steps down to the sacred river below. Then it was on over the Bramagiri hills into Coorg district where, just as the sun set pink over the distant jungle, we arrived at Tata's Cottabetta Guesthouse, a romantic former planter's bungalow on a hilltop. Here we were thoroughly spoilt. As I wrote to Thomas that evening: 'You must be working your magic again. I only met Ratna Krishnakumar once for lunch in London and now – thanks to you – instead of struggling around India on trains and buses, we're being escorted everywhere by jeep and staying in wonderful guesthouses'.

Next morning Glencairn was still suffering from his ankle infection hatched in Polynesia so we called the doctor, a tiny Indian with a Scottish accent acquired when studying in Glencairn's home city of Edinburgh. He spoke Hausa, having worked in Nigeria, had a quirky sense of humour and said, 'Call me guru.' He ordered two days' rest at Cottabetta, partly, I suspected, because he enjoyed Glencairn's company so much. So we had to postpone our plans.

'Let's contact Michael Van Ingen,' suggested Bency. So we did, thanks to telephonic communication impossible when I was last there. Not only did we find Michael at home in Mysore, but we also learnt that Joubert, now 90, had outlived all his brothers and was still living in Bissel Munti where I stayed as a teenager. Michael invited me to stay in his Mysore house and I was keen to set off at once, but there was a workers' lightning strike, *bandh*, in the region that day and Bency insisted I delay. 'The car might be stoned,' he warned, 'and the police won't help if they sympathise with the strikers' cause.'

So it was late afternoon when the driver took me down and down a pot-holed road through bamboo forest, with glimpses of spotted deer, to the hot Mysore plain with its aloes, eucalyptus and bright birds on telegraph wires. Thomas and I had done this journey before. As usual the extreme poverty was depressing, but visions of rural life beautiful to the outsider who doesn't have to live them: graceful women pumping water at village wells and carrying it home on their heads in aluminium pots, their grubby children springing ahead barefoot, thin arms circling huge bundles of firewood; carts pulled by bullocks with painted horns and gaudy drapes on their backs; snow-white egrets on the backs of cattle in paddy fields; circular coracles in muddy tanks; the patterns of clothes drying on bushes looking like a Paul Klee painting; and *Saddhus* in dirty *dhotis* burning incense beneath marigold garlands hanging from the branches of shrine trees. As we approached the city there were more and more stinking lorries with the unnecessary 'Please Sound Horn' painted on their tailboards and, walking beside the road, schoolgirls, with neat plaits and long navy skirts, shouldering huge satchels.

Michael Van Ingen welcomed me into his house, built by his father and unimaginatively called 'The Land'. I found Michael freighted with worry about his rotting coffee. The unrest on his Bramagiri estate stemmed from a typically complicated Indian tale of contested land ownership, powerful unions, resentment of outsiders, bribery and corruption. His court case to prove ownership had been postponed sixteen times so far. I now learnt that we had been lucky to escape attack yesterday.

Michael's metal cupboards overflowed with unsorted paperwork, much of it rescued from destruction by his uncle Joubert. I learnt that the taxidermy factory closed just months earlier. My bedroom at 'The Land' resembled the one I had slept in at Bissel Munti all that time ago. Stone floor, bare table, and a basic bathroom, though hot water now came from a tank, the former tin tub relegated to the garden. Once in the large bed, cocooned by its much-needed mosquito net, I could write to Thomas: 'In my head,' I told him, 'I'm moving between parallel worlds at the moment. Their similarities and differences interweave. There are your experiences in the 1850s, mine in 1970 and of course mine again today. I have with me copies of your Journals and parts of mine unread for 30 years. As so often when looking at your life through mine there have been bizarre coincidences'.

'Of course,' said Thomas. I dreamt of shadows and distant howls of fear.

Next morning I returned to Bissel Munti after a 31 year absence and found it unchanged, apart from the plumbing. Almost unchanged too, was nonagenarian Joubert himself, as spry as when he leapt down from his khaki jeep to greet the naïve skinny teenager that was me in 1970. Joubert was still living for small game shooting, characteristically undeterred by recent laws making it illegal. He was now stuffing his own cartridges with local gunpowder to go poaching, relating this loudly with wicked relish, since the niece and her husband who were 'looking after him' were within earshot and disapproved. He was keeping them waiting to inherit this priceless house as well as Karticulum, the coffee estate I first visited.

Joubert gave me a reprise of the trophy tour in the long gallery, again relating their stories. There was Botha's first tiger, Duwet's first lioness (shot in Africa where the brothers would go for a change of scene), an elephant tusk weighing 96 pounds, a boar speared by Jubert on horseback, a Himalayan black bear – and so on. Among the photos was one of Duwet's 120-pound fish, a record still unbeaten then. The painted plaster-cast head of this fish gawped beside the photo. 'Would you like to see all the trophies I stuffed for the last Maharajah of Mysore?' asked Jubert. 'They're in a private room in the Palace, only visited by VIPs and my guests.' I was game for anything, forgive the pun. Joubert phoned the Director, and dispatched me to the palace, rebuilt since Tom's day.

Back in 1970 I peered at the immense building through locked wrought-iron gates but this time I was inside, being passed up a chain of grumpy petty bureaucrats until I reached the Director's hallowed office. Here I waited for ages for a minder to appear, while people shuffled in and out to fumble for keys in drawers or fill in forms. The minder appeared at last and took me to the Curator's office to fill in my own forms. Finally I was led past no end of gilded thrones and glass cases until we reached a set of double doors behind a rope barrier. My minder unlocked their vast padlock and we stepped into darkness. When he put the light on I gasped. We were in the Armoury and it was full of cases packed with weapons, some ceremonial but most designed to kill, including the sword Tipu Sultan used, unsuccessfully, to defend himself against the future Duke of Wellington in 1799, down the road at Seringapatam. The Trophy Room next door was equally awesome and gruesome, displaying the last Maharajah's hunting trophies, all immaculately stuffed, mounted and maintained by the Van Ingens to seem alive. Hundreds of animals, from giraffes to crocodiles, and including almost more tigers than exist in India today, glared into the claustrophobic centre of the room. Apparently the Maharajah was advised to shoot a hundred tigers to get a son and heir. So he did, and he got one.

With the Van Ingen business just closed and Joubert the sole survivor of his generation, would these trophies slowly disintegrate from then on, with no one to maintain them? And for how long can the next generation of Van Ingens cling to their two coffee estates?

In April 1970 I witnessed an explosion of coffee blossom for the first time. Coffee flowering peaks annually for a single day, following rain, and Joubert had heard via bush telegraph that conditions were ripe at his Kartikulum estate. So we set off at dawn, up the Kubbany River, which flows into Tom's familiar Mananthavady River, with islands mid stream like children's book illustrations. En route we passed elephants captured in the wild to be trained to work. Tethered to trees, they trumpeted loudly, tugging restlessly backwards and forwards on their chains.

I stepped from the jeep into the scent of Paradise. Imagine jasmine and orange blossom blended with something extra. Shaded by tall canopy trees with pepper vines spiralling up their trunks and dangling long catkins of green pepper, were acres of coffee bushes so dense with flowers they seemed coated in snow. Bees and iridescent butterflies were ecstatic with nectar and so was I. It was a day to remember and connect me to Thomas in the future – or is that the past?

My older self in 2001 was enchanted to find Kartikulum's bungalow exactly as before, because Joubert forbade alterations. Transport was by bullock cart and the watchman still used a bow and arrows ('in the Wynaad the ancient art of archery is still upheld' wrote Tom with surprise, even then). We tiffed on the veranda, ringed by shade trees of wild fig, jackfruit and rosewood with swathes of cardamom ferns spreading tentacles of blue-striped flowers along the ground below. The only sound was birdsong. 'Cherry' coffee was drying on wooden platforms. ('Cherry' coffee is black, unlike cherries, whereas what's known as 'fruit' is red – like cherries. By the way, if you want a decent cup of tea or coffee don't go to India where it comes from.)

In 1855, Tom, now managing Smyth's estates of Bon Espoir and 'Wynaad', needs something stronger than a cup of tea or coffee to cheer him up. He misses Bengal with its comfortable bungalows, few but good friends, 'scrupulously clean' natives, and access to books and papers from Calcutta. Besides, he frequently feels 'seedy' with fever and ague and is taking quinine again. (Having often smiled at Tom's use of the quaint adjective 'seedy', I found a diary entry of my own written in Ceylon's jungles in May 1970: 'I've been feeling a bit seedy recently'.) Malaria, cholera and black-water fever threaten during the wet season, but Tom still responds to the jungle's majesty and tries to keep his spirits up. Of Bon Espoir he writes: 'Nothing could equal the damp and discomfort of this bungalow which is over run with rats and saying this much I need say no more on the subject I am here to make the best of it.' He sketches suggested improvements and takes up beekeeping. There's plenty of work and there are frequent visitors, some bearing longed-for letters from home. He writes an article on Wynaad planters for 'The Madras Athenaeum', is secretary/treasurer for the local Planters' Association and starts a book club. It sounds as if they need the latter, since, Tom complains again, his fellow planters' conversation is limited to coffee, hunting, and making money, with no interest in the country they are working in. On the list of subscribers to his club we find Tom Bassano, quoted above, whose surviving letters give a flavour of the kind of planter our Tom complains about. Bassano's sporting interests include hunting down the local virgins.

20. Closing the Gap

There are more things in heaven and earth, Horatio
Than are dreamt of in your philosophy

(*Hamlet, Act 1 Scene 5*, quoted by both Thomas and
me in our diaries, long before we met)

If I were Zen I would leave this chapter blank. The Buddha was surely
right that the best way to express a transcendental experience is to
maintain a 'noble silence'.

There we were, poised to leave the heaven of Cottabetta estate after the
lucky delay. We sat on the terrace wall after breakfast, looking over layers
of gauzy hills, absorbing mingled smells of coffee blossom and spices and
sounds of servants' rhythmic sweeping. Our packed cases were at the top of
the steps, the driver was pointlessly polishing the car and we were chatting to
Bency while waiting for the 'guru' to arrive for farewells. When he appeared
he pronounced himself delighted Glencairn's ankle had healed so well.
'Good,' I said, 'now we can get going at last'. 'Don't be so impatient,' he
laughed, 'this is India! Why not relax for a couple more hours, have lunch
with the new guests on their way up from Tellicherry, and set off after that?
You'll still have time to visit Tellicherry and reach your hotel for the night.'

I forced a smile and looked at Bency, hoping he would insist we should
be off at once. But he just shrugged and looked resigned; he was getting
used to our changes of plan. Since Glencairn was fitting in with my Thomas
timetable the decision was left to me. I felt obliged to give in, so as not to
seem boringly British.

So at midday we were still idling on the terrace with books and tea when a dark car came up the drive and stopped beneath the curving steps. The driver opened a door and a tall middle-aged white man, grey-haired and lithe, stepped out. From the other side emerged an Indian woman in a sari the colour of marigolds, her friendly face framed by a western hairstyle. They climbed the steps to the terrace, where we introduced ourselves. The man, Bernard Imhasly, was a Swiss foreign correspondent based in New Delhi, who had just visited Tellicherry to research its coffee history in the exact period when Thomas was involved in the business. We chatted about this over drinks while Glencairn was talking to Bernard's wife, Rashna Imhasly-Gandhy, who told him she was in southern India promoting her newly published book called *The Psychology of Love*.

Just before lunch we swapped places. 'What brings you to this part of India?' Rashna asked me. In a few sentences I outlined my quest for Thomas. Rashna gave me a sharp look that made me feel uncomfortable, then asked: 'Have you ever thought of exploring your past lives?' I had never been asked such an astonishing question before – let alone by a stranger – and I wanted to reply 'No'. But out of my mouth came, 'No – but yes'. I tried to explain this contradiction. 'Some rather peculiar things have happened while I've been looking at Thomas's life,' I told her, 'but I haven't tried to analyse them and I certainly wouldn't consult some random hypnotherapist in the West.' Pause. 'Anyway,' I continued, puzzled, 'why did you ask me that?'

'I think there's something going on between you and this young man,' replied Rashna. She then explained that as a professional psychotherapist she often did 'past life regressions' with clients, though only if the timing was right and the person was ready for such an exploration. She sensed that I was, but confirmed it by carrying out various tests to do with significant dates. I was intrigued of course, but also extremely wary.

We continued our discussions over lentils at lunch. I learnt about Rashna's rigorous training in Switzerland in Jungian psychology, which she overlays with Oriental wisdom and archetypes. I warmed to her approach, which was straightforward with no hint of feyness. She described what a thorough past-life regression involves. 'Ideally it takes place over four days, though three is possible,' she explained. As we were due to depart for Tellicherry with Bency within the hour, any notion of having sessions with Rashna at Cottabetta seemed impossible, though she calculated she could squeeze in the minimum of three if she changed her programme and we started that afternoon. I looked at Glencairn, who said, 'Why don't you arrange to meet Rashna in Switzerland?' It was a good idea but I knew it would never happen; it was clearly 'now or never'. Glencairn and I worked out that if we altered our schedule again I could manage three sessions with Rashna and we could still reach the tea station at Munnar in Kerala for our planned rendezvous with Ratna Krishnakumar. So we never left Cottabetta that day.

Over the next three days Rashna recorded all I said during the three intensive sessions with her. Just before the first session later that afternoon, I updated Thomas: 'For some reason today's date, the 15th, is circled in my diary,' I told him, 'though I've no idea why. However, it seems that something rather strange is going on, and it's just possible that you and I are going to meet. Or at least that I may be about to understand more clearly the relationship between you and me… if you are around, Thomas, please take your chance. Here goes.'

I'm lying with eyes shut in a quiet room at the back of the house. Rashna puts me into a relaxed state by massaging my head and feet and getting me to focus on my breathing.

Now she says, 'Before we go further back in time, I need you to think first about a period in your own childhood and tell me about it.'

From now on I seem to be in two places and times at once throughout the sessions. I am 'seeing' vividly – as if in the present – settings in the past that I am 'experiencing' yet always aware of Rashna's presence. I even interrupt myself from time to time to interpret for her what I am 'seeing' and make clear which 'I' is talking.

I'm nine years old, and feel that size. I jump down from the high step of the school bus. My white ankle socks look too bright against my dark brown school shoes with their rounded toes and heavy soles. I cross the road and skip down a long drive, past threatening laurels with over-shiny leaves and out into sunshine. Halfway down the drive I drop my leather satchel with its awkward brass clasps, unbuckle my shoes, and squeeze into a field between fat grey fence wires. Lying down on my back I shut my eyes to let the sun dazzle patterns onto my eyelids. When I open them again I see delicate grasses and pale pink ladies' smock flowers through the sunspots still bouncing before my eyes. I pick and chew sweet grass stems tasting of tinned milk, and rub between my thumb and first finger the shiny ribbon that's coming loose at the end of one of my plaits. The grass I'm lying on smells of apples and feels ticklish and moist on the backs of my legs in a comforting kind of way.

When I get home and into the kitchen with its cool red tiles and loud ticking clock that doesn't tell the time, I drop my satchel and Mummy makes me a milkshake. It foams pink and is full of small pips that I push between my teeth with my tongue to bite into one by one before I swallow them. I have no homework. The long light evening might go on for ever.

I have two brothers and wish I was a boy too, except I hate shooting and seeing dead pigeons floppy warm with little feathers sticking to the blood on their soft breasts. I'm always climbing trees or playing in the woodshed that smells of cellar mould. The cellar fascinates and bothers me. When I go down its stone steps into the gloom I'm terrified the door at the top might slam shut and leave me trapped like in a tomb.

I love water. Daddy takes me swimming in an estuary where trees dip right into the water at high tide and seaweed hangs like hair from low branches. I don't mind the feel on the soles of my bare feet of slimy mud we wade through before it's deep enough to start swimming. Nor do I mind cool patches of water that catch me unawares, like ghosts of big fish, and the slippery strands of weed that circle my thighs. Sometimes the pull of the tide makes me frightened in an exciting way.

I'm not that happy at school but at home I feel safe and think this lovely time will never end. I seem to be much more in the present than I am today.

Rashna: Now think of those times in your life where you've experienced most strongly a sense of 'one-ness' with the world, a feeling of being part of something eternal.

I get this feeling when I sit on a cliff looking out to sea, or stand alone in the dark looking up at the sky. It makes you feel so small, yet also part of something huge and timeless. Music can take you there, and sometimes the atmosphere in a spiritual building such as a cathedral or a Jain temple. Most of the time we think too much and too selfishly but occasionally we can be absorbed into something much larger than ourselves.

I've never belonged to any group, always feeling outside events, watching, always watching, and forever writing in my head.

Rashna: Tell me where you are now.

Thomas: I'm in my house near the town, Beverley, where I was born and baptised. I love the large homely vicarage, but my family is quite conventional and I want to do something different.

Jenny: He feels like I did when I was young.

Thomas: The house is always full of people coming and going, but I feel so small.

Jenny: I can feel Thomas's height.

Thomas: Somehow I don't quite fit in. I sidle in and out of rooms and nobody takes any notice of me. My brothers will join the Army or Government Service but I'm a sickly child and they want me to work in an office. I can't bear this life, I want adventures too.

Jenny: Now I understand why Thomas yearned for attention.

Thomas: Each time I came home I didn't feel I fitted in the family any more. My life overseas was so different from the others' that they never really understood me. I felt a bit like a black sheep, not succeeding like my brothers, though I now know that Father had a special feeling for me all along. I don't see Mother. I never had the chance to show her how I overcame my physical weaknesses to become a man and do it on my own.

Rashna warned me not to try and do anything else on the days of our two-hour sessions. It was just as well. I had no idea how drained I would be. Glencairn was shocked by my appearance after the sessions, saying I looked as pale as a ghost. But I found the one thing I needed to do was to write and write. Or at least, we both did. (By 'we' I mean Thomas and me of course.) I found myself using a blue pen for a voice that seemed to belong to Thomas talking to me, and the usual black pen for myself addressing him.

Rashna: Go back to that feeling of the eternal self.

I'm back on the Polynesian island of Fatu Hiva. I'm walking alone on a high mountain path, watching sunlight bounce off the ultramarine ocean far below, and later I'm on the ship's upper deck under the night sky with Moana. I'm feeling a 'one-ness', like an awakening, for the most sustained period in my life. I have no sense of time.

Now I'm aware of something to do with being here in India. I can feel Thomas is close by, just beyond the purple hills.

Thomas: I am not at ease, I was happier in the countryside of Bengal, and I miss the Bengali people. Above all I miss Mr Forlong, who understood me in the way my family, even Father, never could. The eight years I spent with him brought out the best in me.

Jenny: I understand that unease with one's own family, my parents having a social style and outlook I could go along with superficially but which was at odds with what I really felt.

Thomas: Here in southern India there's no one I can talk to as I could to Forlong. I'm trying to do things like starting my book club but it's a struggle on my own. I'm making plans for a new bungalow and beginning to enjoy working with coffee. . oh no, something terrible is happening now.

Rashna: Why are you sobbing like this?

Thomas: Everything's going wrong. I can't talk to my fellow countrymen, they stick together. I can't stand this brutality. British killing Indians, Indians doing inhumane things to the British too. Something's breaking inside me with all this violence, I can't belong to either side. People think I'm weak but I've withstood all kinds of physical hardships, and could kill nature's creatures for food – but how can anyone kill another person?

Rashna: Let's move on. Where are you now?

Thomas: I'm in a hospital bed. I've had another fever. This time it's the end. I've had enough, I'm not going to fight it.

I'm facing a window bathed in sunshine. All the heat and fury of my fever has vanished, in its place I feel limp, almost weightless, and serene. It's a special kind of peace and I know I'm ready to move on. I'm alone in the room apart from two women standing still as statues on either side of my bed. Both are dressed in some kind of uniform. The one to the left at the foot of my bed is a young English nurse of slight build wearing a cap on her head; nearer to me on the right is an Indian nun with a smooth round face beneath her starched wimple. She seems like a guardian angel as she looks down at me with a beautiful expression of pure compassion, not something I've been accustomed to in my life.

The women don't stir as my end draws nigh. They are slowly fading from my sight as I think of Father and can glimpse with my inner eye the sparkling face of my perfect first love, Whyheva. Now I have a vision of my brother Richard, and the bright light from the window is dimming and dissolving. In its place, directly in front of me, I can see a tapering tunnel of dazzling white light. The very last breath is floating from my body and I'm entering this long tunnel. There, right ahead of me, bathed in its light, stands Father. His arms are stretched out towards me. He is waiting to greet me with Acceptance and Love.

This session with Rashna was particularly vivid. When it was over Rashna told me I had not only been sobbing but had also been shaking violently with emotion when describing the effects on Thomas of India's 1857-58 'Mutiny' – or 'Sepoy Rebellion' (the most disastrous episode in British Indian history, a revolt that began with Indian soldiers in the Bengal army of the British East India Company but developed into a widespread and violent uprising against British rule in north and central India).

I had not been aware of my emotional reaction though I had 'seen' a good deal of detail. When I later retold what I had 'seen' I continued to see more.

Having felt as if I had lived through Thomas's death, as it were, I had a question for Rashna: 'Do you think I shall ever dare to visit the place where Thomas died?' 'What are you afraid of?' she asked. 'We have so many things in common that I suppose I'm afraid of dying where he did,' I replied. Rashna put paid to that nonsense. 'You're in your life, not his,' she reminded me. She added: 'Of course you will have to visit the place where he died – but you won't go until you're ready.'

Rashna: Go back again to that feeling of the eternal self.

Jenny: It brings a kind of peace. After yesterday's session Thomas told me not to be afraid of dying – he said it will be alright. I can still see those two women who were with him when he died. The one standing on the right was important for him, for he never abandoned his Christian background.

Thomas: Within her face I found something I'd been seeking all my life. It was what my Journals were all about. When I returned home from abroad I would feel apart from the family, but when I left I would leave my writings behind. I always felt I'd failed the family, especially Father of course, but I hoped that when he read my words he would understand me better. They were so personal, even though I had to leave much out of them of course. When I was alive I never really knew what Father made of them and I didn't believe he could possibly accept me for what I was. Now I know he often wept when he read my words – I can see him weeping by the fireside in his study. I think in some ways he almost loved me best because of my trials and failures but he couldn't tell me that. The last time I went home he wasn't there to talk to, he'd already died. I couldn't know then that he would be waiting for me elsewhere.

Jenny: I don't feel I've completed what I need to in this life yet. Perhaps I might be able to help other people seek out links of their own. They might hear my story and draw their own conclusions.

Now I return to the meaning of *mana*, its connections with nature and my own need to be close to the natural world, something I was deeply aware of even as a child. The *mana* is strongest in association with the sea, so no wonder the Marquesas are suffused with it, being surrounded by the Pacific Ocean. I also return to the subject of forgiveness and compassion.

Again Rashna asks me about people who have been most important to me. I tell her more about my family, recalling painful episodes in my childhood and my own failings as a mother, especially to our daughter. I also talk about my marriage and the joy of sharing (not least, laughter and a sense of the absurd) and then find myself telling Rashna about my closest friend, cellist Naomi le Fleming, and about Susan Bosence, the mentor who set me off down paths I'm still exploring. I describe how she ignited the passion for indigo that would later turn into my passion for Thomas, an affair which had just, in a sense, been consummated.

In Forster's *A Passage to India*, the book that magnetised the teenage me, the heroine Adela Quested goes to southern India in search of a husband but instead has a mystical experience in the Marabar hills. I already had a husband, but I was looking for a young man and had also just had my own mystical experience in the Malabar Hills, thanks to a string of apparently random events and altered plans. Without them I wouldn't have met Rashna, let alone the older Thomas. Once again, the synchronicity of events seems almost heaven-sent, even if one doesn't believe in heaven.

When I got home I looked up the relevant references in *A Passage to India* and was reminded of this conversation between Adela Quested and Cyril Fielding when they were trying to pin down what happened to the former in the Marabar caves:

'Miss Quested: 'It will never be known... I am up against something, and so are you. Mrs Moore – she did know.'

'How could she have known what we don't?'

'Telepathy, possibly.'

The pert, meagre word fell to the ground. Telepathy? What an explanation! Better withdraw it, and Adela did so. She was at the end of her spiritual tether and so was he. Were there worlds beyond which they could never touch, or did all that is possible enter their consciousness? They could not tell... Perhaps life is a mystery, not a muddle. They could not tell. Perhaps the hundred Indias which fuss and squabble so tiresomely are one, and the universe they mirror is one. They had not the apparatus for judging.'

I didn't have the apparatus for judging either. I had to be open-minded about what had happened during the three days spent with Rashna, since such experiences are limited by labels. Since human perception is self-limiting and the nature of consciousness a mystery, how can any of us judge such things? Perhaps we'll find out after we die – whatever 'after' means in this context.

The morning after my last session with Rashna we were, at our third attempt, about to leave Cottabetta. Before we left Thomas took over from me again and wrote more in my diary. He continued to do so rather obsessively over the next few days. Once let out of his bottle like a genie he couldn't stop talking. Or laughing at my absurdities.

Now I no longer know who is writing this book or where the compulsion comes from. It seems fraudulent to claim sole authorship. Perhaps it should be attributed to Jenny Machell, or to Thomas Balfour Paul née Scott. Here I am scribbling away (as Tom would say, though in Latin) and I don't know who is driving the words. Perhaps it doesn't matter who gets the credit.

Leaving the haven of Cottabetta estate we wound back down the mountain slopes through tangled forest towards the Malabar coastal plain, Karnataka's coffee estates vanishing into mist behind our backs. Thomas disliked this journey, the track being in a 'deplorable condition', the jungle overwhelming and the 'poor coolies' forced to carry his traps on their heads. In 1970 I had passed a small bullock train laden with hessian sacks swinging down to the coast through fumes from painted lorries grinding upwards. The sight had seemed a throwback to a gentler time and thirty years later I found Thomas describing the same route when thousands of bullocks carried salt and 'sundries' from the coast, returning with coffee, rice and tobacco.

Green and watery Kerala was known for her ancient spice ports, which Thomas calls 'Coconut towns peculiar to this coast'. In 1683 the British East India Company founded their own first Malabar 'factory', for exporting pepper and cardamom, in Tellicherry (Thalassery today). Soon afterwards they built a fort there, manned by a 'company of Madras sepoys' in Tom's day. All we found beside the neglected fort was a group of small boys playing cricket in the dust. Glencairn joined their game, upholding a tradition dating to the late 18th century when the future Duke of Wellington brought cricket to the region with his Malabar Campaign.

Tellicherry's Victorian godowns, newly redundant after a century and a half of continuous activity, seemed sad silenced spaces, their chunky iron machines for coffee garbling (i.e. sorting) still oiled and poised for action. In Tom's day they were being constructed to process coffee from his neighbourhood and he lodged at the 'Garbling bungalow' in 1855 en route to the North-West Frontier. 'On the coast at Tellicherry, Cochin or Cananore,' he records ('cheroot in my lips, pen in my hands, firing away as usual') 'the coffee is garbled, packed in boxes and shipped for Bombay, the Red Sea or England. The Arabs often buy it and if it is of good quality and colour it ultimately arrives in England as the genuine blue bean of Mocha.' I wonder what Tom would think of today's ubiquitous American coffee chains?

Tellicherry's old Raj guesthouse seemed barely changed since his day. Having climbed up a flight of stone steps with balustrades smothered in mauve bougainvillea, we entered an airless hall full of mahogany furniture and chairs upholstered in maroon velvet protected by white lacy anti-macassars. In the upstairs dining room we were enchanted to find the original *punkah*, made of fringed olive-green satin, still suspended over a large oval table. Even its pulley system was intact, though now operated electrically. We set it swinging slowly back and forth from its old ropes and I couldn't resist crossing my feet on the table's top as we tiffed, aping Thomas in his journal sketch that first led me to him.

After tiffin we made for the sea, holding our noses as we tiptoed over human excrement and stale slimy fish down a crowded alleyway to reach the beach. Squint a little and you see merchant ships of all kinds and from all nations setting sail westwards across the Arabian Ocean, slung low with pepper, nutmeg, cardamom, cinnamon, cloves, cotton and coffee. Thomas looked at this view. He called it 'the high road to home'.

The following day, now further south in the Cardamom hills, we laboured back up the Western Ghats, the ones Thomas viewed from the sea in 1847 and imagined as a 'delightful retreat for the panting European', which they are. Arriving after dark, we finally met up, near the old hill station of Munnar in another former Raj planter's bungalow now a Tata guesthouse, with our hitherto absent hostess Ratna Krishnakumar. Ratna was longing to hear about the trip and I told her everything. Being Indian, she took it all in her stride, 'past-life regression', the lot. Back in UK I soon learnt to keep my mouth shut. India's rush towards Western materialism may be stifling her soul, but one can't help feeling that her collective unconscious will always be nearer the surface than it is in the West. Let's hope so anyway.

Next morning Thomas hijacked my diary again.

'19th March, morning. Now you see why I woke you up so early. You couldn't have missed the sight of the chill blue mist turning pale peach as it floated off the hill to reveal emerald-green tea slopes that half an hour earlier you didn't realise were there beyond the bungalow lawn. Can there be any more perfect experience than to live through such a dawn in a country like this?

'Since the sessions with Rashna you are 'seeing' more and more clearly, which helps us both. Rashna told you that not everything would come at once, because I (that is, you) would need time for it to sink in. Now you are beginning to look properly at the wider picture. Above all you are starting to understand your – our – relationship with India, its excitement and mystery.

'Incidentally, it was amusing watching you struggle to pronounce some Malayalam yesterday. I spent ages trying to master it when I lived in the

Wynaad. It was easier for me because I already had my background in Hindi and Bengali and I'm a better linguist than you. Besides, I had much time for study during those long lonely evenings.

'*Bedtime*. I enjoyed your visit today to the tea estates and to the Aranya centre for disabled children. That's the kind of thing I would have liked to have done myself.

'Do you remember the day you found my Journals and came up short when you read my sentence saying I hoped some 20th century descendant might come across them in some dusty library and find them of interest? You immediately sensed that that person was you, but were puzzled by the word 'descendant'. Now you see how you couldn't have been a closer relation. You cut it a bit fine by finding them just as the century was ending, but you wouldn't have been ready for them before. You needed to have your indigo career and do your travels in India, Arabia, China etc. first. So what timing eh?'

Jenny on the steps of the former Raj guest house in Thalassery (known by the British as Tellicherry), a commercial town on the Malabar coast in Kerala, formerly a spice town and a centre for coffee processing and export.

21. Between the Known and the Unknown

The practise of science happens at the border between the known and unknown… there are no untouchable truths; there is no certainty.

(*The Wonders of the Universe,* Professor Brian Cox, particle physicist)

Back in Britain I told a few close friends about my encounter with Thomas while it was fizzing on the surface, then pushed it below. However, I explored many sources that provide intriguing evidence for 'past life' experiences, whatever they are, and found the concept accorded not only with eastern religions but also with early Christian thinking and the more mystical gospels discarded when the Nicene Creed was created (by men) for political reasons. Christian thinkers who believed in 'reincarnation' were then dismissed as heretics because free-thinkers are a threat to religious leaders, institutions and states, their ideas ill-suited not only to man's desire for control but also to his fear of the mysterious and unknown.

Like Thomas, I am both amazed and amused by the dogmatic certainties of some religious people, atheists and scientists on the big questions of life, which for others remain wide open. I enjoyed a conversation with a Dean of York (a position also held by Tom's elder brother incidentally), who talked of a 'third level, out of time and beneath daily life and the imagination', where you connect in some way with others from the past. He called the phenomenon 'intercession', and also spoke of times when we're given a 'shove forward' in life, and how experiences viewed in retrospect often seem to have happened for a reason. His name for this was 'Spirit', whereas Thomas and I call it destiny. Just words.

Believers in 'reincarnation' include Socrates, Plato, Voltaire, Nietzsche, Tolstoy, Benjamin Franklin, Jung, Ralph Waldo Emerson, Balzac, Henry Ford, Norman Mailer and millions of others. One notable Christian luminary who came to believe in psychic phenomena was the late theologian, Hugh Montefiore. The writer A N Wilson told me he often met the Bishop for lunch and related how one day their meeting had an extra resonance. That day the Bishop appeared perfectly healthy, but was, said Wilson, giving off a 'powerful aura' as he talked about death and reincarnation throughout the meal. The following day Wilson received in the post a book by Montefiore called *The Paranormal: A Bishop Investigates* – posted just hours before he died. In the book's introduction Montefiore, who scrutinised a mass of evidence, challenges the sceptics: 'The upshot of this enquiry has been that the paranormal seems to me a subject of real importance, and I find it deplorable that scientists deride it and that religion ignores it. I hope that this book might contribute to altering such negative attitudes.' He criticises the Christian church's lack of interest and considers the 'negative attitude of most scientists' to be 'unscientific' in itself. His extensive investigations led him to conclude that 'there is no compelling scientific or philosophical reason' to refute the idea that the 'soul' continues to exist in some way after death. He found the idea of reincarnation helpful rather than something to be feared and wrote: 'It is the present that matters… Reincarnation is important for our search for the truth about life, not for living it.' Reading that sentence I reflected upon how my Thomas explorations had opened my own mind to new possibilities, ways of living in the present and, indeed, seeking that elusive, numinous 'truth' that forever defies all manmade measuring, definitions and divisions and intersects with the strangeness of the quantum world.

Whatever the explanation of my 'Malabar moment', I marvel at the way my life's path joined seamlessly with Thomas's to extend his life's ambitions into the present. And remember his idea, expressed in 1852, of writing 'a novel in the form of an autobiography'? If this is it, it will have taken not just a few years to write, but a century and a half, which may be a world record.

22. Beginning of the End

I have trod the upward and the downward slope;
I have endured and done in days before;
I have longed for all and bid farewell to hope;
And I have lived and loved, and closed the door.

(from *Songs of Travel* by Robert Louis Balfour
Stevenson)

When I had discovered, thanks to the unlikely source of the Mormon archives, that Thomas had died six years after his last Journal entry it had initially been a blow, even though I was pleased he hadn't died as young as I had originally assumed. With the absence of records, his final years – and indeed his death – seemed frozen. I was initially frustrated by this truncation of his life story, not least because it came just before the 'Indian Mutiny' / 'Sepoy Rebellion', but soon the 'missing' years turned into a challenge. I was able to create a skeleton of Tom's lost years by ferreting around in libraries and archives, but it had no flesh. Instinct had, however, sent me searching for clues in the place where Thomas had bent over the pages of his last surviving Journal (Volume Five in the British Library) and the chance to re-tread my own youthful path in southern India had reinforced the urge.

Goodness knows what I had hoped to uncover. Characteristically I hadn't thought it through before I set out, but I confess to harbouring that daft dream of actually finding parts of Tom's missing Journals somewhere in the Wayanad, though I had no idea how long he had remained in southern India after he had written his last surviving entry. Had I really imagined ancient bundles of papers lurking on a high shelf in some cobweb-strewn room like Miss Havisham's, waiting for me to climb up to them, blow off the dust and find they had been written by Thomas?

Back in UK after this trip to southern India that, like my 1970 one, hadn't turned out at all as anticipated, I returned to the British Library, seeking more clues, or even corroboration of events I had described to Rashna. The Victorians in India, it seems, recorded everything; the challenge is locating information buried in one of millions of documents.

I began with the maps. The misinformation about Bon Espoir that had deflected me from consulting old maps before embarking on the trip had led to the reconnection with the Van Ingens and with their Kartikulum estate where I had first experienced coffee's exotic habitat. That was a lucky turn of events, but I still needed to know exactly where Thomas was living when he wrote his final Journal entry.

I hardly expected to find a map that actually marked individual estates in the small Wayanad area, but to my surprise that's just what I did find. The scale of the map is so large that it actually marks individual estates near Mananthavady. Made ten years after Thomas was involved in pioneering coffee and was considering trying cotton, tea and silk, the map focussed on the latest crop, which was quinine-yielding cinchona. Luckily for me, the map-maker, Mr Clements Markham, had selected Smyth's Bon Espoir and the Van Ingen's Karticulum estates among those for his trials with cinchona seeds and plants collected in South America.

And what did this map reveal? That the two estates were so close they were a mere 'dog's cart ride from Mananthavady in the dry season', as the mapmaker put it. I might have known, given all the Thomas coincidences so far, that thanks to an undelivered letter in 1970 and a misleading email thirty years later, I had twice smelt Tom's coffee. Now I see that my serendipitous teenage visit to the Van Ingens had created the setting to connect me both with Tom and with my former self when the time, like the coffee, was ripe.

Next day I sought clues to Thomas' last years. Since his last journal entry had been penned in the Wayanad in December 1856 I expected his name to crop up somewhere in the countless sources on southern India covering 1856-1862. After all, he had been in coffee for less than 18 months when he wrote that entry so it seemed likely that he spent more time in that post. However, my assumption was wrong and the search was futile.

The librarian on duty suggested I check the even more extensive records on northern India. Every Englishman who ever resided in any street in any town there seemed to get a mention. Yet 1857, 1858 and 1859 yielded nothing. Where was he? Then, as the Library was closing that day, on page 202, part X of the New Calcutta Directory for 1860 I spotted the name Thomas Machell at last. He was listed as resident in Calcutta's Moffusil district, working as 'agent for the commercial transport association, Jubbulpore'. That same year, under the heading 'Mirzapore/Commercial', an entry records his old friends the Howard brothers as joint partners in 'Howard Brothers, Merchants and commission agents, bullock train to Jubbulpore etc'. Directories for the following two years reveal that Tom joined the partnership. So this gap was closing; I had now established Tom's whereabouts and occupation in the last three years of his life.

I found Jabalpur (in today's spelling) to be in Madhya Pradesh, with the remote town of Narsinghpur (it has numerous English spellings) less than fifty miles west – one of the two 'Nursingpores' on the Victorian atlas I had looked at when I had found mention, both on the family tree and on the brass inscription in Etton Church, of a memorial to Thomas in 'Nursingpore'. On the atlas both towns with that name had looked improbably remote, with no obvious connection with anything I knew about Thomas's life. But now it made sense – clearly the town near Jabalpur must be the site of his grave, since there was no reason now for him to be in Orissa's Nursingpore.

I spent the following day turning the pages of legions of old photograph albums of India that just post-dated Tom's time, commercial photography having got going around the time of his death. (How he would have loved to have a camera and how glad I am he didn't have one.) Raj characters surrounded by acolytes, turbaned natives and dead game gazed out, held forever in their foxed and faded sepia images. I was looking through a mass of photographs of Officers of Empire when I suddenly found Thomas in uniform! At least, it looked like a macho version of him but closer inspection revealed it to be a formal photograph of Lance in a three-quarter pose identical to one of the Journal sketches of Thomas. The uncanny likeness of the brothers, down to a kink in the thick hair at the back of the head, endorses Colesworthy Grant's sketch, done – or 'taken', to use the jargon then – in 1850. But how I longed to see just one photograph of Thomas. Trust Lance to trump him even in this.

Rashna had predicted I would be so affected by Thomas after the sessions with her that more would appear thereafter. Soon after my library visits, I was listening to music one day and suddenly 'understood' that Thomas had suffered a nervous breakdown. I began to write, not knowing what would come. Thomas seemed to be dictating every detail, and surprised me by being back in Bengal in 1857, contrary to my assumptions and where I wanted him to be.

What follows is what Thomas and I wrote together in the months after our reunion in southern India.

'I think it very probable that... I shall leave behind me some seven volumes of manuscript papers which will neither be published nor opened'. I penned that passage more than ten years before I died. I was guessing of course but it turned out truly prophetic because in the last six years of my life I did indeed write two more volumes (making seven altogether) though the last was never completed. And these two can be neither published nor opened because not long before I died I burnt them both, convinced my Family would be embarrassed by them were they ever to read them.

It was a torpid afternoon in 1862. I constructed a small fire out of sticks and shrivelled leaves and then when it was burning nicely very deliberately placed Volume Six (unbound) of my life onto the flames. I squatted native fashion and watched the pages slowly turn the colour of shoe-leather edged with an orange glow. The pages curled inwards as if alive and devouring themselves, growing ever darker as they obliterated my words, my record, my life. I felt totally calm almost numb. When Volume Six was reduced to ash I watched my swarthy hand stretch slowly forward to place Volume Seven (unfinished) onto the fire it were as if the hand belonged to a stranger. A hot breeze got up and this smaller bundle burnt rapidly. Twas soon over. I closed my eyes and the smell that filled my nostrils brought back remembrances of the childhood fireside at Etton.

Four years of my life lay in a tiny pile of ash in a wood in Central India.

It had a kind of Truth for over the years my Journals had almost come to define my very existence. You could say they were more alive than I was myself and I truly believe that from that moment in the woods my spirit began to leave me and I started to die from inside out. By the time of my actual death a few months later there was little of me left – merely a carcass and the remnants of a soul that had been slowly wafting out of my body like smoke from a lazy autumn bonfire.

Those who chance upon the last surviving volume of my Journals (the fifth) to find its way to England might find the conclusion puzzling with its dull passage noting vegetable prices at market in the coffee hills of Kerala. Of course I intended to conclude that Journal like the others, but I left my unfinished pages behind with my possessions at Bon Espoir on my unplanned departure, expecting to return ere long to resume my life there. By the time I retrieved them I had long since embarked on Volume Six.

"At thirty-two I feel older than many I have seen with ten more years on their shoulders," I penned on 20th September 1856. I was far from well and in those fever ridden jungles it was little surprise when I was struck down once more. Too enfeebled to work, the only place in India where I could take refuge was with my faithfull friends the Howards.

On my arrival in Calcutta I found that all was not well in Bengal. There was unrest in sepoy regiments as well as on the indigo concerns and on 12th of May 1857 news reached Calcutta so terrible that at first many refused to believe it. News traveled fast with the new electric telegraph – so just two days after the event we learnt that there had been a truly fearful native Uprising against the British in Meerut. Imagine sepoys not just disobeying orders but turning on their own English Officers, and even townspeople joining in the dreadfull frenzy. It seemed that once the killing began there was no stopping it and a few days later came news of an attack on the city of Delhi itself, with great slaughter of men women and innocent children.

All summer long when Delhi was in Turmoil reports came thick and fast. Officers, soldiers and families who had escaped the sieges reached Calcutta with rags on their backs and lurid tales of woe. It seemed as if Punjab itself so hardly taken might soon fall from British hands. Ofttimes did I hear mention of Lance's own regiment the Bengal Horse Artillery and I knew my other dear brothers must also surely be called to Arms with all the troops from far and wide.

No one knew if our soldiers had numbers sufficient to overcome the mutineers or if the whole of India would go up in flames, and the great City of Palefaces be ravaged like Delhi. One Sunday came a rumour that angry mutineers were marching in hundreds towards our City and every terror-struck White man woman and child fled the city, though the rumour proved false. Little cared I for my own life but what of India moreover Bengal where I had made my home

Into my fevered brain came crowding memories I thought long since forgotten. In a half sleep rose visions of the outrages daily reported mingled with scenes I hoped never to recall of slaughter and vengeance I had witnessed in those far-off days in China when scarce a man. Now those times that began when dear Mother was alive seemed once again as if of yesterday and I could not wipe the bloodshed from my sight. It was more than I could bear. From the past too came recollections of violent brawls and rapacious attacks on defenceless women I had borne witness to in the seaports of the world, and the distressing acts I had myself been forced to partake with Bully Roberts, which had so cruelly taken away my childhood innocence. As news reached us daily of the brutalities being carried out in India they joined with all the other pictures in my mind until I truly believed that I was going mad.

So weary was I of this world of bloodshed that I yearned for death that would not come. My anxious friend Howard declared that I was ill but he knew not the cause. Alas Mrs Howard was no longer with us to provide succour with her tender ministries. Besides, what were my puny troubles when all around whole families were being cut down in their prime? To my shame I would oftimes weep bitter tears all was confusion in my mind and in my body as I sat and brooded in my little room while the troops and carriages passed beneath my window the street sellers pedaled their wares and flies buzzed incessantly round my head.

As the weather grew hotter and my frail body yet weaker my ever dear friends Bernardt and Ranolph Howard insisted I reside at their abode at Mirzapore, less fetid than Bengal's swamps. Little did it matter to me where I laid my head each night.

In my feverish state I could not count the days but as the months passed I began to recover my senses. In September came news came of the recapture of Delhi and as the year of 1857 drew to a close the Crisis was past. I thought again of returning to the Wynaad jungles but the Howards declared twould be best to remain with them.

With the Uprising all but quelled the new Government rushed to ensure that such a perfidious mutiny against the British could never happen again. In 1854 when I took the new iron road to Burdwan I wrote: 'Though there are a number of people employed they seem to work very slowly they say it will take six years to open the line as far as Benares and two or three generations to unite it with the Bombay line'. I penned this before the Upheaval but once the Troubles commenced twas clear the movement of our troops was far too slow. Thus the decision was taken to construct the railways in all possible haste. The Howards saw their chance to provide transport from Calcutta inland to where the east-west railways would meet. I befell me to oversee new bullock trains between Mirzapore and Jubbelpore and on to Nursingpore with its coal and iron mines and military encampments. Having nowhere I could call a home, what mattered it where I lay my head and right glad was I to repay the debt I owed my true friends. My humble post as agent was of use to them and in the last year of my life I became a partner in their modest company. Not much of an achievement for a Machell but well it suited me in the twilight of my life to be amongst men of such generous spirit.

Before I commenced my novel employment Bernardt suggested I should pay a visit to Lance for the Bengal Horse Artillery was at that time stationed not far from Raniganj where the railway from Calcutta ended. I took a pony from the rail's end and rode in the direction of the camp. At length I espied in the distance beside a bend in the river bright red coats and white hats of officers moving among many tents in neat rows and Men washing down horses at the water's edge.

I was excited but anxious too. I had never felt at ease with Lance as you know and was uncertain how he would greet his unannounced visitor. I rode into camp on my pony, handed the reins to a khalasi and walked towards the large mess tent, feeling upon my back the eyes of officers resting outside their tents. The moment I dipped under the flap I knew I was making a mistake and wished to retreat but alas twas too late. Lance was standing behind a long wooden table strewn with the remains of tiffin the coolies were clearing. He sported a white shirt, the collar loosened at the neck, his hair was disheveled, his skin darker than before, his moustache luxuriant and he looked as ever confident and at ease. He was discoursing with a companion who saw me first and nodded his head in my direction with a quizzical air. Lance followed his gaze to where I stood and I caught in his look both astonishment and embarrassment at the unwelcome sight of his strange elder brother standing hesitatingly within the door flap. When I later re-lived that moment I realised what a paltry figure I must have looked; all skin and bones in my loose Indian trousers and dusty muslin shirt, with my old cotton bag slung across my shoulders. Lance hastily disguised his expression of disgust, excused himself and skirted around the end of the table to come and greet me but the damage was already done for we were both aware he felt shame not joy at the sight of his brother.

After expressing surprise I had journeyed so far to seek him out, Lance offered me some tiff and led me off to sit with him on low wooden stools beneath a spreading banyan tree. I sensed his desire to keep me apart from his companions. We began to talk – much had happened since we had last met and I felt a desperate desire to unburden myself of my troublesome thoughts. I related how I had come to be residing in Calcutta during the Troubles, of my mind's weakness I revealed but little but I tried to explain my thoughts on the brutal actions of the Mutineers which had not commenced without provocation said I. Surely outrage would follow any suggestion that pork and beef fat might sully their lips. "How could Christian Officers have contemplated the idea?" I declared rather too hotly. "My dear deluded brother," said Lance, "Are you attempting to make excuses for those beasts the Mutineers?" "Of course not," said I, "but remember we are not blameless – was it wise of Lord Dalhousie to annex the Kingdom of Oudh where so many of the Sepoys came from – after all, when Cumbria was invaded by the Scots and Crackenthorpe threatened did we not feel anger that our native land should be thus taken by Outsiders?" "That is a very different case," cried Lance, "for these men were in our Army and had sworn allegiance to our Crown." He was keeping his temper in check but I could see the warning signs I knew too well (the raised vein in the neck, the rubbing of the jaw, the flash in the eye). I should have stopped there and then but could not help myself.

"We did not treat the sepoys well enough," said I. "Look at the poor huts in which they were accommodated, the meagre pay and food they received for loyal service. Must there not be limits to how much even the poorest native will accept?"

"Enough of your nonsense brother," declared Lance. "Safe in Calcutta you did not see what we were forced to see – not just soldiers but innocent women and children defiled and hacked to pieces. No excuse in the world can forgive that."

"Of course not," cried I in reply, "but as good Christians we should set an example by showing restraint and respect for other religions – yet to gain revenge we acted like Barbarians ourselves, hanging the Hindu burning the Moslem and defiling their women as they defiled ours. We forced captives to lick the blood of Christians before they were executed and the Moslem to swallow pork and the Hindu meat. And how on God's earth can you defend the punishment meted out in your own regiment of strapping human beings to the barrels of your cannon and blowing them to pieces? And the old emperor Shah's three sons were all shot dead by William Hodson – a clergyman's son. In the eyes of the Lord in whose service our dear Father and Richard tirelessly work does not all this make us as bad as the worst of them?"

Once I had commenced I was unable to prevent myself from pouring out my bewildered sorrow at the events that had so recently taken place. I had vainly hoped for fraternal understanding but seeing me thus agitated was too much for Lance. He gave way to his anger in the manner that would frighten me when we were children together in our Etton bedroom. By this time he was on his feet and leaning over me, he no longer cared whether or not we were overheard. He shouted out his worst feelings about me, his embarrassing older brother. How I had been so misguided when we ran away together, how my day-dreaming at school had unsettled his nerves, how my propensity to cry when teased as a child had been girlish and could hardly be excused by my birth defect, how ridiculous I looked in native clothes, how soft I was in the head to think I could make true friends with Indians and Arabs, how pointless it was to spend so much time learning all those languages since East and West were worlds apart and the rebellion had proved that.

He saved the worst taunts till the last: 'No wonder you never married,' he shouted, 'the only woman you ever got to love you – if such creatures are capable of love – was a naked savage South Sea islander from a tribe of cannibals! How shaming that was to our dear Father and all the family. Compare yourself to Richard, a pillar of the Church married to a Lady and begetter of three fine Machell heirs. And look to your other brothers, risking their lives as I have done to defend our Great Empire following in the footsteps of many brave Machells before us who battled at Bunkers Hill, Badajos, Waterloo and in the Crimea.' With a venomous snarl he almost spat out the final sentence – 'What have you done to uphold the proud name of our family?'

Lance stopped there as abruptly as he had begun. He had vent his opinions and I could tell he realized he had gone too far even though he would never admit it and in any case twas too late. Our fragile brotherly bond was finally broken beyond repair. Lance spun on his heels and strode back to his tent as I sank to my knees in the dust my hands covering my face and fervently wished I could die there and then. Then I got to my feet and stumbled away from that camp in the evening sunshine, my face hot with tears. Over and over I could hear like a terrible refrain those wounding words of Lance's ringing in my ears. 'What have you done to uphold the proud name of our family?'

He was right, I had achieved nothing despite all my struggles and I knew that from then on my estrangement from the family would grow. Was this what they all thought of me? Was I such a failure even in the eyes of Richard and of our Father? It was almost too much to bear.'

23. Rowing into Eternity

The dead are always looking down on us they say,
while we are putting on our shoes or making a sandwich,
they are looking down through the glass-bottom boats of heaven
as they row themselves slowly through eternity.

They watch the tops of our heads moving below on earth,
and when we lie down in a field or on a couch,
drugged perhaps by the hum of a warm afternoon,
they think we are looking back at them,

which makes them lift their oars and fall silent
and wait, like parents, for us to close our eyes.

(*The Dead,* Billy Collins)

You can imagine my state of my mind after that ill-starred meeting with
my brother. Fortunate was it soon after that my kind old friend Forlong
was on a visit to the City of Palefaces as was I. I told him of my illness
and wept without shame as I recalled those cruel words of Lance and
my desolation at failing my beloved Father.

Forlong too was bowed down with woe for great were his burdens. All
he worked so hard for was threatened by the foolish greed of the owners
of the indigo Concerns and the bankers and merchants of Calcutta.
Would that I could have accompanied him to Neechindapore but I was
obliged to return to Mirzapore and thence to Jubbelpore to muster up
my bullock train.

Just after the rains of 1859 alarming reports reached us that once more the native was up in arms, this time twas the ryot turning on the indigo planters and zamindari in Bengal. Great was my anxiety about Forlong, but he was not harmed and not long before my death he moved northwards to the state of Bihar.

Close on these indigo disturbances in those troubled years preceding my own death I learnt the worst news of my life. Twas the end of May I was in Mirzapore's dusty square near the godown where we kept our stores, sat on a hard low wooden stool leaning my sorely aching back against a mud wall and imbibing a cup of sickly sweet tea. My head ached from the incessant beating of the sun the constant chatter all around me and the ceaseless buzz of insects. Then I espied the postman. Those days I received letters but rarely but as he approached I could see he bore one addressed to me: *Thomas Machell esq., c/o Office of Howard and Howard, Dillywallah Road, Mirzapore, Central Provinces, India.* I reckognized Richard's careful script and knew at once from the black around the edge that it must enclose bad news.

Slowly I opened the envelope with my dry fingers and removed the letter. It bore the news of Father's death on 15th April.

This was the moment I had dreaded all my life but only then did I realise that my efforts to live up to Father had been the mainstay of my existence. As I writ in 1850: Surely no love is purer and none cherished with more confidence, and yet how rarely is it that we see a perfect confidence between father and son?

I walked away from the bullock train, sank to the ground beneath the spreading branches of a pepul tree bowed my head and closed my eyes. Father's weary kindly face floated before me as I pictured a sombre procession file into Etton's church and the pallbearers gently place Father's coffin in front of the altar where he presided for twenty years. The sun shone through the window in memory of our beloved mother to shed coloured specks of light onto the coffin's polished lid. Ill at ease in formal English attire I saw myself in the old family pew as Richard delivered a reverential tribute from the pulpit. Then the pallbearers shouldered the coffin and walked jerkily down the aisle, through the ancient porch and out into spring sunshine.

The double tombstone had been moved aside in readiness. The coffin was lowered deep into the tomb next to Mother's and the huge stone heaved into place, its surface now completed, chiselled with these words:

Here lies Robert Machell, born 21 October 1797, died 15 April 1860, who served the parishes of Etton and Leckonfield diligently for 20 years. United at last in the eyes of our Lord with his beloved wife Eliza... Sit mihi sit tecum sedes intrare piorum Tecum. Nam sine te gaudia nulla juvant.

It gave me solace to know my parents were reunited in the tomb Father prepared so long ago to be the final resting place of their earthly bodies. The celandines were shining in the grass like a whole firmament of little yellow stars and I heard a thrush in the old yew tree singing its heart out for Father's soul.

All this and more I saw as I sat in the dirt while the bullock train was being prepared for another trek southwards. Only that night did I truly weep for the greatest loss of my life.

Six weeks later the promised letter from Richard arrived describing for me the actual Funeral. Twas not as I had imagined for it had neither taken place in Etton nor had our beloved Father been laid to rest beside Mother in accordance with his own instructions. Instead the service had been conducted in the church of Marton-in-Cleveland where Father was Curate when he died and his body laid beside the south porch in that churchyard as Madre wished. Now Mother will lie in her tomb with a space beside her forever vacant.

Less than two years later at the beginning of 1862, the year in which I too died, my little nephew Guy Lawrence, Richard and Emma's fourth son, passed away at almost three months old. Though Richard was Vicar of Barrow-on-Humberside he buried his son in Etton churchyard close by that of the grandmother he would never know.

By then my own life too was drawing towards it close. Years of illnesses had worn my body out and I was already grown weary of life before I heard of Father's death. After that news I seemed to exist in a twilight world and in December 1861 I made my will though I had little enough to leave. Everything I possessed I left to Richard so my modest collection with its flavour of the East might entertain my nephews. In the year that followed I burnt the last two Volumes of my Journals in an act I have already described.

Twas early in December when I succumbed to another fever and was taken to Narsingpore. All my life I had battled hard to shake off illness when it came my way but this time I welcomed it and waited for my end. I had written to Father at the close of 1850: 'You my dear father have become to me the silken thread on which I string my beads... all are unworthy of the thread they hang on but still I string on with blind affection hoping that some chance may place a jewel within my reach which shall compensate for all the dross'. That jewel alas eluded me.

As the end drew nigh my thoughts flew more and more to Etton, the place I loved the most, its church that had once been my solace and the old house filled with children's laughter before our Mother was taken from us. I could not forget the moment when I stood beside her grave and realised the loss of her but it gave me comfort to end my life at the same age and on the same day of the week as my own dearest Mother.

The day before I departed this World my ever faithful friends the Howards paid me a final visit. Their humble goodness had forever shone a beacon of light in the darkest of times. Bernhardt expressed a wish to remain at my bedside but I begged him to return to his work. Do you recall that Journal entry of April 1850 when I was musing on the fate of those who died alone and very far from home? I wrote then: 'We cling at all times to the memory of those we love and who knows whether the selfish desire of seeing them one last time does not greatly outweigh the relief we should feel that those who love us are spared the grief of seeing us die'. As it turned out my own death proved far from lonesome howsoever it may have been thought of by those I left behind. Tis true that I closed my life in a small town in central India lacking companionship of family or friend but in the end that did not matter. And in 2001 I lived again through Jenny my last moments on earth.

I died on 14th December 1862 while the rest of the world went about its usual business. I had turned thirty-nine years of age the month before. Twas the third Sunday in Advent – Father would have liked that. On 30th June 1850 I wrote these words to him: The long wide sea which separates us seems like the blank leaf between the volumes of my journal. Now at last the blank leaf could be filled.

24. Into the New World

A different silence has come to some
Close friends, but sealed inside my head
They live, talk, laugh. I know they'd rather
Be thought of that way than as dead.

(*Letter to the family*, Glencairn Balfour Paul)

In spring 2002, Crackenthorpe house itself suddenly provided a missing link. Every source I consulted had told me that the Crackenthorpe Machell family line had expired. Then, out of the indigo blue one day, I learnt that the former caretaker had just come across an old Machell calling card among paraphernalia accumulated in the back of a drawer.

The card was twenty years old. It was a long shot, but I picked up the phone and dialled the American number on the card. A woman answered at once: 'Claudia Machell speaking.' Wow – the number not only worked but led to a Machell. 'I'm phoning from England and you don't know me but… ' I began (as so often) before explaining my quest. 'I'm Fred Machell's wife,' said Claudia, 'but the people you should call are his parents, Nancy and Reg, who live in Houston, Texas. They know all about the family history.' She gave me their number and I phoned straight away.

To my surprise and delight the phone was answered directly by Reginald (Reg) Machell, who told me he was the current head of the ancient family of Machell of Crackenthorpe! He was, he explained, the grandson of Thomas's nephew, Reginald Willoughby Machell (Richard Beverley's third son), an artist who for some reason had come to roost in the USA. I outlined my Thomas mission to Reg and his wife Nancy and after a couple more calls they invited me to stay (a characteristically intuitive gesture I would later discover), ignoring the advice of their children, who were understandably uneasy at the idea of their elderly parents having a total stranger in their house. They even urged them to do a British police check on me.

I surged with other passengers past officials at Houston airport and spotted an elderly couple walking forward to greet me. A short slim woman with auburn hair set off by an immaculate white trouser suit moved closer with both hands outstretched. She looked at me with piercing green eyes, smiled broadly and exclaimed in a Texan drawl: 'Hi, you must be Jenny – I'm Nancy Machell. I hope you had a good flight?' 'How did you recognise me?' I asked. Nancy laughed, 'It's obvious, Jenny!' She turned her gaze tenderly to the frail old man beside her and introduced him: 'This is my husband Reg.' I found myself looking into one of the gentlest faces I had ever seen, a face holding the genes of his great-great-Uncle Thomas. I already knew the visit would be a success. I felt like a returning long lost Victorian relative, which I suppose I almost was, since I was acting as intermediary to introduce them to Thomas. (Nancy's first email after my visit said: 'Dear J/T, We missed you when you left. It was like having a favourite niece – or Great Uncle – visit.')

Crossing the threshold of the Machell's home I found myself face to face with Crackenthorpe Hall and its gardens, painted by Reginald Willoughby just after their construction by Tom's brother James. (They are the only pictures showing the house in its heyday). There was also a portrait of Reginald's father Richard Beverley (Tom's brother) and John Thomas greeted me in his Waterloo uniform. He's the one whose 'horse was shot under him' and who later became a partner in the Machell family bank.

Nancy led me into a luxurious guest bedroom, full of mod cons but its walls adorned with old family pictures. I moved towards a faded photograph of a man in a high-necked Indian jacket whose serene face with its fine features and generous lips I seemed to know. The thick hair had that distinctive dip at the back of the crown. 'Yes, that's Thomas's nephew Reginald Willoughby,' answered Nancy before I'd asked the question. 'Come and see his painting of Bacchante.' I followed her into her own bedroom suite and there over the bath hung a reproduction of a daring painting of a full-frontal sprawling naked goddess. I was intrigued. What inspired Reginald Willoughby to paint something so totally different from the conventional scenes of Crackenthorpe in the hallway?

Nancy and Reg may have needed to meet Tom but I also needed an introduction to Tom's nephew.

Firstly, though, I needed a drink. I stroked the white deep-piled poodle lolling beside my chair on a matching white deep-piled carpet while Nancy mixed a cocktail at the kitchen counter. 'Do you believe in reincarnation, Jenny?' she asked as she handed me a glass. What a startling question from a near-stranger, and in that thoroughly modern and western house. 'Why do you ask?' was my rhetorical response, stalling as I tried to gauge what had prompted this. I was asked the same question by Rashna in the Malabar jungles. I sipped my drink, gave a non-committal reply and the moment passed.

We returned to Reginald Willoughby. In our brief email and telephone exchanges Nancy hadn't explained why he emigrated to America. I had gathered he was disinherited for being an artist, but this didn't sound sufficient reason to abandon his country. Even if his father disapproved of his career choice Reginald Willoughby could surely have continued painting in Britain or in Paris where I had heard he studied? Now, sunk in a deep armchair with her own drink, Nancy gave me the answers.

'Reginald Willoughby didn't leave England just because he was an artist, there was much more to it than that – but I decided to wait until we were face to face before telling you about it,' she said. And what a story it turned out to be – exotic enough for a book of its own and too long to relate in detail here. In summary, in the late 19th century Reginald Willoughby, at that time a classically trained prize-winning painter, had an encounter that radically changed not only his own life but those of his descendants' too. This was meeting in London in 1886 the elderly Madame Blavatsky, a larger-than-life character who had formed a new movement based on her studies with masters in Tibet. Her philosophy was what Reginald Willoughby was seeking and he soon joined the Theosophical Society she had founded in 1875. Its first two objects are: 'To form the nucleus of a Universal Brotherhood of Humanity without distinction of race, colour, or creed' and 'To encourage the study of comparative religion, philosophy and science'. By the time Blavatsky died in 1891, Reginald Willoughby had decorated her London Hall with Oriental symbols and was entertaining eastern mystics in his studio.

Blavasky's successors divided. Henry Alcott and Annie Besant moved east to the Theosophical Society-Adyar headquarters in Madras, while William Judge moved to America. Here his follower Katherine Tingley soon went her own way and after Judge's death established the Theosophical

Painting of the Indian goddess Lakshmi by Reginald Willoughby Machell, 1890s.

Society in San Diego in 1896, four years later launching a kind of New Age colony overlooking the ocean at Point Loma. Here the Theosophists created a self-sufficient community, planting trees and crops on formerly barren land, building a school, America's first open-air amphitheatre, a Temple of Peace, working buildings and a renowned university. (The Society and university moved to Covina near Los Angeles in 1942.)

Reginald Willoughby, enticed to 'Lomaland' from UK, was greatly involved from the start, fully applying there his wide talents as sculptor, artist, writer and dramatist for the expanding community that soon became a highly influential centre of music, culture and education.

Soon after meeting Blavatsky Reginald Willoughby had developed an entirely new painting style, abandoning traditional landscapes and portraiture in favour of huge symbolist paintings (some exhibited in the Royal Academy in London when he was a member of the Royal British Society of Artists). Later he incorporated Eastern decorative forms into his murals, architectural ornamentation and carved furniture. I wondered out aloud if Thomas's attraction to Islamic architectural decoration had any influence on his nephew. Nancy filled me in on all this as we pored over Reginald's sketchbooks, some showing Lomaland in its heyday, and looked at pictures of his carved furniture and large paintings now in museums or private collections. On his death in 1927 Reginald Willoughby left an important legacy in writing and art. Theosophical Society magazines frequently reproduce his huge Blake-like painting called, appropriately, 'The Path'. Today it dominates the Theosophical Society's headquarters in Pasadena, California. Other Machell paintings and also carved furniture, such as his enormous doors saved when the temple burnt down, are now with the California Historical Society in San Diego.

When Reginald Willoughby turned his back forever on England and Crackenthorpe in 1900 (thereby relinquishing the family seat) he left behind his elder son, who completed his public school education, followed in his ancestors' military footsteps and became another victim of World War I. Reginald Willoughby's younger son, Montagu Arthur, was the lucky one. Taken to the States with his father and educated in Lomaland's 'Raja-yoga school', he became a professional cellist and married a pianist, Cora Lee, in the first marriage of two Lomaland students. Having left the Colony to pursue musical careers, but never abandoning Theosophy, the pair had one son, Reg (my host), who became a distinguished aeronautical engineer. I gathered *en passant* that Reg had rescued Nancy, only daughter of a woman she described as 'a classic southern belle and flapper', from a difficult childhood. Both Reg and Nancy greatly admired Reg's talented and broad-minded late parents and grandfather.

Reginald Willoughby had found in Theosophy a belief system, based on compassion, which united the divided religions of East and West by recognising the essential one-ness of all beings – thereby resolving Thomas's own lifelong preoccupation. Reginald Willoughby's essays almost take over ideas penned sixty years earlier by Thomas. For example, in his essay 'Cosmic Justice', Reginald Willoughby wrote: 'The religions of the world have not succeeded in showing man the harmony and fitness of nature's workings… In much of the Orient justice was known thousands of years ago under the name karma and was made intelligible by the doctrine of reincarnation.'

Perhaps it's as well Reginald Willoughby didn't know that the Theosophist's Lomaland campus, which brought Buddhist ideas to the West, would become today's Point Loma Nazarene University, a college affiliated to the evangelical Church of the Nazarene.

The whole story was a revelation to me. I hadn't given Theosophy a thought for thirty years, but suddenly I was back in Madras in 1970 when for some bizarre reason I had chosen to take refuge from the midday heat in the World headquarters of the Theosophical Society. I recalled the buildings, the library, the symbols embracing all the main faiths, and sitting beneath the world's largest banyan tree in the shady gardens reading a leaflet about Theosophy that probably featured a painting by Reginald Willoughby Machell.

Once I told Nancy and Reg about Tom's life and interests things fell into place for them. Both Nancy and Reg felt sure that Reg's grandfather was inspired to follow his own path after hearing tales of his Uncle Tom, whose Journals from the East he could have read in Crackenthorpe Hall. According to my research Reginald was in the womb when Thomas made what I assume was his last trip to England, in 1854. Oddly, though, I had a mental picture of Thomas taking his nephew on his knee and telling him in person many tales of his life in exotic lands – but I must have been imagining that. It seemed that nephew had followed his uncle as a free-thinker questioning family and society's expectations. Thomas went East, as befitted his time, and tried to bridge the gap between east and west by studying eastern ideas. Reginald travelled westwards geographically, but only to steep himself in philosophies, religions and arts of the East and be a major figure in the first movement to 'unite the philosophic Orient with the practical West'. Reginald was the biological son of Richard Beverley, straight-laced Dean of York, but in spirit far more like the son Thomas the seeker never had.

'I wonder what Reginald's father thought when his son embraced the Theosophical movement, being such an upright pillar of the Church himself,' I said. (What's more, what did he think of Reginald Willoughby's hasty marriage to a Yorkshire clergyman's daughter in Paris when only twenty two, let alone her alcoholism and their subsequent divorce?)

Nancy laughed. 'Come and have another look as his portrait,' she said.

We returned to the entrance hall and looked up at Richard Beverley, who in turn glared down at us with disapproval. His son had portrayed him in formal attire, boxed within a book-lined study. 'I'm afraid in our family we always refer to him as the archetypal tight-arsed Englishman!' said Nancy. Poor Richard Beverley; he probably didn't approve of his third son's way of life, but he seemed to get a bad press.

Had Reginald left behind his younger son, like the elder, with his mother in England instead of taking him to the New World, things would have been so different. Now I undertood why James bequeathed Crackenthorpe to his younger nephew Percy (which meant it all landed on Roger's lonely shoulders after his mother died, because he was an only child and had no offspring himself). Had it not been for Madame Blavatsky, there might be English Machells in the old house to this day. As it is, the next head of the Crackenthorpe Machells would be an American heart surgeon, Nancy and Reg's oldest son, Chuck (Charles).

We now talked about the fate of Crackenthorpe house. Reg and Nancy, like Reg's parents, had always longed to go there but had never made it. When they visited Reg's cousin Roger in London in the 1980s, his first question to Nancy had been: 'I hope you don't have a nanny for your children?' She had assured him she didn't and asked what prompted the question. 'I spent years alone in the nursery wing of Crackenthorpe in the care of a horrible nanny,' he had replied, the memory still haunting him decades later.

My head was whirring as I climb into bed that night.

The next morning Nancy drove me into Houston city. She took her winter furs to the furrier for summer storage and me into a vast over-cooled shopping Mall for lunch. She looked at me over our pink milkshakes and said: 'Now Jenny, please tell me more about Thomas and yourself.'

On leaving home, Glencairn had asked me if I was going to tell the Machells about my 'past-life' experience with Rashna. 'Definitely not,' I had replied, 'they'd think I was mad.' But now I knew about Reg's background,

Nancy's unexpected question about re-incarnation yesterday fitted into place and I decided to risk telling her everything. I needn't have worried, it seemed normal to Nancy, since Reg was brought up with those ideas and she had had psychic experiences of her own.

'Now tell me more about Reg,' I asked. Nancy revealed the reason for his frailty. 'He's battling severe leukaemia' she told me, 'but had a blood transfusion before you arrived because he was determined to be strong enough to welcome you into our home.' This news brought tears to my eyes, Thomas-fashion. What inner strength did this dignified man possess? He seemed to have inherited a Machell gene that combines gentleness with determined courage to forge a new path away from the norm. Each time Thomas returned to his comfortable surroundings in England, he had driven himself back East, despite increasing ill health. Likewise, his nephew Reginald Willoughby had foregone both a successful career as traditional artist and a ready-made home at Crackenthorpe Hall to make a new life on another continent. As for Reg, he had also boldly changed career, resigning a naval commission to join NASA's pioneering Skylab space programme.

We returned home to wait for Reg. Despite being in his seventies and weak with leukaemia and its horrible treatments, he had driven a round trip of several hours to work as consultant on an aeronautical programme that day. Yet when he returned home, visibly exhausted, he insisted on taking me out to dinner.

Five days after my visit Reg Machell suffered a stroke that marked the beginning of the end, and the following summer, 2003, Nancy wrote to tell me he had died (she survived him by five years). His last words to me, on hearing my Thomas tale just before I left for the airport, were: 'That makes you and me related in a way for which there is no definition'.

The late Susan Bosence, hand-block textile printer, resist-dyer, teacher and Jenny's mentor, dyeing indigo in the courtyard of her Devon farmhouse, UK in the early 1980s.

Amrita Mukerji, who was part of the Thomas trail from the start. She founded Kolkata's organization SUTRA, dedicated to preserving India's textile heritage; her hand dipped in indigo marked the inauguration of the SUTRA 2014 event called 'Colours of Nature'.

The banks of the Hooghly river at Babu Ghat (built 1830), where Thomas's ships berthed on arrival in Calcutta, India. In the distant haze is Howrah suspension bridge, 2010.

Patakabaree nilkuthi, *indigo planters' house, north of Kishenagur on the Ganges tributary of the Jellingee, where Thomas lived in 1846 when he was learning about the manufacture of indigo.*

The ruins of Patakabaree house, found by Jenny, Amrita Mukerji, the late Glencairn Balfour Paul and Monoleena Banerjee in February 2000 during their nilkuthi *hunt in Bengal, India.*

'Indigo planters after tiffin'; Thomas's sketch of himself and his French boss Mr Verplough at Patakabaree, imagined from the viewpoint of the humble punkawallah *whose job was to pull the ceiling* punkah *to and fro, with a rope on a pulley, to fan his employers.*

Jenny in 2001 emulating Thomas, beneath a punkah, *now powered by electricity, in a Raj bungalow (see page 215 for the exterior) in Thalassery (known as Tellichery by the British), a spice town on the Malabar coast in Kerala, India.*

A merchant's house in Alleppy, Kerala in 2001, unchanged since Thomas's time.

Thomas's self-portrait showing the town barber of Suez sprucing him up after his long voyage by dhow *from Jeddah, Saudi Arabia, in the Red Sea.*

Thomas's sketches of houses in Wellesley Street in 1850. On the right is Number 45.

Left: Old colonial houses in Rafi Ahmed Kidwai Road (former Wellesley Street) in Kolkata.

Right: Jenny looking at Number 45, the modern building that replaced the house where Thomas used to stay with his friends the Howards; a video shop at street level in 2000, but run down by 2014, videos having already had their day.

Thomas's sketch of dancers in 1850 at a wedding party of Boonah local people at Rooderpore village, near Jessore in present day Bangladesh.

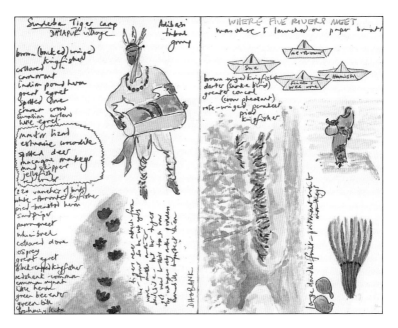

A notebook page of Jenny's from February 2014 showing a village dancer, tiger pug marks and other scenes in the Ganges delta of the Sunderbans, the world's largest tidal mangrove swamps, home to the Bengal tiger and a UNESCO world heritage site. They were teeming with wildlife when Thomas travelled there in the 1840s and 1850s.

Thomas's sketch of a tiled tomb at Hyderabad, made during his journey from Karachi, in present day Pakistan, to Kashmir and the Northwest Frontier in 1855.

Jenny's 1975 sketch of a Persian star tile.

Thomas's painting of an Indian in lower Bengal leaning against a date tree considered holy because its shape resembled the trident wielded by the Hindu God Shiva.

View from the boat when Jenny and her daughter Finella were going through the Narmada River marble gorges near Jabalpur, during their trip to search for Thomas's grave at Narshinghpur in Madhya Pradesh in October 2003.

One of the many obstacles encountered on the road from Japalpur to Narsinghpur, this one a lorry collision near Bhopal junction.

A goatherd who had walked hundreds of miles from Rajasthan with his flock. On the road from Bhopal junction to Narsinghpur.

Finella in the derelict old British cemetery at Narsinghpur, looking for Thomas's grave with little hope since almost all the graves had vanished, were badly damaged or smothered by undergrowth.

Reginald Machell's painting, The Path, *that symbolizes 'the way by which the human soul must pass in its evolution to full spiritual self-consciousness'. Of oil and gesso, 6'2" x 7'5, it is now hanging at the International Headquarters of The Theosophical Society in Pasadena, California.*
A stained glass window at the Theosophical Lodge in Leeds, England, features this design.

David Wheeler, Jenny and Simon Dorrell in 2005 with dogs Toby and Roly, in the part of the garden at Bryan's Ground, near Presteigne, that Simon created for David's 50th birthday to commemorate Crackenthorpe Hall.

Etton church yard in Yorkshire. with the Machells from America. Peggy Machell Aalund cleaning the grave of Guy Machell, brother of her great-grandfather, Reginald Willoughby, with Jenny, Troy Aalund and the late Nancy Machell.

The Machells from America visiting the ancestral home of Crackenthorpe Hall in Cumbria in July 2005. Seated from left: the late Glencairn Balfour Paul, Troy Aalund, the late Nancy Machell; standing: Jenny, Rebecca Steele, Peggy Machell Aalund holding Maggie Steele, and Tony Aalund.

December 30th 1847 On Board the Bogolah
Fot el Khair Captain Mahommed bin Ahomed
Casim. Bound from Linga in the Persian
Gulf to Jeddah in the Red Sea.
I came on board last night accompanied by
my friend Kapında the mate of the Hamoody.
For whom I have a very sincere regard and so
great was my sorrow at parting with my dusky
friend that I was obliged to look over the stern
of the vessel as if seeking for fish for some

Thomas's sketch of the baghlah, *a large deep-sea merchant dhow, he sailed in with Arab merchants from Muscat in Oman to Jeddah in Saudi Arabia in 1848, with a cargo of dates, tobacco and carpets.*

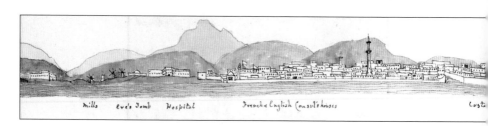

mills   eve's tomb   Hospital   French & English Consul's houses   Custo

Thomas's sketch of Jeddah in Saudi Arabia from the sea in February 1848.

Port Said container port - looking
towards Suez Canal, 28 Jan 2010

6pm Great oval sunset like a blood orange,
reflected in snatches of the lake behind Port Said.
Have seen the whole day through, imprisoned
in the ship! Eased up the port in a soft
creamy dawn, having anchored all night in the
Mediterranean, lights of the Egyptian coast just
visible, & birds wheeling around in the ship's
lights - presumably catching insects attracted by the light.

Jenny's picture of containers being loaded onto the container ship CMA-CGM Coral *at Suez,
Egypt in January 2010, with a view south of the start of the Suez Canal. Jenny had taken passage
on this ship to travel from UK to India via the Mediterranean, Red Sea and Indian Ocean.*

Arish Diwan   Yemen Gate   Christian Burial ground

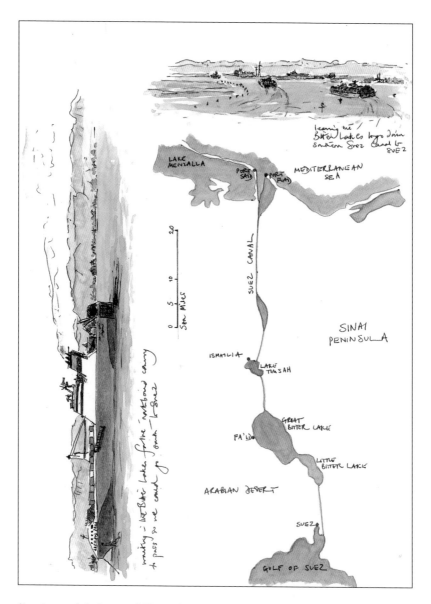

Jenny's map of the Suez canal, Egypt with sketches of cargo ships waiting in the Bitter Lakes for the northbound convoy to pass and heading down the southern section of the canal to Suez, January 2010.

Thomas's painting of the Omani harbour of Muscat as seen from the dhow Hamoody *on its approach by sea at the end of December 1847.*

Jenny in the Calcutta Cricket and Football Club,
one of the oldest sporting clubs in the world. Jenny
had just acquired the colonial hat in a bric-a-brac
shop in Park Street.

Thomas's sketch of himself in his colonial hat,
hunting birds in the bheels *(Ganges flood waters)*
of Bengal in 1850.

Left: A sketch of Krishna by Thomas and one by Jenny (right)
of the Krishna image in the shrine of Birla Mandir,
the Hindu temple built in Ballygunge in Kolkata in 1970.

25. Back to the Beginning

Long long be our hearts with such memories filled
Like the vase in which roses have once been distilled
You may break you may shatter the vase if you will
But the scent of the roses will hang round it still.

(*Irish Melodies*, Thomas Moore, quoted
by Thomas)

In the 'Indian summer' of 2003 Glencairn and I headed to Etton and Crackenthorpe via eastern England this time, dropping in en route on various Machells not yet visited.

First stop was Newmarket, a town that smells of horse and where civic statues commemorate jockeys rather than generals. We paid homage to James at the famous stables he created at Bedford Cottage and Machell Place (formerly Chetwynd House) and at his grave in Newmarket's enormous cemetery before we drove on north through the fenlands of Lincolnshire to drop in on Richard at his parish of Barrow-on-Humber in a backwater on the southern side of the Humber estuary. Richard presided over this parish for forty-five years, longer than Tom's entire life.

We crossed over the Humber and drove east to Kingston-on-Hull. After losing Crackenthorpe, Grandfather Christopher did well to marry a daughter of Christopher Scott, sheriff and mayor of the city as well as merchant and property owner. The Neaves guided us to various remaining Scott and Machell haunts, including a street still named Machell Street after the family, and a prominent merchant's house called Blaydes House, where Thomas's great-aunt Kitty, wife of a wealthy shipbuilder, lived.

Leaving Hull for city planners to wreck, we turned west and returned to Etton's rectory, which felt like a homecoming. On our first visit, when the Wilsons lived there, it had been a surprise to find the nameplate 'Thomas' attached to the door of the room I was convinced had been Tom's. When the new owner, Lynn Elvidge, led us to the same room she said: 'Our son Thomas chose this as his bedroom,' and pointed to a new nameplate saying 'Thomas'. Of course, I thought, glancing at Glencairn. Lynn asked us why we were smiling.

Downstairs in the drawing room we explained the smiles. I thought how young Lynn looked in her leather jacket and tight jeans, yet in her late thirties she was the age at which Thomas's mother died after giving birth to her twelfth child in the room above us. Lynn must have read my mind. 'When I'm upstairs alone in the house I often hear the voice of a child downstairs calling out "Mummy",' she said, suddenly.

She mentioned plans to re-roof the house and I told her of my fading hopes of finding in an attic any papers or mementos relating to Thomas.

I crossed the lane to clean up Eliza's grave. The half blank gravestone still didn't feel right.

One of Thomas's last gestures shows how Etton was on his mind at the end of his life. A notice in the Beverley Guardian of Saturday January 10th 1863, under the heading 'Etton: Christmas Liberality' thanks him for his generous gift of £5 'to be distributed among the poor of this village'.

Next stop was York, where, stepping into the space, light and colour of its mediaeval Minster, I was overlaying both Tom's visits when Richard was Canon and my own when a student in the city. Then we headed further north to Marton-in-Cleveland, once a North Riding village, but now engulfed by Middlesbrough. Its old rectory and church of St Cuthbert are marooned in dreary modern suburbs and the modest grave of its former vicar Robert Machell also seemed marooned.

It was a relief to travel west towards the setting sun. Westmoreland's fells were dissolving in a pinkish gold dusk when we reach Crackenthorpe to find rabbits still hunched on the lawns and the familiar crows settling into the woods for the night. The Balfours handed us the keys to the main house, inviting us to make ourselves at home. Pushing open the heavy front door, we passed the pantry and entered the central hall with its billiard table, the felt top bleached by time. Was one-armed Christopher Machell glad to see us back? The drawing room, the size of a skating rink, is far too big for two, but as I sank into one of its large sofas I saw Victorian and Edwardian Machells strolling around the room in tweed waistcoats, puffing at their cheroots and chatting of estate matters. From the terrace outside I could hear children laughing and crying. In this room that evening the silence was filled with the sound of Machells.

I got up early and went round the house like a Victorian maidservant, drawing back faded velvet curtains and folding heavy concertina shutters with cracking varnish. In the dining room I trailed my fingertips over the Braille of the embossed wallpaper panels, before heaving open the lower sash window – a strangely clumsy arrangement – to step over the high sill and onto the moss-coated paving stones of the terrace.

Countess Valda's fountain, made by her sculptress sister, stopped singing long ago. It is throttled by ivy, which also competes with Russian vines and red roses to parcel up the house façade. But the summerhouse had been cleared since our last visit, revealing the date 1891 carved into its stone lintel, and rusted lawnmowers in the shade within. I could smell mock orange and honeysuckle blossom as I stepped barefoot onto the dewy lawn, surprised to find it warm underfoot. This drew me down to the circular lower terrace whose paving lay under a counterpane of turf, past the old lead statue, on down the remnants of steps which once linked a series of terraces designed for aristocratic strolling, over the silted-up leat, and finally down to the Eden, sliding at snail's pace with bubbles on its surface after the unusual summer heatwave. I was joined again by generations of Machells who descended those terraces before me down to the uncaring river below.

At the end of the woods we have to duck beneath dark laurels and watch out for rabbit holes like snares. Percy strolls ahead of us through these beech woods, which shimmer in spring with bluebells. Can you see him rounding the last bend in the path and pointing with pride to the pump-house that is providing his household with the first electricity in the area? There it is, arching over what is now a bramble-filled ditch but back then was the race, diverted from the main river, flowing strongly to power the horizontal wheel driving the pump. Notice how the Machell coat of arms with his and Valda's stone initials are still sharp chiselled.

Let's leave Percy at his pump-house and return up the path behind the widowed Countess and her son in 1928. Arm in arm they are walking towards the house. In this adieu both are conscious of the ancestors who have followed this same path for almost a thousand years. With Roger's departure the line of Crackenthorpe Machells living on their ancestral land is ending. But they know the right decision has been made. World War I changed not just their lives, but the whole country's. Life in a stately home, even one as modest as

Crackenthorpe, is no longer tenable. Most of the gardeners who maintained the terraces, cleared the woods and pruned the roses died in the trenches – several beside their master Percy himself. The survivors moved on to other occupations, and wives and widows chose better jobs than blackening grates and ironing satin sheets. As we know, the house expired with its master's death, Valda taking her shattered dreams to London, renting out the main house and leaving Roger with that sadistic nanny.

Roger is now a young man of 20. The house reproaches him with its neglect. In some ways the decision to sell feels like a betrayal of Uncle James, who used his wits and bravado to return the family to their rightful home. Can that be just 50 years ago? It seems much more. He and his mother are about to turn their backs forever on a place filled with memories of the husband and father who inherited it. Roger was six when Percy went to war. He treasures the last father-and-son photograph, father in his Lonsdale Officer's uniform, himself in a replica uniform made especially for him. His father spent much time with his clever, twinkling only child. Roger can vividly recall the sensation of sitting on his father's knee while together they read poems aloud from the Golden Treasury, their favourite book. He can still smell his father's waistcoat, a reassuring blend of woodland and tobacco, and feel against his cheek the hard bulge of his father's gold fob watch in the waistcoat pocket, its ticking loud in his ear. He remembers too the bond he felt when standing next to Father in muffled evening hush, swallows dipping overhead while their fishing lines swished and settled on the river's surface and the reels purred. Sometimes they saw a kingfisher skim upstream, entrancing as the dragonflies dancing in from nowhere. On the way back to the house before nightfall, Roger would hold Father's hand, chatting away, secure in the knowledge that life would continue forever that way, secure in his father's protective presence.

At his side, his mother is submerged in her own nostalgia, recalling the bustle of arrivals at Penrith station on the train from London. The deferential driver standing to attention as he held open the door of the carriage shaped car that had come to meet them, and her European maid tucking a cashmere blanket around her knees, fearful her mistress might catch cold in this northern county. Valda's heart always leapt at the sight of the fells her husband loved so much, though she never felt truly at home among them. The car would edge through the gates of the Hall and there on the steps ahead were the servants waiting to greet their master and his glamorous wife. The gundogs barked in excitement, fires blazed, trunks were unpacked – and London soon seemed very far away.

Valda remembers especially the gaiety when friends and family came to stay; how the women chatted and laughed, her artist sisters sketched and the men relaxed into fishing and shooting, striding towards the house in long boots followed by keepers carrying the day's haul of salmon, trout, pheasant and pigeons. The men strolled along the terrace on fine summer evenings with brandies and cigars. On rainy days they played cards and billiards and she could still hear the endless click of the balls in the hallway below while she dressed for dinner in a floor-length gown and her maid put up her hair with a profusion of pins. How her heart would lift when Nanny brought her miracle baby to her room for a goodnight kiss – he smelt of innocence and talcum powder. Later he would put his head round the door, a toddler with a smile. Then it was down the wide staircase and into the dining room where candlelight bounced off the wallpaper's gilt, to share game pies, sides of glazed salmon served on huge oval plates, jellies and exotic pineapples. After the meal Valda delighted her guests with her accomplished singing. She remembers the joy of sending her voice soaring across the room from the platform at its curved end right over to the portraits on the far wall. At Christmas time the staff brought their families to the house for cakes, ale and presents, the merry children bringing, she thought, the very fabric of the building alive.

Softly, in the dusk, a woman is singing to me;
Taking me back down the vista of years, till I see
A child sitting under the piano, in the boom of the tingling strings
And pressing the small, poised feet of a mother who smiles as she sings.

(from *Piano*, D H Lawrence)

'Do you remember the cobweb?' asks Roger suddenly, interrupting the intense silence between them. Valda laughs for the first time in days. 'How could I ever forget it?' she replies. The morning both remember so vividly came just weeks after Percy had left for war with his Lonsdale men. It was September, the valley a veil of mist. Roger ran across the wet lawn to investigate a surprising patch of pink at its farthest end, leaving little footprint dashes in the grass. The pink was a clump of autumn crocuses, not that he knew nor cared. All that interested him was the startling way the egg-yolk yellow stamens stood out against the papery petals the colour of the sugar-pink mice in his Christmas stocking. Looking up, his eye was caught by a cobweb suspended between two tall thistles, its intricate oval

Watercolour of Valda Machell and her son Roger Victor in 1911 by Valda's sister, British sculptor and designer Feodora (Lady Feodora Georgina Muad Gleichen b. 1861, d. 1922).

maze pricked out by thousands of tiny dew beads glistening in sunshine. He remembers being spellbound for several minutes before running back over the lawn as fast as he could to share this miracle with his mother. He had found Valda in the drawing room, arranging scented roses in a crystal vase on the round table in the big bay window. 'Mama, Mama, you must come quickly,' he had yelled excitedly. 'My dear, what is it?' she had asked, startled by the child's urgency. 'Something magic,' he had replied.

Valda followed her son across the vast lawn, holding up her skirts to save the hems from getting wet, while Roger, on his awkward little legs, looked back over his shoulder to urge her on. He recalls how fearful he had been lest the cobweb should vanish before his mother reached it. But it was still there, sparkling more brightly than before. Mother and son crouched side by side on the edge of the ha-ha and stared and stared. They found to their mutual delight that by tilting their heads at certain angles they could see rainbows in each droplet. 'Come dear,' said his mother, after many minutes had passed, 'I have something to show you now.' Roger remembers how intrigued he had been as his mother led him back to the house, enfolding his tiny hand in her large silky one, feeling the hard ridge of her wedding ring. Still hand in hand, not stopping to wipe their feet, they had climbed the wide front staircase like fellow conspirators and entered the enormous master bedroom, whose size always overawed the small boy. Valda pulled open a drawer and took out a lacquered jewellery box Roger had never seen before. Until then he had had no idea where his mother kept the necklaces she would wear in the evenings when guests were staying. He had held his breath as she opened the lid and pushed aside several strings of pearls, diamonds and emeralds until beneath them she found the necklace she sought. She held it up to the light, so the morning sun shone through it. 'Look,' she said, 'what does this remind you of?' And of course the string of moonstones, brought back years ago from India by Roger's great-uncle Thomas as a gift for his sister, looked just like the cobweb dewdrops now being absorbed by sunbeams in the garden.

This memory had been boxed along with all the others in a treasure chest whose lid was slammed shut in 1914 when Valda was still a young woman and Roger a small child.

It was now our own last afternoon at Crackenthorpe Hall. I didn't expect to be here again and I assumed it would soon have new owners because the Balfours were putting it on the market. Glencairn was reading Kipling on the terrace and quoted out loud:

... if you enter the woods
Of a summer evening late,
When the night-air cools on the trout-ringed pools
Where the otter whistles his mate...
You will hear the beat of a horse's feet,
And the swish of a skirt in the dew,
Steadily cantering through
The misty solitudes,
As though they perfectly knew
The old lost road through the woods...

I set off to look for 'Peg's stone'. It only rises out of the riverbed in dry summers like the one we had been having, when water levels are exceptionally low. It's the large granite boulder underneath which Elizabeth ('Peg') Sleddal's corpse, exhumed during one such dry summer in the early 18th century, is said to have been re-buried in order to keep her troublesome spirit out of mischief for nine hundred and ninety-nine years, though the effort wasn't entirely successful.

With hauntings on my mind I headed down towards the Eden, this time veering to the right, leaving green and gold meadows behind as I re-entered the gloomy woods. The further I penetrated, the more overgrown it became. There was a musty smell, like wardrobes filled with dead uncles' suits, and I could hear the oyster catchers crying out over the water. Drawn onwards, I was now forced to duck beneath overhanging trees and scramble over fallen logs. My heart was beating faster than usual, but I couldn't resist glancing back over my shoulders from time to time, half expecting – almost daring – a figure to be standing in the half light at a curve in the path. I had to slither clumsily down the steep bank through stinging nettles and thistles to the bend in the river beyond which rises Peg's Stone. I reached the bottom of the bank and got to my feet.

There in the wide water, the river stretching on beyond downstream, was the boulder. And right beside it, upright and motionless, a grey cape pulled tight around its hunched shoulders, stood a lonely figure. I froze.

But it was only a heron. Releasing my breath, I watched sunlight skip around it on the water's pewter surface until it somehow sensed my presence. It lifted slowly off the riverbed and glided low over the water before curving away to disappear into the brooding woods of Crackenthorpe Hall.

26. Moments of Epiphany

'Now' is Simple.
'Then and When' is Complicated

(*'Humanism Excellence Forum'* of R K Gupta)

Like a Russian doll Narsinghpur town sits in the belly of Narsinghpur district, which sits in the belly of the State of Madhya Pradesh, which sits in the centre of India.

I confess I was wary of venturing to Narsinghpur on my own, in case Rashna was wrong and a lonely death awaited me there too. A friend offered to accompany me but had to pull out, so with reluctance I resolved to brave it alone. However, soon afterwards I had a call from our daughter, Finella, then living in Australia. 'I'm longing to go to India,' she said, 'I'll come and join you there.' I very much doubted she would make it as her life was so busy, but in the end we did indeed rendezvous in Kolkata to head together into unknown territory.

I kept my fears to myself. They weren't entirely irrational because central Madhya Pradesh retains a touch of the dodgy reputation that in the 1820s caused the British officer William Henry Sleeman to declare war on Thugee – akin to President Bush's 2001 declaration of 'War on Terror'. Sleeman's crusade was against a notorious cult called 'Thugs' (the English word comes from the Hindi). They lurked in the region's forests and strangled countless unfortunate travellers, reputedly in the name of the Hindu goddess Kali, though they were probably ruthless robbers grabbing British treasure amassing from Central India's opium crops. Sleeman launched his famous man-hunt in Narsinghpur, a town so forgotten today that it doesn't merit even a passing mention in guidebooks. Back in 2000, having found out that Thomas was apparently buried in a town of that name, I had asked my Indian friends about it. None of them had even heard of it, and neither had any of my well-travelled British friends until I mentioned it to writer and traveller Bruce Wannell, who knows everybody. 'You should get in touch with my friend Kevin Rushby,' he said, 'because he's just been travelling in remote parts of central India and I believe he's been to a place called Narsinghpur. He'll be back in Yorkshire now, unless he's already departed for Yemen. I'll give you his mobile phone number.'

I rang Kevin at once, wondering if his mobile phone would work in Yemen. 'Call me back on a landline' he said, dictating a number to me. 'But that's the same code as ours,' I exclaimed in surprise, 'where on earth are you?' 'In Crediton,' was his reply. Crediton is our home town, and it turned out that Kevin was breakfasting just down the road from our house, assessing a hotel for a tourist guide! Less than half an hour after I made contact with him, Kevin Rushby was sitting at our kitchen table telling us tales of Narsinghpur, which he had just visited while researching Sleeman and Thuggee practices for his next book.

'What does it look like?' I asked Kevin. He bent down and rummaged in the bag on the floor beside his chair. 'I'll show you,' he grinned. 'I haven't had time to unpack since I got back, so my camera full of pictures of the town is still in my bag'. A press of a button took us down the town's old-fashioned streets and into Sleeman's own courthouse, but not the cemetery. Kevin confirmed Narsinghpur's obscurity, describing gleefully how it remains in such a time warp that sights and encounters that might seem strange anywhere else are the norm there. 'It's the kind of place,' he declared, 'where you'll be served in a café by a waiter with thirteen toes. Or you'll walk down a street and come across a sacred bull that has two extra legs dangling from its hump.' 'Look,' he said, clicking onto a picture of the sacred bull, adorned with cowrie shells and pom-poms, bestowing blessings on a shop. That did it. And since it was a lost town filled with crumbling vestiges from the time of the Raj, as Kevin confirmed, then an old English cemetery might still exist, though it was discouraging to hear that Kevin hadn't come across one. His depiction of the town as a 'peculiar' threatening place of ill omen was hardly reassuring.

I didn't expect to find Thomas's actual grave since all the odds were against it, but I believe in what I term 'negative research'. Thomas's absence from the extensive London records of burials in India is made more conspicuous by those of his relatives recorded there, including brother Lance, who didn't die a hero's death on the battlefield but succumbed to 'Apoplexy' in the Himalayan foothills two years after Thomas's death. The chances of finding a remote old cemetery, let alone a grave, were very slim. And even in Calcutta, where Raj cemeteries are still cared for, I had, in the Victorian Scottish cemetery, witnessed laundry strung between illegible gravestones and tombs desecrated, empty, their lids tossed around the undergrowth like scattered dominoes. In any case, Indian towns have expanded so much since Thomas's day that an obscure, untended British cemetery would probably have been colonised by squatters.

Before I left for India I made one last desperate stab at trying to establish whether it really would be worth going all that way to Narsinghpur just to search for an unlikely lost grave. Thanks to a chance conversation in Crediton High Street I heard of a local dowser, Fred Saunders, renowned for his ability to locate everything from shipwrecks and lost purses to... graves. With nothing to lose (but my pseudo 'academic' reputation) I paid him a visit.

It was an intriguing experience, tense with concentration. First the dowsing ('divining') rods had to 'lock on' to Thomas by mysteriously locating his energy, wherever it was; then Fred instructed me to ask 'yes/no' questions via the rods. In their movements they appeared to respond to my questions with conviction. I built up to the crucial question. 'Did Thomas die in India?' The rods swung inwards, for yes, as I expected. Next I asked, 'Does his grave still exist in Narsinghpur cemetery?' At this, the rods shot out sideways and backwards. This indicated a most emphatic 'no'. I was very disappointed, but was beginning to form new questions in my head when Fred, exhausted, called a halt. 'Come back with a map,' he said, 'so the rods can locate for you the exact spot where Thomas died.'

Remembering that the name Narsinghpur applied not just to the town itself but also to the large surrounding district, I now wondered whether Thomas might have died elsewhere in the district and been buried in some forgotten location. After all, the family tree and plaque in Etton church said 'died in Nursingpore', not Narsinghpur town, and I knew Thomas was constantly on the move with his bullock trains.

Joined by Glencairn, I returned to Fred's house with two maps, one of Narsinghpur district in Thomas's day and the other of the town itself in the early 20th century, including its old cemetery then. Once again the rods mysteriously 'locked themselves' onto Thomas, while I held a pencil over the maps. 'Was Thomas buried somewhere in Narsinghpur district?' I asked the rods. To my surprise they swung out for 'no'. This floored me again but I ploughed on with other questions and a plausible story emerged from the yes/no indications of the rods. According to these, Thomas had been fatally kicked in an accident involving bullocks, and his embarrassed Indian employees, anxious to conceal their negligence, had cremated his body on an isolated hillside. Guided by the rods' magnetism my hand drew a cross in the eastern corner of the map of Narsinghpur district, apparently indicating where Thomas had been reduced to ash.

I left Fred's house feeling puzzled and thrown off course. Where did this leave the very different account I had, as it were, received about his own death from Thomas himself? He had never let me down before. If I believed the dowsing rods it made the forthcoming trip even more futile. Now fully resigned to finding nothing in Narsinghpur town, it seemed I must explore the wider district too, where 'x' was now marked on the map. Secretly I hoped that if I made the effort to go there, Thomas might just come to my rescue.

17th October 2003. Our pilgrimage starts at midnight in Kolkota's grandiose Howrah station, terminus of India's East Indian Railway and the only station in the world where cars drive right along the platforms. Tonight the Howrah-Mumbai mail train pants off along Thomas's short line, and then way beyond. By dawn Finella and I have passed through Varanasi and just left Mirzapore, where Thomas lodged near the *ghats*. With our backs against the open door of the slowly moving train, we are the audience at an open-air cinema showing a film of rural poverty, to a background rhythm of clanking wheels. Scenes unfold and repeat themselves in endless variations; buffalo ploughshares folding soil the colour of condensed milk; women drying cowpat cakes on wooden boards in rows neat as on a baker's tray; girls in bright dresses drawing water at a pump; men squatting; small boys with skinny legs leaping gleefully into monsoon pools; and sacred cows meandering in and out of the frame.

A party atmosphere often develops on a long-distance Indian train journey. Seats are ferociously fought over at the station, but with the journey under way the carriage community relaxes and a new film starts running. Beneath a regiment of grey fans seats are swapped, shoes removed, picnics spread on sheets of newspaper are shared, children play 'peek-a-boo', babies change laps. A mini-drama occurs. Who are the two figures in scarlet following the *chai-wallahs* down the carriage? Men or women? Larger and coarser than women, they nevertheless wear saris, jewellery, caked powder, rouge and red lipstick. They approach people at random, clapping loudly when eyes are averted. They are *hijras*, eunuchs from the outskirts of society who scrape a living by causing embarrassment to people until they are paid to go away. Thomas knew what it was like to feel an outcast. I think of him in the last years of his life, supervising his bullock trains as they plodded up and down nearly three hundred miles of dirt roads in all weathers.

We lean once more against the frame of the open door, satisfyingly breaking British 'Health and Safety' rules. I gaze down and suddenly blurt out to Finella, 'I have a feeling we're literally on Thomas's tracks'. She is getting used to such remarks, gives a quizzical half smile inherited from her father and takes a slow drag of her cigarette.

It is long after dusk when we reach Jabalpur, India's Crewe Junction, where the East Indian and Great Indian Peninsular main lines from Kolkata and Mumbai intersect. When we alight most passengers, heading for Mumbai, have settled down for a second night on the train. As our train is several hours late I am not surprised there is no sign on the deserted platform of Deepak Rai, the English-speaking guide I have booked to accompany us, so it's a relief to find him waiting patiently outside the station. On the way to our hotel he warns us of recent trouble on the streets and talks of frequent curfews. 'Why did you choose to launch a travel company in such a town?' we ask. 'I have no rivals,' he replies, 'in a town notorious for crime 'n all.' It seems he will be a reassuring and entertaining companion and his company name, 'Wild Expedition', seems appropriate for our own probable wild goose chase.

Jabalpur might be 'remarkably little visited' by foreigners today, according to the guidebook, but it certainly wasn't in Tom's day. Back then it was packed with soldiers, officers, engineers and civil servants (not to mention humbler workers like Thomas), all keeping the peace and joining up the scattered dots of Queen Victoria's great Indian Empire. Centuries earlier it had been the capital of several mediaeval kingdoms, being a major crossroads on the Narmada, one of India's holiest rivers, which defies the rules of the region's geography by flowing from east to west.

The town feels sleepy today, despite its reputation for crime; a place where cycle rickshaws and bicycles far outnumber motorised traffic. Deepak ferries us from one spacious part to another, many still known by Raj names such as Napier and Wright Towns and Circuit and Civil Lines. The vast and monstrous mock-Gothic courthouse reflects the problem of administering justice in the area, then and now, just as the quantity of laundry strung across acres of parade grounds reveals the size of the army now occupying former British barracks and Officers' Messes. We meet an army Major friend of Deepak's from Dera-Dun who tells us without irony that the Indian Army is 'more British than the British'. Certainly it appears to have seamlessly carried on here where the British left off after Independence. On street corners and roundabouts Pakistani tanks captured in the 1971 war cosy up to tanks and cannons leftover from earlier British battles. Ordnance factories and depots flourish as ever and the old circuit bungalow, railway headquarters, churches and schools have been absorbed into modern Jabalpur along with the simpler houses of the type I assume Thomas lodged in. Some Raj residences are, however, gently decaying, their red tiled roofs caving in and verandas filling with rubble while mauve-flowered bougainvilleas thuggishly strangle them.

British Society life in India revolved around its clubhouses, 'oases of refuge to the White Man, burdened as he was with the grave and onerous responsibilities to rule and to civilise', to quote from the memorial centennial publication of Jabalpur's Nerbudda Club, its editor getting his own back on India's colonial rulers. The sarcasm continues: 'That his travails were entirely of his own making, and that the subject peoples had their own views – quite often superior and justifiably so – on these momentous issues mattered not a whit to him.' The Nerbudda Club was built thirty years after Thomas's death, but had it existed in his day, as a non-official he wouldn't have qualified for membership, for we read that it was 'undoubtedly the most famous, the best equipped and the most exclusive of the Central Indian Clubs'. In the past Finella and I would have been excluded too on account of our sex. Nowadays the club is less rigid, but it still comes as a surprise when Deepak suggests we join the lads in a game of snooker. This is no ordinary offer; it transpires that we are being invited to play on the hallowed table on which the game of snooker itself was invented in 1875 by a subaltern of the Devonshire Regiment called Neville Chamberlain (no relation). Apparently he was playing a game of Black Pool at the time, but decided to add a coloured ball. One player failed to pot an easy shot and Chamberlain called out 'Why, you're a regular snooker' (meaning 'new cadet') but added, to soothe his feelings, 'we're all snookers at the game so let's call it 'Snooker''. In a moment to treasure, we find ourselves pitted against the resident expert. I don't even know the rules, and Finella's not much better, but somehow I manage to pot my very first ball, and Finella pots her first two. Such flukes are of course unsustainable and we're soon snookered ourselves. I note in my diary: 'What I love most about travelling in India are the unexpected Happenings that occur like an art form.' Our experience surely rivals Thomas's of November 29th 1854: 'Escorted by

four or five outriders all armed in Cavalry fashion we drove up to the
Maharajah of Burdwan's country house and landed at the Billiard room
which is built between the house and the private appartments. We were duly
challenged by the Maharajah and Major Smyth took up the cue.'

This evening I call on Jabalpur's resident historian, the elderly Dr
Choubey (a medical doctor) in his villa of Dickensian dinginess in Napier
Town. It seems that the few researchers who make it to Jabalpur all end up in
Choubey's gloomy study and all mention him in their subsequent books, so
here am I upholding the tradition. Rushby notes in his book that Choubey's
first question to him was 'Oxford, or Cambridge?' Choubey peers at me
through spectacles of thick pebble glass and asks 'Oxford, or Cambridge?'
(I also disappoint him). He pulls down from sagging shelves endless books of
obscure historical interest, all privately published or out-of-print. Thanks to
assiduous scholarship he can show me a photocopy of a list of inscriptions
on all the British Tombs and Monuments in the region, published by British
Government Officials in Nagpur in 1932, and so rare there isn't even a
copy in London's Indian Office collections [I later give them a photocopy
of Choubey's photocopy]. To see several pages listing over a hundred graves
in Narsinghpur cemetery is a heart-stopping moment. Surely Thomas must
feature here. I work my way down the dates preceding his death. Hugh
Fraser died in 1842 on Thomas's birthday, then Augusta Otway Mayne
and Edward Charlton in 1849. Next comes a baby in 1851 and a three year
old boy in 1857. The following year it's the turn of John Henry Fitzgerald
to die. I have almost reached 1862, the year of Thomas's death. I turn the
page. No Thomas. The next name on the list is W.F. Ireland, who died in
1865. Now I look more closely and see that all those listed were officials or
their family members. Private box-wallahs like Thomas didn't even count in
a modest community far from the main cities.

19th October. To compensate for this latest piece of negative research we
decide to join the Gujarati holidaymakers on a river jaunt, since Deepak
is longing to show us Indian Jabalpur, especially a local beauty spot called
'Marble Rocks'. The 'rocks' are towering gorges of milk-white marble
through which the Narmada squeezes her swollen belly. They should be
seen under a full moon but you can't have everything, and the river is raging
in full spate so it's as well to be on it – or rather, her – in daylight. Being
rowed against the current is thrilling. The more the gorge narrows towards
'Smoke Cascade' waterfall, the more our boat whirls around uncontrollably.
Deepak's wife warned us yesterday that the Narmada, because of her
unmarried status, is 'wild and active'.

After that excitement we climb a long flight of steps to a rare 10th-century circular mandir on a high hilltop above the river. We have it to ourselves. It's not every day you find yourself surrounded by sixty-four ancient stone Yoginis, luscious naked female attendants of the goddess Durga. I notice a well used brass bell on the central temple platform. 'What's this for?' I ask Deepak. 'People ring it to get the attention of the gods,' he explains, 'because they too are preoccupied with their wives 'n all.' Also circular is the modern Jain temple down below, its interior a maze of painted miniature mountains with mythical creatures perched on top. We are told it represents the 'Eighth Geography'; it looks more like a Jain version of *The Lord of the Rings*.

Since Jabalpur didn't feel remotely threatening by day, we decide to test it by night. The goddess is in a calmer mood upstream from the waterfall and we row gently several times around her shrine in the middle of the river. Returning to the ghats, we find a group of exuberant women drumming and dancing for a mini-Kartik celebration beside the sleeping forms of their menfolk. Deepak tells us they dance by the river to entice its goddess to join them. 'You'd think they might have noticed by now that it never happens,' whispers Finella. Back in the town centre the streets are deserted apart from groups of sacred cows peacefully curled up in the dirt like overgrown cats.

20th October 2003 – D-day. We get up early as planned, but Deepak is late. When he eventually appears he tells us the direct route to Narsinghpur is so badly eroded by the recent exceptional rains that we shall have to make a huge detour, adding three hours to the journey. I realise at once that it also means we shall not now be passing anywhere near the spot marked 'x 'on my map where the dowsing rods indicated Thomas had died. An inauspicious beginning, I think to myself, as I surreptitiously remove from my shoulder bag the divining rods the dowser gave me. He taught me how to use them (I located a gas pipe under his floor at my first attempt!) and told me to consult them when we reached the spot. I haven't even mentioned them to Finella lest she think her mother is completely round the bend. The rods have been a reminder in the bottom of my suitcase whenever I delve deep for clean undies. At least I'm wearing the lucky necklace, the silver hand of the Prophet Mohammed's wife Fatima, given to me by Glencairn when we sailed away from Tunisia on our third wedding anniversary. It's a good luck talisman throughout North Africa and I have worn it on every trip abroad since 1977.

We head west in the direction of Bhopal. I am conscious it's Finella's first proper outing in the Indian countryside and it's starting badly. Despite our late start, the devout Deepak insists we stop to pay homage and rupees to Krishna at a mildewed old temple.

We drive past flat fields of wheat, dhal, rice and sugarcane, occasional simple villages and simpler wells. The verges are smothered with coloured creepers and blood-red hibiscus, Kali's flower. And so it goes on for two hours. Rare stretches of reasonable road, newly tarmaced for the coming local elections, soon revert to the default of chronic potholes.

Things begin to look up when we reach the Harun River. We stop on the bridge to look towards the borders of Narsinghpur district, recalling its website's claim to have the most fertile land in Asia, as well as an admirable lifestyle: 'Here life is very simple. Living standard is not the show-off kind.' ('An understatement of an entry' comments Finella.) Swallows draw invisible circles in the stale air beneath the arches of the bridge as we enter the district I've long dreamed of reaching, and the road sloughs off its last attempt at tarmac to become a gravel track winding down through a landscape described in the website as 'mixed forest of herbs, sherbs and scurbs'. I can't identify sherbs and scurbs but we see a mongoose, lots of monkeys and peacocks with scruffy – or even scurby – tails.

We're making good progress until we're blocked by a huge lorry that has expired across the track, its axle inevitably snapped in half under the weight of two of the largest chunks of marble I have ever seen. As our jeep slithers past the lorry Deepak decides to entertain us with a favourite joke from a Kushwant Singh Joke Book. He twists to face us from the front seat and quotes with a twinkle:

Young man to Santa Singh: 'Guess what? Men have just landed on the moon.'
Santa Singh: 'That's nothing.'
Young man: 'What do you mean, that's nothing?'
Santa Singh: 'We Sikhs can go to the sun.'
Young man: 'But the sun is hot – you would melt.'
Santa Singh (triumphant): 'No we wouldn't, we would go at night!'

Deepak laughs so hard that we laugh with him, rather than at the joke. We reach the bottom of the hill and regain tarmac of sorts only to find our route blocked by a vast herd of white cattle, a thousand sickle moons balanced on the craters of their bony shoulders. It takes ages to thread through them and we only bump on beyond for a few minutes before we're forced to another emphatic halt. This journey is beginning to resemble a theatrical drama. Ahead of us as far as the eye can see is a solid queue of motionless lorries. It looks as if this might be it, for hours, if not days, or weeks, or forever. We climb down from the jeep in despair and hang about watching the mass of cattle we have just passed surge towards us while our driver goes off to talk to the lorry drivers. 'Two lorries falling over and blocking road' he announces gravely on his return. He follows this with a daring offer to try and squeeze our jeep along the narrow and deeply rutted mud verge beside the road. It's either this or abandon the journey, Narsinghpur *et al*. I daren't even think about Thomas.

The verge is for animal traffic, but we bump in and join a line of gunmetal grey buffalo straining up the ruts. At least we are lurching forwards, if at alarming angles and at buffalo speed, by-passing the envious lorry drivers. At last we reach the source of the impasse. A speeding lorry has overturned, scattering across the road enough boxes of photocopying paper to supply the whole Mumbai stock exchange. Another impatient lorry, in a reckless attempt to get by, tipped over beside it, adding its own load of gas canisters to the general mess.

Next stop is a tea break at a particularly squalid roadside café at the Bhopal-Narsinghpur road junction. Deepak and the driver sit with a group of swarthy truck drivers to drink buffalo milk tea and from the jeep I watch Finella cross the road to join them. With her long golden hair and a flowing white scarf draped around her neck and spreading down her back, she looks like an angel in a Nativity play.

Tea over, we turn south. We are over halfway and heading in the Narsingphur direction at last. We achieve at least five miles before the next obstacle. This time our route is barred by an enormous flock of goats with a magnificent blood red turban rising out of the middle. And beyond that are more of the same. The turbans crown tall thin herdsmen who have trekked on foot hundreds of miles to Madhya Pradesh from their native Rajasthan, arms hooked over crooks lying across their shoulders. Deepak explains that Narsinghpur district has a large Muslim population, which means the unsuspecting fattened goats that have escaped sacrifice to the goddess Kali during her recent puja will be slaughtered at the imminent Eid marking the end of the Muslim holy month of Ramadan. Indians celebrate every festival in an exuberantly all-inclusive Indian way – Hindu pujas, Muslim Eids, Christmas, the lot. Finella observes with envy: 'All these gods – the perfect excuse to party.' The Narsinghpur website agrees, declaring that 'festivals are celebrated in a gorgeous number'.

Deepak fits in another Sikh joke before the next excitement.

It turns out that we and the goats aren't the only creatures on a long pilgrimage from home. Ahead of us, again straddling the entire road, are camel caravans on the same journey. The disdainful beasts are led by the nose by nomadic women also wearing huge nose rings, and fluorescent pink plastic bracelets from wrist to shoulder, bright skirts with glinting mirrorwork embroidery and sexy tight embroidered bodices. Their camels too wear a kind of embroidered bodice and pink pom-pom necklaces. All the household goods are piled onto platforms created by balancing on the camels' humps inverted wooden beds with carved legs. On top of the goods perch tiny children clasping young or poorly goats. It's not easy passing large camels with precarious wide loads when massive lorries are approaching from the opposite direction.

We reach a bottleneck at the long narrow bridge over the sacred Narmada River. In a rash moment Finella and I opt to cross on foot, negotiating goats, camels, herdsmen, nomads, cattle, cars and lorries all crowding in *en masse*. We are amazed the dangerously leaning railings can contain the press of animals each time a flock parts to allow a cranky oncoming lorry to nose through. We look down at the fast-flowing water far below, the colour of brown lino, parts of its bouldered edge hewn into flat platforms for washing *ghats*. Primitive dugout boats strain at their leashes in eddies near the shore. In the distance lie Narsinghpur's hills and forests, dotted with an occasional

Camel caravan from Rajasthan on the road to Narsinghpur, south of the Bhopal junction, Madha Pradesh, 2003.

white shrine. Turning our attention back to the bridge we see a small boy grab one of the goats and run off with it at lightning speed.

Soon after crossing the Narmada we come up behind a large group of the jolliest gypsy carts we have ever seen. Every wooden surface, shaft and wheel spokes included, is newly painted with enchanting designs in glossy primary colours. Balanced on top are more inverted beds holding family goods and chattels, upturned aluminium pots providing fat finials to the wooden bed legs, and women in shiny shawls are crowded on top. The carts are hauled by bullocks with bones projecting like tree roots, horns painted and necks circled by beaded collars holding large wooden cowbells playing jaunty tunes. It seems that every man, woman, child and beast on the road to Narsinghpur is in festive mood today.

> Santa Singh to his wife: 'I am sick of all these jokes with me in them.
> Can't you tell me one in which I am not involved?'
> Santa Singh's wife: 'Yes - I'm pregnant.'

Deepak is still chuckling when we reach the outskirts of Narsinghpur town. The journey has taken five hours.

Narsinghpur town. So This, I think, is It – whatever This, or It, may be.

There is little traffic and glimpses down side streets reveal old-style Indian houses with wooden verandas, a type long since demolished elsewhere. Rising above them are tall domes of mosques and temples, the oldest being a mandir dedicated to the presiding god, Narsimha, after whom the town is named. We find this lion-headed manifestation of Vishnu depicted on gaudy Bollywood style posters in its inner temple. Exploring its ancient arched corridors that smell of damp, old incense and bat droppings, we crawl through an Alice-in-Wonderland doorway into the innermost sanctuary of Shiva to ask for protection. We sense we may need it.

Incongruously mixed in with Old India are remains of rural colonial British architecture. Our next stop is the simple whitewashed church of St. Catherine's, now attached to a modern convent. Seeking inscriptions inside, I find wall plaques commemorating contemporaries of Thomas. Across the road is the circuit guesthouse, formerly Sleeman's residence, which looks so airy and comfortable with its wide verandas and high ceilings that I wish we were staying there. It can't have changed much since Thomas's day, and neither has the Deputy Collector's Courthouse, the only building with pretensions of grandeur, though two pillars have just collapsed in the monsoon. We're invited inside to see the dark panelled offices with marble floors where Sleeman waged his ruthless anti-terrorist campaign, in full swing when Thomas arrived in India. It resulted in the capture of three thousand Thugs, nearly five hundred of whom were hanged. Clearly little happens in the Courthouse today, though this does not prevent files from piling up and up until the end of time. Old-fashioned fans whirr below the high ceilings and I'm delighted to find pulleys for the former *punkahs* still *in situ*.

The delight is short-lived. We step onto the courthouse portico intent on heading across town to the cemetery, using the only town map I could find, that 1920 British touring map I had taken to the Devon dowser. The moment of truth is about to happen – or so I think. However, Truth remains as elusive as ever. I notice Deepak's mood darken. Suddenly he looks worried and tugs nervously at his cap. 'What's up?' I ask him. 'Police,' he replies. Sure enough, a group of policemen awaits us at the foot of the Courthouse steps. My heart begins to race and I kick myself for not having headed for the cemetery first, instead of saving it for last, as if unconsciously postponing the inevitable disappointment for as long as possible. Now it looks as if I might have blown it.

The police usher us towards the former British Police station, in the opposite direction from the cemetery. We are led into a dismal room clogged with large desks and shelves stacked with curling papers literally tied up in red tape. 'Sit down!' orders the scowling boss behind the largest desk. We do as we are told and glance anxiously at Deepak, who is looking helpless, again pulling at his cap 'n all. 'What are your names? Where are your passports? Where's your permit to visit the town?' Of course permits to visit are not necessary, but the sight of foreigners in Narsinghpur is such a rarity it makes the police suspicious. Or more likely, as Finella whispers to me, 'They're just bored.' At least we have our passports on us. I produce mine first, and the Chief examines every single page with excruciating slowness. Unfortunately it is full of strange visas for China, Indonesia, Mali and so on, so this takes a long time. Watching the charade, Finella mutters, 'Thank heavens my passport's brand new.' We wait in frustration as all details are painstakingly copied into a large maroon ledger. The next bombshell is the pronouncement that our passports have to be photocopied (why?) and, since there is no facility for this in the police station, they will have to be taken elsewhere. Through the open door we watch them vanish in the dust, clutched in the hands of a police minion riding pillion on the back of a scooter.

I have travelled in India often enough to know that it is wise to have a fallback contact when venturing off the beaten track. Being a little anxious about the area's reputation and remoteness, I had been relieved when Amrita in Kolkata had mentioned she knew the Head of the Archaeological Survey for Madhya Pradesh, who lives in Bhopal. We weren't intending to go anywhere near Bhopal, but he would be an emergency contact, so I jumped at Amrita's offer to phone him, and this produced a fax that included both his name and that of his Jabalpur representative. I don't have the fax with me, but leafing through my notebook I find the phone numbers.

'The head of the Archaeological Survey team gave us permission to visit Narsinghpur,' I announce triumphantly, handing the Chief the Bhopal phone number. He dials and we wait, looking pretend calm. 'He's not there – he's away in Delhi for two days and out of touch,' pronounces the Chief with satisfaction. Round Two to him. 'I have the number of his Jabalpur representative too,' I declare. The Chief dials the number and finds the representative not only in, but actually confirming that his boss in Bhopal gave us permission to visit Narsinghpur (not that he did). 'Phew!' as the cartoons say.

Now we wait and wait for the reappearance of our passports, in a scene of agonising inertia. In Sleeman's day a policeman's job was non-stop activity, with arrests, imprisonment and hangings. Today there can't be much to do. It crosses my mind that the police might wish to spice up their jobs by sending Finella and me off to join the young offenders who today occupy Narsinghpur's jail. In that very prison, reformed Thugs made for Queen Victoria the world's largest handloom carpet, which to this day adorns the Waterloo Chamber of Windsor Castle. Offenders still use the looms, so I picture Finella and myself ending our days weaving hearthrugs for the royal corgis.

Suddenly we hear the buzz of the returning scooter and are ridiculously overjoyed to be reunited with our passports. But still we can't escape. As the most crucial afternoon in my four-year search for Thomas continues to wear away, we have to smile and drink cups of sugary tea. The farce ends with all of us posing for photographs beneath a lurid picture of Kali wearing a necklace of severed heads.

At last we are released and, now under police escort, drive across town to the old cemetery. We park in a scruffy street and walk down a narrow lane towards the entrance pillars. The gates have gone. I am braced for the worst, but even so the sight that greets us is more than dispiriting and my heart sinks to my sandals. 'I can't believe I've come all the way from

Australia for this,' comments Finella dryly as she stands beside me to survey a scene of dereliction. I have dragged her across India on a long and hazardous journey to find this old cemetery that has, predictably, become a waste ground jungle of weeds and shrubs, out of which a few decaying monuments rear up forlornly. And to think I could have taken her to the Taj Mahal.

Near the cemetery entrance a family of bristly pigs scavenges among a stinking pile of rubbish, and beyond we see a chestnut cow meandering around piles of fallen stones, followed by nosing dogs with scimitar tails. Small boys appear over the dilapidated walls. The cemetery's filling up with the living, though most traces of the dead have gone.

'Watch out for snakes!' warns Deepak as we pick our way along the central pathway through rubbish and shit, both human and animal. It is soon depressingly clear that even the few surviving tombstones won't yield clues about the occupants in the ground beneath them, since inscribed stucco has crumbled after decades of weathering to expose bare brickwork, and marble insets have been pillaged. In the middle of the cemetery we're therefore astonished to find one round marble plaque miraculously intact. It is tiny, and only survives because it is so deeply inset into a fluted obelisk on top of the largest remaining tombstone. We peer at the words: Ann Whitehead, 13.10.1835. Aged 6 years, 3 months, 1 day. I begin to compose in my head the ending to this book – it will relate the poignant bathos on finding, after such a long journey, not Thomas's grave in the lonely cemetery but instead this monument to one innocent child of the Empire, who died aged six years, three months and one precious final day.

'I suppose we had better plough on towards the end of the cemetery,' I suggest without hope. I doubt we shall find anything more, but Deepak comes across the weathered base of a gravestone whose stark inscription is just legible, and I find one more. This one is chiselled in stone on the side of a rectangular tomb tipped over at an alarming angle. I promised the organisation in London that records British graves in India to note what I found here, if anything, since none of their recorders has ventured this far. I don't blame them. I kneel down to take a photograph. It is now obvious that even if a grave for Thomas had ever existed, it would long since have vanished like almost all the others. I am now growing anxious. We wasted hours in the police station and have a very long drive ahead of us, much of which will now be in the dark, but we ought at least to try and get clear of the steep forest track before dusk falls. 'Click' goes my camera, capturing the death of Augusta, wife of Lt Charles Ofway Mayne, who died aged 24.

An ever-lengthening row of small boys, scabby legs dangling, stretches along the high surrounding wall to watch this unexpected entertainment. While I take pictures and fret about the return journey, I call out to Finella: 'We really must go now, this is hopeless.' But my angel has floated off in open-toed sandals through the snake-filled undergrowth towards the farthest end of the cemetery, white wings angled over her shoulders. Then comes the Annunciation: 'My God – I've found Thomas!' I freeze where I am, kneeling in the dirt. 'You must be joking,' I shout back. 'No – really – YES, it says Thomas Machell – there surely can't have been two Thomas Machells?' comes the distant reply. She has first glimpsed the word 'Thomas', then moved closer and seen the full name. I still don't believe her, despite knowing that even she wouldn't tease me about this. I drop my bags and notebooks onto the rubbish and run towards her through the long grass.

'Look,' says Finella, pointing to a low stone plinth. And there it is. If ever there was a eureka moment, this is it. We are surrounded by undergrowth, yet here is the base of a grave with space around it, almost as if someone has cleared it for us. A hole on top of the plinth indicates a missing cross or urn, but the plinth itself is intact. The simple inscription is as legible as when it was first chiselled.

THOMAS MACHELL
BORN 12TH NOVEMBER 1824
DIED 14TH DECEMBER 1862

I sit down on the plinth beside Finella and lean on her shoulder. She confesses to feeling somewhat 'teary' herself. 'I'm so pleased for you,' she says, meaning it. Deepak, the policemen, the cows, the pigs, the dogs and all the boys who have leapt down off the wall stand around us in complete silence. We must look like a nativity tableau, minus the baby.

We make our way back up the path and I notice one of the boys has woven some strips of palm leaf into an exquisite ornament. He offers it to me and I retrace my steps through the undergrowth to place this modest wreath at the base of the grave. This will make Thomas smile.

He died alone in India, with no grieving relative to hold his hand, on a quiet Sunday nearly a century and a half before our visit. There were few mourners at his burial two days later, and none of his extensive family would ever have visited his grave. But now, on another Sunday, in the year

2003, his surrogate family, mother and daughter, have converged from the opposite sides of the globe on this remotest of cemeteries in the heart of India. In 1854, musing on his own destiny, Thomas wrote: 'There are some who are hustled out of the beaten track and must therefore endeavour to break a track of their own.' His contemporary, the American philosopher Emerson, took the words out of his mouth when he wrote: 'Do not go where the path may lead; go instead where there is no path and leave a trail.'

Following the trail left by Thomas has been long and sometimes complicated, but now everything suddenly seems simple. As I stand among the weeds, gazing at my young man's grave, I am aware that Now, Then and When have become One.

Jenny and her daughter Finella on the grave of Thomas Machell, which Finella had just found in the derelict Raj cemetery in Narsinghpur, Madha Pradesh, in Central India, October, 2003.

Further Endings

27. Eureka!

Why do you travel so far for what is most near?
The smallest coin in your purse buys what is most dear.

(*A Visit to Stratford*, Charles Causley)

The day came to meet my agent, Gillon Aitken, soon after my explorations in southern India. Over lunch in a London restaurant I related Thomas's story. I knew I must risk telling him everything, even if I sounded like a witch and put him off. 'There are some rather strange aspects to the tale that I left out of the proposal I sent to you,' I admitted, while twiddling slippery spaghetti round and round a fork. 'Try me!' he challenged. So I stopped twiddling and told him about my 'past life' sessions with Rashna. An alarming pause followed. I thought I had blown it. 'Now where does that leave my story?' I ventured, tentatively. 'Should I put all this in?' Gillon looked straight at me and said, 'But of course you must tell the whole tale'.

Over coffee I tried something else. I showed Gillon a copy of Roger Machell's Will. It turned out that Gillon had worked for the publishing firm of Hamish Hamilton, where Roger Machell, Thomas's great-nephew, had been a partner. So Gillon had actually known Roger well. He instantly recognised several names in the Will, including the main beneficiary, a David Wheeler, who, he explained, had been Roger's close friend for the last thirteen years of his life. This was news to me. 'I wonder if David Wheeler could possibly still be alive?' I mused out loud.

'Roger was considerably older than David. I've met him several times and found him a charming young man – and I know he's very much alive.'

'I happen to have David Wheeler's addresses in my office,' he added.

I sent an email to Mr. Wheeler, asking if he had any family papers and what Roger had told him of his time at Crackenthorpe. His reply was surprising: 'Most curious about Crackenthorpe. Roger led me to believe it had burnt down years ago, leaving no trace; maybe he "burnt it" from his memory, for he certainly had a lonely childhood there. As an adult Roger was entirely "Londoncentric"... and felt uncomfortable anywhere much beyond the bend in the Kings Road.' So here was confirmation that Roger had indeed been glad to turn that key and head south to London in 1928. Even so, pretending the house had literally burnt down seemed exceptionally drastic.

In the email David mentioned that Roger had burnt stacks of papers on a huge bonfire when he knew he was dying and that this had worried him because Roger had corresponded with many well-known literary figures. But, wrote David, Roger had assured him the destroyed papers were of no significance and had, accordingly, entrusted to him a box of papers. However, David, when clearing out Roger's Albany flat after his death, had one day descended into the old cellar and come across a chest crammed with old documents that he had never seen before. David said he had hung onto both box and chest, taking them with him whenever he moved house, each time lodging them in the attic because he was saving the task of going through them for a mythical 'rainy day'. He ended the email by telling me that he believed the box was full of Roger's mementos and papers relating to his royal Gleichen ancestors but he had no idea what the chest contained. A box and a mystery chest in an attic! This news was almost too much.

When I received no reply to several subsequent emails and letters I feared I had pried too much, and the papers would remain agonisingly out of reach. There was nothing to be done other than back off for a while, though this was hard. Many weeks passed before an email popped up one morning on my computer screen after I had almost given up hope. It was from David. What a relief it was to be back in contact. However, in the brief message David explained that he had been working hard to fulfil a deadline writing a history of Glyndebourne Opera and he warned me that the house and garden, Bryan's Ground in Herefordshire on the Welsh border, where he lives with his partner Simon Dorrell, was keeping them both extremely busy. He concluded by mentioning that the house happened to feature in the current issue of *Country Life* magazine if I wanted to take a look.

I went straight out and bought a copy. It was even more tantalising being able to see, in a full page picture of a lovely 'Arts and Crafts' house, the actual attic that just might hold a little piece of Thomas. But I was clearly being kept at arm's length by David and didn't know what to do next.

I only had to wait two days for another twist of fate. A friend of mine, Lucy Goffin, a textile artist with whom I did indigo dyeing each summer, just happened to phone for a catch-up chat. She and her husband, Graham Gough, live in East Sussex where Graham created 'Marchants' Hardy Plants' nursery. At the end of the conversation Lucy mentioned an unusual artwork commission she had just received from nearby Glyndebourne Opera House. Hearing that name prompted me to ask if by any chance she had come across a David Wheeler. 'How extraordinary that you should mention that name,' she exclaimed. 'It so happens that we met him and his partner, Simon, for the first time just a few days ago at a supper party with Glyndebourne friends. We got on so well that they visited "Marchants" next day and David was so impressed by our garden that he's asked Graham to write a piece for his eclectic garden magazine, *Hortus*.' Small world again. I explained my predicament to Lucy and wondered if this lucky conjunction might just tip the balance.

The following day Lucy was back on the phone. 'Guess what!' she said excitedly, 'we've just been invited to dine with David Wheeler again when he returns to Sussex later this week. Do you think it might help your cause if I tell him about you and Thomas and that amazing weekend we spent at Crackenthorpe for your fiftieth birthday?' After the meal she reported back at once. She said David had almost fallen off his bar stool when she had told him not only that she and Graham knew me (and Thomas) well, but also that they had actually stayed at Crackenthorpe Hall.

The personal connection with Lucy was the breakthrough I needed. David emailed to suggest we popped in when next travelling in the area.

Many months later, in May 2004, the time finally came. Glencairn and I would be en route to Scotland, to do a round of relatives and, knowing that David would have completed his book by then, I suggested passing by Bryan's Ground simply to introduce ourselves and explain my mission. I didn't expect him or Simon to find time to delve into the box and chest as I knew they were preparing to open their garden to the public. But on the eve of our departure from Devon I received a surprise email from David, who had just climbed down with Simon from their dusty attic. 'Heavens!' it read, 'we have just rooted through the attic and found rather more Machelliana than I imagined, some of it going back two hundred years. Clever Ol' Rog to have kept it safe.' Clever old Roger indeed.

This was thrilling news, especially since the previous week I had re-read Thomas's tantalising reference to a collection of family correspondence in a 'little closet'.

'*4th May, 2004.* Nature's greens are almost too luminous in sharp sunshine as we approach Bryan's Ground. The house, comfortable in its worn ochre overcoat, sits just inside England but reaches out to the hills of Wales beyond its garden, laid out, David told me in an email, in contrasting rooms including the one they call Crackenthorpe.

David, tall and smiling broadly, greets us in the wide stone-flagged porch and introduces us to Simon (slighter in build, also smiling in welcome while quietly taking us in) and three hounds (it had to be three) – Roly, Toby and Diva. Stepping into the hall we feel the creativity of the household and immediately encounter Machell family and their in-laws. Mementos of them are everywhere. Here is an elaborate Machell family tree decorated with hand-painted crests (greyhounds galore) opposite one tracing Countess Valda's royal lineage, and a portrait of Uncle John, who fought in Wellington's army, next to one of Valda's German relatives. Passing into the dining room, the 17th century wife of Thomas Sterne of York, Thomas's ancestor on the maternal line, glowers at us over her starched white neck ruff. Here David shows us a series of watercolours painted in Cumbria and the Lake District by Thomas's grandfather, matching the ones donated by Valda to the Victoria and Albert Museum. On the polished dining table are two large porcelain platters rimmed with green and gold, their centres decorated with the familiar Machell crest – and of course the greyhound trio.

We follow David and Simon into a long low sitting room filled with large sofas, books, plants, pictures, a grand piano and an old oak chest in the centre. Yes, it's THE Machell family chest Tom mentions, its wood burnished shiny as roasted coffee beans. Carved into the lid is the date 1640. I wonder how many Machell fingertips I'm overlaying by tracing the contours of this ancient graffito, adding to its patina made smooth from centuries of touch.

The tabletops inside this lovely room are piled high with heaps and heaps of Machell papers, brought down from the smaller chest and boxes in the attic. It's hard to know where to begin, and I am also talking to David, who is showing me glossy photos of famous actors and literary figures who crossed Roger's path during his long career in publishing. I pick up a packet labelled 'Letters: 1844-1880', which therefore covers Thomas's period. The very first letters I pull out were written by his father, Robert – last time I saw that handwriting was in the Beverley archives over two years ago. Now I find Thomas's watercolour sketches of the memorial windows for Eliza and her son in Etton church. Simon holds up a naïve-style painting of a Georgian house, unfamiliar to him and David, but which I instantly

Jenny reading through Machell family papers brought down from the attic at Bryan's Ground near Presteigne, Herefordshire by David Wheeler and Simon Dorrell, 2004.

recognise. 'Goodness, that's The Elms!' I exclaim, 'where the family lived before they moved to Etton rectory when Thomas was nine. I've been inside it but this old view from the garden isn't one I've seen before.'

Simon continues to rummage quietly in the boxes and comes towards the chair where I'm now sitting, bearing a huge leather-bound book. He places it open on my lap without saying a word. I look down at the page. It seems to be some kind of family record but I'm flabbergasted to recognise the handwriting. The page appears to have been written by my Thomas about himself. I begin to read. 'Oh, I recognise all this,' I tell the room, 'it's the *résumé* of Thomas's life up to 1852 that appears in an appendix to the Journals: I was born on the 12th of November at the Minster Parsonage Beverley. Owing to an unhappy defect...' etc. I skip-read the familiar account but see that it continues to 1854, so Tom clearly updated the page on his life's activities just before he headed back to India after his last visit home.

I turn the page. What's this? The account is continuing beyond 1854, but still in Thomas's hand. How can this be? He died in India, and was last in England in 1854, wasn't he? Yet here is Thomas telling me in his own words what happened to him during the 'missing' six years between 1856 and his death: 'Colonel Smyth offered me employment on his estates in Wynaad under his manager Mr Becher with whom I lived one year after which I returned to Calcutta in August 1857. Very ill ordered to leave Bengal again and went to Mr B Howards at Mirzapore in the N.W. Provinces.' This is almost too uncanny even for me. 'I just don't believe I'm reading this. Tom's account matches what I have already written from "imagination" without knowing the facts,' I announce in astonishment to David and Simon, who have noticed how shaken I am. I think back to last summer when I embarked on the difficult chapters covering the mystery years. I remember telling Glencairn that something strange was happening as I wrote: 'I assume Thomas was still working on the coffee estate in Southern India in 1857 since he had only started the job the previous year,' I had told him, 'yet now I have started writing the chapter in his persona I feel compelled to put him in Calcutta that year, I have no idea why.' Not being a fiction writer, I assumed then that that was what 'fiction' writing was like. The following day I had had the 'realisation' that Thomas had suffered in 1857 what today we would call a nervous breakdown and that he had retreated to recover with the Howards. I remember rushing home to my study and letting the words flow as I entered Thomas's despairing and confused state of mind. I wrote this last year.

I read on. Thomas continues: 'After recovering from my illness I entered into business with Messrs Howard Brothers and opened a Bullock Train from Mirzapore to Central India.' I had learnt about the bullock train in the Calcutta Records and had imagined it carrying all sorts of goods to service the military cantonments and civilian personnel in the region. But when Finella and I travelled by train on the stretch from Mirzapore to Jabalpur last October, something else had happened. It was when we were standing together at the open doorway of the train as it moved slowly through the countryside. Do you recall how I had looked down at the tracks and suddenly declared to her: 'I don't know what this is about but I have a strong feeling that we are literally on Thomas's tracks'? Now look what Thomas tells me: 'In 1860 I joined Mr Williams of Jubbulpore in carrying out a contract for supplying sleepers of the Great Indian Peninsular Railways Company.' I feel stupefied, to borrow a Thomas word.

When I was writing the chapters covering Thomas's six lost years, there remained almost a year that I somehow couldn't manage to describe even from 'imagination'. I was pretty sure Thomas was in India then but I couldn't 'see' him there. Now I find him providing the answer himself. 'In January 1862 having been taken severely ill I was ordered home to avoid another hot season and arrived in England on 15th March'. So the reason I couldn't visualise Thomas in India that year is because he wasn't there! Now he tells me that during that gap in the India story he was once again quietly convalescing, taking refuge with Richard, whom he never expected to meet again. This means that he could indeed have visited Etton after Father had left the rectory, as I/he had mentioned to Rashna during the 'regression', and that Richard's son Reginald Willoughby, born just after his Uncle Tom had last been in England, had, after all, been able, aged eight, to get to know his Uncle before he died, just as I had pictured when I had visited Nancy and Reg in 2002.

Thomas's handwritten report ends here in England in 1862, but not the summary of his life because Richard's looping script takes over and fills in the last months for me. 'Thus far my dear brother wrote the account of his own life, he passed the spring and summer in England with his family and friends, and returned to India overland in the autumn, he arrived at Bombay Nov. 13th 1862. His last two letters to me were dated P. and O. steamer Massilia Oct. 25th 1862 and Aden Nov 4th.' So now I find I was even in Tom's footsteps when I first went to India overland as a teenager. Richard concludes: 'The next account I received of Thomas was from his friend Major Moxon of Jubbulpore with the sad tidings of his death – He was engaged in his duties at Sohagpur where on Dec. 13th he came into Camp Garurwara very ill and on Sunday evening Dec. 14th 1862 he died. He was buried at Nursingpore on Dec. 16th a monument is erected over his grave in the burial ground at the station Nursingpore in the Central Provinces of India. By his will dated Dec.29th 1861 he left all his real and personal property to me – just before his death he expressed a wish ['which was immediately carried out,' added Richard to this account] that five hundred pounds should be given by me to his brother Henry at that time on his voyage round the Cape to join him in India. Signed Rich. B. Machell'.

I have seen the 1861 Will in the British Library, but why the last-minute bequest to Henry, I wonder. And Camp Garurawa eh? This gives me another jolt because last year the Neaves in Beverley sent me an extract from a Gazetteer mentioning the town of Gadawara (mis-spelt by Richard) with a covering note saying: 'It seems that a branch line of the Great Indian Peninsular Railway was built from Gadawara to nearby coal mines in 1862, the year of Thomas's death – could he have been involved in this?' How right they were. Have the Neaves too come under his spell? Thomas was not only involved in the railway, but now I find he actually died in the town the Neaves alerted me to. And he didn't die in an accident but from a severe illness, just as I described to Rashna. (On the journey back from Narsingpur to Jabalpur last year I had felt almost sick when I suddenly remembered that because of the delays and excitement in the cemetery I had failed to seek out the old hospital and look for the room where Thomas died. Now I find he died in Gadawara in any case.)

So here, literally as well as metaphorically fallen into my lap, is a summary of Thomas's last six years – and nothing deviates from what I have already written. Staring in amazement once again at Thomas's page, trying to grasp what I am seeing, I now notice a small extra sheet of paper glued into the page. What can this be? I flip it over. Goodness – it's a drawing of Thomas's grave. Someone, perhaps Major Moxon, must have sent it to the family, or maybe Richard selected the design. I am transported back to Nursinghpur's cemetery. I am sitting arm in arm with Finella on the edge of Thomas's plinth. There's a hole on top where something is missing. 'I wonder what kind of monument was originally on the grave,' I had mused to Finella. 'Well, that's something you'll never know,' she had replied, 'just be content that we've found the grave.' And indeed I was. But now, literally to crown it all, I find a sketch of the entire grave with a large, simple Celtic cross on top. Thomas would like that.

'I'm so sorry,' I apologise to David and Simon. I am trying not to cry.

The last brief entry in the weighty book is Roger's. It tells us that on July 25th 1908 he was born in St James's Palace, and among the sponsors were the Earl of Cromer and his Uncle, Count Gleichen. A *Times* cutting describes Roger's October baptism with Jordan water in the Palace chapel where his parents married, and a sepia photograph shows him in christening gown in the arms of Mrs Couch (a nanny? the nanny?) with a fat dog at her feet. (Trust there to be a dog in the final entry.) I'm tempted to seize a pen right now and fill in Roger's page. After this come many blank pages. I wonder whether the story of *émigré* Reginald's American descendants will ever be added to the book? Or will it – indeed should it – forever end when the family's Cumbrian roots were yanked out of the soil of Crackenthorpe Hall because of the battles of World War I?

'One last puzzle remains,' I tell David. 'Thomas was born with an unspecified 'birth defect' as he calls it. I've deduced it was probably a foot deformity, but have found nothing to confirm this.'

'How very odd you should say that,' replies David, 'because Roger also had a birth defect that caused permanent problems with his feet. All his life he wore special shoes and walked with an awkward kind of shuffle.'

Same day, later. It is now nightfall, and I'm standing on a lonely Scottish hilltop in the gloaming, with the moon right before my eyes, yet I cannot make it out. What is unfolding on this May evening at the end of perhaps the most extraordinary day of my life is like a metaphor; Thomas's life and my search to uncover it seem to be mirrored in this rare total lunar eclipse that is showing me that Thomas's life did not vanish with his death, it was just eclipsed for a while by time and history, patiently waiting to come into view again. It is now that point at dusk when time seems suspended, though everything in nature is very very gently on the move. Dew is chilling the air, slowly settling on grass and on my skin, mist is stealing up the valley, and the sheep stand absolutely still, scarcely seeming to breathe, their coats glowing whiter as dark descends. Behind me in the western sky Venus, the planet of Love, outshines all the other stars, as she should.

Now the sky is turning a little darker, and suddenly I can make out the ghost of the hidden moon. It is exactly where I have been staring all along, but it was obscured for a time and I couldn't see it. Now it acquires an ethereal deep red glow. Slowly, slowly the shadow of the sun is peeling across its surface, starting at the bottom. The moon is growing brighter and brighter before my eyes. Now the very last slice of shadow lifts off its shoulder and the whole is revealed.

Two full moons later we were welcomed back to Bryan's Ground by David and Simon, who made us feel part of their extended family, which, in a peculiarly extended way, perhaps we are. In the evening we dined off the worn green and gilt Crackenthorpe plates and I felt at home.

Gillon's response to my ecstatic email after our first visit to Bryan's Ground was: 'Having a pre-lunch dry martini in heaven, where he surely is, Roger will be very happy…' Roger would have time for many more heavenly martinis during this second delve into his family's papers.

We spent several days immersed in Machelliana. In the sitting room Rose, the ancient bony cat, daily feigned death on an old velvet cushion, and the irregular buzz of lazy bluebottles on windowsills vied with the metronome ticking of the Crackenthorpe grandfather clock in the hall.

I found most of the family information conveniently gathered into three leather-bound books. And guess who wrote all of them? Thomas of course.

It was bachelor Thomas, when in England convalescing from his various illnesses, who had time to work on the new family history. (His namesake 'Thomas the Antiquary' having compiled the previous one two centuries before). He managed to write and illustrate all three large volumes, the last updated after his death by Richard and his successors until that final entry on Roger. It had taken me four years to piece together Tom's family history, and now I found it written down in one place, and by Thomas himself. I could almost hear him laughing at – or with – me.

I particularly enjoyed letters referring to Tom's brother, Harry (it's amusing to find all these references to Tom, Dick and Harry, the nicknames Thomas, Richard and Henry used). From hints and snippets it sounds as if Harry's life story bears some resemblence to that of my own elder brother, Graham.

I've gathered that Harry, like Graham, rejected his respectable middle-class British origins in favour of a restless search for adventure overseas that often went wrong. Both men lived mainly in tropical rain forests, surviving on their wits (when not bailed out by family) and getting into scrapes with women and the law, sometimes due to being too kind-hearted or gullible. I think I now understand why Thomas left his money to his feckless brother, but wish I knew more about this Black Sheep whose outrageous behaviour must have embarrassed his respectable Victorian family, not least Richard, who, as the eldest, seems to have borne the brunt.

As for the childhood haunts, as well as old photographs I found two touching sketches of Etton, annotated by Richard, dated 1843, two years after Eliza's death. One shows the family 'vault' with its large horizontal tombstone, at that time surrounded by a low iron railing. This picture solved the mystery of the lack of graves for Rosamund, Kathleen Anne and Hugh Devon, because a note in Richard's hand tells us they all lie together in the vault, though it's strange they aren't named on the tombstone. The other sketch shows the widowed rector with four of his younger children being greeted by a maid at the rectory's original front door.

Not only is there all the Machell stuff plus Roger's records, but how about the Gleichen side? Among their mass of papers I was intrigued to find a list of presents given to Percy and Valda for their royal wedding, not least because I'm pretty sure I actually own one of them, unlikely as this seems. This is a shawl given to Valda by none other that King Edward VII himself.

One day I had a surprise call from Fiona Thwaytes in Appleby. She thought I would be interested to know about a forthcoming local auction that was going to include items from Crackenthorpe Hall. The descendants of Valda's 'adoptive' daughter Molly were putting up for sale such items as the doll's tea set that Queen Victoria had given Valda as a child, and that Valda had passed on to Molly as she had no daughters or grandchildren of her own. Fiona thought I might be interested in a Reginald Willoughby painting of a view of Crackenthorpe estate across the Eden River. I did make an online bid for this but it sold for a large sum way out of my price range. However, I also bid, on impulse, for a Paisley shawl, because I thought it might have been an Indian gift from Thomas to his sister. However, when the shawl arrived by post it wasn't what I expected. I had instead acquired an exceptionally luxurious pure silk European Paisley shawl in mint condition. When I showed it to two experts they both dated it to the time of Valda and Percy's wedding and it matches the description on the wedding list. This is surely another unused gift of Valda's passed on to Molly and stashed away in a drawer for a hundred years until it found its way to me.

In the quiet of the dining room, sitting on its low window seat, I tackled Gleichen correspondence, piling it into little towers around my feet. Each time I picked up a small envelope and eased out a letter I felt intrusive and moved. Unfolding the thick paper and reading the inked words on its page, one enters the correspondents' lives as voyeur and time-traveller, joining their present while knowing their future; luckily they don't.

I had already pictured the goings-on at Crackenthorpe in its Edwardian heyday but it was good to find confirmation in the light-hearted pre-war correspondence between Valda and her unmarried artist sisters, notable sculptress Feodora and painter Helena, who later became *châtelaine* of haunted Hellens Manor in Hertfordshire. They clearly enjoyed their sister's unusual marriage, leading to visits to the atmospheric estate they fondly called 'Crak', and to the wondrous gift of a nephew. A watercolour by Feodora shows three year old Roger sitting beside his mother on a piano stool, feet dangling far off the floor. Today the three sisters are reunited in name on a memorial plaque in Golders Green crematorium.

Their brother, Major-General Lord Edward Gleichen, distinguished soldier and author, wrote many letters from the trenches to Valda after Percy was killed. What was it like to be a grieving young war widow? Some sensitive private correspondence made me witness to Valda's enduring devotion to Percy. The correspondence began in July 1916 with her approach to Sir Fabian Ware, founder of the Imperial War Graves Commission, on a 'delicate matter', which was a plea for an exception to be made to the rules so her ashes could be added to Percy's remains in Warloy Ballion when her time came.

In 1927, she returned to the subject when drawing up her will.

St James's Palace, 2nd April 1927.

Dear Sir Fabian Ware,
I hope you will forgive me for writing to you again on a matter that I consulted you about in July 1916… after my husband Lieut.Colonel P.W. Machell C.M.S., D.C.O… was killed on the Somme… You very kindly answered that you thought 'the matter might be taken up privately after the war.

Valda went on to say that she believed her wish to be unique and offered her written undertaking to keep the matter top secret. After considering the request for several months, Sir Fabian finally granted her wish:

'If I am alive at the time and in my present position I shall offer no objection officially to your ashes being laid in your husband's grave… and I think you may safely leave it to any successor of mine to regard the request with the same sympathy.'

Valda's reply assured him that only her brother and son knew about the plan.

Time and another World War didn't lessen Valda's devotion. In a 1954 letter to Sir Fabian, she sought reassurance that her husband's grave had survived the war and that her 'heavy bronze wreath' hadn't been stolen, and informed him of her brother's death and her son Roger's promise to carry out her wishes. Sir Fabian reassured her on all counts, but died two years before Valda. Under the terms of their agreement there was no need to involve the Commission officially again so it remains a mystery whether Roger honoured his mother's wishes. I like to believe that he did.

Looking through all this stuff at Bryan's Ground made me understand why Roger packed it away and got on with his life among the London literati. His unhappy childhood memories of Crackenthrope Hall were one part of his story, but he was also crushed in the pincer of two family lines with exceptional histories that ended with him. To be sole guardian of so much history from both ancestral lines must have been overwhelming.

Bryan's Ground, 1st July 2004, last day of my search for Thomas. Slipping early out of the house, notebook in hand, I head for a quiet corner of the garden, but the hounds have other ideas and insist I take them to the river. I have just learnt that it's known locally as one of the five Rivers of Paradise. First we cross 'Little Eden' stream, named by David and Simon after Crackenthorpe's Eden River. I'm reminded of my final dawn walk at Crackenthorpe, but this time three live hounds gambol around me in the long wet grasses, and I'm heading for a spot along the Lugg riverbank where Simon says otters can be spotted. I don't glimpse one, so I turn back towards the house, recalling that unforgettable vision of the heron silently rising off the Eden's riverbed last autumn. I lift my eyes from the grass to the river and incredibly (or not) memory transmutes into reality, as a heron suddenly appears from a bend in the river and glides away upstream. It seems as if Crackenthorpe's ghosts have followed me to Bryan's Ground.

In a flash I realise that today surely marks the completion of my tale of searches within searches. Roly and Diva lollop back into the house but faithful little Toby, like Thomas's Blucher, follows me along the terrace in front of the house, through an opening in the tall hedge, and into the 'sulking house' in Crackenthorpe garden, an appropriate place to complete my tale, to the sounds of a distant orchestra of wind in tall trees, insistent birds and soft moans of sheep by the river. It is strange how I chose to celebrate my fiftieth birthday by staying in Crackenthorpe Hall, while Simon marked David's by constructing this mock-Gothic temple in a gloomy part of the garden named after their image of the vanished 'burnt' Crackenthorpe, a house that for them had acquired mythical status, like Mandalay or Wuthering Heights. Simon could have no idea a colonnaded stone summerhouse exists at Crackenthorpe, yet his temple is like a tall version of it. Its musty interior, with shredded velvet drapes and cushions faded and coated in dust and leaf debris, is certainly brooding.

Everything has miraculously come together with the families regrouped here at Bryan's Ground, including, in a different way, myself and Thomas, five years after our story began.

Glencairn wanders into Crackenthorpe garden just as I am completing this entry on the temple steps. 'This time I really have written the very last chapter,' I announce. He is so delighted (and relieved?) that he immortalises the great moment with a photograph. As if on cue, David appears along the mown path bearing a tray of refreshments, like an Edwardian waiter, and I remember I haven't had breakfast. We join Simon and the dogs on the terrace, where, smelling fresh coffee and catmint, I read aloud extracts from my chapter that mentions Roger and Valda, to check the accuracy of my hunches then. I realise this is the moment to tell David and Simon about my episode with Rashna, including, though it is hard to voice, my sense of Thomas's death. Glencairn has heard the tale many times, but as I relate the deathbed scene his eyes once again fill with tears. Silence follows, softened by the garden's low hum. Then, as we are marvelling at the string of coincidences that have led us to Bryan's Ground with its chest of Machell papers, David glances at the book Glencairn is holding and his eyes widen. It's a life of Glencairn's ancestor Robert Louis (Balfour) Stevenson. Its title? *Dead Man's Chest.*

Later the same day, back home. We arrive around midnight in pouring rain and I open the boot of the car to remove my bag. Lying on top is something extra. I find that Simon, in his thoughtful way, has secretly placed there for me a touching memento. It's one of the flags he made years ago out of an old biscuit tin, to adorn his herb garden. On them he painted, against a woad blue background, the three Machell greyhounds.

Uppincott Barton, 3rd October 2005. Once again I thought I had completed a chapter but have unearthed new information. This story doesn't want to end.

We had no plans to revisit Bryan's Ground this year but an invitation to David's sixtieth birthday party was irresistible. I didn't expect to see any Machell papers during a social weekend but neither did I expect to find the old tin chest full of letters still in the sitting room, unmoved since dug out for our visit many moons ago. Of course I homed straight to it. David came into the room and caught me in the act. He suggested I might like another peek when the guests had gone, and lugged it upstairs to Simon's studio where I could later delve undisturbed.

I wasn't alone, though, because the old cat Rose, looking younger at seventeen than she had the year before, kept vigil once again. This time I found her curled up right among the Machell papers, and she stayed all morning, which amazed Simon because Rose had only ever ventured into his studio once in twelve years. Another little bit of Machell magic perhaps.

I was still puzzled by that deathbed legacy of Thomas's, leaving most of his money to his wayward brother Harry. Why the last minute change of heart? And since describing Tom's death to Rashna I was hoping to find confirmation that he had died in the way I/he had so vividly described.

Surrounded by all the folders I thought I had already been through I wasn't sure where to start re-examining them, but for some reason I was drawn to the least promising package, a tattered envelope fashioned from a Victorian newspaper and labelled 'Gee-Sterne'. I had dismissed it last time after a quick look revealed dull papers relating to Eliza's godmother's affairs, but now I noticed an unmarked envelope buried within the other papers. I pulled this envelope out and found it stuffed with letters in tiny envelopes. The first I extracted was a palimpsest of European and Indian postmarks, official stamps, instructions in Richard's hand and many re-directions. Richard was clearly anxious that this letter should catch up with the addressee. It seems almost miraculous that such minute and near-illegible envelopes ever did reach their destinations.

So what important news did this little letter contain, and why the urgency? Sitting on the floor next to Rose I unfolded a single sheet of thin paper and found I had zoomed straight in on Thomas's death. I got quite a frisson, and it wasn't caused just by the freezing temperature in Simon's studio.

Barrow on Humber, England, Jan. 26th 1863

My Dear Harry,

I send this on the chance of its finding you at Calcutta – I feel very anxious to know what you will do and advise you to go on to Allahabad and consult with Launce; - Major Moxon of Jubbulpore has sent me the sad tidings of poor Tom's death, which took place on Sunday evening December 14th 1862 at Camp Garurwara, where he had come in very ill the day before from Sogapore. He was buried on Dec. 16th at Nursingpore and the doctor reported the cause to be inflammation of the bowels and of the Peritoneum.

I have received from Major Moxon a copy of Tom's will in which he leaves everything to me, and I have written to Major Moxon to ask him to act as Tom's executor, and to preserve any of his things which would be interesting as memorials to be distributed among his family. I am told that the will must be sent to the Administrator General at Calcutta, and that nothing can be done about his property for a year. I should like you to have anything you wish for as a remembrance of dear old Tom.

So Thomas had, after all, died from fever in a hospital bed as I had pictured it. And I was back with Tom, Dick and Harry again. All the place names and forwarding directions on the envelope show that Richard was trying to intercept Harry en route from England to India, taking the sea route to India (unlike Thomas) and travelling on overland to Jabalpur. It's clear that the letter missed Harry in Calcutta. How did he feel when he arrived in Jabalpur after so many weeks on the move and found that Thomas had just died? And why was Harry making that long trip just then to visit his brother in central India?

I pulled out the rest of the letters and in their to-ing and fro-ing Harry's story came alive.

I found that Harry spent many years in South America on the run from the British law. Due to unspecified 'misdemeanours', he had been put under guard aboard the navy ship he was serving on in the River Plate but had jumped overboard, disappeared into the bush, and become a 'brigand chief'. He had cut all ties with his homeland. Long-suffering Richard clearly tried every avenue to track him down, re-doubling his efforts after Father died in April 1860. Not only did Richard correspond with officials in Montevideo, but he even placed an advertisement in the *Times* appealing for contact: 'Henry, your father is dead...' etc. It was all to no avail.

However, a year later Harry had a dream that prompted him to renew contact at last. He sent a letter to Father, who was long since dead. In it he tells Father that he appeared to him when he was asleep and when he awoke he was full of remorse at how much he had upset Father and let him down. He begs for Father's forgiveness. It was too late for that of course, but thanks to this letter Harry was at last tracked down and Richard arranged for him to be given an official pardon so he could return to England to collect Father's inheritance. Most of it he squandered at once on fine clothes.

With Harry back in England and unemployed, the family had to keep him out of mischief. So they did the time-honoured thing and packed him off to India. Now I know that Thomas was in England in 1862 I realise the brothers would have been reunited for the first time in years, and I presume Thomas suggested that Harry might come and stay with him in India and have a fresh start. The letters reveal that Harry anticipated making his fortune by ranching sheep in central India, but that Thomas was sceptical, no doubt expecting this to go the way of all the other madcap schemes his brother had tried.

As I'd learnt from the family book, Thomas travelled to India overland that last time. I find he was followed in October by Harry, taking the sea route and fleeing from another scandal, having just seduced a young woman he refers to as 'L'. Clearly Richard received news (by the 'overland steamer'

Thomas mentions in the Journals?) of Thomas's death while Harry was still en route, hence his letter attempting to intercept him before he headed for Japalpur.

Now I understood Thomas's deathbed change of heart, which overrode the terms of his Will. Knowing he wouldn't be able to help Harry get back on his feet, he was trying to soften the blow by bequeathing him the residue of his estate (£500). One hopes Harry at least appreciated Tom's gesture but it didn't serve its purpose. True to form, Harry lost no time in begging Richard to send out Tom's money as soon as possible, but he soon squandered the bequest and, unemployed as usual, had to resort to sponging off Lance in northern India for a while. Harry then returned to Britain, where, to Richard's chagrin, the scandal with Laura (L) resurfaced. In a letter written at the end of 1863 Richard, who appears to have been an unwilling go-between between Harry and Laura, writes to Harry, 'I am sorry you are in a rage with me as I have always been a good friend to you'. The following year Harry fled the country in disgrace again, both craving and rejecting Richard's affection in a letter. He says he is off to Montevideo with his hounds and rifles to become a trapper on the wild and lawless frontier with Argentina.

So how did this tale end? Much as it began, and we shall never know whether Thomas, had he lived longer, would have been able to help his brother get on track. Harry returned to his old swashbuckling ways in South America, writing very occasionally to Richard, either to demand money or to goad him, or both. He tells Richard he looks a complete ruffian and is among 'bandits and brigands'. One exceptionally defiant letter describes all the 'fighting and throat-cutting etc going on here and says that he has himself been laid up 'with a bullet under my left jaw'. 'You ought to take a turn out here one day, it would do you good,' he writes provocatively. There is another gap of several years before Harry resurfaces again. He hasn't changed, declaring he still prefers 'dark to light'. It says something for Richard that he continued to keep faith with Harry and meticulously dated and preserved all these letters (so why isn't there a stash from Thomas?).

After reading all this I wasn't surprised to learn that Harry died a violent death, his wayward life having ended in 1868 when he was fatally stabbed 'by a native' in a drunken brawl. One can't help feeling Richard must have heaved a sigh of despairing relief when this news reached him in York.

Poor old Richard had done his best to help the most troubled of his siblings, but Harry wasn't the only one to shame the family. Sister Matilda caused a scandal of her own by cheating on her Officer husband and fleeing to Paris with her lover, and even brilliant Lance fell from grace. An icy letter of his to Richard, written on the eve of his return to England in 1864, announces that Susey has left him. The tone of the letter implies that Susey has also had an affair. His letter ends: 'I will never darken your doors again for which I think you ought to be very much obliged… I do not dislike you because I think you are a bad fellow… but you have foiled me twice and I never forgive.' Oh dear, I wonder what this is all about. Was Richard really a holier-than-thou, moralising busybody or was he a tolerant older brother? I cannot tell, but I do now have a better picture of Thomas within his wider family.

It is odd how later generations have made a stereotype of stuffy Victorian family life. The widely differing lives and vagaries of Thomas and his siblings are proof that they were just as various as the rest of us today.

Roger Victor Machell, born 23rd July 1908, son of Lt Col Percy
Wilfred Machell and Lady Victoria Alice Leopoldine Ada Laura Gleichen
(known as Valda). Roger was the last in the long line of the Machells of
Crackenthorpe in the UK.

28. Machells Reunited

Close both eyes in order to see with the other eye

(Rumi 1207-1273)

When I met Reg Machell in 2002 he was already too frail to travel overseas to Crackenthorpe. Nancy had therefore planned to mark the first anniversary of his death by reconnecting her American family with their ancient roots. However, various obstacles prevented this and I was surprised to receive an email from Nancy early in 2005 that declared: 'The Balfours are still at Crackenthorpe and we're determined to come over from the States this summer – when can you join us?' Between then and the summer two more Machell descendants were born.

In warm sunshine on 3rd July Glencairn and I were waiting anxiously on the road below Etton church, where we had arranged to meet the Machells. Nancy's son-in-law Tony, a Houston boy born and bred, had never been to the UK before, but was braving the narrow Yorkshire lanes in a hired car. It appeared with minutes to spare, and out clambered four generations of Machells: spry great-grandmother Nancy, her daughter Peggy, Tony, Troy their teenage son, Becky, Peggy's daughter by her first husband, and in her arms her four-month old Maggie. (At the last minute the present head of the Crackenthorpe Machells, and his son, sole male of his generation to carry the family name, had to pull out of the trip.)

Like a clucking chicken I ushered the brood up the church path, trying to calculate when last a Machell had trodden that way. On cue the vicar, a Victorian figure in his outsize frizzy grey beard, stepped from the porch to greet them. As the service began I looked around and realised the Machells formed half the congregation. (A bemused Tony told me later that the average attendance at his church in Houston was over a thousand.)

The Revd Thorpe aimed his sermon at the Machell pew. 'Your ancestor, Robert Machell, was an ordinary parish priest,' he began. I hoped the family were not taking offence. 'Ordinary,' he emphasised, to my increased discomfort. 'But,' he continued, 'the church only survives thanks to such humble curates who work among the people, not because of the hierarchy of archbishops, bishops and so on. They could all disappear tomorrow and it would make no difference.' The theme was clearly heartfelt as he empathised with Robert Machell and his other predecessors. 'Remember,' he concluded, 'that the church depends not on the High-ups but on the Low-downs.'

I thought of Low-down Robert, his son Thomas (another Low-down) sometimes at his side, tramping in all weathers between his two parishes of Etton and Leckonfield. Even in those days Thomas says the latter's bell summoned 'a very small and sleepy congregation', in contrast to the 'high state of fidget' of Hindus preparing for the Durga Puja.

I showed the Machells their family memorials in the church before leading them outside to the gravestones. Eliza's was already clear but Peggy and I knelt side by side in the grass to clean up the little grave of Guy, brother to Peggy's great-grandfather Reginald Willoughby who had crossed the seas to live in America. Five years had passed since I had compulsively uncovered Eliza's tombstone. Crossing the road to the old rectory we found it once again lacking a maternal presence, because Lynn Elvidge had left it soon after our last visit. Jonathan Elvidge told me he checked for boxes in the attic when the house was re-roofed but found nothing. 'Don't worry,' I reassured him, 'it was the wrong attic.'

After lunch we skipped around Beverley in sunshine, again guided by the Neaves. The great churches, the Georgian brick houses, the wide streets, all seemed warm and familiar.

It made a change exploring Etton and Beverley with living Machells. And next stop was the family seat itself.

En route, while the Machells explored York, Glencairn and I spent a night nearby with the Denyers, joined by Bruce Wannell. This also felt like a circle closing since we had been joined by them for that visit to Etton and Beverley four years earlier, when Thomas first took me over.

I should have got used to being high-jacked during each new Thomas escapade, but I was caught by surprise once again. Glencairn spotted a handful of issues of the now defunct *Blackwood's Magazine* beside our bed at the Denyers. Picking up the top copy he found to his amazement that the very first article was 'The Lyon's Tale', written by his own grandfather, Sir James Balfour-Paul. Delighted by this coincidence, since hundreds of Blackwood's volumes were published between 1817 and 1980, he showed it next morning to Isa, who told us she had just rescued a few issues from a large pile her father had been burning on a bonfire. After breakfast I quickly scanned the contents lists on the other Blackwood's covers just in case one contained an article I was seeking on the Opium Wars. On the third issue I picked up, dated October 1975, what did I find listed but 'Coals from Newcastle' by none other than – THOMAS MACHELL! I could hardly believe this; it was my original title for my chapter on our joint trip to the Marquesas Islands. Though he had been dead for over a century when this article was published, it seemed as if Thomas was getting his own back by usurping my own writing. And since I thought I was the first person to draw on Thomas's Journals, the find was unnerving.

I took the incredible chance discovery of this Blackwood's article as a direct hint from Thomas to get on and complete our story.

On returning home I contacted the Centre of South-Asian Studies at Cambridge University, since a biographical note with Thomas's Blackwood's article says its editor was, in the 1970s, 'scouring eastern Scotland for forgotten fragments of Scots-Indian history on behalf of the Centre when he came across Thomas Machell's story of the South Seas in the possession of Iain Dunbar, who kindly allowed its publication.' Who was this presumptuous person claiming ownership of the Journals? It was annoying and puzzling since I had assumed that Roger owned them until their sale to the British Library. Making enquiries, I learnt that the editor of Tom's Blackwoods' article, a Scot called Malcolm Stuart, had since died, but that his notes at Cambridge described a visit to Iain Dunbar, bookseller in Fife and apparently then owner of Thomas's Journals. Stuart's notes mention four volumes, ending in 1852, so how did Mr Dunbar get hold of them and how did they become separated from Volume Five (1852-56), yet somehow get reunited in the British Library less than ten years later? And did this Mr Dunbar by any chance have any other writings of Thomas's in his possession?

I soon found out that Mr Dunbar had long since died, and I even tracked down the dealer who bought up his collection of books on India. He said there had been no manuscript papers among them, so that particular sidetrack ended in a cul-de-sac, to my chagrin. However, I marvelled how the Journals (four anyway) nearly ended up in Cambridge, where I would never have heard of them.

A year later things turned even more bizarre when another extraordinary coincidence occurred.

This came about thanks to the publication of Glencairn's memoirs, *Bagpipes in Babylon*. They brought several relatives out of the family woodwork, among them Glencairn's long-lost first cousin, nicknamed Snookie, with whom he had had no contact for over half a century. However, Snookie's daughter, Jane Burnett wrote to Glencairn after seeing an article about *Bagpipes* in an Edinburgh newspaper. They invited us to stay.

Snookie had just celebrated her 100th birthday but her mind was sharp. She reminisced about the years she had spent in Thomas territory in Bengal, both before and after Partition, because her husband (whose name I hadn't taken in) had been a prominent official there. Just before bedtime on the eve of our departure two days later, a chance remark startled me; Jane mentioned that her father had travelled around Scotland in the 1970s collecting information for the future Centre of South-Asian Studies at Cambridge University. I almost choked on a piece of fudge when I heard this. 'Goodness, was your father Malcolm Stuart?' I asked Jane. 'The very same,' came her reply. So the husband of Glencairn's first cousin was the mystery man who had found Thomas's Journals and liked them so much he had published a section of them before me.

'My father left boxes of papers, one of which I have here,' volunteered Jane. Glencairn groaned 'not again'. I read through them into the wee hours and next morning rummaged through more piles of papers under Snookie's late husband's desk. I found his completed book manuscript called *The White Nawabs*, along with a file of publishers' and agents' rejection letters, including one from Roger Machell of Hamish Hamilton Ltd. Stuart's subject matter was unfashionable then, coming too soon after Indian Independence and the end of the British Empire. The young William Dalrymple's timing was luckier. I even came across his letter thanking Stuart for sharing his *White Nawabs* manuscript and extensive research notes (many culled from private collections in ancestral houses) on 18th-century Scottish *nabobs* in India. Thomas's Journals were outside Stuart's main research remit, but having chanced on the four volumes with Dunbar he had been so captivated that he had borrowed them to study, and published Tom's Marquesas chapter with Blackwood's. Stuart's papers reveal a humane official concerned about how the British behaved in India. He outlined ideas for a sequel to his

White Nawabs, to be titled *Step-children of the Raj,* one of its themes being that at least some Victorians in India had moral scruples. A chapter in this proposed book was to be about Thomas. After his disappointing failure to find a publisher, Stuart deposited most of his papers with the National Library of Scotland.

So I found myself connected by Thomas as well as by marriage to this cousin-in-law who had also been drawn to Thomas's life story and had even had his Journals in his possession for a while. If he had bought them from Dunbar they would have been the property of my own family! (Snookie moved to a nursing home very soon after our visit and died weeks later. Yet again, Thomas-timing had worked in its mysterious way.)

We rendezvoused at Crackenthorpe with the Machells on 4th July, three years ago to the day since I had held my birthday party there. This time I was toasting US Independence Day (and the anniversary of the day Glencairn proposed to me) with my adoptive American family.

Becky daringly chose to sleep in the haunted King's bedroom. 'Whenever my mother sleeps in that room she lodges a chair against the cupboard concealing Peg the ghost's preferred entry point through the blocked window,' said David Balfour with a twinkle. I copied this gesture for Becky as a precaution.

We exchanged stories by the fireside. I told the Machells about the coincidence concerning Thomas's article in *Blackwood's,* and Nancy recounted the bizarre story of her lonely childhood with an adoptive mother who later turned out to be her biological mother, and a stepfather, her real father having disappeared from her life before she was three. 'After an awful childhood a wonderful thing happened to me' she said, and related how, at seventeen, she escaped into the arms of gentle Reg. It was only when she needed a passport years later that her aunt (her mother, who had refused to give her her birth certificate, having died by then) revealed her birth surname. But it was this trip to Britain, with all the talk of Machell family reconnection, that had inspired Nancy to trace her own roots and find out what happened to the father she always longed to know. Helped by her unusual surname, as I was in my Machell searches, she eventually discovered she had a living half brother and sister. They had longed to trace Nancy when they learnt of her existence after their parents' died, but had nothing to go on, knowing neither her adopted nor married surname. When the call came from Nancy they said: 'You took your time to find us – seventy-five years!'

All this happened when Nancy was preparing for the present trip. She had a premonition that something ominous might happen in UK and so she travelled to California to be reunited with her long-lost family just two weeks before leaving USA. Nancy, an only child who for years believed she was adopted, said: 'It's fabulous to feel whole at last.'

Now I understood Nancy's passion for family roots and her enthusiastic support for my own quest.

On 7th July, having spent three nights at Crackenthorpe and taken the Machells to the family haunts around Appleby, Glencairn and I were poised to drive home, leaving the family for a last night in the ancestral seat before they set off to sightsee in London en route back to USA.

It was not to be. After breakfast, with our car packed, I decided before we left to try once more to telephone David and Simon to confirm that the Machells didn't have time to visit Bryan's Ground as they had hoped. I expected the usual answerphone, but this time Simon answered in person. The first thing he said was: 'Have you heard the news?' 'No,' I replied, 'we're about to leave and we haven't put the radio or television on since we arrived here.' 'Well, put it on now,' urged Simon, 'London's under attack from terrorists as we speak.' I rushed into the Hall to convey this news and we switched on the television. On the screen were scenes of mayhem. 'Bombs are detonating on underground trains and a bus has just been blown up,' came repeated announcements. Unfolding before us was the inevitable terrorist attack on London that everyone had been dreading since Bush and Blair decided to wage their provocative war on Iraq. We all thought it was another September 11th. 'Don't leave us!' pleaded Nancy, clutching my arm. And clearly we couldn't possibly abandon our American friends, not least since the carnage appeared to be centred on King's Cross, the station they were booked to travel to.

I did the British thing and made a pot of tea. As the morning passed it became clear that although London had just suffered its first attack by suicide bombers, with, as it turned out later, over fifty killed and hundreds injured, the carnage wasn't on the scale of New York in 2001. It was, nevertheless, the biggest disaster in the city since World War II. Transport was in chaos, not least because several underground trains were blown up, including one directly beneath King's Cross station. Maybe this explained Nancy's premonition about the trip.

We spent several hours helping the Machells make new arrangements.

Bizarrely, it was due to the London tragedy that they were forced to change their plans and now had time to connect with more of their family heritage at Bryan's Ground.

I heard later that the visit to Bryan's Ground was a great success. David and Simon displayed all the 'Machelliana' inherited from Roger and presented a delighted Nancy with a 'family pedigree' she planned to frame alongside the chunk of old Crackenthorpe oak floorboard the Balfours had already given her (trodden on by centuries of Machells and maybe King Henry VI, since it came from just outside his bedroom.) David remarked happily: 'Becky let me carry baby Maggie round the garden – 21 years since I had a Machell in my arms!'

As for me, I took advantage of the extra morning at Crackenthorpe to get up early for a last walk before sitting at a wooden table in the King's neglected garden to write another final book passage that turned out not to be:

'*8th July 2005*. Last morning at Crackenthorpe. Everything is quilted with tiny cobwebs. I have just walked down to the river, trying to reconcile in my mind the violence of yesterday's bombings and with this perfect summer dawn.

When I entered the woods they seemed almost benevolent. Cooing doves had temporarily replaced the raucous crows and narrow shafts of sunlight were piercing the gloom. I looked back and saw, framed by foliage at the entrance to the wood, a triangular shadow cast by the house across the lawn. Beside it, in a faint mist, was a path of my own footprints, green in the silvery dew. The sun will soon melt them away, but their invisible imprints will remain forever with countless others.

Suspended wholly in this present moment, I realise that my journeys into the past with Thomas are finally over, but that the wider trail into the future will never end.'

29. Pirates of the Arabian Seas

Why should we grieve that we've been sleeping?
It doesn't matter how long we've been unconscious.
We're groggy, but let the guilt go.
Feel the motions of tenderness
Around you, the buoyancy.

(*Buoyancy*, Rumi)

'Thomas Machell sounds more like a friend,' said my fellow passenger this morning, as we leant over the ship's bow, delighting in a family of dolphins leaping for joy. Christine Fehr joined the ship yesterday and we were exchanging reasons for choosing the slow route to India. I had just outlined my search for Thomas.

'I suppose he is, in a way,' I replied. I haven't thought of him quite like that before, but we've certainly shared many good and bad times together. I didn't attempt to elaborate on the kind of friend he has become.

A week earlier, just after New Year's Day 2010, I had left Southampton in searing cold, the only passenger on *CMA-CGM's Coral*, a huge new freighter transporting containers between Europe and Asia.

There were several reasons for choosing this voyage. Once again I'm being drawn back to Kolkata. Travelling by sea forces me to slow down.

Glencairn's death on 2nd July 2008 set me off on a new and painful inner journey. 'A mountain keeps an echo deep inside itself, that's how I hold your voice wrote the Sufi poet Rumi. For the first six months I couldn't penetrate grief's barrier. The only book that helped, called *Walking backwards into your future* (Kath Beattie), described the feeling of days marching forward while you face backwards with arms outstretched to the dead person, the death itself, and times before that. You don't even want a future. The only way forward was to keep constantly busy.

When Big Ben chimed in the New Year, 2009, I was in a friend's kitchen in Sussex. While celebratory fireworks were exploding over Lewes castle, the radio was broadcasting news of bombings and pointless deaths in Gaza. It put my personal plight in perspective, highlighted my over-comfortable surroundings, and gave me the resolve to make more effort not to increase the planet's negative stock. In any case, the miserable, self-centred widow I had turned into was boring myself, as well as those around me. I had learnt the value of family and true friends, but they too have lives to lead, problems to solve, futures to walk into.

It was time, therefore, to steer the juggernaut around, look for new work and try to reconnect with Thomas, whom I had neglected for far too long.

So on January 20th I made myself return to his Journals, picking at random the place where he talks of the school he has recently created in Bengal, based on the Lancastrian system. This launched his dream – soon to be shattered by his forced departure with cholera – of using education to help poor children have a better life. My heart wasn't in the writing and I took a break from my university office. On my return I decided to dash home to hear the inaugural speech of America's new President, Barack Hussein Obama, live on television. A last email check revealed an unfamiliar one from an Andy Russ, 'artistic coordinator' of the 'Silk Road Project', an organisation I hadn't heard of. The subject of the message was 'Indigo as an educational model'.

It was a long email that began: 'I am writing to ask about your possible interest and involvement in a new education initiative based around the story of indigo'. I skip-read the rest. Andy set out the background to the Silk Road Project – an educational organization founded in 1998 by cellist Yo-Yo Ma, which 'takes inspiration from the historic Silk Road trading route as a modern metaphor for multicultural and interdisciplinary exchange' – then described the indigo initiative. It seemed that Ma, seeking to inspire 'passionate learning' in children in 'under-served' schools in New York City, had decided that 'the incredible story of indigo' was the perfect spark – 'a gateway to connect the personal experiences of our everyday lives (for example our own ubiquitous blue jeans) with the history, geography and culture of the whole planet.'

The email ended: 'It goes without saying that your book has been a great inspiration for Yo-Yo and the Project, and so we were eager to get in touch with you... perhaps we can even entice you to join Yo-Yo, members of the Silk Road Project and a number of invited artists and educators at a brainstorming session in Cambridge, Massachusetts this February.'

Astonished by this email, I sped home, coinciding with Hamish's arrival from London. I told him about the email while switching on the television, and at that very moment we found the cameras zoomed in on none other than Yo Yo Ma, playing his cello in a trio just before the presidential speech.

I looked up the Lancastrian system that Thomas chose for his school, only to find that it was the basis for New York City's own education system. Joseph Lancaster, born in 1778, was a British Quaker and radical thinker who championed free education for the poor. Beginning in London, he developed a system of teaching large numbers of pupils by using, among other things, peer tutoring to keep costs down. In the first decades of the 19th century his influential ideas spread to the eastern States of USA, beginning in Providence, the base, incidentally, of the Silk Road Project. Soon New York was establishing its first schools, based on Lancaster's principles, forerunners of today's 'normal schools' in the USA.

In 1838, when Thomas was 18, Lancaster died in New York. I flew there with a member of Ma's Silk Road Ensemble, British storyteller Ben Haggerty, whom I hadn't met before. On my 22nd birthday, when flying east to Jordan with Glencairn, I wouldn't have believed I would share my life with him for the next thirty-four years. But nor would I have believed that 35 years later I would be flying west and about to spend a birthday with Yo Yo Ma and Ben Haggerty and dine in the Harvard Club, instead of bathing in self-pity at home.

I learnt that an indigo story had started the whole thing off. Ben has a repertoire of over three hundred stories but, by chance several years earlier, he had recounted to Ma an African tale of how indigo came down to earth from the sky so that people could capture its colour in their clothes. This story had, apparently, given inspiration and focus to Ma's overall vision to connect the young, East and West, through cross-cultural education.

In 1848, Thomas, anticipating Ma's objectives, wrote the following on board an Arabian *dhow*:

> The effendi was very curious in enquiring how I being a Christian should be so desirous of acquainting myself with Oriental Literature. I explained to him that as a liberal minded man I took an interest in studying the books and opinions of all nations where learning is to be

found… Every man clings tenaciously to his own faith whilst we do so let us tolerate the opinions of others. From the wise of all faiths and nations knowledge can be obtained… the more we enlarge our minds by communing with the sages of the world the less likely we are to remain in darkness.'

Now, almost a year after becoming a partner in Silk Road Connect, which drew me west from Europe to be among new people and play my own small part in west-east connectedness, I'm ready to change pace and confront the inner loneliness, on a slow journey to the east. I also hope to cross paths with Thomas and with the young woman who made the long maritime voyage between India and Europe 40 years ago.

9th January 2010, approaching Le Havre, northern France.

Dear Thomas,

For the last five days I've been aboard a modern cargo ship called a freighter, wondering how to reconnect with you after a long gap. Indeed, wondering whether I ever would find the kind of connection we had before. And if I did, how I would incorporate this latest voyage into our story, which has already had several last chapters that turned out not to be the last.

I've spent five days in the North Sea, shivering, sleeping and absorbing my new temporary home, *CMA-CGM Coral*. Subconsciously I suppose I've also been waiting, like a hopeful jilted lover, for you to return to me. And today you have, though you've taken your time – in earthly terms I mean; less than a week is nothing to you, I know. Meanwhile I've had ideas about weaving this new journey into existing chapters.

First I'll tell you a bit more about the ship, as you will want to compare her with yours. Even by today's standards the *Coral* is large; at almost three hundred metres long and over thirty wide, 60,000 'dead weight' tonnage and carrying over four thousand containers, she would amaze you; but the new 'Chinamax' freighters will carry 400,000 containers. And to think that in your day shipbuilders from the Persian Gulf to the Red Sea calculated the size and tonnage of *dhows* on the number of baskets of dates to be transported.

Crew (me included) live in a tall narrow central block, overlooking containers fore and aft, stacked thirteen deep, water ballast in the lowest. This is how most cargo travels these days. It is quick, efficient, inhuman and polluting. So much energy is consumed in big ports that they have their own power stations, smoking day and night like volcanoes, or like our Captain, whose curved pipe never leaves his lips.

A ship like ours was crewed by forty not long ago, which won't sound much to you, but is pared to twenty and still shrinking to save costs. It's too bad we didn't stick to wind that's free, instead of filthy oil. By the way, the *CMA-CGM Coral* is Korean built, British registered, French run and Lebanese owned. That's how international shipping has become. Conditions are comfortable and pay good but the crew complain non-stop about life aboard their floating prison – four month stints for an Officer but nine for the Filipino ratings, who still manage to smile and sing. This is the last and only freighter taking passengers between England and India.

Taking this slow route, in sea's time-limbo, to India after a loss makes me empathise with how you felt on your first voyage to India after losing Father, your anchor (or 'world's secret centre', to quote Glencairn about love). Why did you risk India's dangers that last time when you were so unwell – is it because one takes more risks when caring less for one's own life? When I went for long walks those first months after Glencairn died, I remember feeling like a tiny boat adrift in an ocean with no shores, though I wasn't seeking metaphors. Is this how you felt too after Father died?

Alone. The word is life endured and known.
It is the stillness where our spirits walk
*And all but inmost faith is overthrow*n.
(from Siegfried Sassoon's *When I'm Alone*)

I've had more time than you to work out how to convert loneliness into aloneness.

Picture me alone in a cabin about the size as yours on the *Rajah* returning to Calcutta in 1849. Alas mine's not made of 'Spanish mahogany with gilt mouldings' like yours. You scratched away with your quill whereas I'm tapping at a computer keyboard. What I'm not doing is curing large seabirds to send home to a museum as you sketch yourself doing, writing that 'they stink infernally.' I bet they did.

13th January.

Hello Thomas,
Sleepless night in the Bay of Biscay due to badly stowed cargo because we left Le Havre in a rush to beat workers' strikes and forecast storms. Huge row at supper between Chief and Captain, the latter yelling: 'If the

Coral sinks in high seas tonight I shall be blamed'. Hardly reassuring. We have taken on board a secret cargo of two large military tanks (aggressive vehicles designed for the roughest ground, just up Lance's street.) They're probably destined for the North-West Frontier. Yes, we're fighting – and losing – another war there, just as in your day. Don't learn much, do we?

Passing through the Straits of Gibraltar after a rough passage from Finisterre I pictured you aboard the 700 ton barque *Junior of Liverpool* you took from Alexandria on the last leg of your Arabian journey home. You said she was carrying cotton and beans, whereas most of our cargo is a mystery, but at least we're spared your weevil problem.

17th January.

Felt nostalgic skirting the coast of North Africa, where we lived in the 1970s. I kept glimpsing you as we moved east through the Mediterranean where you sailed west. You talk of being becalmed and rowing to nearby islands. We've been 'drifting' near those same islands, not for lack of wind but to 'lose time' because we're ahead of schedule.

Next day at 6a.m. Perfectly balanced between two worlds, readied for our rendezvous on the Red Sea, Thomas. At dawn we dropped anchor in the Bitter Lake, midway down the Suez Canal, midway between the Mediterranean and the Red Sea, midway between Europe and Asia, and midway too in this last voyage to India with you.

23rd January.

Hello again. Awoke to air with no chill. The sky pales as it meets the sharp line of the horizon, where our fellow ships are miniatures, looking as if towed along on invisible strings. In between, I see you in your clumpy *dhow* tacking laboriously northwards through this Red Sea, as blue as blue this cloudless morning. Can you see me coming towards you in my equally clumpy giant freighter? You won't be able to hear the constant chug of our motor above the sound of the wind in your canvas sails and the swish of the waves. Only a century and a half, or nothing at all, separates us.

You wrote your 'Talking Papers' because you needed to share with the person you most loved. Maybe that's why I'm turning to you on this first long journey without Glencairn to share it with. I'm closer to you right now, because we're in the same place doing the same thing.

Jeddah, now in Saudi Arabia, was on our original schedule but now we're neither delivering nor collecting 'Guns drugs and spices', main exports in your day. I had hoped to copy you and sketch its profile from the sea since I wouldn't have been allowed to go ashore as you did because I am an unaccompanied female! Can this be possible today I hear you ask. Yes, truly. It would be funny if it wasn't so absurd.

We enter Yemeni waters tonight, but shall see nothing of the country, though we hear plenty in the news. Just as in your day there's internal fighting as Government forces grapple with 'Al Qaida in Yemen', the latest offshoot of Al Qaida in Afghanistan (i.e. the Taliban, descendants of those radical Wahabis you warned us about). Remember the civil turmoil when you rather bravely ventured into Hodeidah in this same month but in 1849?

As for pirate danger, let's compare notes tomorrow.

I'm re-reading Forster's *A Passage to India*, which influenced my adolescence and led to you. Written sixty years after you died, when the British were still running their Empire with patronising certainties, in many ways it's nearer to your experiences than to mine. The two main female British characters embarrass their community, as you did, by wishing to explore 'the real India'. It's forty years since I first read the book and made my own first passage to India, ignorant as the main young English character, Miss Quested. Now I've almost turned into her companion, Mrs Moore (also widowed with two children), and can relish her perspective: 'She did not take the disappointment as seriously as Miss Quested, for the reason that she was forty years older, and had learnt that Life never gives us what we want at the moment that we consider appropriate. Adventures do occur, but not punctually.'

Thin clouds today, the sea mussel grey with pools of sunlight. A more subtle beauty than showy sapphire beneath clear skies.

25th January.

Sense of foreboding this morning now we're in Yemeni waters. I wondered if it was my imagination, but I've just been on the bridge and the Captain appeared, looking very serious, saying: 'On our present course we'll reach the southern end of the Red Sea after dark, passing the place where a German vessel was recently captured by pirates... and I wanted to pass through the Bab al Mandeb in daytime.' With a pair of compasses he calculated distances and timings on the chart, wrote figures on a scrap of paper and disappeared down to his cabin. We shall know his decision later. I've been re-reading your Red Sea Journal in the quiet of the ship's bow and find we're in perfect synchronisation today. On this exact same date in 1848 and 2010 we both go on pirate alert off the coast of Yemen.

Mid-afternoon. Languor has descended on the *Coral*. The good news is that we're drifting now in order to reach at dawn the Straits where two continents shake hands across the water. We're commanded to assemble later on the bridge for pirate drill. Zabid, Ibn Batuta's favourite town in Yemen, and ours too, is on our latitude as I write this.

Evening.

While we've been doing pirate drill you've had pirates on board. This is how you put it if you recall:

> We had just dropped anchor for the night when a smart looking boat came spanking down and sent on board two suspicious looking villains with long matted hair hanging over their shoulders their heads covered with coloured handkerchiefs and their dress a patchwork of rags. They were Bedouins of Yemen the wildest of Arabs. I saw their keen eyes taking note of the number and strength of our crew and whilst engaged in conversation with the Nacoda keeping a sharp lookout They discovered my weapons in a minute I saw their sharp eyes often turned on the English rifle and long-barrelled pistols which they know never misfire… "their practice" said the Navigator " is to swim off from their encampment at night and cut the cable, then when the vessel drifts on shore they can wade aft and overpower us by numbers and having cut our throats they will take possession of our merchandise."

Today's brigands are just as fierce as yours but nowadays they fire rockets at the bridge, board with machine guns blazing and force captains at gunpoint to race to the bay off Somalia where captured ships and crew (currently eight hundred of them) are held while ransoms are agreed. This can take months or years. Ransom demands are for up to seven million pounds, which finance Somali criminals and terrorists descended from your pirates. Western hostages increase the price – hence our instructions to hide in the secret place in the ships' bowels during the critical time when vessels from the international anti-piracy force race to intercept captured ships before they reach the bay. It's real life 'cat and mouse'. If you were here on your *dhow* it would probably get captured by pirates for their use as a 'mother ship'. It is amazing that around two hundred ruthless pirates using tiny fishing boats are causing such havoc in the vast Indian Ocean. Yearly it gets more dangerous, so that companies are now considering transiting around the Cape of Good Hope, as in your day, despite the extra cost (£200,000) and additional three weeks.

And so to bed. The whole ship's on alert tonight, though Captain and Cookie still got in their evening game of 'ping-pong'. For the next five nights watches will be increased and on the bridge we'll be using our alarm known as the 'Dead Man's Button'. It lights up every twelve minutes and has to be switched off manually by the watch, to prove he's awake. It reminds me of what you wrote in the same situation: 'I was amused by the way they secure the vigilance of the sleepy-headed watch. He performs a constant solo for two hours by blowing on a reed which sounds like the chanter of a bagpipe.' Dead Man's Pipes?

I don't have pistols at the ready like you on this same night, but have knife and torch by my bunk, dollars sewn into my jacket lining, and have memorised our latest logged position, all this following advice from a Royal Marine General just before I left home. Let's hope we outwit the pirates as you did.

26th January.

At dawn we passed through the Bab el Mandeb Straits, Africa to starboard, Arabia to port. As the Straits narrowed we could, tantalisingly, see Djibouti's hills and even its houses through binoculars. The Captain was delighted to be skipping this strategic, beleaguered colonial outpost, but I was disappointed.

Once we entered the Gulf of Aden we were in the official 'pirate corridor', over five hundred sea miles long and patrolled by international warships and helicopters. We're now at full speed, twenty-three knots in a headwind, consuming 140 tons of crude oil a day. You should see the ship's chart for this area last year – covered in pencil crosses with 'pirate attack' or 'ship hijacked' and their dates.

We by-passed Aden, still an important port, because of Yemen's security problems. You mark this southern coast of Arabia on your maps as Arabia Felix, but it's not so felix now, Thomas. Neither was I today. I recalled your words, written on this same journey, when you describe the particular type of loneliness that sometimes overwhelms a traveller miles from home among strangers.

27th January.

The Master has just told us he received a red alert last night from the international anti-piracy agency because a pirate 'mother ship' has been spotted off the coast of Yemen's Socotra Island. This is south of the patrolled pirate corridor, which, incidentally, we shall soon be leaving, making an attack more likely. So the crew (and Christine Fehr, the other passenger who joined us at Le Havre, and I) are more tense than ever, and every little fishing vessel is still being examined closely through binoculars because pirates use speedboats too small to appear on the radar screen. We're in the exact spot where a ship was high-jacked by pirates last month, just six hours after the *Coral* passed through. Our Master heard the alert but naval vessels were already on their way.

28th January, Salalah.

After troubled Yemen, gentle Oman. Ibn Battuta found the inhabitants of old Salalah 'men of good dispositions with affection for strangers.' Their main export was 'thoroughbred horses' and then, as today, they wore cloth traded from India. After two weeks aboard, we had at last a few precious hours on shore. While the Captain checked the price of tobacco, Christine and I bought frankincense and myrrh in the soporific midday suq. Fresh fish for supper, caught by two of the Filipino crew in the filthy harbour water.

30th January.

Last night I finished reading *A Passage to India*. I dreamt that Mrs Moore, Miss Quested, you and me were so intermingled I didn't know who was who; at the same time we all seemed incredibly isolated, trapped in our heads by our individual thoughts. Alone or at one? I couldn't tell.

We've spent almost two days back at normal speed, a sedate fifteen knots, chuntering up the long coast of Oman while you've been waltzing with the wind in the opposite direction. We passed Ras al Hed this morning, on 22nd December 1847 your first sight of land after leaving India's coastline. With the *Hamoody* becalmed you spent a lonely Christmas among Muslim crew before reaching Muscat.

I love your sketch of Muscat around three sides of the page. Now I'm approaching ports by sea I realise it's the truest view. Today it was the turn of Khor Fakkan, up the coast from Muscat and just over the Omani border.

In your day, and indeed when Glencairn was here, Khor Fakkan was a village on a barren coast. You won't believe what it's grown into in twenty years.

31st January.

Another Sunday. Woken by the ship's horn, not a church bell. Leapt out of my bunk, looked out of the porthole and there you were! The horn was warning an old wooden *dhow* of our approach. It was 'beating about', as you would say, on a choppy sea. I'm sure you were aboard, smoking your meerschaum, talking to Father in your head and feeling homesick for Sundays at Etton. Did you send me a message in a bottle?

2nd February.

Back in the Indian Ocean after a day in Jebel Ali, the world's largest manmade harbour. We meet again, Thomas, in the last full day of sea-limbo and last few days of our shared slow journey to India.

Ibn Battuta said that 'the sea between Dhofar and the land of India can be crossed with the aid of a wind in a month'. It took you that too, whereas with oil and the Suez Canal ships can make the whole passage from England in that time.

3rd February, Pakistan, morning.

We're sliding up river in the Indus delta. At the estuary's mouth Pakistani naval ships were stationed beside buoys like guard dogs beside kennels. This country didn't exist in your day but you've been here, travelling up and down the Indus on that horrible visit to Peshawar with Lance and his new bride. Can you see me now, near to you in 1855?

Later.

We're passing mudbanks either side of the wide estuary, beyond are mangrove swamps, glints of distant water, and, on the horizon, industrial smog. As we barge past like a swaggering bully, trios of men, squashed into meagre fishing boats, are looking at us looking at them as they try to make a living on the point where the tide sparkles on the turn.

Lunchtime, Bin Qassim. We've arrived at this nightmare container port that's expanding as I write this. The air smells acrid but sea eagles circle overhead. I'm now listed, with Christine, as a lowly crew 'super', because Pakistan port rules prohibit passengers on freighters, but I don't have to holystone the decks like you. Trapped in my cabin until tomorrow morning, I shall think of your journey to these parts – and where we've got to since then.

4th February, midday.

We've just returned to the ocean, our last sight of Indus delta sandbanks the same as yours: women wading the shoreline in saris, and further out, where river meets sea, wooden fishing boats, nets tugging their bows, profiles of men, bundles, tattered flags, simple awnings. As we left the noise and stench of the port, another freighter immediately took our place in the relentless need to serve humanity. I sat in the bow as we went down river, the only place on the ship where you hear the sound of water instead of the engine. Herons motionless in the mud flats; a flashback to Crackenthorpe. How long can this wilderness survive shipping like ours? Joined the birds' cries for nature's wildness and for home.

Evening. I've returned to the bow to share the sunset with you, and to read a poem of Glencairn's about love that's called 'Sunlight on Water'.

Jenny's crew pass for CMA-CGM Coral, *the last freighter to take passengers from the UK to India.*

30.Come Back Yesterday

Think of that lone Bengali
Dancing and dancing, not
For his own delight but for
His god's and he dances dances
Till he knows he's wholly one
With the Being he's dancing for

(*The Thing that it's About*,
Glencairn Balfour Paul)

From: Balfour-Paul, Jenny
Sent: Monday, February 15, 2010 02.24 AM
To: Balfour-Paul, Jenny
Subject: to THOMAS MACHELL ESQ

Dear Thomas,

'Welcome Home,' said a friend of Amrita Mukerji within half an hour of my arrival in Kolkata. How did he know?

Now I've been in your Kolkata for four days (let's call it Calcutta from now on, since that's the name you're familiar with). I flew here from Mumbai, where I was cradled once again by Rashna Imhasly-Gandhy and Ratna Krishnakumar, who are melded into our story. I'd planned to join you in the peace of the Bengali countryside to complete our book. However, as an organiser of the 'Sutra' seminar next weekend has fallen ill and since, as Amrita keeps reminding me, it's my fault this seminar is happening, the least I can do is help her. Though, as I remind her, the person to blame is YOU, who first led me, with Glencairn, to this mad, fascinating city exactly ten years ago. 'Sutra', by the way, is a Sanskrit word for 'stories, connections, and threads' and this is the second Sutra gathering to draw me back to your city of former palefaces.

I've been too busy since getting here to see much of you. So today I decided that I'd better communicate directly with you this time by the quick, modern way of email. In any case, after all the time I've spent in the past with you, it's time for you to join me more fully in the present. You'd have loved email. I can picture you teaching Father how to use it to communicate instantly, instead of waiting six weeks for letters to come by sea. You would lean over his shoulder and place your suntanned hand over his pale old one to guide him with the 'mouse'.

You should have seen me having tea with Amrita yesterday in the Bengal Club, where the snobbish Army Officers and Company officials with their stuck-up wives looked down on you. It looks much the same with ornate ceilings and chandeliers, huge oil paintings of notable Brits, and waiters in crisp white, with pleated turbans.

The main reason we're assembling here from all over the world is to do with your century, when the most renowned British dyer was Sir Thomas Wardle, dyer to William Morris, founder of the 'Arts and Crafts movement'. His favourite dye was indigo (of course) and Wardle, who travelled all over India studying textiles and dyes, taught Morris how to use it. Then, when there was a big colonial exhibition in 1880s London, Wardle made three sets of three thousand dye samples for the occasion. The two sets sent to England have long since been lost, and the third set was assumed lost too. However, last year I had a surprise call from an excited Amrita who had just returned from the old Botanical Survey of India, a museum of Economic Botany at the back of the huge India museum, which you may have visited. One of the directors, a Dr Debnath, had just shown her a miraculous recent find – the lost stack of Wardle's eighteen great leather volumes dumped on a lavatory floor. Though damaged, they had survived more than a century of monsoon damp, insects and dirt and contain all the dye colour samples, meticulously labelled. When I spread this amazing news to those who would be most interested, I didn't know that by a wonderful coincidence it was the centenary year of Wardle's death. So the Sutra conference has expanded to encompass all this. Just up your street.

And talking of streets, today I walked up the one where you lodged and saw again the ugly building that replaced the Howard's house. Last time I came it was a video shop but now even videos are old fashioned. Of the two nearby colonial buildings I photographed then, one's a building site, the other about to be demolished. Traces of your time are daily crumbling and being absorbed as the city charges on. In the countryside too the Bengali waterways are washing away the traces of the British who briefly made their mark there, including much of the garden of the former indigo planter's house where we stayed at Plassey, and the planter's grave there.

From: Balfour-Paul, Jenny
Sent: 22 February 2010 21:48
To: Balfour-Paul, Jenny
Subject: to THOMAS MACHELL ESQ

Dear Thomas,

This has been quite a day. Celebrations and a few tears too. But mainly joy in this complex city of filth, heart-breaking poverty and delight, known as the City of Joy.

I was interviewed today by Soumitra Das of the *Calcutta Telegraph*, for an article about you and me. At the end of the interview Soumitra repeated the question he's asked several times in emails over the past years: 'When are you going to finish your book about Thomas Machell?' The moment he asked the question I found that at last I had the answer. 'Right now,' I replied. 'Dust in the air suspended/Marks the place where a story ended', wrote poet T S Eliot.

Today was also the end of Amrita's seminar and everything seems to have connected up. I've been re-reading what you wrote about your love of Bengal and your sense of a destiny to fulfil in India, 'the land of my pilgrimage' as you call it. Are these Sutra gatherings, inspired by you, the fulfilling of your destiny? People have come from all over the world to share a passion for natural dyes, exotic weaves, Indian craftsmanship, education and exchange of knowledge. And for me, it was an extraordinary coincidence of timing when I remembered it was my birthday, which makes it forty years ago to the day that I climbed into an old jeep in London to travel overland on my first passage to India. And ten years exactly since Glencairn and I began that memorable day in the Calcutta police station in the small hours, reporting the theft of our suitcases when searching for your indigo headquarters; a day transformed by a note from Amrita, whom we barely knew, announcing she would join us in your indigo footsteps.

That birthday evening we were invited to dine in the Calcutta Club by a stranger, the descendant of the Maharajah of Burdwan you'd been introduced to by your future boss Smyth. It was towards the end of the meal that the chef, on learning it was my birthday, had found in the kitchen a small chocolate brownie for a makeshift cake and stuck a stub of candle on top. The smallest, most spontaneous and delightful birthday cake I have ever had.

And this evening, another spontaneous party, echoing that one. A woman I barely knew (called Neela – female version of the Sanskrit word for indigo) was holding a leaving party at a famous restaurant and invited me at the last minute, on hearing someone mention it was my birthday. She even insisted on sharing her big chocolate cake, showy elder brother to the baby brownie of a decade ago. Both are part of the generosity I've found time and time again in Bengal.

Back at the Mukerji's flat after the party, Amrita, known as the 'angel in a sari', gave me the *Bhagavad Gita*, which led to talk of Hindu gods. I thought of you with your Hindu pundit. She explained how Krishna (whose colour is indigo, of course) personifies 'everything to do with love'.

Remember, Thomas, how our journeys together only started thanks to the single word 'indigo', a word linked with intuition, spiritual knowledge and the 'third eye', as well as love? You would relish a Buddhist expression (from the *Lotus Sutra*) I learnt about today. It takes the way that things dipped in indigo become bluer than the dye itself as a metaphor for the intensity of Buddhist practice, for students to surpass their teachers or mentors, and also for moving forward in life. The expression is: 'from indigo, an even deeper blue'.

I was watching so-called 'invisible darners' demonstrating their work this afternoon, connecting threads so intricately that the structure is held together but the threads cannot be seen on the surface. As I left, one of the darners waved and called out to me, 'Come back yesterday'. 'I shall,' I promised. But maybe I already have?

31. Twist in the Tale

It's who you are
not where you are.

(Buddhist saying)

In May 2010 I turned my attention to Thomas's illustrations. I was selecting images for an exhibition so I needed to see the colour originals, not grey microfilm.

I requested the volumes in advance to save time.

I was longing to see again Tom's watercolours of the Arabian maritime voyage I had so recently undertaken myself, and had already started designing a commissioned exhibition banner to feature our joint journeys to India.

'Do you have the manuscripts I ordered?' I asked.

'Yes – here they are,' said a librarian, handing me five small boxes containing a set of microfiches identical to the ones I have at home.

'Sorry,' I said, 'but I've come to London to see the original volumes, and have email correspondence about this.'

'Oh – it must be a mistake. Can you come back in two hours, because it takes time to fetch them from the basement?'

Later I duly returned to the desk.

'Are they here now?' I asked.

'We have three of the volumes ready for you,' was the reply.

The librarian handed me Volumes Three, Four, and Five, though I had ordered One and Two, the ones covering Thomas's time in China's Opium Wars, his first spells in India, his journey home on Arabian *dhows* and his first job in indigo.

'I'm happy to look at these volumes while waiting, but it's the first two volumes I requested and need to see,' I said, looking at my watch and trying to be patient.

The librarian disappeared, promising to retrieve these as quickly as possible, but when the library closed for the day they still hadn't arrived.

'We seem to have mislaid them temporarily,' she said, 'but don't worry, they're probably with the Reproduction department so we'll fetch them from there first thing tomorrow.'

Tomorrow morning came – and went. The Volumes were not with the Reproduction department and a big search by several library staff couldn't locate them elsewhere. They appeared, incredibly, to be lost.

It was unbelievable. A main theme of my book is the mystery of the missing last two volumes and now the first two volumes seemed to have been spirited away from the safety of the British Library's manuscript store.

Clearly keen to distract me while the hunt went on, the librarian asked me if I was aware that a few photographs had been removed from the back of one of Tom's Journals in the 1990s and placed in the Department of Prints and Drawings. I didn't know this.

A librarian from that department appeared, holding a flat box. He led me into a side room with a large display table, pulled on a pair of white gloves and removed the lid of the box. He picked up the top photograph to show me and I found myself looking straight at Thomas Machell.

To my amazement I realised that the photographs must have been taken during the 'missing' last years of Tom's life. I had assumed that no photographs were ever taken of him, not only because he only refers to sketches but also because his last surviving Journal volume dates to just before commercial photography got going in India (hence only finding a photograph of his younger brother Lance). I had spent ten years with Thomas and had to imagine what he might have looked when he had aged. Now, when I thought my search was complete, I could see in this single, unlabelled photograph what he actually did look like towards the end of his life. It was uncanny seeing this unexpected apparition. Also, I had deduced that Thomas had a limp, and in the picture he is indeed holding a walking-stick. I was glad a librarian hadn't assumed the person in the picture to be Lance; it would have been typical for Tom to be upstaged by his younger brother even in death.

When I looked again that evening at inadequate black and white photocopies taken from the microfilm I was reminded just how many priceless watercolours were in the Volumes still not located. What if they didn't find them? How could they be lost when readers are only allowed to see them at special supervised desks because they are so valuable?

Could they have been spirited away?

With no sign of the missing volumes, I left London to visit my brother-in-law in Scotland. When I drove this elderly man to his boyhood haunts in Glencairn parish he marvelled, with an infectious childlike joy, at sharp new greens of beech leaves, cloud bruises on distant hills, lichens on stones, a field of golden dandelions, and the scent and structure of a tiny flower. 'Look thy last on all things lovely', was that favourite de la Mare quotation of Glencairn's. As it turned out, poignantly, his brother was looking his last on all things lovely in the landscape he had known for so many decades; the following week he was dying in hospital.

This visit took my mind off concern about the Journal volumes and I wasn't too worried when I left London because the librarian seemed confident they would locate them on the wrong shelf before the week was out.

But they didn't.

The next week the horrible thought dawned that maybe the first two volumes really were properly lost or stolen. This was compounded when an internal British Library email was forwarded to me in error:

Subject: RE: Mss Eur/B 369

I have noticed on a previous order that we had for this item last year that the originals were already missing then. Don't know if this helps at all.

From my point of view it helped to make me much more alarmed. Once I saw this email stating that the two volumes had been missing since the previous year I understood why the microfilms had been produced when I first arrived at the library and why everyone had looked so worried when I protested and asked to see the requested originals. The fact they hadn't found them last time they were requested made it much less likely that they would find them now.

It looked as if this book that began with a tale of two missing volumes of Thomas's would end with a similar enigma.

However, after an extensive search lasting several weeks, the volumes did at last turn up on the wrong shelf and are now reunited with the rest. It seems they needed to be lost for a while so that Thomas could show me what he looked like at the end of his life.

British Library, 10th May 2010.

Dear Thomas,

I am in the library where I have connected with you many times over the last decade. But I am looking for the first time at the single existing photograph of you. It is faded and unlabelled, and I am the only person who would recognise it as you. The poet Lawrence Sail writes in *Sift*, his memoir of childhood: 'Most families know the true history of time and chance – the sift of who and what survives, what is spoken of or glossed or glossed over… the photographs making it through to anonymity.' But here I am reversing that sift by finding a photograph that made it through to anonymity and restoring it to the person, that is, to you.

Buddhists describe the body as the guesthouse and the person's mind, or spirit, as the guest. You feel more complete now I can see your guesthouse just before you, its guest, departed. But no one can know where your guest, or ghost, has got to now.

The only known photograph of Thomas Machell, taken in Jabalpur, a major city of Madha Pradesh, in 1862, the last year of his life.

Acknowledgements

The world may be tough, but I have been touched by kindness again and again over the years and am grateful to everyone who joined my travels along the Thomas trail in one way or another.

The late Susan Bosence started it all by passing on her passion for indigo, and Paul Auchterlonie, librarian extraordinaire, unwittingly led me to Thomas Machell's Journals in the British Library.

Lawrence Sail tackled the first baggy draft of the completed manuscript and has been a constant support and provider of invaluable advice. I also owe a huge debt to Penelope Hoare for her encouragement and exemplary edit of the final draft (done, by coincidence – or not – at Roger Machell's desk, bequeathed to her when he knew his life was ending).

Gillon Aitken, of Aitken Alexander Associates, has remained steadfast in his belief in me and Thomas since our first meeting in 2002. This has meant a lot to me, as has A N Wilson's interest in the story, and his generous comments on reading the completed manuscript. I am also most grateful to Kevin Rushby and Nick Smith for their feedback.

Finella Balfour Paul, Jenny Quinton, Liz Rogers, Valerie Rambaut, Jill Scott, Isabella Whitworth, Graham Barrett, Nita Wendover and Sue Harbour-Robertson commented on the text at various stages, as did Beverley historians David and Susan Neave, who also helped greatly with Machell family history.

Those who have spurred me on include Peter and Susie Barrett, Clara Semple, Sara McDonald, Steve and Sue Sims, Hilton and Anita Whittle, Anthony and Naomi le Fleming, Anna Worden, Jackie Herald, Hilary Barnard, Joss and Jayne Graham, Michael Honnor, John Harris, David Treadaway and Dominique Cardon.

The following people became part of the story in various ways:

In India: Rashna Imhasly-Gandhi, who opened all my eyes when our paths first crossed on a coffee plantation in the Western Ghats in 2001. She and her husband Bernard provided a welcome haven in New Delhi the following year and in Alibag in 2010 when I disembarked in Mumbai's container port of Nhava Sheva after five weeks aboard the freighter *CMA-CGM Coral* dodging pirates and masquerading as crew in Pakistan with fellow passenger Christine Fehr.

The generosity, support and friendship of Ratna and K K Krishnakumar, Anjan, Amrita and Kanika Mukerji, and Ruby and Farhad Ghaznavi has meant much more than I can put into words. Tracking down Thomas Machell's indigo haunts either side of the Bengal/Bangladesh border with Amrita, Ruby and my late husband Glencairn, provided experiences never to be forgotten and Liz and Stephen Bichieri-Colombi's hospitality in Bangladesh seemed Heaven-sent. My thanks are also due to Bency Isaac, Michael and Jubert Van Ingen, Monoleena Banerjee, Deepak Rai, Victoria Vijayakumar, Darshan Shah and Soumitra Das.

In the UK: Bruce Wannell, Isabel Denyer, Lucy Goffin and Graham Gough, the late Anthony and Ski Harrison, the late Lance and the late Fiona Thwaytes, Sue Farrington, Gail White and, last but not least, Valerie Rambaut, Andrew and Sally Wilson and Lynn and Jonathan Elvidge at the former Machell home at Etton Rectory, Richard and Carol Hudson at 'The Elms' in Beverley, and David and Angela Balfour at Crackenthorpe Hall, ancestral seat of the Machells of Crackenthorpe.

In USA: the late Reg and the late Nancy Machell welcomed me as family into their Texan home, and it was a joy reconnecting Nancy to the family roots at Etton and at Crackenthorpe Hall along with her daughter Peggy (with Tony and Troy), granddaughter, Becky and great-granddaughter Maggie.

David Wheeler and Simon Dorrell were incredibly generous, not only allowing me to disrupt their lives as I delved for days into the 'boxes in the attic', but also with their hospitality – including David's delectable meals – and friendship.

The music and vision of Yo Yo Ma and members of his Silk Road Project team provided inspiration when it was most needed.

The award of a British Academy grant enabled the whole project to get off the ground, with extra financial support from the Charitable Trust of the Worshipful Company of Dyers and the Institute of Arab and Islamic Studies (thanks especially to Tim Niblock) where my Honorary Research Fellowship has been invaluable. I also treasure my Fellowship of the Royal Geographical Society (especially the encouragement of Alasdair MacLeod), the Royal Asiatic Society and New York's Explorers Club.

The many public archives consulted include: Beverley; Carlisle (including the Regimental Museum at the castle); Hull; York; London's Public Record Office, Victoria and Albert Museum and Guildhall Library; and San Diego's Historical Society. At the British Library I would like to single out Jackie Brown, and John Falconer, Lead Curator for the Visual Arts, for his support.

Thank you to everyone at Medina Publishing Ltd, especially directors Peter Harrigan and Kitty Carruthers and my patient and creative editor Richard Wood. They have all been a delight to work with, from beginning to end.

My children, Finella and Hamish, have tolerated and encouraged my passions and obsessions for decades, and the companionship and love of Glencairn enriched my life in every way.

Last, but certainly not least, I thank the late Thomas Machell himself, for writing his Journals and for taking me on many exciting journeys, overland and by sea and in time and space.

Picture Credits

TMJ = ©The British Library Board, Mss Eur B369

JBP = © Jenny Balfour Paul

Machell family papers = © David Wheeler, Machell family papers at Bryan's Ground, Herefordshire

Theosophical Society = © Archives of the Theosophical Society, Pasadena. Reproduced by permission

Main Text

8	TMJ, Vol One/299
19	Machell family papers
30	Simon Michell
32	TMJ, Vol One/6
42	TMJ, Vol One/33
54	TMJ, Vol One/10; JBP
58	Machell family papers
84	JBP
93	Glencairn Balfour Paul
96	Machell family papers
108	TMJ, Vol Three/115v
121	TMJ, Vol One/187
129	TMJ, Vol One/261
137	JBP
138	TMJ, Vol Two/6
144	TMJ, Vol Two, *frontispiece*
152	TMJ, Vol One/138
173	TMJ, Vol Two, *frontispiece*
188	TMJ, Vol Five/309
200	TMJ, Vol Five/76
216	Glencairn Balfour Paul
236	Rebecca Steele
246	Machell family papers
259	JBP
265	Deepak Rai of 'Wild Expedition'
270	Glencairn Balfour Paul
283	Machell family papers
302	JBP
311	TMJ, 4B (2)

Plate Sections

i	TMJ, Vol Two/6
ii	Simon Michell
iii	JBP
iv	JBP
v	(top) JBP; TMJ Volume One/32v and Volume Three/34
vi	(top from left) TMJ, Vol One/38v; Vol One/45; Vol One/38v (bottom) JBP
vii	(top) Machell family papers; (bottom) JBP
viii	Machell family papers; JBP
ix	(clockwise from left) 1, 2 & 3. Machell family papers; 4. Glencairn Balfour Paul
x	(top) Glencairn Balfour Paul (bottom) JBP
xi	JBP
xii	JBP
xiii	JBP
xiv	(Clockwise from left) 1. Peggy Machell Aalund 2-5 Machell family papers
xv	Machell family papers
xvi	JBP
xvii	JBP
xviii	TMJ, Vol One/141; JBP
xix	TMJ, Vol One/142; Glencairn Balfour Paul
xx	JBP; (sketch) TMJ, Vol One/258v
xxi	TMJ, Vol Two, page Two/50v; JBP
xxii	TMJ, Vol Two, page Two/68; JBP
xxiii	(clockwise from left) 1. TMJ, Vol Five/316; 2. JBP; 3. TMJ, Vol Two/134
xxiv	JBP
xxv	JBP
xxvi	Theosophical Society,
xxvii	(clockwise from left) 1. Glencairn Balfour Paul; 2. Tony Aauland; 3. David Balfour
xxviii/xxiv	(clockwise from left) 1. TMJ, Vol One/217; 2. JBP; 3. TMJ, Vol One/247v-248
xxx	JBP
xxxi	TMJ, Vol One/211
xxxii	(clockwise from left) 1. Janie Lightfoot; 2. TMJ, Vol Two/17; 3. JBP; 4. TMJ *owned by* JBP

Endpapers

TMJ, Vol One/frontispiece

Contemporary 'chart of the world' map bound into the beginning of the first Volume of Thomas's Journals, on which he marked voyages to India (both via the Cape of Good Hope on British merchant and passenger sailing ships and via the Red Sea on Arab *dhows*), to southwest China and to the Polynesian Islands of the Marquesas (outward passage via Cape Horn, return through the Strait of Magellan).

Jenny returned from Mumbai in India by passenger ship via the Cape of Good Hope in 1970 and took passage there on a container ship via the Suez Canal and Red Sea in 2010. She also travelled to the ports of Kolkata, Hong Kong and Xiamen like Thomas, and explored the Marquesas Islands in his wake by cargo ship from Tahiti in 2001.

Chronology

Some key personal and world events during Thomas Machell's lifetime.

1100-1200 First mention of members of the Machell family (then known as le Machel) owning land at Crackenthorpe near Appleby-in Westmorland in Cumbria, northern England. (Henry VI takes refuge there in 1464 during the Wars of the Roses.)

1824 Thomas is born in Beverley, Yorkshire, UK on 12th November and christened in Beverley Minster, which has memorials to Machell family members.

1837 Queen Victoria succeeds to the British throne, aged eighteen.

1838-39 Charles Dickens' *Nicholas Nickleby* is published in instalments.

1840 Thomas enters into service as midshipman on board an East Indiaman, the *Worcester*.

Queen Victoria marries Prince Albert.

1841 Thomas, still aboard the *Worcester*, now a troopship, arrives in Hong Kong and witnesses major battles of the First Opium War (or 'Anglo-Chinese War') begun in 1839.

1841 Thomas's mother dies in August, aged 39, following the birth of her twelfth child. Robert Peel, the modernising Tory, becomes Prime Minister (until 1846) for the second time, replacing Lord Melbourne's Whig administration.

1842 France, under Admiral Dupetit-Thouars, claims the Marquesas Islands in the South Pacific for the Empire. Herman Melville jumps ship and stays four weeks on the Marquesan island of Nuku Hiva, which inspires his semi-fictional novel *Typee* (published 1846).

British Army of the Indus is defeated and slaughtered in Afghanistan (in the First Afghan War, started in 1839).

The First Opium War ends in August with the signing of the Treaty of Nanking, witnessed by Thomas. The *Worcester*, with Thomas aboard, returns to England in 1843 via Calcutta and the Cape of Good Hope.

1844 Thomas sails before the mast on The *Ganges*, transporting coal from Newcastle around Cape Horn and along the West coast of America to fuel French steamships controlling the Marquesas Islands.

1844-5 The *Ganges* returns to England, collecting guano off the coast of Peru, and rescuing two British missionaries stranded in Patagonia in the Straits of Magellan. Dickens completes *Martin Chuzzlewit*.

1846 Lord John Russell's Whig-Radical coalition replaces Peel's Tory administration.

1847 The Marquess of Dalhousie, at 35, becomes the youngest ever Governor-General of India, taking over from Sir Henry Hardinge. Dalhousie extends British control by improving communications – building railways, expanding the postal service and introducing the telegraph – as well as abolishing internal trade barriers, and such practices as suttee and female infanticide.

1847-8 Thomas, assuming an Arab *alias*, spends four months travelling with Muslim merchants from Calcutta to Suez by Arabian *dhow*, then travels on to Alexandria by camel and Nile boat.

1849 Britain annexes Punjab (British troops having defeated the Sikhs in 1848, and annexed Sind in 1843).

1850 Thomas unsettled, with no fixed job, travels around Bengal until he is offered the job of manager of Rooderpore estate, near Jessore in today's Bangladesh.
Death of Sir Robert Peel.

1851 Thomas opens a school at Rooderpore.

1852 Thomas gets cholera and returns to UK to convalesce.
Following the 2nd Anglo-Burmese War Britain annexes Pegu, renaming it Lower Burma. Russell resigns and Lord Derby forms a minority Conservative government that is defeated in December and replaced by Lord Aberdeen's coalition.

1854 Thomas returns to Calcutta in March, hoping to work in the Himalayas, but instead is offered a job in coffee in the Wynaad (Wayanad), north-west Kerala, India, and travels there on a *recce* overland from Madras.
Britain and France enter the Turkey-Russia war (begun 1853) on Turkey's side.

1855 Thomas travels overland to Kashmir and the North-West Frontier with his younger brother Lance, returning by boat on the Indus.
Palmerston becomes Prime Minister in February. Fall of Sebastopol in September.

1856 Thomas starts working at Bon Espoir, his friend Major Smyth's new coffee plantation near Mananthavady in Kerala's Western Ghats.
The Crimean War ends. Dalhousie's application of the Doctrine of Lapse to annex Oudh (Awadh) causes discontent that leads to the Mutiny the following year.
In February the Viscount (later Earl) Canning succeeds Dalhousie as Governor-General of India.

1857 Sepoy uprising in India commonly known as the 'Indian Mutiny'.

1858 Palmerston's Liberals defeated and replaced by Lord Derby's Conservatives, but Palmerston returns to power in 1859 until his death in 1865. Authority over India transferred from the Honourable East India Company to the British crown with the India Bill, Canning becoming the first Viceroy.

1859 'Indian Mutiny' ends. Indigo peasant farmers revolt against their masters in Bengal, in what is later known as the 'Blue Mutiny'.

1860 Revd Robert Machell (Thomas's father) dies.

1861 Prince Albert dies.

1862 Thomas dies aged 39 at Gadawara, Central India on 14th December and is buried two days later in the British cemetery in Narsinghpur (or Narsimhapur), Madhya Pradesh, in central India.

Select Family Tree of Machells of Crackenthorpe
from Thomas's grandfather Christopher

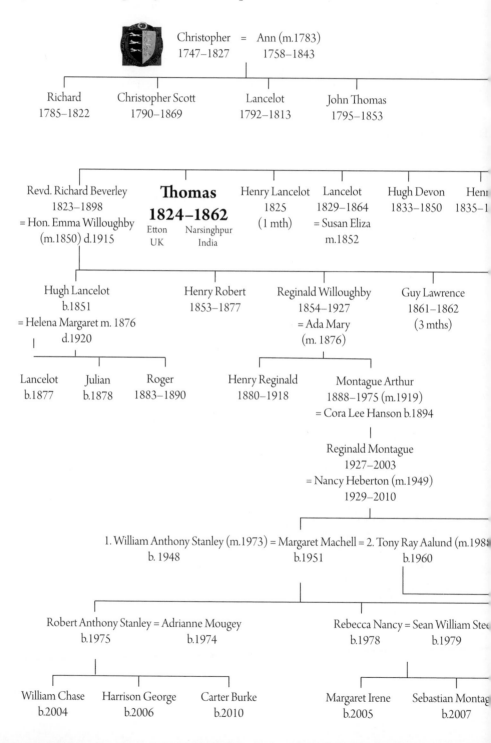

Christopher = Ann (m.1783)
1747–1827   1758–1843

Richard
1785–1822

Christopher Scott
1790–1869

Lancelot
1792–1813

John Thomas
1795–1853

Revd. Richard Beverley
1823–1898
= Hon. Emma Willoughby
(m.1850) d.1915

Thomas
1824–1862
Etton   Narsinghpur
UK   India

Henry Lancelot
1825
(1 mth)

Lancelot
1829–1864
= Susan Eliza
m.1852

Hugh Devon
1833–1850

Henr
1835–1

Hugh Lancelot
b.1851
= Helena Margaret m. 1876
d.1920

Henry Robert
1853–1877

Reginald Willoughby
1854–1927
= Ada Mary
(m. 1876)

Guy Lawrence
1861–1862
(3 mths)

Lancelot
b.1877

Julian
b.1878

Roger
1883–1890

Henry Reginald
1880–1918

Montague Arthur
1888–1975 (m.1919)
= Cora Lee Hanson b.1894

Reginald Montague
1927–2003
= Nancy Heberton (m.1949)
1929–2010

1. William Anthony Stanley (m.1973) = Margaret Machell = 2. Tony Ray Aalund (m.198
b. 1948   b.1951   b.1960

Robert Anthony Stanley = Adrianne Mougey
b.1975   b.1974

Rebecca Nancy = Sean William Stee
b.1978   b.1979

William Chase
b.2004

Harrison George
b.2006

Carter Burke
b.2010

Margaret Irene
b.2005

Sebastian Montag
b.2007

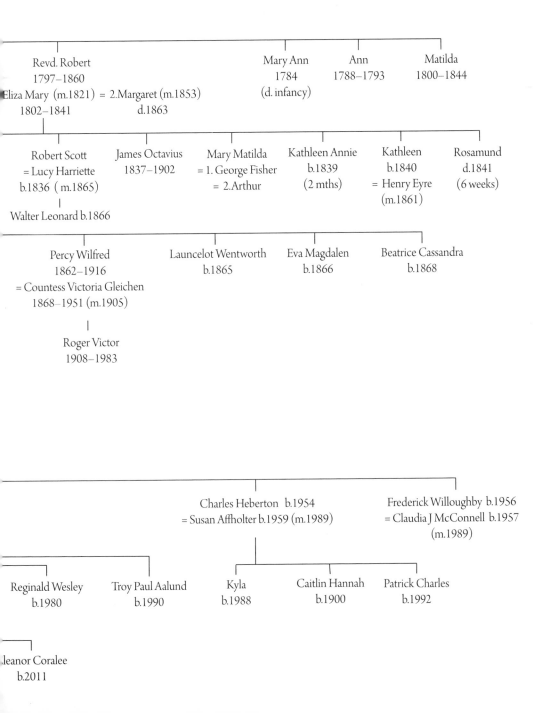

Revd. Robert
1797–1860
Eliza Mary (m.1821) = 2.Margaret (m.1853)
1802–1841   d.1863

Mary Ann
1784
(d. infancy)

Ann
1788–1793

Matilda
1800–1844

Robert Scott
= Lucy Harriette
b.1836 (m.1865)

Walter Leonard b.1866

James Octavius
1837–1902

Mary Matilda
= 1. George Fisher
= 2.Arthur

Kathleen Annie
b.1839
(2 mths)

Kathleen
b.1840
= Henry Eyre
(m.1861)

Rosamund
d.1841
(6 weeks)

Percy Wilfred
1862–1916
= Countess Victoria Gleichen
1868–1951 (m.1905)

Roger Victor
1908–1983

Launcelot Wentworth
b.1865

Eva Magdalen
b.1866

Beatrice Cassandra
b.1868

Charles Heberton b.1954
= Susan Affholter b.1959 (m.1989)

Frederick Willoughby b.1956
= Claudia J McConnell b.1957
(m.1989)

Reginald Wesley
b.1980

Troy Paul Aalund
b.1990

Kyla
b.1988

Caitlin Hannah
b.1900

Patrick Charles
b.1992

Eleanor Coralee
b.2011

Glossary

Chow-Chow: old slang for Chinese

godown: warehouse in parts of Asia, especially India

gunjah: cannabis

jamdanis: an exceptionally fine hand-woven Bengali muslin patterned with rich motifs

khalasi: in South Asia, manual worker

khansamah: Anglo-Indian for a house steward or male servant

lathiyal: literally one who wields the *lathi* or stick, often functioning as a strongman of the *zamindar*

mandir: a Hindu temple (house of a deity)

mela: in India, a gathering or fair

meerschaum: a soft mineral resembling sea foam, used mainly for the bowls of pipes known as meerschaum

mofussil: 'up-country' or provincial

ryot: in India, a tenant farmer or peasant

tiffin: Anglo-Indian for a light meal, or lunch

zamindar: In Bengal the word denoted a landowner and hereditary tax collector for the East India Company who could retain 10 percent of the revenue he collected from the *ryot*.